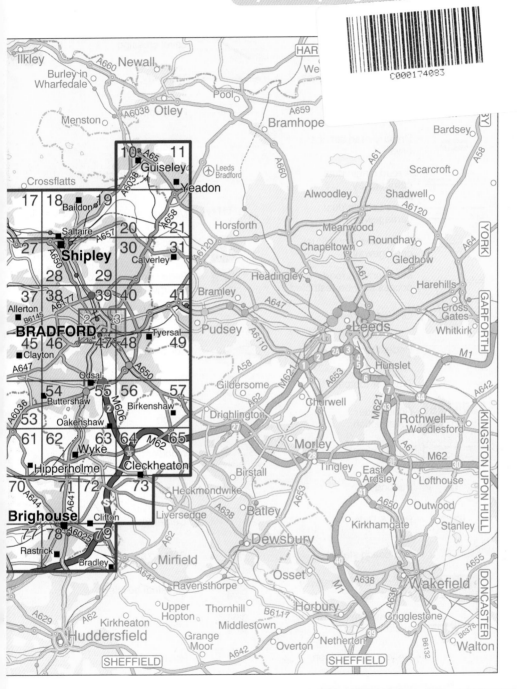

4.2 inches to 1 mile

Scale of main map pages **1:15,000**

| 0 | 1/4 | miles | 1/2 | 3/4 | 1 |

| 0 | 1/4 | 1/2 | kilometres | 3/4 | 1 | 1 1/4 | 1 1/2 |

iv

Junction 9	Motorway & junction	LC	Level crossing
Services	Motorway service area		Tramway
	Primary road single/dual carriageway		Ferry route
Services	Primary road service area		Airport runway
	A road single/dual carriageway		County, administrative boundary
	B road single/dual carriageway		Mounds
	Other road single/dual carriageway	17	Page continuation 1:15,000
	Minor/private road, access may be restricted	3	Page continuation to enlarged scale 1:10,000
	One-way street		River/canal, lake, pier
	Pedestrian area		Aqueduct, lock, weir
	Track or footpath	465 Winter Hill	Peak (with height in metres)
	Road under construction		Beach
	Road tunnel		Woodland
P	Parking		Park
P+	Park & Ride		Cemetery
	Bus/coach station		Built-up area
	Railway & main railway station		Industrial building
	Railway & minor railway station		Leisure building
	Underground station		Retail building
	Light railway & station		Other building
	Preserved private railway		

Street by Street

BRADFORD HALIFAX

BINGLEY, BRIGHOUSE, KEIGHLEY, SHIPLEY

Baildon, Calverley, Cleckheaton, Cullingworth, Elland, Guiseley, Haworth, Hipperholme, Queensbury, Saltaire, Sowerby Bridge, Wyke, Yeadon

3rd edition January 2006
© Automobile Association Developments Limited 2005

Original edition printed May 2001

Ordnance Survey® This product includes map data licensed from Ordnance Survey® with the permission of the Controller of Her Majesty's Stationery Office. © Crown copyright 2005. All rights reserved. Licence number 399221.

Published by AA Publishing (a trading name of Automobile Association Developments Limited, whose registered office is Fanum House, Basing View, Basingstoke, Hampshire RG21 4EA. Registered number 1878835).

Mapping produced by the Cartography Department of The Automobile Association. (A02548)

A CIP Catalogue record for this book is available from the British Library.

Printed by Oriental Press in Dubai

Ref: ML013y

Key to map pages	ii-iii
Key to map symbols	iv-1
Enlarged map pages	2-5
Main map pages	6-79
Index – towns & villages	80
Index – streets	81-99
Index – featured places	99-101
Acknowledgements	102

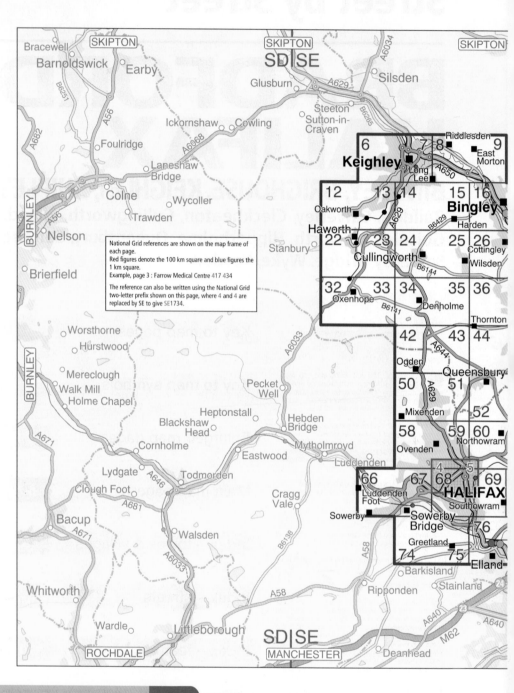

National Grid references are shown on the map frame of each page.
Red figures denote the 100 km square and blue figures the 1 km square.
Example, page 3 : Farrow Medical Centre 417 434

The reference can also be written using the National Grid two-letter prefix shown on this page, where 4 and 4 are replaced by SE to give SE1734.

| 0 | | 1/4 | | miles | | 1/2 |
| 0 | | 1/4 | | 1/2 | kilometres | 3/4 | | 1 |

⊓⊓⊓⊓⊓⊓	City wall		♜	Castle
A&E	Hospital with 24-hour A&E department		⊞	Historic house or building
PO	Post Office		Wakehurst Place NT	National Trust property
📖	Public library		Ⓜ	Museum or art gallery
ℹ	Tourist Information Centre		🏃	Roman antiquity
ℹ	Seasonal Tourist Information Centre		⊥	Ancient site, battlefield or monument
▮ ▯	Petrol station, 24 hour Major suppliers only		🏭	Industrial interest
✝	Church/chapel		❃	Garden
🚻	Public toilets		◉	Garden Centre Garden Centre Association Member
♿	Toilet with disabled facilities		🌷	Garden Centre Wyevale Garden Centre
PH	Public house AA recommended		🌲	Arboretum
🍴	Restaurant AA inspected		🛒	Farm or animal centre
Madeira Hotel ▄	Hotel AA inspected		🦌	Zoological or wildlife collection
🎭	Theatre or performing arts centre		🦜	Bird collection
🎥	Cinema		🦆	Nature reserve
⚑	Golf course		🐟	Aquarium
▲	Camping AA inspected		V	Visitor or heritage centre
🚐	Caravan site AA inspected		🎉	Country park
▲🚐	Camping & caravan site AA inspected		⌒	Cave
⛲	Theme park		✲	Windmill
⛪	Abbey, cathedral or priory		🛢	Distillery, brewery or vineyard

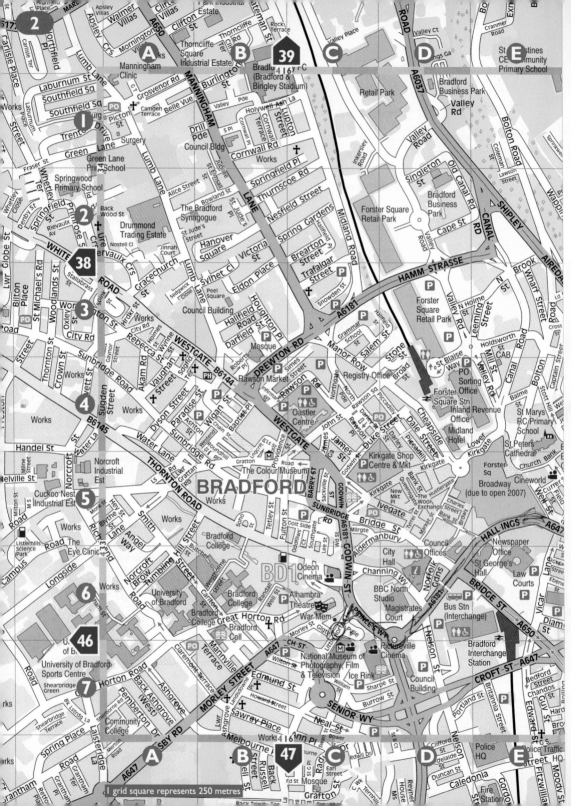

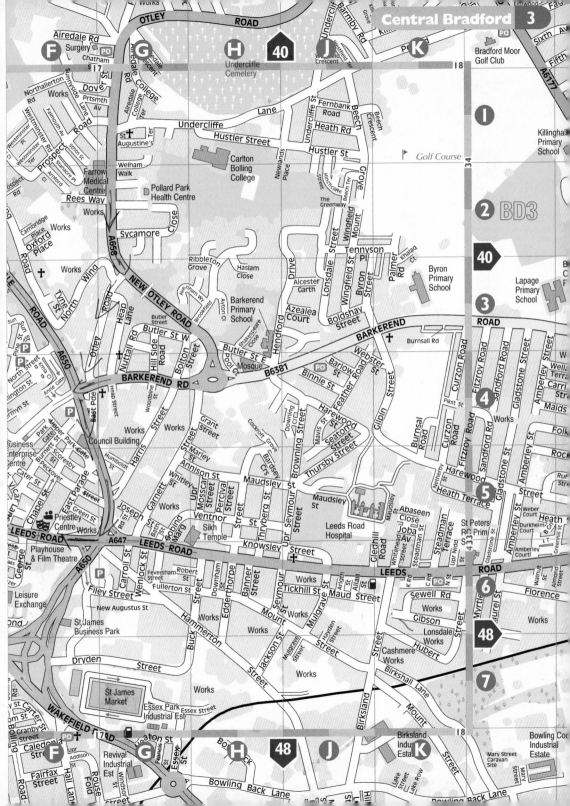

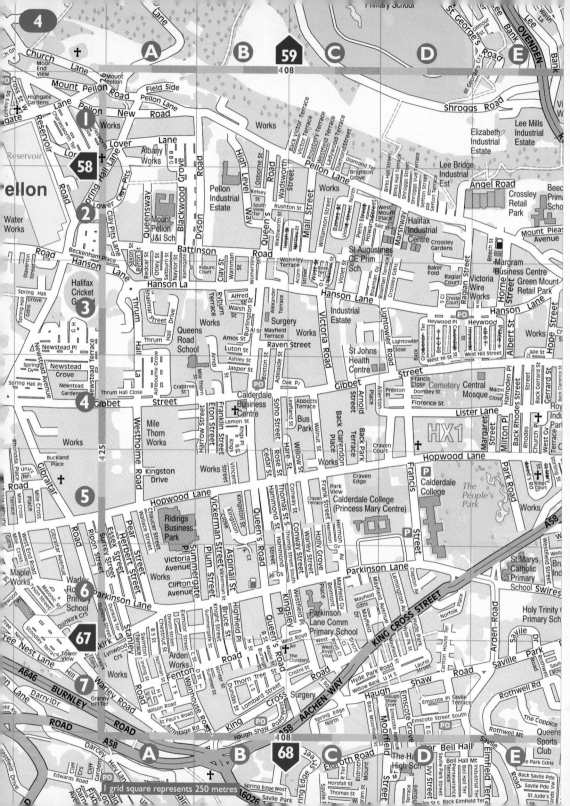

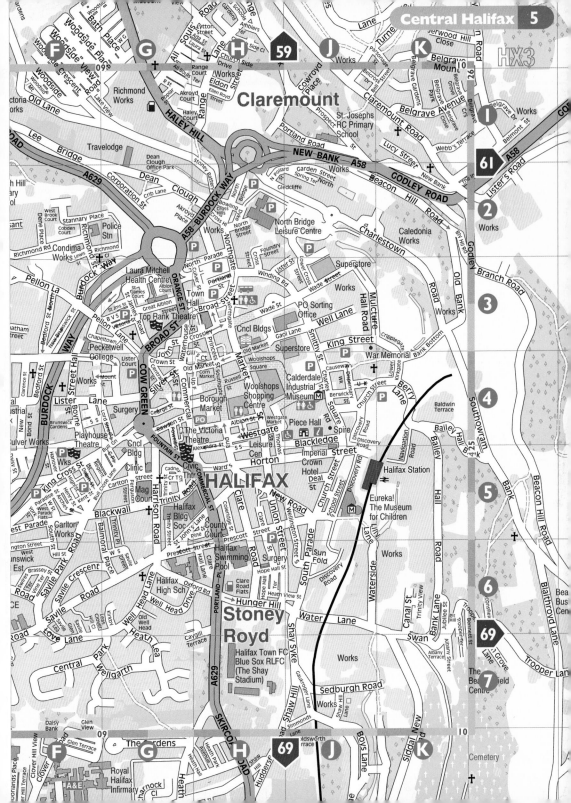

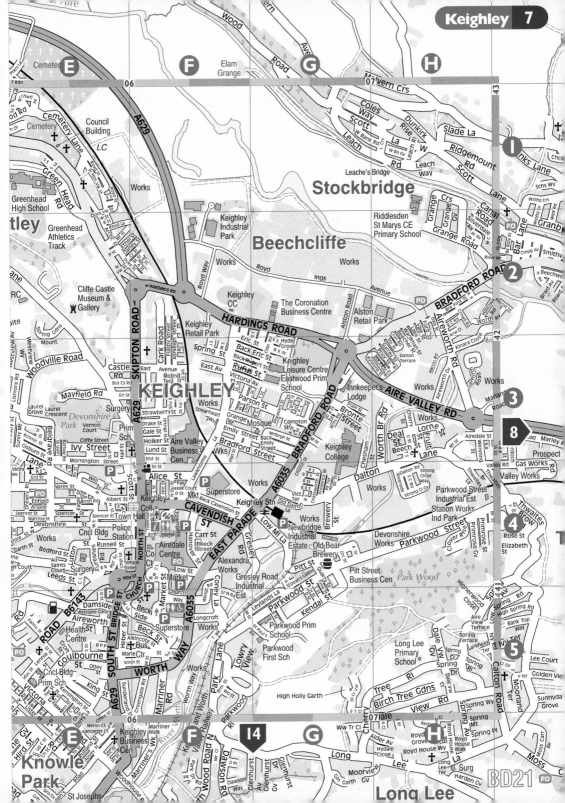

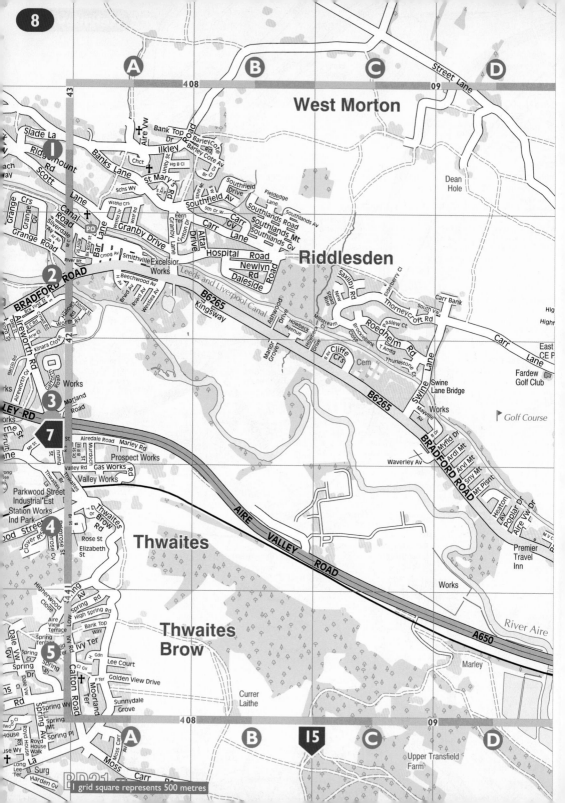

8

West Morton

Street Lane

Dean Hole

Slade La
Ridgemount Rd
Scott Lane
Banks Lane
Aire Vw
Bank Top Dr
Ilkley
Barley Cote
Barley Cote Av
St Mary's Rd
Chct
Schs Wy
St H F
Southfield Drive
Southfield Av
Fieldedge Lane
Southlands Road
Southlands Av
Southlands Mt
Southlands Gv
Grange Crs
Grange Gv
Grange Road
Canal Road
Silverdale
Bar Lane
PO
Granby Drive
Wstfld Crs
Wstfld Rd
Fern Ter
Granby Lane
Altar Drive
Carr Lane
Carr Gv
River Mt
Cmpg Av
Smithville
Excelsior Works
Hospital Road
Newlyn Rd
Daleside
Newlyn Road

Riddlesden

Ashwood Drive
Saxilby Rd
New Sheep Row
Stead Rd
Thorneycroft Rd
Carr Bank
South Vw
Elderberry Ct
Roedhelm Rd
Paslew Ct
Brackenbank
Amtg
South Rd
High
Carr Lane
East CE P

2
BRADFORD ROAD
Aireworth Rd
Worth Av
Kinara Close
Beechwood Av
Brwd Av
Rswd Av
Wstea Av
B6265
Kingsway
Leeds and Liverpool Canal
Manor Grove
Howbeck Avenue
Howbeck Grove
Millstream
Cliffe Crs
Cem
Thurlestone
Swine Lane
Swine Lane Bridge
Mayville Av
Works
B6265

Fardew Golf Club

Golf Course

3
EY RD
Marland Road
Works

7
Airedale Road
Marley Rd
Murgroyd
Prospect Works
Valley Rd
Gas Works
Valley Works
BRADFORD ROAD
Myfld Dr
Arcl Mt
Arvl Mt
Sny Mt
Mt Pl'snt
Waverley Av
Heaton Av
Poplar Dr
Aire Vw Dr

4
Parkwood Street Industrial Est
Station Works
Ind Park
Clover Rd
Primrose Gv
Primrose St
Rose St
Elizabeth St
Thwaites Brow Rd

Thwaites

AIRE VALLEY ROAD

Premier Travel Inn

Works

River Aire
A650
Marley

5
Highwood Close
Aire View Terrace
Spring Av
Spring Gv
Spring Rd
High Spring Rd
Bank Top Way
Ivy Ter
Spring Mt
Dale Vw
Spring Dr
Spring Wy
Moorland Road
Calton Road
Lee Court
Golden View Drive
Sunnydale Grove
F Ter

Thwaites Brow

Currer Laithe

Upper Transfield Farm

A **B** **I5** **C** **D**

BD21

1 grid square represents 500 metres

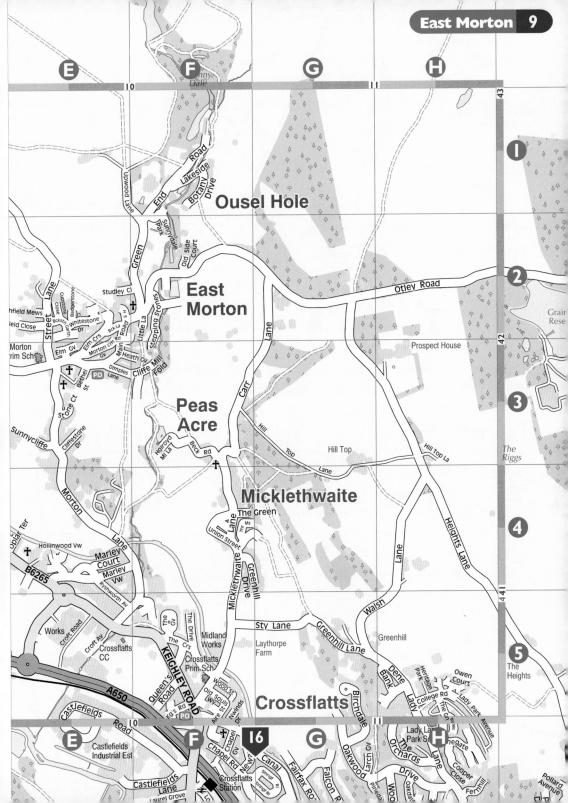

E   F   G   H

Ousel Hole

Sunny Dale

Lakeside Drive
Botany Drive
End Road
Green Lane
Sunnydale Park
Old Side Court

East Morton

Studley Cl
Whitestone Dr
Badgerstone Close
Cupstone Close
hfield Mews
Street Lane
field Close
Morton Prim Sch
Elm Gv
Elm Crs
Morton Gv
Heath Gv
Dimples Lane
Little La
Main Road
Cliffe Mill Fold
Stepping Stones

Bethel St
Stone Ct
Cliffestone Dr
PO

Peas Acre

Sunnycliffe
Morton Lane
Horovd M La7
Beck Rd

Carr Lane

Prospect House

Otley Road

Graii
Rese

The Riggs

Hill Top Lane
Hill Top
Hill Top La

Micklethwaite

The Green
Union Street
Thr
Ms

Poplar Ter
Hollinwood Vw
Marley Court
Marley Vw
B6265

Mickleth Drive
Greenhill Drive
Lane

Walsh Lane
Heights Lane

Works
Croft Road
Croft Av
Crossflatts CC
The Crs
The Drive
The Cl
Queen's Road
KEIGHLEY ROAD
Midland Works
Crossflatts Prim Sch
Sty Lane
Laythorpe Farm
Greenhill Lane
Greenhill

Dene Bank
Birchdale
Heritage Park
Lady Park
College Rd
Owen Court
Lady La
The Heights

Crossflatts

A650
Castlefields Road

Queen's Road
Kg's Rd
PO
Wood St
old sols Vw
Nwinds
Are St

The Orchards
Lady Lane
Park Sch
The Drive
Fernhill
Cooper Close
Pollard Avenue

E   F   16   G   H

Castlefields Industrial Est
Castlefields Lane
Chapel Rd
Newcastle
Canal
Crossflatts Station
Chapel La
Fairfax Rd
Falcon R
Oakwood
Larch Gv
Pinedal
Oakdale
Wo
Laurel Grove
Snigil Rd

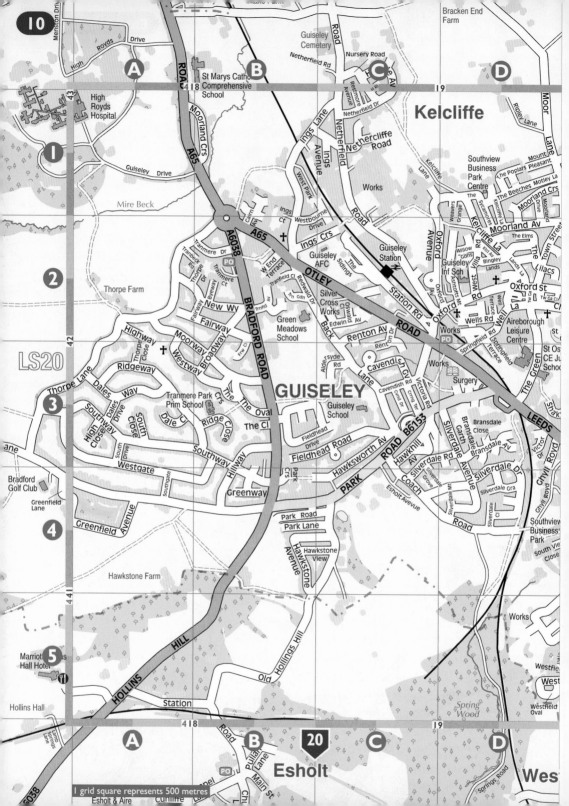

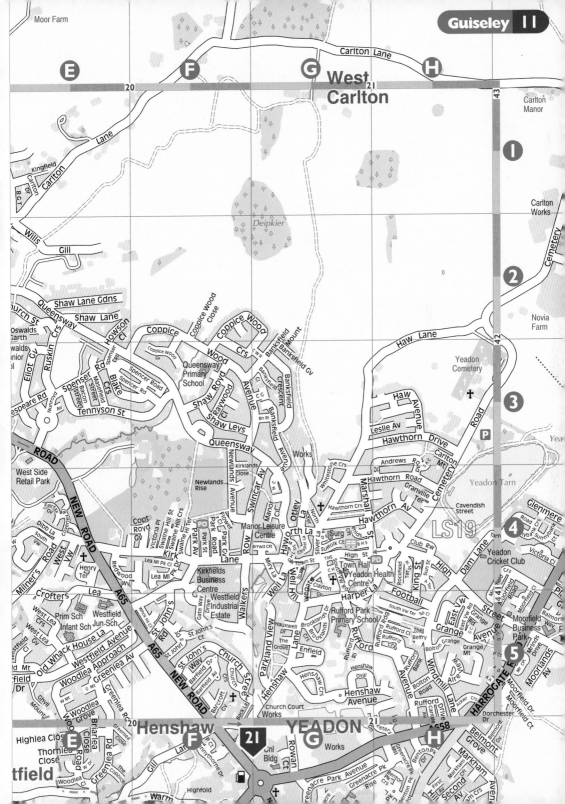

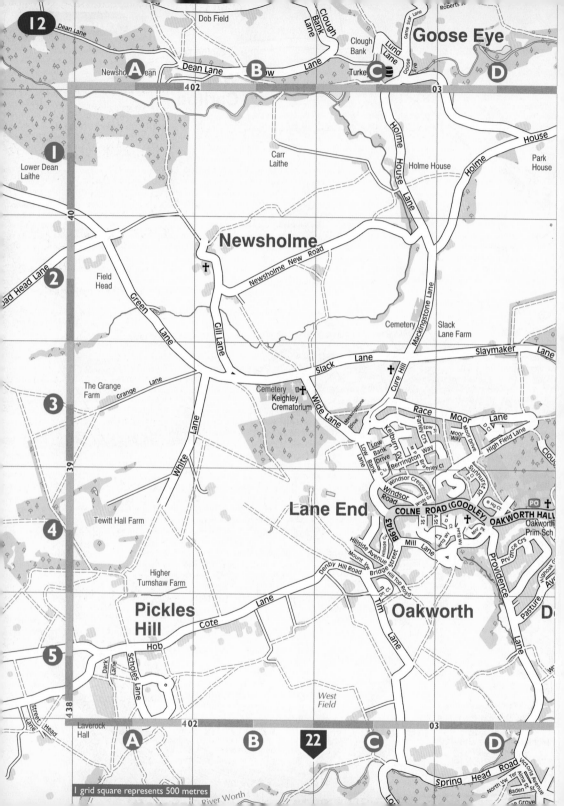

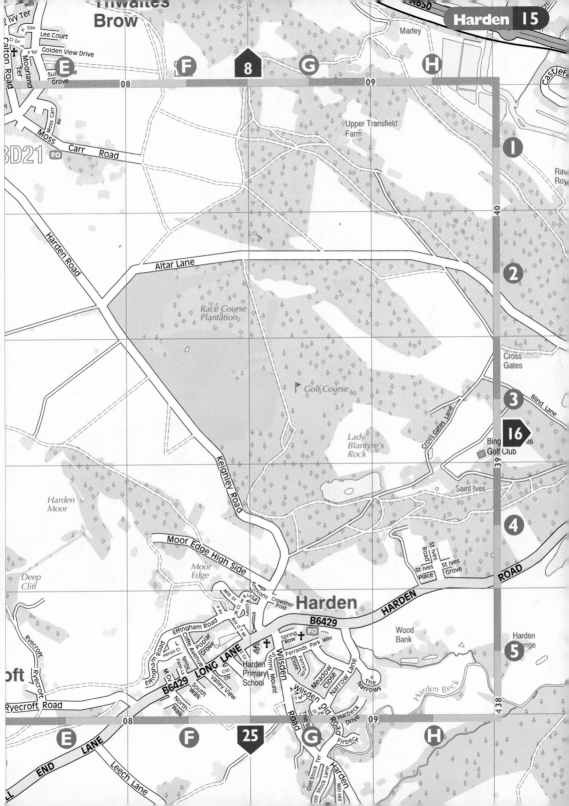

Thwaites
Brow

A650

Marley

Ivy Ter
Lee Court
Golden View Drive
E
F
8
G
H

Moorland Ter
Calton Road
Surmmer
Grove

Moss Carr Av

Upper Transfield
Farm

I

Moss Carr Road
BD21
PO

40

Harden Road

Altar Lane

2

Race Course
Plantation

Cross
Gates

Golf Course

3
Blind Lane

Lady
Blantyre's
Rock

Cross Gates Lane

16
Bing
Golf Club

39

Harden
Moor

Saint Ives

Deep
Cliff

Moor Edge High Side

4

Keighley Road

St Ives
Road

St Ives
Place

St Ives
Grove

ROAD

Moor
Edge

Anthony La
Crowther
Fold

Mild Dr
La Lat
CSSW

Harden

HARDEN

5

Harden
ange

Effingham Road

Cliffe Avenue

Poplar
Grove

B6429

Spring
Row

PO

Ferrands Park Way

Wood
Bank

Harden Beck

Ryecroft

Heron Cl

L

M Cl

LONG LANE

Spring
Farm Cl

Crnry Mount

Wilsden

Ferrands
Close

Meadow
Close

Narrow Lane

Harden
 range

Ryecroft Road

B6429
Effingham Road

South
Walk

Valley View

Cstl

Crt

Harden Primary
School

Wilsden

Old Road

Harbeck
Drive

The
Narrows

North
Walk

E
LANE

F
25
G
H

END
Leech Lane

The
Fold

Wilsden Old Road

Golt Stock Ter

Firbeck

Harden Mill Hill

08
09
438

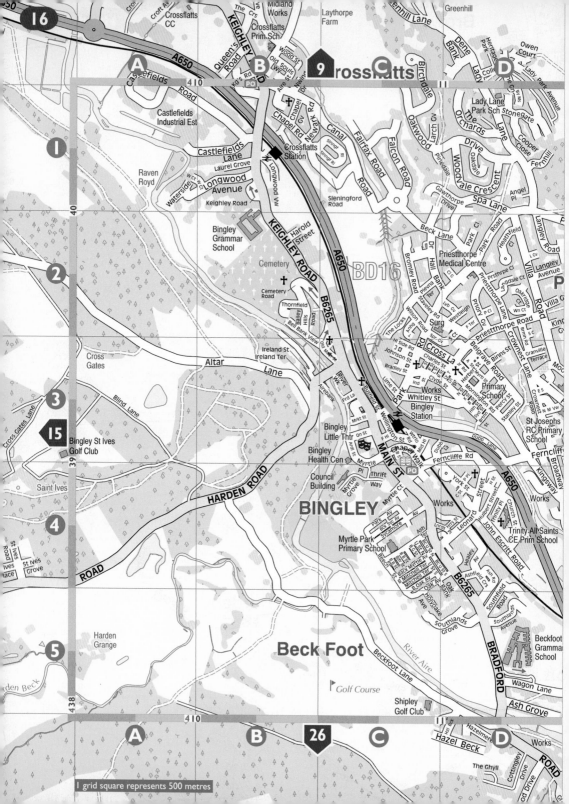

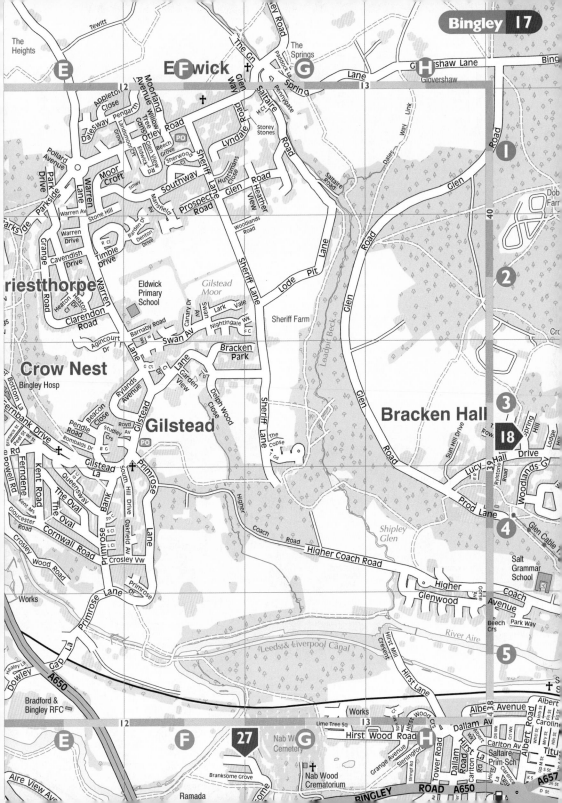

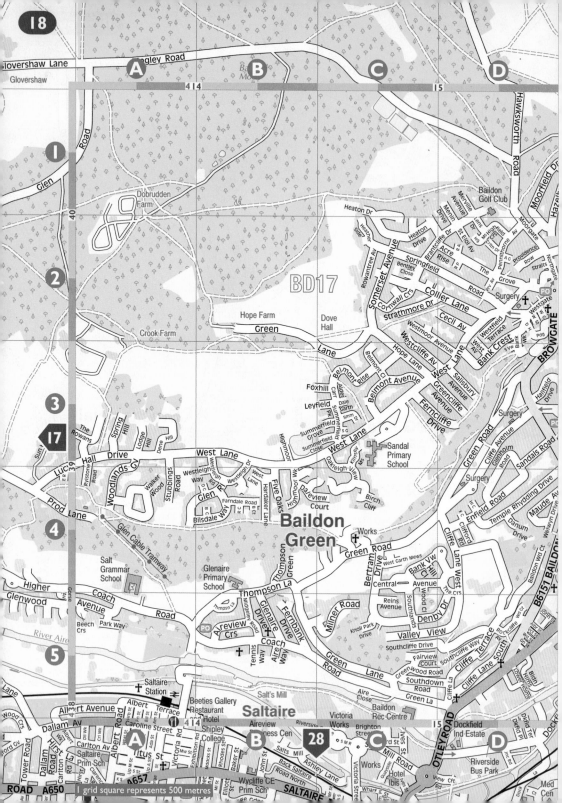

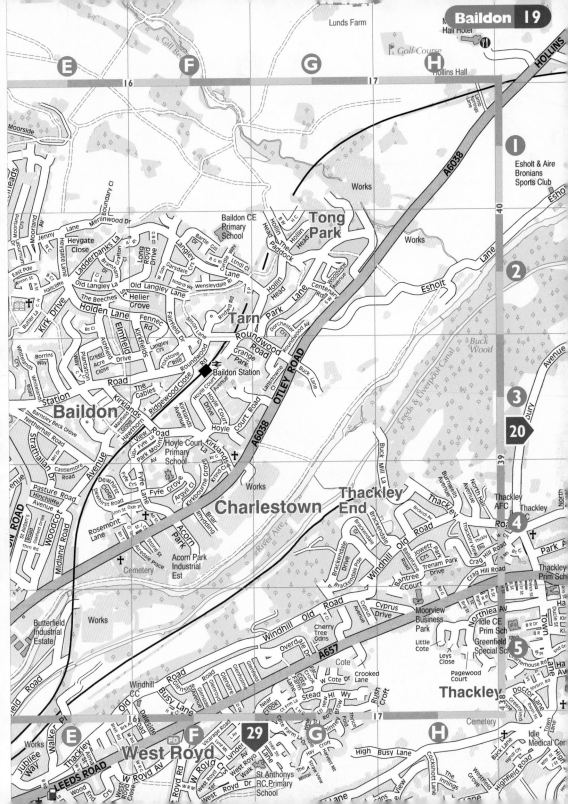

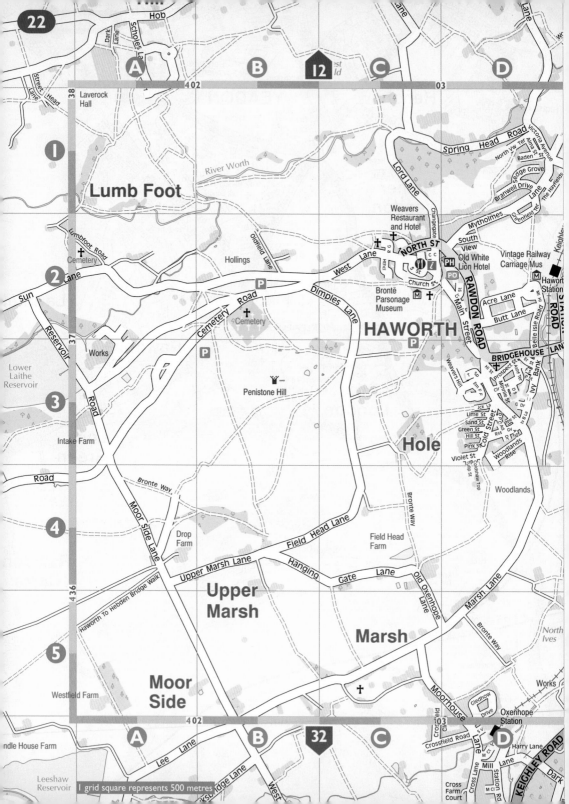

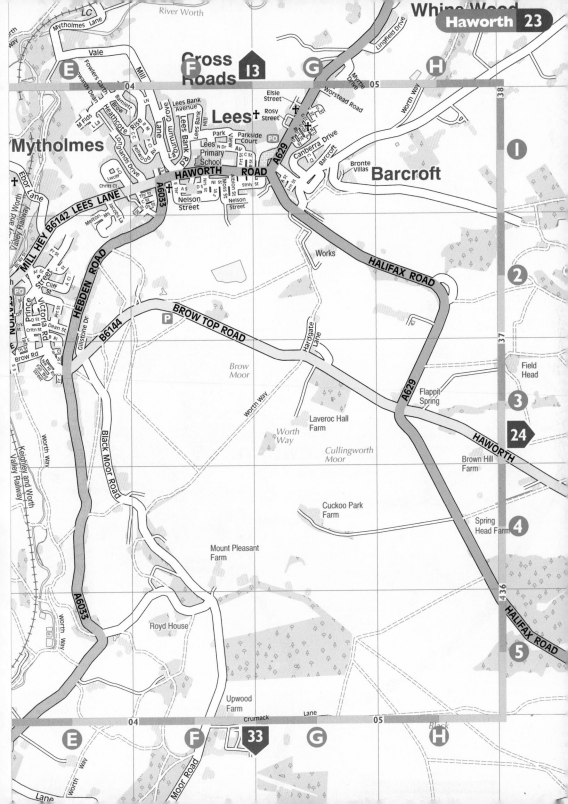

River Worth

Whins Wood

LC
Mytholmes Lane

Vale

E

Fowlers Garth

Edwards Dean

Heathcote

M Flds

Longlands Drive

Mytholmes

Ebor Lane

Cross Roads 13

F

Lees Bank Avenue

Lees Bank Rd

Lees Bank View

Lees †

Park View

Parkside Court

Lees Primary School

HAWORTH ROAD

Nelson Street

Nelson Street

Jacob La

Melton

MILL HEY B6142 LEES LANE

A6033

HEBDEN ROAD

Lingfield Drive

G

Worstead Road

Myrtle Drive

Elsie Street

Rosy Street

PO

Canberra Drive

Barcroft

†

Stnly St

A629

Bronte Villas

H

Worth Way

I

Barcroft

2

HALIFAX ROAD

Works

A629

37

Field Head

3

Flappit Spring

24 HAWORTH

Brown Hill Farm

Hardgate Lane

Worth Way

Laveroc Hall Farm

Worth Way

Brow Moor

B6144

BROW TOP ROAD

P

Gillstone Dr

Black Moor Road

A6033

Dean St

Brow Rd

Prince

Victoria Rd

PO

Keighley and Worth Valley Railway

Worth Way

Cullingworth Moor

Cuckoo Park Farm

Spring Head Farm 4

436

HALIFAX ROAD

5

Mount Pleasant Farm

Royd House

Worth Way

Upwood Farm

Moor Road

Crumack Lane

E

F 33

G

H

Black

Ryecroft
Cliffe Avenue
Poplar Grove
LONG LANE
Spring Row
Wilsden
Ferrands Park Way
Wood Bank
Harden

E
F
15
G
H

Ryecroft
Ryecroft Road
B6429
Heron Ci
Effingham Road
Farm La
South
Valley View
Norton Walk
Harden Primary
Snowy Mount
Meadow Close
Ferrands Close
Narrow Lane
The Narrows
Harbeck Drive
Firbeck
Harden Beck

END LANE
Leech Lane
Gott Stock Ter
Gott Stock Lane
The Bluffield
Harden Road
Mill Hill Top
Wilsden Road
Sandy Banks

I

Garden Centre
Leisure Centre
Cherry Tree Row
Bank Top
Lee Lane

2

Lower Bents Farm
Cross Lane
Coplowe Lane

Bents Lane
Birchlands Grove
Stoney's Fold
Mayfield Grove
Lee Close

Coplowe Hall

3

Middle Bents
Birchlands Avenue
Florence Avenue
Stapper Green
Smithy Lane
Manor House Road

26

Hallas Bridge
Tan House Lane
owthg st
Moss Row
Chapel Lane
Mansing Rd
Spring Park Road

Hallas Lane
Dye House Lane
Wilsden Hill Road
Sp MS
W S
PO
Tweedy St
Wilsden Primary School

Hallas Cote Farm
High
Meadows
Surgery
North View
Firth St
Main Street
Albion Fold

4

Hewenden
WILSDEN
West
Royd
Hornsea Drive
Royd Street
Lingfield Road
Emily Hall Gdns
Lingfield Grove

Bents Head Farm
Mrs Rd
Laurel
Main St
Ling Pk

5

B6144
Brown Lee Lane
St Matthews Close
Wellington Road
Crooke Lane
Farndale Road
Derwent Av
Albert St
Victoria St
Queen St
Laurel Pk
Ling Pk
Meadow Green

Hare Croft
HAWORTH ROAD
LANE SIDE
B6144

Station Road

E
F
35
G
Ne H Holland

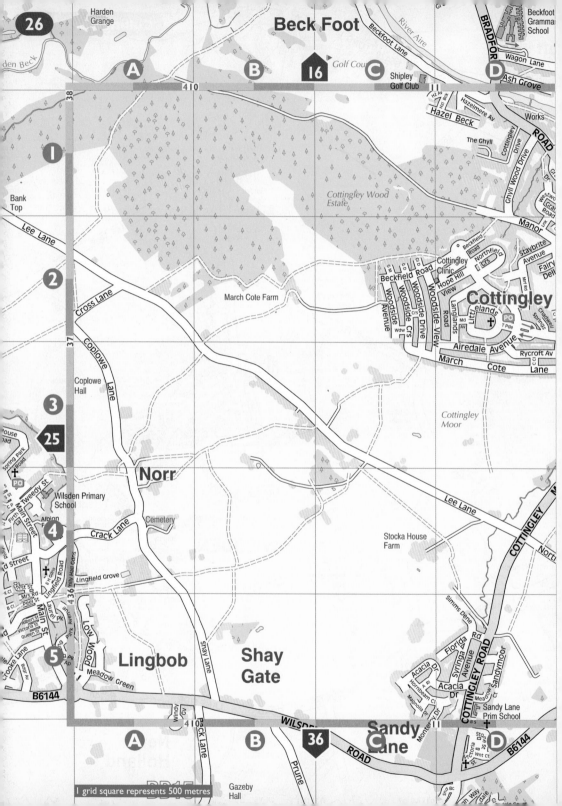

26

Harden
Grange

Beck Foot

River Aire

Beckfoot Lane

BRADFOR

Beckfoot
Grammar
School

Wagon Lane

A

410

B

Golf Cou

16

C

Shipley
Golf Club

D

Ash Grove

Hazel Beck

Hazelmere Av

Works

den Beck

38

1

Bank
Top

Cottingley Wood
Estate

The Ghyll

Ghyll Wood Drive

Westwo
Gra
Road

Manor

ROAD

Lee Lane

2

Cross Lane

March Cote Farm

Cottingley
Clinic

Hope Hill

Cottingley
View

Beckfield Road

Woodside
Avenue

Woodside
Crs

Woodside Drive

Woodside View

Beckfield
Road

Langlands
Road

Northfiel
Crs

Staybrite
Avenue

Fairy
Dell

Cottingley

ield
C D

Md
AV

elands

Little

Chenwell
Springs

PQ
T Pde

Rycroft Av

Cottingley
Moor

37

Coplowe Lane

Coplowe
Hall

Airedale Avenue

March
Cote
Lane

3

25

Spring Park
Road

PQ

Norr

Wilsden Primary
School

Tweedy St

Firth
St

Main Street

Albion
F

Lee Lane

Cottingley

Cottingley

Nort

ROAD

4

Crack Lane

Cemetery

Lingfield Grove

Lingfield Road

436 mly Hall Gdns

Stocka House
Farm

Simms Dene

d Street

St

Qrst St

Mrs Rd

Peel St

Laurel
Pk

E Gdns

Florida
Rd

Syringa
Avenue

Sandymoor

COTTINGLEY ROAD

5

Crooke Lane

Main St

Albert St

Victoria St

Queen St

Low Wood

Meadow Green

Shay Lane

Lingbob

**Shay
Gate**

Acacia
Dr

Hornbeam Cl

Acacia
Dr

A Rd

Magnolia Dr

Meadow
Ct

Monterey Dr

Sandy Lane
Prim School

B6144

Windy

Beck Lane

A

410

B

36

WILSDE

ROAD

C

**Sandy
Lane**

D

B6144

Victoria

Wnt Ct

BD1

Gazeby
Hall

Prune

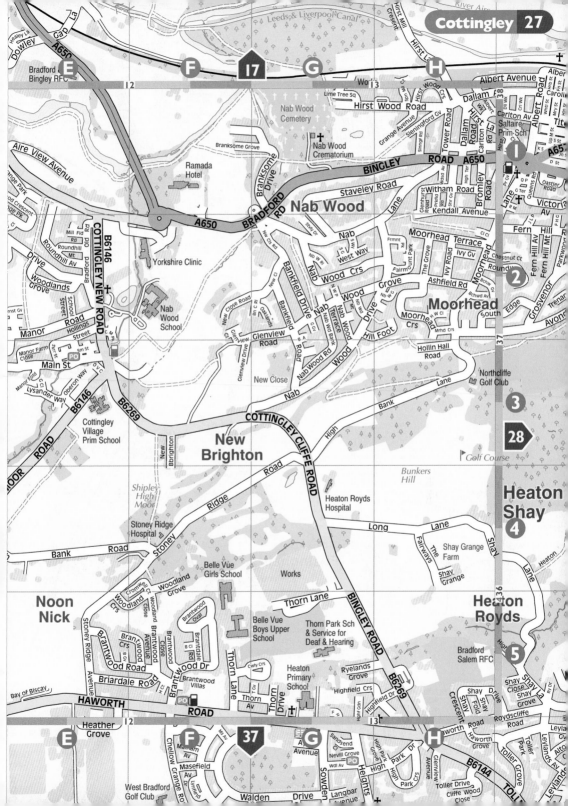

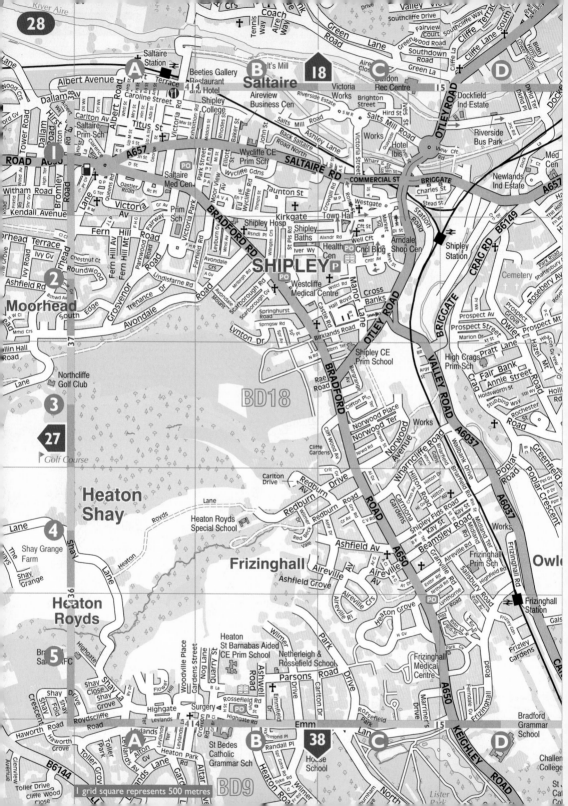

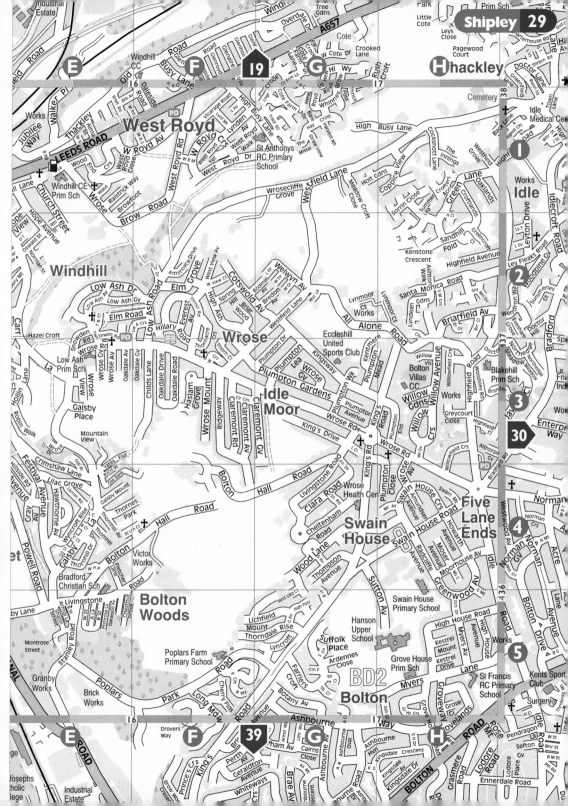

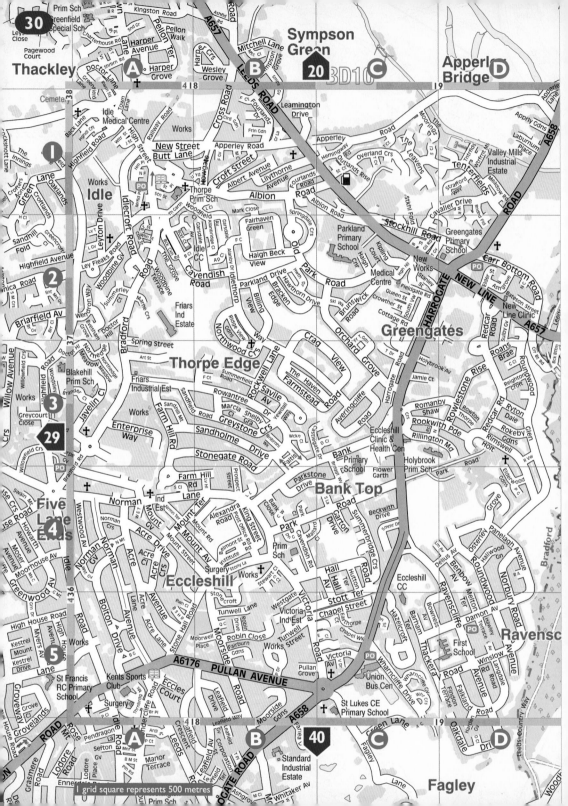

1 grid square represents 500 metres

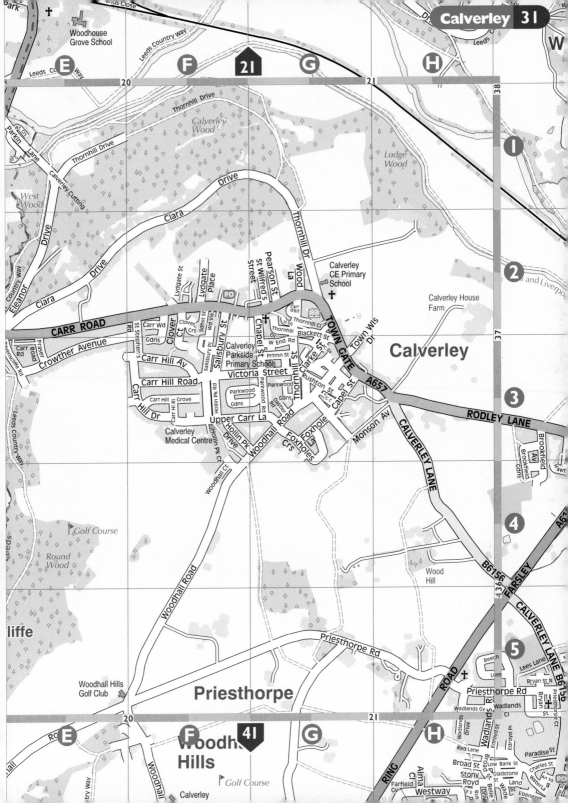

W

Woodhouse Grove School

Leeds Country Way

E

20

F

21

G

21

H

38

I

Thornhill Drive

Parkin Lane

Thornhill Drive

Calverley Cutting

Calverley Wood

Lodge Wood

2

West Wood

Clara Drive

Clara Drive

Eleanor Drive

Country Way

Clara Drive

Drive

Thornhill Dr

Wood La

Thornhill Dr

Calverley CE Primary School

Calverley House Farm

and Liverpool

37

Lydgate St

Lydgate Place

Pearson St

St Wilfred's Street

St Wilfred's Street

PO

CARR ROAD

Crowther Avenue

Carr Rd

Fraser Road

Foxerscliffe Rd

Carr Rd

Carr Wd Gdns

St Stephen's

Salisbury Pl

Clover Crs

Sdhst St

Salisbury St

Carr Rd

Chapel St

Clover Ct

Carr Hill Av

Carr Hill Road

Carr Hill Rl Grove

Carr Hill Dr

Carr Hl Rl

Hollin Pk Rd

Hollin Pk Dr

Hollin Pk Drive

Calverley Parkside Primary School

Victoria Street

Parkwood Gdns

Upper Carr La

Calverley Medical Centre

Woodhall Ct

Woodhall Road

Leeds Country Way

Golf Course

Round Wood

cliffe

Woodhall Road

W End Rd

Prtmn St

Parkwood Road

Parkwood Crs

Woodhall Drive

Thornhill Cl

Blackett St

Carr Rd

Thornhill

Clarke St

Oastler St

TCC

Rushton St

Foxhole La

Foxholes Crs

TOWN GATE

Town Wis

Town Wis Dr

Capel St

Monson Av

Calverley

Calverley

A657

RODLEY LANE

3

Brookfield Av

Brookfield Gdns

Brookfield

4

Wood Hill

B6156

FARSLEY

A65?

CALVERLEY LANE

CALVERLEY LANE B6156

5

Priesthorpe Rd

Beech Lees

Lees Lane

Bryan St N

Bryan St

Priesthorpe Rd

Priesthorpe Ct

B6156

Wadlands Gv

Wadlands Cl

Priesthorpe Rd

Priesthorpe

Woodhall Hills Golf Club

Round Wood

Golf Course

Calverley

E

20

F

21

41

Woodh. Hills

G

21

ROAD

RING ROAD

H

Wadlands Drive

Red Lane

Broad St

Farfield Gv

Stony Royd

Alma St

Westway

Wadlands Drive

Edroyd Pl

Edroyd St

Charles St

Low Bank St

An Sq

Gladstone St

Waterla

Wade La

Ebenezer St

Paradise St

PO

Priesthorpe

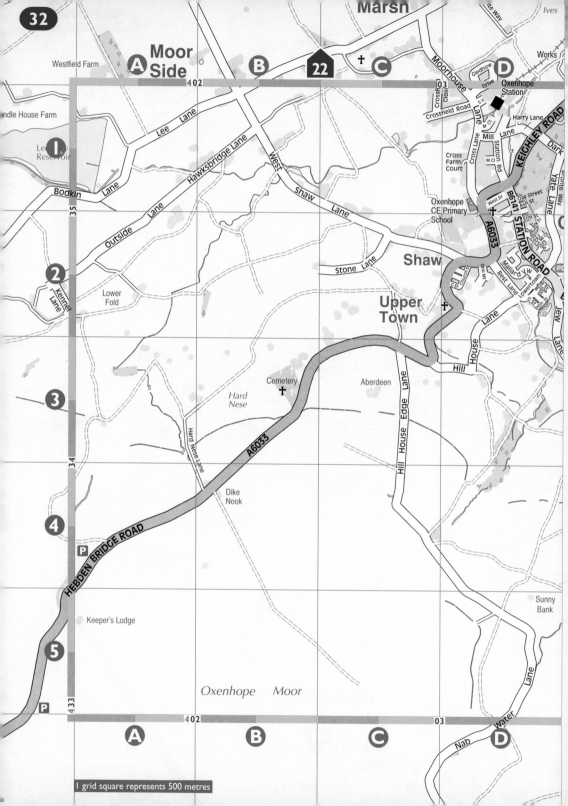

Marsh

Ives

Moor Side

Westfield Farm

ndle House Farm

Lee Reservoir

Bodkin

Lee Lane

Hawksbridge Lane

Outside Lane

Kennel Lane

Lower Fold

West Shaw Lane

Stone Lane

Shaw

Upper Town

Cemetery

Hard Nese

Hard Nese Lane

A6033

Dike Nook

HEBDEN BRIDGE ROAD

Keeper's Lodge

Aberdeen

Hill House Edge Lane

Hill House Lane

Oxenhope Moor

Sunny Bank

Moorhouse Lane

Oxenhope Station

Gledhow Drive

Harry Lane

Crossfield Road

Cross Lane

Station Rd

Mill Lane

Cross Farm Court

Oxenhope CE Primary School

KEIGHLEY ROAD

STATION ROAD

B6141

A6033

Oak Street

Ash St

Elm St

West Dr

Mallard

Lowertown

Best Lane

Jew Lane

Yate Lane

Dark

Nab

Water Lane

Oxenhope Moor

1 grid square represents 500 metres

402

35

34

433

03

402

03

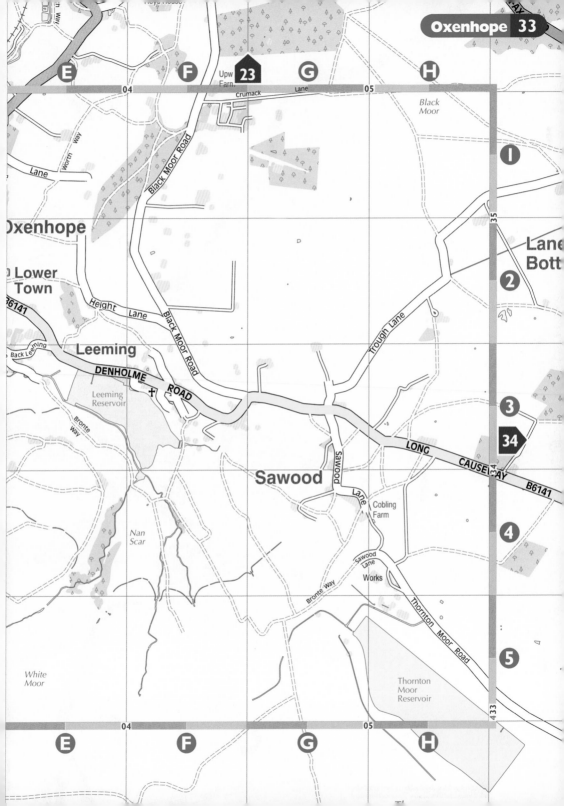

E · F · 23 · G · H · I

Upw Farm.

Crumack Lane

Black Moor Road

Black Moor

Oxenhope

Lane
Worth Way

Lane

Lower
Town

B6141

Height Lane

Leeming

Back Leeming

DENHOLME ROAD

Black Moor Road

Trough Lane

Lane Bott

Leeming
Reservoir

Bronte Way

Sawood

Sawood Lane

Cobling Farm

LONG CAUSEWAY B6141

34

Nan
Scar

Bronte Way

Sawood
Lane

Works

Thornton Moor Road

Thornton
Moor
Reservoir

White
Moor

E · F · G · H

04 · 05 · 433 · 35

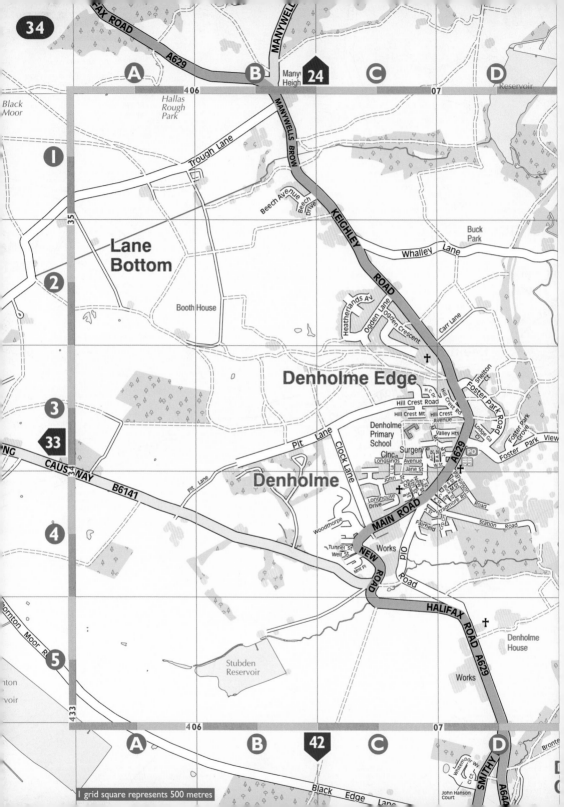

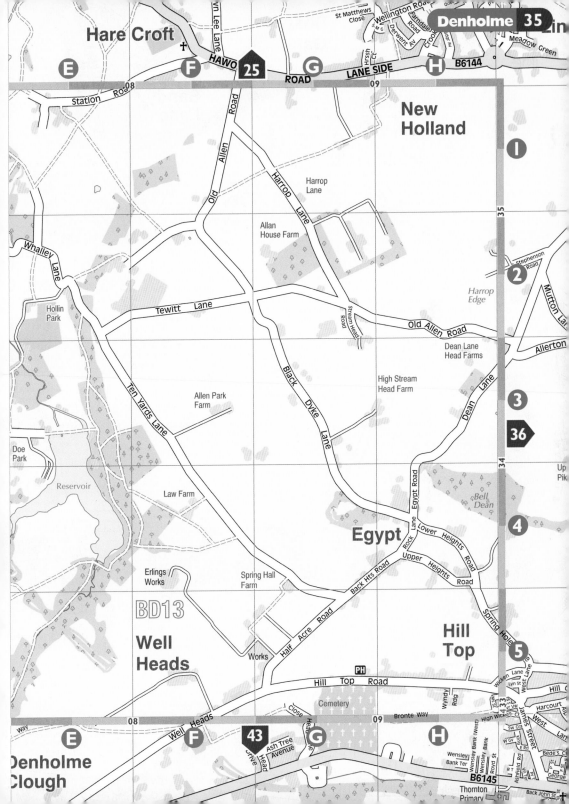

Hare Croft

E   F   HAWO **25** ROAD   G   LANE SIDE   H   B6144   Meadow Green

St Matthews Close   Wellington Road   Arndale
                                       Derwent Av
                                       Crook

New Holland

I

Station   Road   08   09

Harrop Lane   Harrop Lane

Allan House Farm

Old Allen Road   Harrop Lane

Whalley Lane

Hollin Park

Tewitt   Lane   Stream Head Road   Old Allen Road

Harrop Edge

Stephenson Road

2

Mutton Lan

Allerton

Dean Lane Head Farms

3

Ten Yards Lane

Allen Park Farm

Black Dyke Lane

High Stream Head Farm

Dean Lane

36

34

Up
Pik

Doe Park

Law Farm

Egypt Road

Bell Dean

4

Reservoir

Erlings Works

Spring Hall Farm

Egypt   Lower Heights Road

Rock Lane

Upper Heights   Road

Hill Top

Spring Hole

5

BD13

Well Heads

Back Hts Road

Half Acre Road

Works

Hill   Top   Road

PH

Wicken Lane   Lyn St

James Street

West Lane

Hill C

Harcourt

33

Denholme Clough

Well Heads   08   F   **43**   G   09   Bronte Way   H

Cemetery

Ash Tree Avenue   Wyndy Rdg

Wensley Bank (West)   High Wicken

Wensley Bank Ter   Wensley Bank   Royd St   Ashfield Rd   George   Bede's C   Back John St

B6145

Thornton Primary

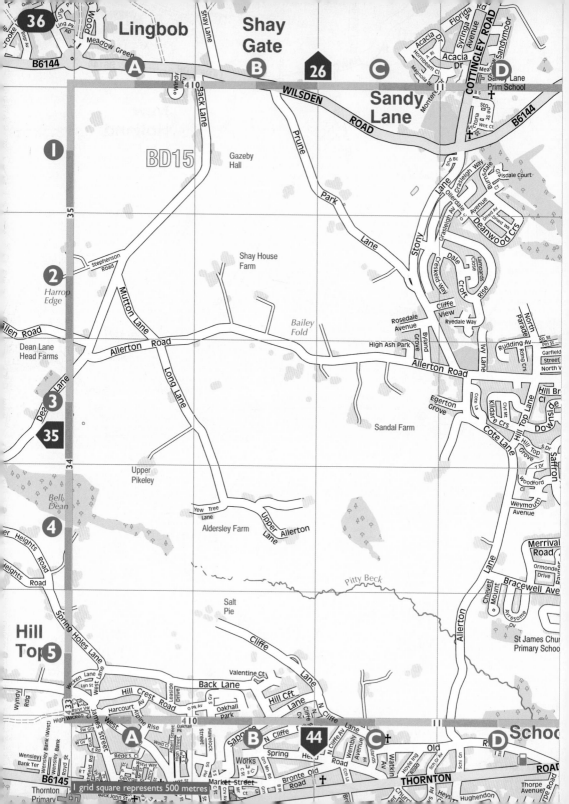

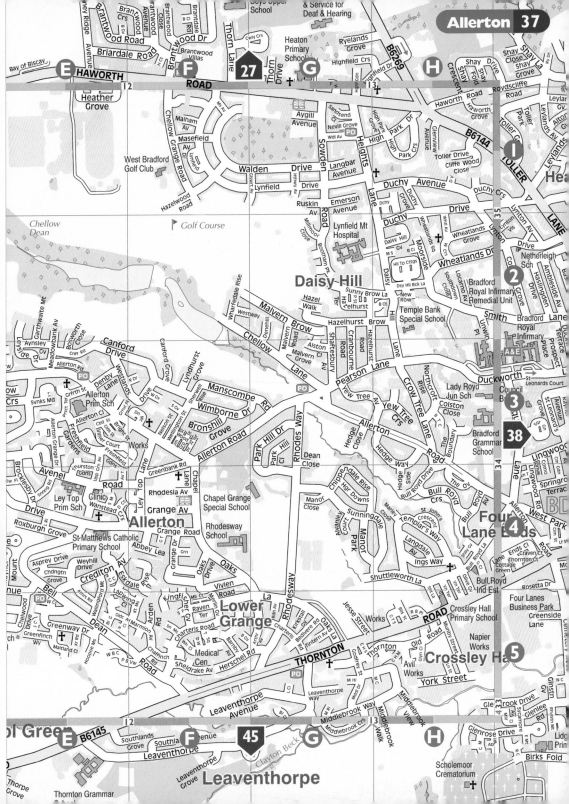

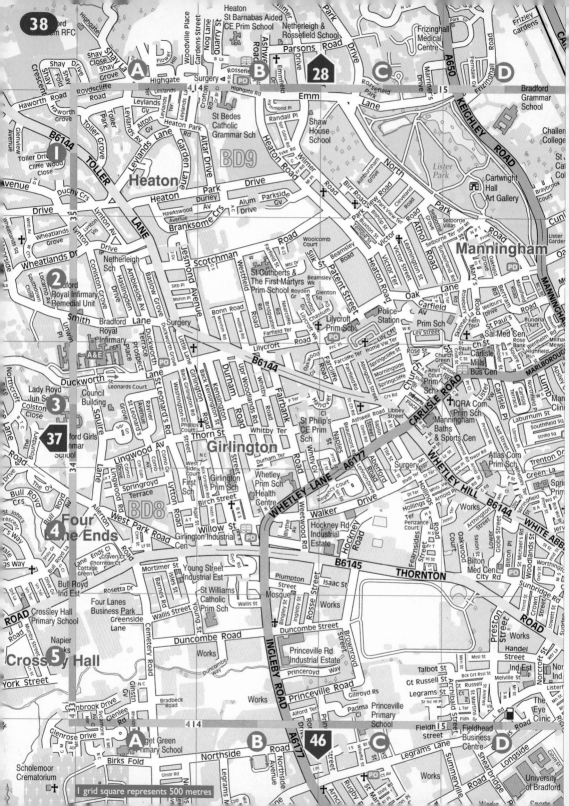

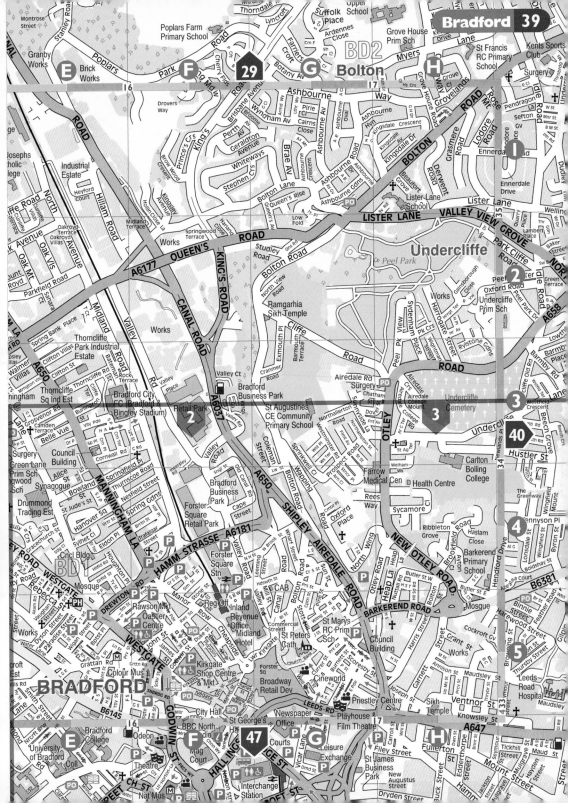

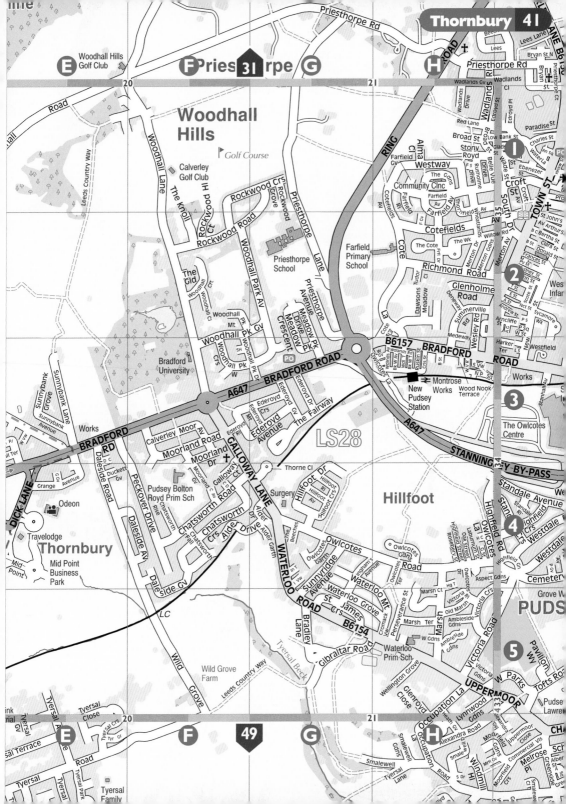

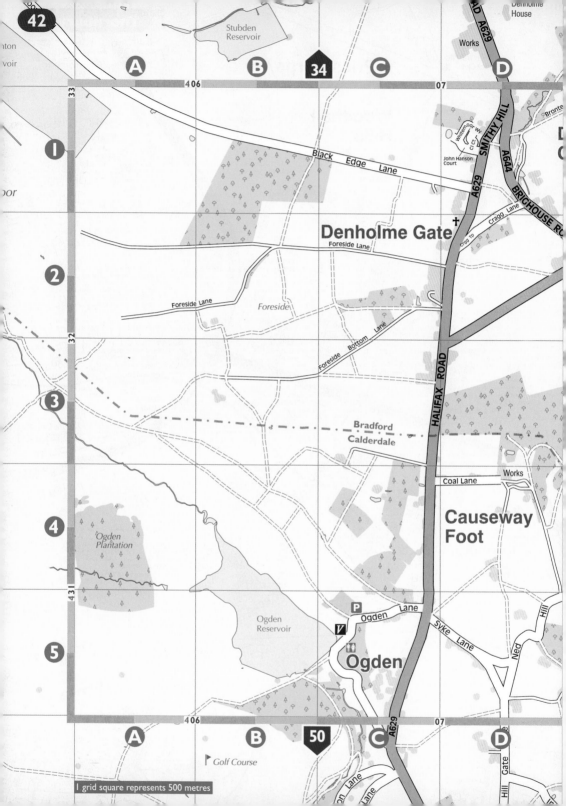

42

A 4 06 B **34** C 07 D

Stubden
Reservoir

Denholme
House

Works

A629

Bronte

Whitemoor Wy
Cl Ct
John Hanson
Court

SMITHY HILL

A629

A644

BRIGHOUSE RD

1

Black Edge Lane

Denholme Gate †

Cragg Lane

Crag Tp

Foreside Lane

2

Foreside Lane

Foreside

Foreside Bottom Lane

HALIFAX ROAD

32

3

Bradford
Calderdale

Works

Coal Lane

4

Ogden
Plantation

**Causeway
Foot**

431

Ogden
Reservoir

5

P

Ogden Lane

V

Ogden

Syke Lane

Ned

Hill

A 4 06 B **50** C 07 A629 D

Gate

Golf Course

Hill

1 grid square represents 500 metres

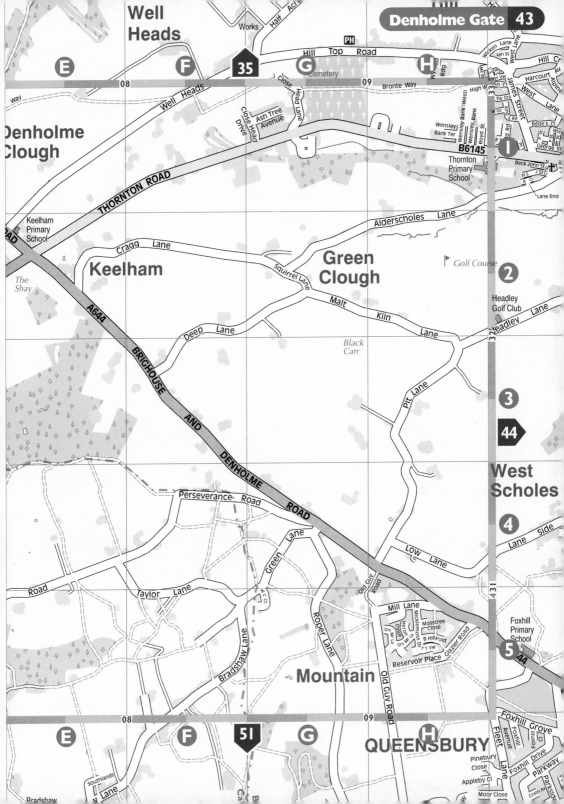

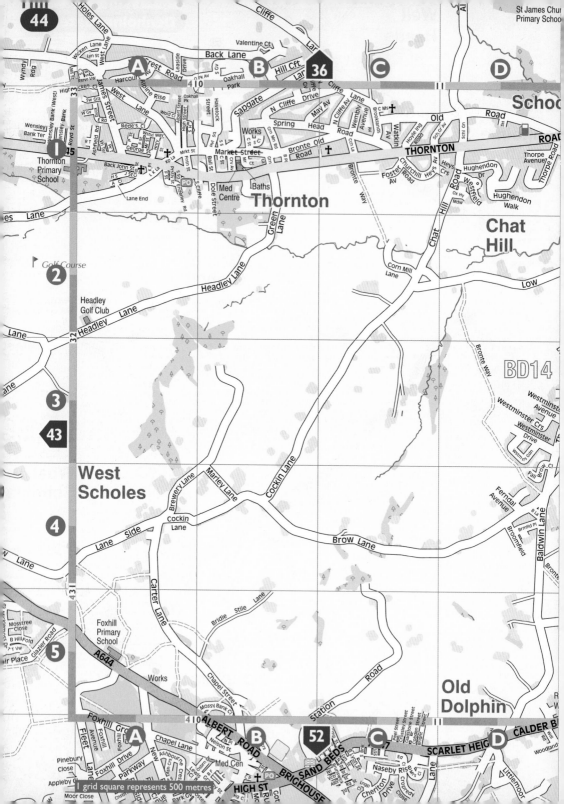

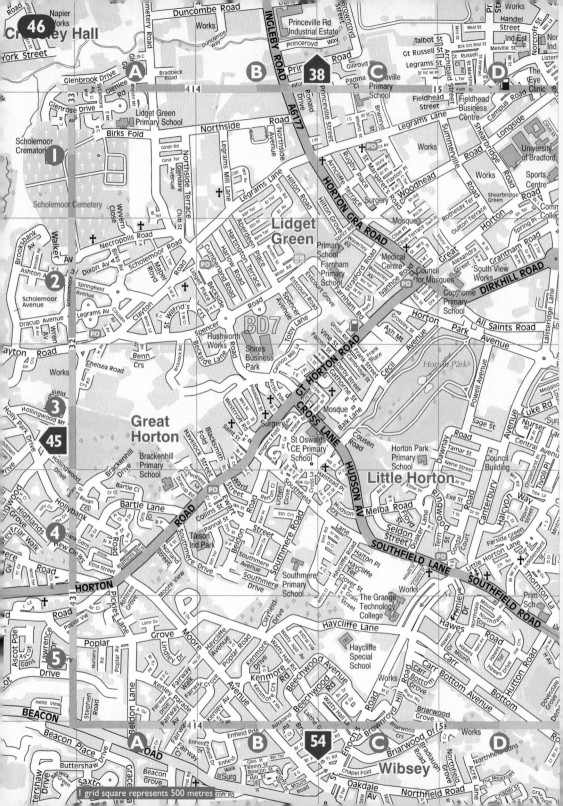

1 grid square represents 500 metres

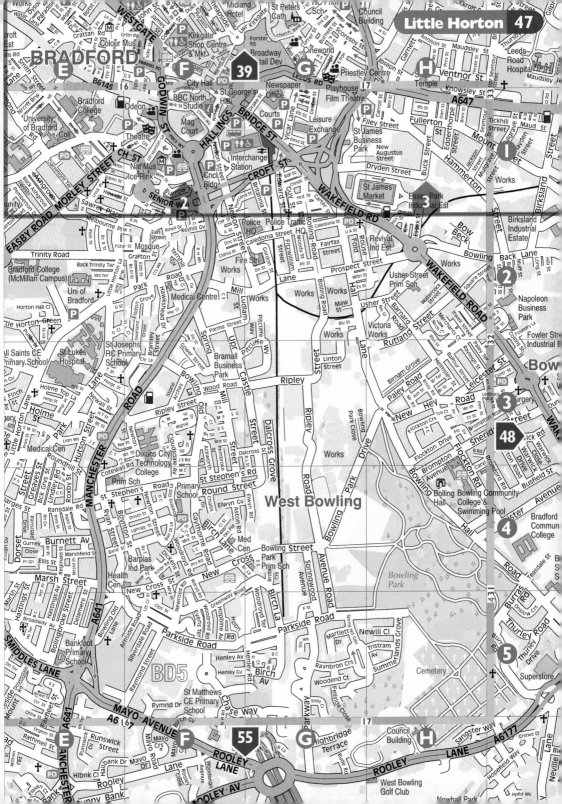

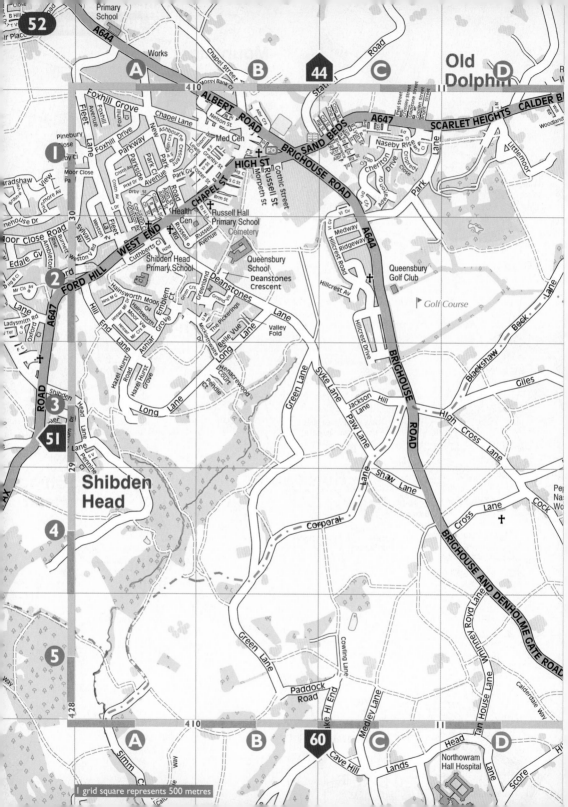

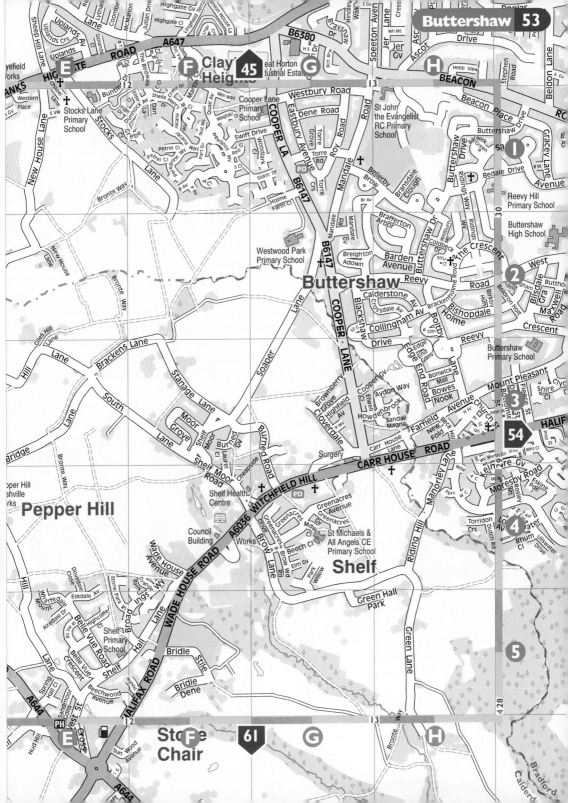

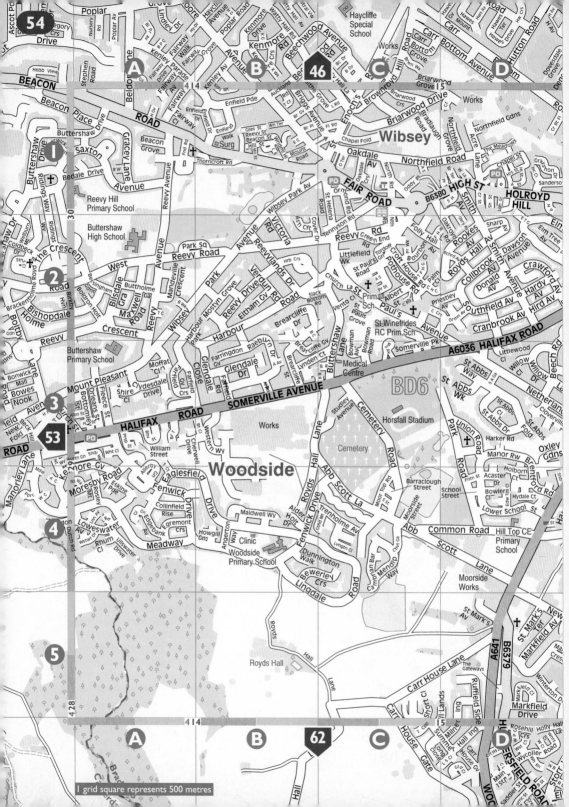

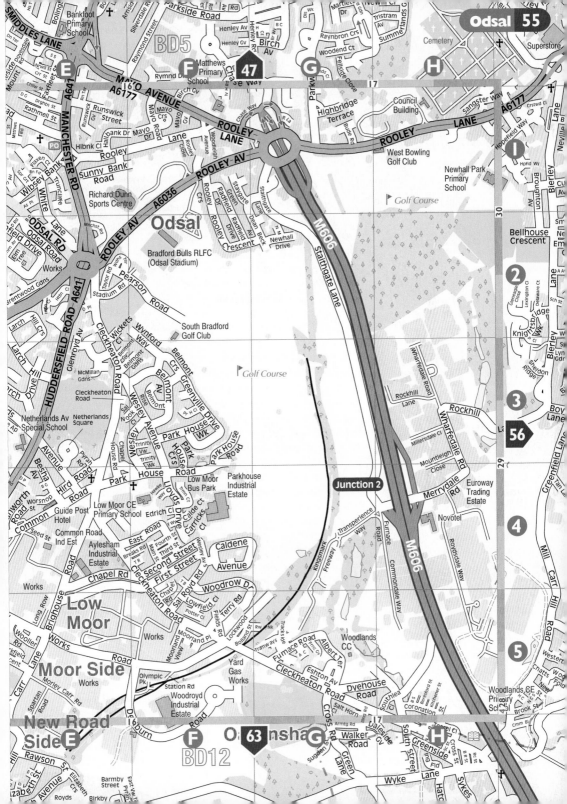

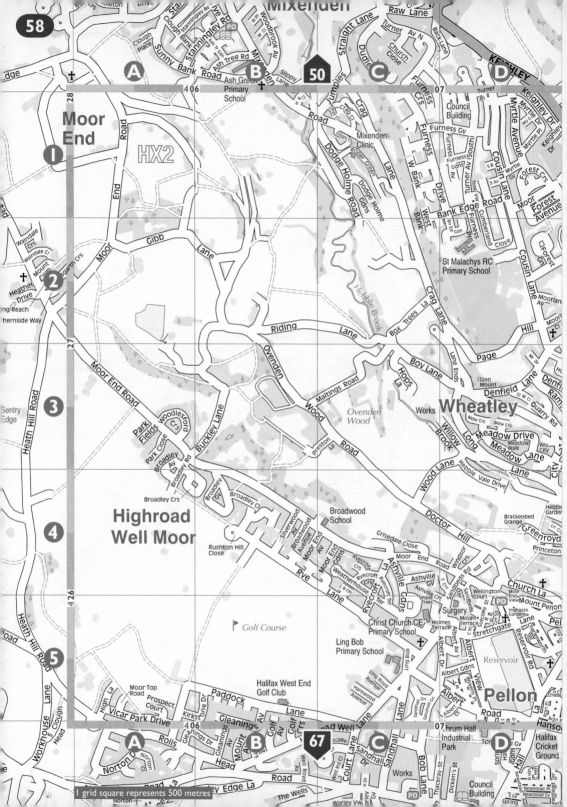

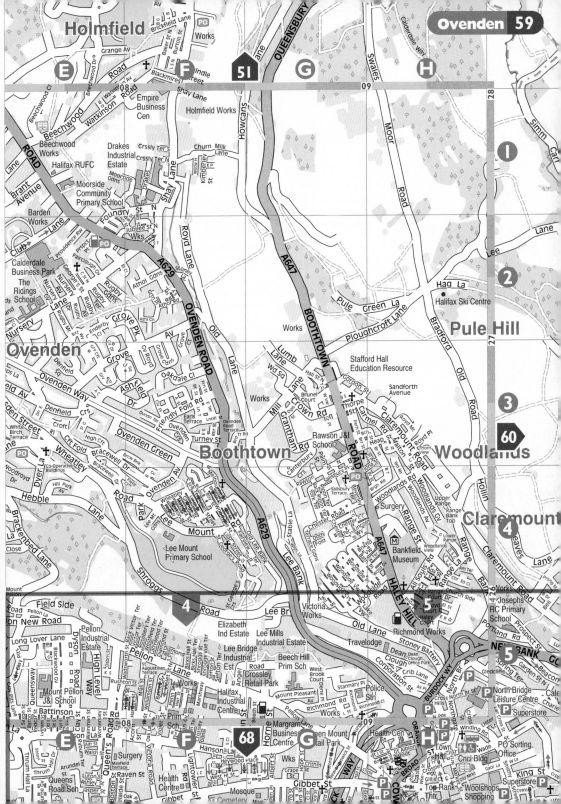

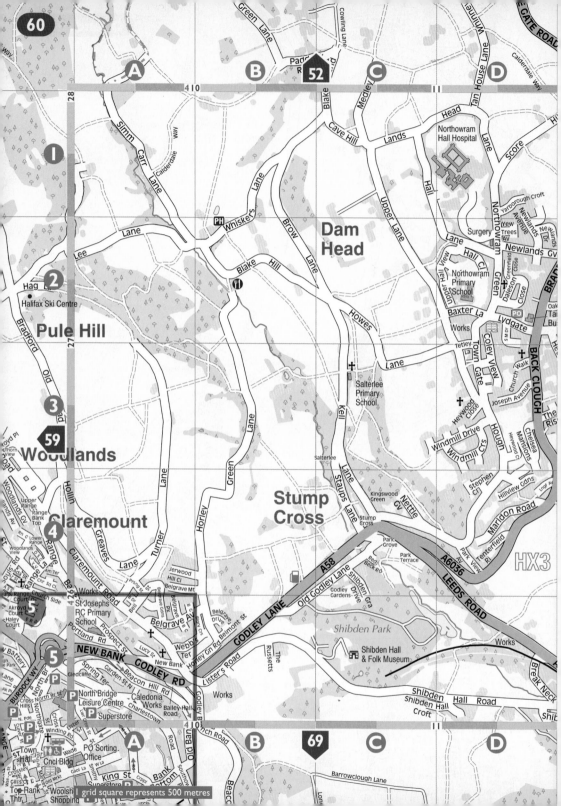

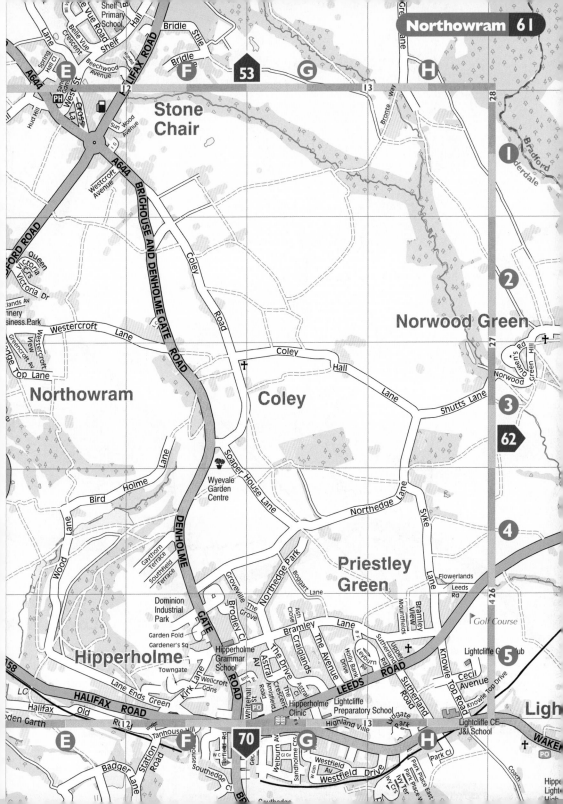

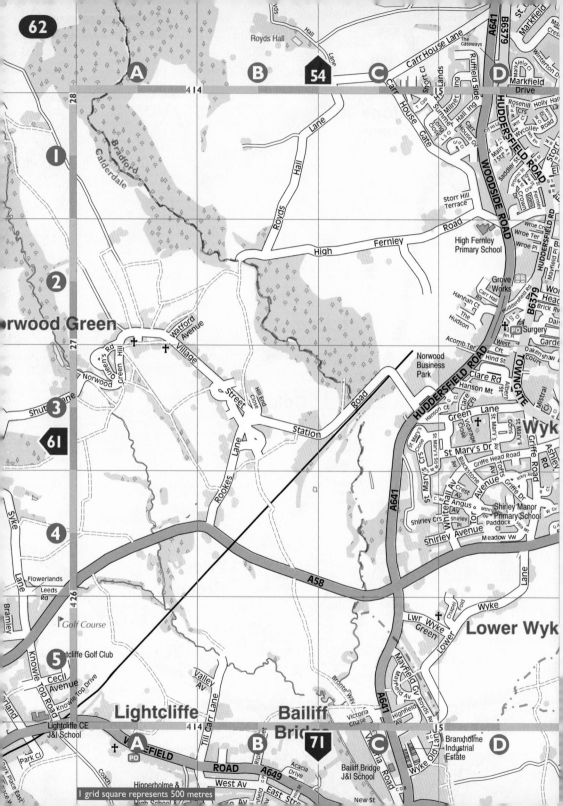

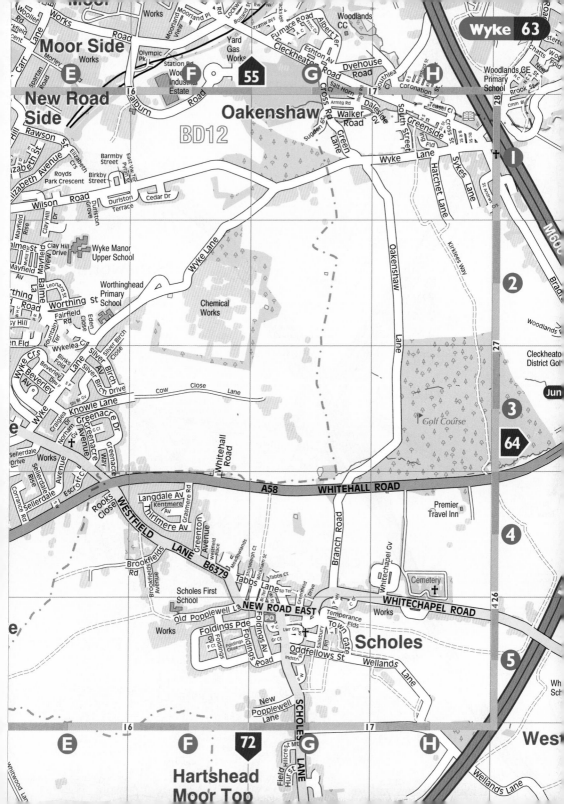

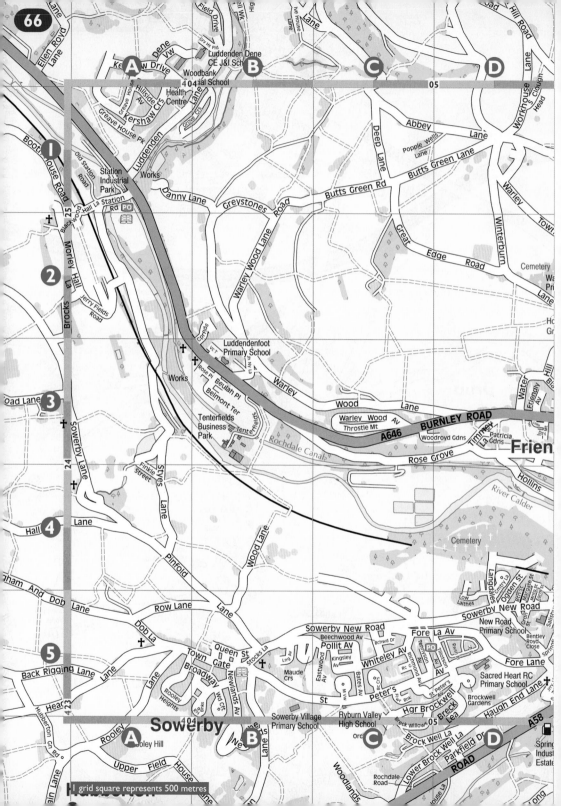

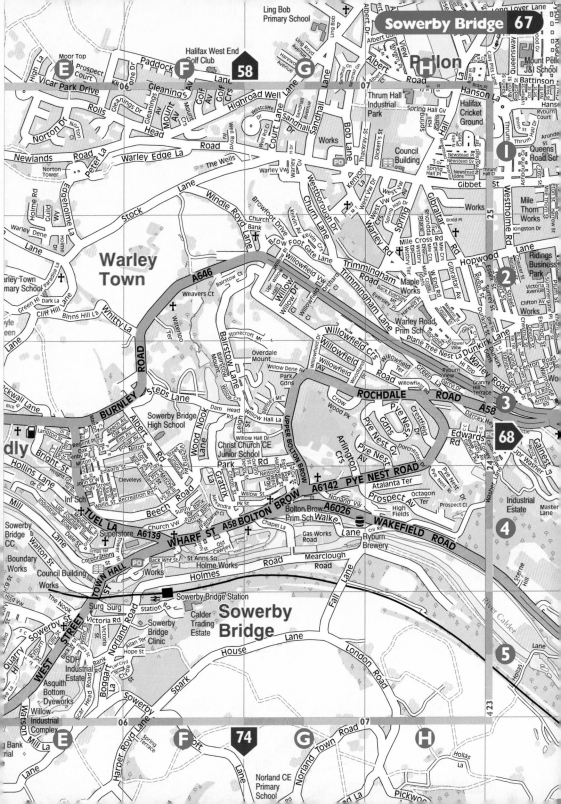

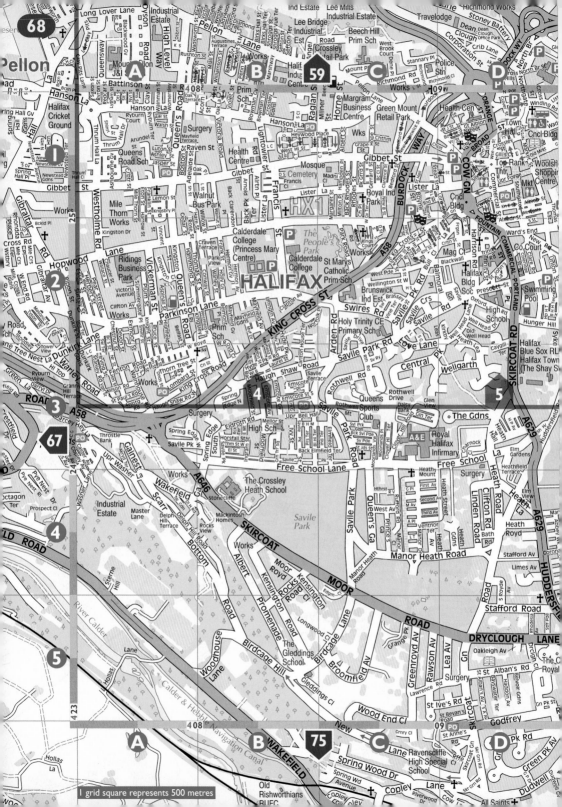

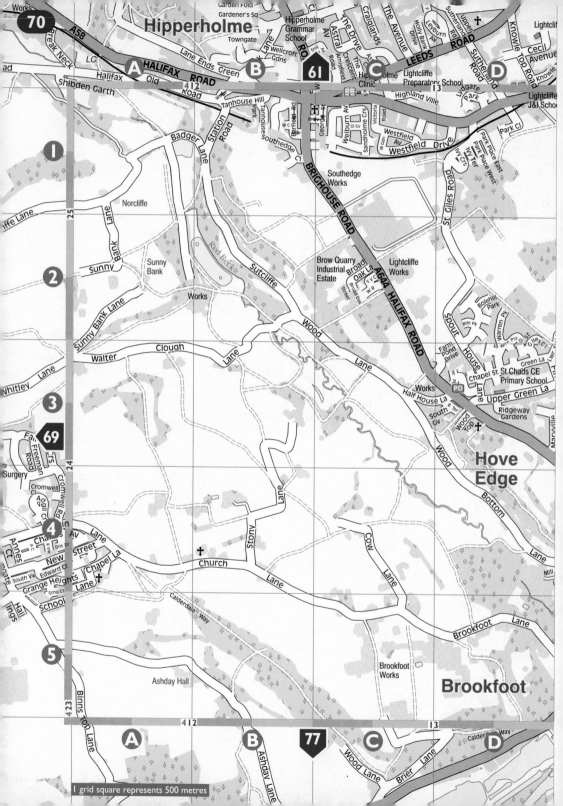

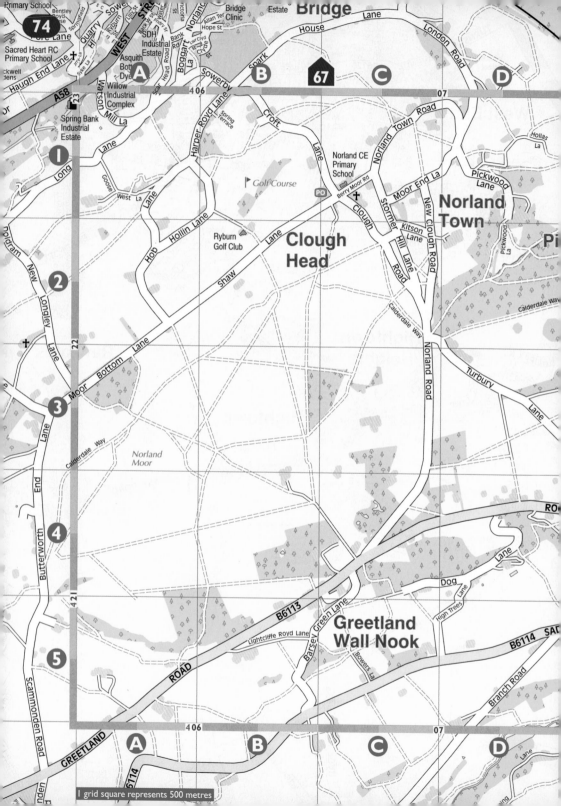

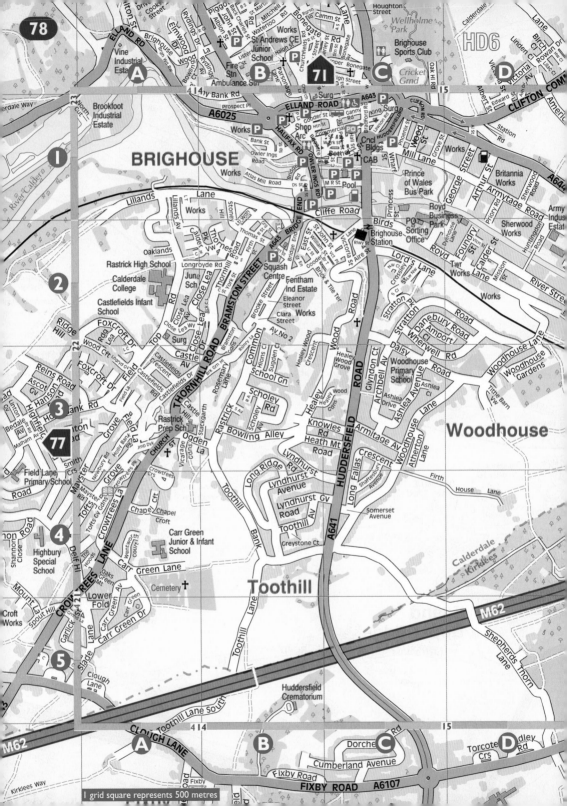

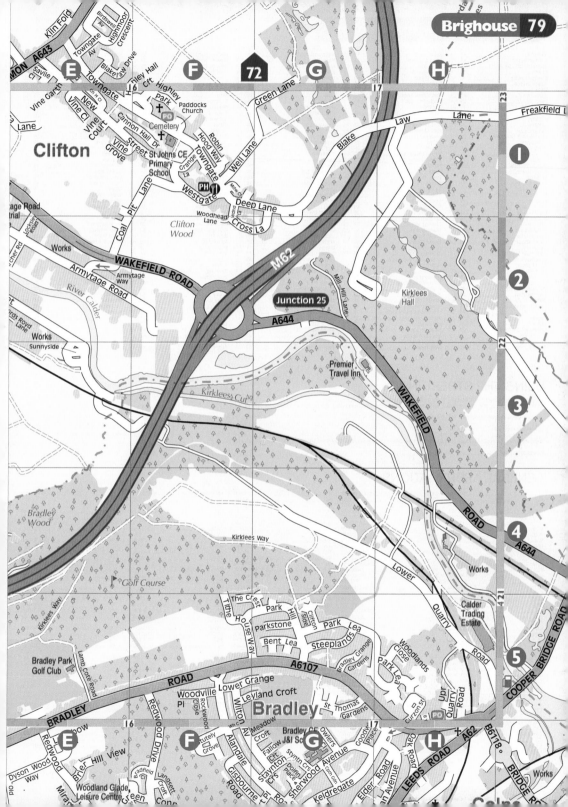

Allerton 37 F4
Ambler Thorn 51 G2
Apperley Bridge 20 D5
Baildon 19 E3
Baildon Green 18 B4
Bailiff Bridge 62 B5
Bank Top 30 B4
Bank Top 68 C3
Barcroft 23 C1
Beck Foot 16 B5
Beechcliffe 7 G2
Bierley 56 A1
Bingley 16 B4
Birkenshaw 57 G4
Birkenshaw Bottoms 65 H1
Birkhouse 71 H2
Black Hill 6 C2
Bogthorn 13 F2
Bolton 29 G5
Bolton Woods 29 F5
Boothtown 59 F5
Bowling 48 A3
Brackenbank 13 G3
Bracken Hall 17 H3
Bradford 2 A5
Bradley 79 G5
Bradshaw 51 E1
Braithwaite 6 A3
Brighouse 78 A1
Brookfoot 70 D5
Brookhouse 50 A2
Buttershaw 55 G2
Cackleshaw 13 E4
Calverley 31 H3
Catherine Slack 51 H4
Causeway Foot 42 D4
Charlestown 19 F4
Chat Hill 44 D2
Claremount 3 H1
Clayton 45 F3
Clayton Heights 45 F5
Cleckheaton 64 D5
Clifton 79 E1
Clough Head 74 B2
Coley 61 G3
Copley 75 F1
Cottingley 26 D2
Cromwell Bottom ... 77 F2
Crossflatts 9 G5
Crossley Hall 37 H5
Cross Roads 13 F5

Crow Nest 17 E3
Cullingworth 24 A3
Daisy Hill 37 G2
Damems 13 G4
Dam Head 60 C2
Denholme 34 B4
Denholme Clough ... 42 D1
Denholme Edge 34 B3
Denholme Gate 42 C2
Dockroyd 12 D5
Drub 65 E3
Dudley Hill 48 B5
East Bierley 57 E3
East Morton 9 F2
Eccleshill 30 A4
Egypt 35 G4
Elland 76 D5
Elland Lower Edge .. 77 F4
Elland Upper Edge .. 77 E5
Esholt 20 B1
Exley 75 H1
Exley Head 13 G1
Fagley 40 C1
Fell Lane 6 B5
Five Lane Ends 29 H4
Four Lane Ends 37 H4
Friendly 66 D3
Frizinghall 28 B4
Gilstead 17 F3
Girlington 38 B3
Gomersal 65 H5
Great Horton 46 A3
Green Clough 43 G2
Greengates 30 C2
Greetland 75 F3
Greetland Wall Nook 74 C5
Guard House 14 B4
Guiseley 10 B3
Hainworth 14 B3
Hainworth Shaw 14 C3
Halifax 5 H1
Harden 15 G5
Hare Croft 25 E5
Harewood Hill 13 F4
Hartshead Moor Side 72 D2
Hartshead Moor Top 72 B1
Haworth 22 C2
Heaton 38 A1
Heaton Royds 27 H5
Heaton Shay 28 A4
Henshaw 21 F1

Highroad Well Moor .58 A4
Hightown 73 G3
Hightown Heights ... 73 F2
Hillfoot 41 H4
Hill Top 35 H5
Hipperholme 61 E5
Holdsworth 51 F4
Hole 22 D5
Holme 49 E5
Holme Wood 49 E4
Holmfield 51 E5
Hove Edge 70 D3
Hunsworth 64 D2
Idle 30 A1
Idle Moor 29 G5
Illingworth 50 D4
Ingrow 13 H3
Keelham 43 E2
Keighley 7 F3
Kelcliffe 10 C1
Knowle Park 14 A1
Laisterdyke 48 C1
Lane Bottom 34 A2
Lane End 12 B4
Leaventhorpe 45 F1
Leeming 33 E3
Lees 23 F1
Lidget Green 46 B2
Lightcliffe 62 A5
Lindwell 75 H3
Lingbob 26 A5
Little Horton 46 C4
Little London 21 F5
Long Lee 14 D1
Lower Grange 37 F5
Lower Town 33 E2
Lower Wyke 62 D5
Low Green 21 H3
Low Moor 55 E5
Lumb Foot 22 A1
Manningham 38 D2
Marsh 22 C5
Merchant Fields 64 D4
Micklethwaite 9 F4
Mixenden 50 B5
Moorhead 27 H2
Moor Side 22 A5
Moor Side 55 E5
Mountain 43 G5
Mytholmes 23 E1
Nab Wood 27 G1

Nether Yeadon 21 F1
New Brighton 27 F3
New Holland 35 H1
New Road Side 63 E1
Newsholme 12 B2
Noon Nick 27 E5
Norland Town 74 C1
Norr 26 A4
Northowram 61 E3
Norwood Green 61 H2
Oakenshaw 63 F1
Oakworth 12 C5
Odsal 55 F2
Ogden 50 A1
Old Dolphin 44 D5
Ousel Hole 9 F1
Ovenden 59 E3
Owlet 28 D4
Oxenhope 32 D2
Peas Acre 9 F3
Pellon 58 D5
Pepper Hill 53 E4
Pickles Hill 12 A5
Pickwood Scar 74 D2
Priesthorpe 31 F5
Priestley Green 61 G4
Priestthorpe 16 D2
Pule Hill 59 H2
Queensbury 51 C1
Rastrick 77 H2
Ravenscliffe 30 D5
Rawdon 21 H3
Rawfolds 73 H5
Riddlesden 8 B2
Ryecroft 14 D5
Saltaire 18 B5
Sandy Lane 36 C1
Sawood 33 G4
Scholemoor 45 H2
Scholes 63 G5
School Green 44 D1
Shaw 32 C2
Shay Gate 26 B5
Shelf 61 G4
Shibden Head 52 A4
Shipley 28 B2
Siddal 69 F5
Southowram 69 G4
Sowerby Bridge 67 F5
Stockbridge 7 G1
Stone Chair 61 F1

Stoney Royd 5 H6
Stump Cross 60 B4
Swain House 29 G4
Swincliffe 65 F1
Sympson Green 20 B5
Tarn 19 F2
Thackley 19 H5
Thackley End 19 G5
Thornbury 41 E4
Thornhills 71 H4
Thornton 44 B1
Thorpe Edge 30 A3
Thwaites 8 A4
Thwaites Brow 8 A5
Toftshaw 56 B2
Tong Park 19 G2
Tong Street 56 C1
Toothill 78 B5
Tyersal 49 E2
Undercliffe 39 H2
Upper Brockholes ... 50 B2
Upper Marsh 22 B5
Upper Town 32 C2
Utley 6 D2
Warley Town 67 E2
Well Heads 35 F5
West Bowling 48 A4
West End 73 E1
Westfield 20 D1
Westgate Hill 57 F2
West Morton 8 B1
West Royd 29 E1
West Scholes 44 A4
West Vale 76 A5
Wheatley 58 C3
Whins Wood 13 H5
Wibsey 54 C1
Wilsden 25 G4
Windhill 29 E2
Woodhall Hills 41 F1
Woodhouse 14 C1
Woodhouse 78 D3
Woodlands 59 H3
Woodside 54 B4
Wrose 29 F3
Wyke 62 D5
Yeadon 21 G1

USING THE STREET INDEX

Street names are listed alphabetically. Each street name is followed by its postal town or area locality, the Postcode District, the page number, and the reference to the square in which the name is found.

Standard index entries are shown as follows:

Aachen Wy *HFAX* HX1 ....**4** C7

Street names and selected addresses not shown on the map due to scale restrictions are shown in the index with an asterisk:

Abbotside CI *IDLE* BD10 * **30** B3

GENERAL ABBREVIATIONS

ACC	ACCESS	CTYD	COURTYARD	HLS	HILLS	MWY	MOTORWAY
ALY	ALLEY	CUTT	CUTTINGS	HO	HOUSE	N	NORTH
AP	APPROACH	CV	COVE	HOL	HOLLOW	NE	NORTH EAST
AR	ARCADE	CYN	CANYON	HOSP	HOSPITAL	NW	NORTH WEST
ASS	ASSOCIATION	DEPT	DEPARTMENT	HRB	HARBOUR	O/P	OVERPASS
AV	AVENUE	DL	DALE	HTH	HEATH	OFF	OFFICE
BCH	BEACH	DM	DAM	HTS	HEIGHTS	ORCH	ORCHARD
BLDS	BUILDINGS	DR	DRIVE	HVN	HAVEN	OV	OVAL
BND	BEND	DRO	DROVE	HWY	HIGHWAY	PAL	PALACE
BNK	BANK	DRY	DRIVEWAY	IMP	IMPERIAL	PAS	PASSAGE
BR	BRIDGE	DWGS	DWELLINGS	IN	INLET	PAV	PAVILION
BRK	BROOK	E	EAST	IND EST	INDUSTRIAL ESTATE	PDE	PARADE
BTM	BOTTOM	EMB	EMBANKMENT	INF	INFIRMARY	PH	PUBLIC HOUSE
BUS	BUSINESS	EMBY	EMBASSY	INFO	INFORMATION	PK	PARK
BVD	BOULEVARD	ESP	ESPLANADE	INT	INTERCHANGE	PKWY	PARKWAY
BY	BYPASS	EST	ESTATE	IS	ISLAND	PL	PLACE
CATH	CATHEDRAL	EX	EXCHANGE	JCT	JUNCTION	PLN	PLAIN
CEM	CEMETERY	EXPY	EXPRESSWAY	JTY	JETTY	PLNS	PLAINS
CEN	CENTRE	EXT	EXTENSION	K	KING	PLZ	PLAZA
CFT	CROFT	F/O	FLYOVER	KNL	KNOLL	POL	POLICE STATION
CH	CHURCH	FC	FOOTBALL CLUB	L	LAKE	PR	PRINCE
CHA	CHASE	FK	FORK	LA	LANE	PREC	PRECINCT
CHYD	CHURCHYARD	FLD	FIELD	LDG	LODGE	PREP	PREPARATORY
CIR	CIRCLE	FLDS	FIELDS	LGT	LIGHT	PRIM	PRIMARY
CIRC	CIRCUS	FLS	FALLS	LK	LOCK	PROM	PROMENADE
CL	CLOSE	FLS	FLATS	LKS	LAKES	PRS	PRINCESS
CLFS	CLIFFS	FM	FARM	LNDG	LANDING	PRT	PORT
CMP	CAMP	FT	FORT	LTL	LITTLE	PT	POINT
CNR	CORNER	FWY	FREEWAY	LWR	LOWER	PTH	PATH
CO	COUNTY	FY	FERRY	MAG	MAGISTRATE	PZ	PIAZZA
COLL	COLLEGE	GA	GATE	MAN	MANSIONS	QD	QUADRANT
COM	COMMON	GAL	GALLERY	MD	MEAD	QU	QUEEN
COMM	COMMISSION	GDN	GARDEN	MDW	MEADOWS	QY	QUAY
CON	CONVENT	GDNS	GARDENS	MEM	MEMORIAL	R	RIVER
COT	COTTAGE	GLD	GLADE	MKT	MARKET	RBT	ROUNDABOUT
COTS	COTTAGES	GLN	GLEN	MKTS	MARKETS	RD	ROAD
CP	CAPE	GN	GREEN	ML	MALL	RDG	RIDGE
CPS	COPSE	GND	GROUND	ML	MILL	REP	REPUBLIC
CR	CREEK	GRA	GRANGE	MNR	MANOR	RES	RESERVOIR
CREM	CREMATORIUM	GRG	GARAGE	MS	MEWS	RFC	RUGBY FOOTBALL CLUB
CRS	CRESCENT	GT	GREAT	MSN	MISSION	RI	RISE
CSWY	CAUSEWAY	GTWY	GATEWAY	MT	MOUNT	RP	RAMP
CT	COURT	GV	GROVE	MTN	MOUNTAIN	RW	ROW
CTRL	CENTRAL	HGR	HIGHER	MTS	MOUNTAINS	S	SOUTH
CTS	COURTS	HL	HILL	MUS	MUSEUM	SCH	SCHOOL
SE	SOUTH EAST
SER	SERVICE AREA
SH	SHORE
SHOP	SHOPPING
SKWY	SKYWAY
SMT	SUMMIT
SOC	SOCIETY
SP	SPUR
SPR	SPRING
SQ	SQUARE
ST	STREET
STN	STATION
STR	STREAM
STRD	STRAND
SW	SOUTH WEST
TDG	TRADING
TER	TERRACE
THWY	THROUGHWAY
TNL	TUNNEL
TOLL	TOLLWAY
TPK	TURNPIKE
TR	TRACK
TRL	TRAIL
TWR	TOWER
U/P	UNDERPASS
UNI	UNIVERSITY
UPR	UPPER
V	VALE
VA	VALLEY
VIAD	VIADUCT
VIL	VILLA
VIS	VISTA
VLG	VILLAGE
VLS	VILLAS
VW	VIEW
W	WEST
WD	WOOD
WHF	WHARF
WK	WALK
WKS	WALKS
WLS	WELLS
WY	WAY
YD	YARD
YHA	YOUTH HOSTEL

81

POSTCODE TOWNS AND AREA ABBREVIATIONS

AIRE	Airedale	BTLY	Batley	GTHN	Great Horton	KGHY	Keighley	SHPY	Shipley
BAIL	Baildon	CLAY	Clayton	GTL/HWG	Greetland/Holywell Green	LM/WK	Low Moor/Wyke	WBOW	West Bowling
BFD	Bradford City Centre	CLECK	Cleckheaton	HFAX	Halifax	LUD/ILL	Luddenden/Illingworth	WBSY	Wibsey
BFDE	Bradford east	CUL/QBY	Cullingworth/Queensbury	HIPP	Hipperholme	LVSG	Liversedge	WIL/AL	Wilsden/Allerton
BGLY	Bingley	ECHL	Eccleshill	HTON	Heaton	MIRF	Mirfield	YEA	Yeadon
BIRK/DRI	Birkenshaw/Drighlington	ELL	Elland	HUDN	Huddesfield north	PDSY/CALV	Pudsey/Calverley		
BOW	Bowling	GIR	Girlington	IDLE	Idle	RPDN/SBR	Ripponden/Sowerby Bridge		
BRIG	Brighouse	GSLY	Guiseley	ILK	Ilkley				

Index - streets

Aac - Avo

A

Aachen Wy *HFAX* HX1 4 C7
Abaseen Cl *BFDE* BD3 3 K5
Abbey La *LUD/ILL* HX2 66 C1
Abbey Lea *WIL/AL* BD15 37 F4
Abbey Wk *HIPP* HX3 68 D4
Abbey Wk South *HIPP* HX3 68 D4
Abbotside Cl *IDLE* BD10 * 30 B3
Abbotts Ter *HFAX* HX1 4 C4
Abb Scott La *LM/WK* BD12 54 C4
Abelia Mt *GTHN* BD7 45 H1
Abel St *LM/WK* BD12 62 D1
Aberdeen Pl *GTHN* BD7 46 B2
Aberdeen Ter *CLAY* BD14 45 G3
GTHN BD7 46 B1
Aberford Rd *GIR* BD8 38 C3
Abingdon St *GIR* BD8 38 C3
Acacia Dr *BRIG* HD6 71 F1
WIL/AL BD15 26 D5
Acacia Park Crs *IDLE* BD10 21 E4
Acacia Park Dr *IDLE* BD10 21 E4
Acacia Park Ter *IDLE* BD10 21 E4
Acaster Dr *LM/WK* BD12 54 D4
Acer Wy *CLECK* BD19 63 G5
Ackroyd Ct *CUL/QBY* BD13 * 44 A1
Ackworth Av *YEA* LS19 11 H5
Ackworth Crs *YEA* LS19 11 H5
Ackworth Dr *YEA* LS19 11 H5
Ackworth St *WBOW* BD5 47 F3
Acomb Ter *LM/WK* BD12 62 D2
Acorn Cl *WBSY* BD6 53 H4
Acorn Pk *BAIL* BD17 19 F4
Acorn St *HFAX* HX1 4 C3
Acre Av *ECHL* BD2 30 A4
Acre Cl *ECHL* BD2 30 A4
Acre Crs *ECHL* BD2 30 A4
Acre Dr *ECHL* BD2 30 A4
Acre Gv *ECHL* BD2 * 30 A4
Acrehowe Ri *BAIL* BD17 19 E2
Acre La *ECHL* BD2 30 A5
HWTH BD22 22 D2
WBSY BD6 54 D1
Acre Ri *BAIL* BD17 18 D2
Acres St *KGHY* BD21 7 E5
Acton St *BFDE* BD3 40 B5
Adam Cft *CUL/QBY* BD13 24 C3
Adam St *WBSY* BD6 54 C1
Ada St *BAIL* BD17 19 F4
CUL/QBY BD13 52 A1
HIPP HX3 59 H4
KGHY BD21 6 D4
SHPY BD18 28 A1
Addison Av *BFDE* BD3 40 C3
Addison Dr *HWTH* BD22 22 D3
Addi St *BOW* BD4 48 B4
Adelaide St *HFAX* HX1 4 B4
WBOW BD5 47 F2
Adgil Crs *HIPP* HX3 69 H4
Adwalton Gv *CUL/QBY* BD13 52 C1
Agar St *GIR* BD8 38 A4
Agar Ter *GIR* BD8 38 A4
Agincourt Dr *BGLY* BD16 17 E3
Agnes St *AIRE* BD20 7 F2
Ainley St *ELL* HX5 76 C5
Ainsbury Av *IDLE* BD10 20 A3
Ainsdale Gv *CUL/QBY* BD13 24 D3
Airebank *BGLY* BD16 16 B3
Aire Cl *BAIL* BD17 18 C5
Airedale Av *BGLY* BD16 26 D3
Airedale College Mt *BFDE* BD3 39 H3
Airedale College Rd *BFDE* BD3 39 H3
Airedale College Ter
BFDE BD3 3 G1
Airedale Crs *BFDE* BD3 39 H3
Airedale Dr *HIPP* HX3 53 E5
Airedale Mt *AIRE* BD20 8 D3
Airedale Pl *BAIL* BD17 19 F4
Airedale Rd *BFDE* BD3 39 G3
KGHY BD21 8 A3
Airedale St *BGLY* BD16 16 C3
ECHL BD2 40 A1
KGHY BD21 7 H3
Aire Gv *YEA* LS19 11 H5
Aire St *BGLY* BD16 16 B1
BRIG HD6 78 C2
HWTH BD22 23 E2
IDLE BD10 19 H5
KGHY BD21 7 G3
Aire Valley Rd *KGHY* BD21 7 H3
Airevalley Rd *KGHY* BD21 8 D5
Aire Vw *AIRE* BD20 8 A1
YEA LS19 11 H5
Aire View Av *BGLY* BD16 27 E1
SHPY BD18 28 B1
Aireview Crs *BAIL* BD17 18 B5
Aire View Dr *AIRE* BD20 8 D4
Aire View Ter *KGHY* BD21 7 H5
Aireville Av *SHPY* BD18 28 C4
Aireville Cl *AIRE* BD20 6 D1
SHPY BD18 28 C4
Aireville Crs *HTON* BD9 28 C4
Aireville Dr *HTON* BD9 28 C4
Aireville Gra *SHPY* BD18 28 C4
Aireville Gv *HTON* BD9 28 C4
Aireville Mt *AIRE* BD20 8 D4
Aireville Ri *HTON* BD9 28 C5
Aireville Rd *HTON* BD9 28 D4
Aireville St *AIRE* BD20 6 D1
Aire Wy *BAIL* BD17 18 B5
Aireworth Cl *KGHY* BD21 7 H3
Aireworth Gv *KGHY* BD21 7 H3
Aireworth Rd *KGHY* BD21 7 H2
Aireworth St *KGHY* BD21 7 E5
Airey St *KGHY* BD21 6 D4
Akam Rd *BFD* BD1 2 A4
Aked's Rd *HFAX* HX1 4 E5
Aked St *BFD* BD1 * 3 F5
Akroyd Ct *HIPP* HX3 5 G1
Akroyd Pl *HIPP* HX3 5 G2
Akroyd Ter *LUD/ILL* HX2 68 A3
Alabama St *HFAX* HX1 4 B3
Alanby Dr *IDLE* BD10 30 B2
Alban St *BOW* BD4 48 A3
Albany Ct *AIRE* BD20 6 D3
Albany St *HIPP* HX3 5 K7
WBOW BD5 * 47 F3
WBSY BD6 54 D1
Albany Ter *HIPP* HX3 5 K7
Albert Av *IDLE* BD10 30 B1
LUD/ILL HX2 58 D5
SHPY BD18 17 H5
Albert Ct *LUD/ILL* HX2 58 D5
Albert Crs *BIRK/DRI* BD11 65 G1
CUL/QBY BD13 52 B1
Albert Dr *LUD/ILL* HX2 58 C5
Albert Gdns *LUD/ILL* HX2 58 D5
Albert Pl *BFDE* BD3 40 D4
Albert Prom *HIPP* HX3 68 B4
Albert Rd *CUL/QBY* BD13 44 A5
LUD/ILL HX2 58 D5
RPDN/SBR HX6 67 F3
SHPY BD18 28 A1
Albert St *BAIL* BD17 18 D5
BRIG HD6 71 H5
CLECK BD19 * 64 C5
CUL/QBY BD13 44 A1
CUL/QBY BD13 52 C1
ELL HX5 76 C5
HFAX HX1 4 E3
HWTH BD22 23 G1
KGHY BD21 7 E4
LM/WK BD12 62 D3
WBSY BD6 54 C2
WIL/AL BD15 25 H5
Albert Ter *LM/WK* BD12 55 G5
SHPY BD18 18 A5
Albert Vw *LUD/ILL* HX2 58 D5
Albert Wk *SHPY* BD18 27 H1
Albert Wy *BIRK/DRI* BD11 65 G1
Albion Ct *HFAX* HX1 5 G3
Albion Fold *WIL/AL* BD15 25 H4
Albion Rd *IDLE* BD10 30 B1
Albion St *BRIG* HD6 71 F5
CLECK BD19 73 H1
CUL/QBY BD13 34 C4
CUL/QBY BD13 52 A1
ELL HX5 76 D5
HFAX HX1 5 H4
HWTH BD22 23 F1
WBSY BD6 53 H3
Alcester Garth *BFDE* BD3 3 J3
Alder Av *KGHY* BD21 14 C1
Alder Carr *BAIL* BD17 18 C3
Alder Dr *PDSY/CALV* LS28 41 G4
Alder Garth *PDSY/CALV* LS28 41 G4
Alder Gv *LUD/ILL* HX2 50 D4
Alder Holt Dr *WBSY* BD6 54 B4
Aldermanbury *BFD* BD1 2 C6
Alderscholes Cl
CUL/QBY BD13 44 A1
Alderscholes La
CUL/QBY BD13 43 H2
Alderson St *WBSY* BD6 53 H3
Aldersyde Rd *GSLY* LS20 10 C3
Alegar St *BRIG* HD6 78 D1
Alexander Sq *CLAY* BD14 45 E3
Alexander St *WBSY* BD6 54 C2
Alexander Ter *HFAX* HX1 4 B3
Alexandra Cl *RPDN/SBR* HX6 67 F4
Alexandra Crs *ELL* HX5 77 E4
Alexandra Gv
PDSY/CALV LS28 41 H5
Alexandra Rd *ECHL* BD2 30 B4
PDSY/CALV LS28 49 H1
SHPY BD18 28 C2
Alexandra St
CUL/QBY BD13 * 52 B1
GTHN BD7 46 D2
HFAX HX1 5 G5
Alexandra Ter *ECHL* BD2 40 B2
YEA LS19 11 H4
Alford Ter *GTHN* BD7 38 B5
Alfred St East *HFAX* HX1 * 5 J4
Alfred St *BRIG* HD6 71 G5
GTL/HWG HX4 76 A4
HFAX HX1 4 B3
Alice St *CLECK* BD19 64 C5
GIR BD8 2 A2
HWTH BD22 22 D3
KGHY BD21 7 F4
Alkincote St *KGHY* BD21 7 E5
All Alone Rd *IDLE* BD10 29 G2
Allanbridge Cl *IDLE* BD10 30 B2
Allandale Av *WBSY* BD6 54 B3
Allandale Rd *WBSY* BD6 54 B3
Allan St *BFDE* BD3 3 J6
Allan Ter *RPDN/SBR* HX6 67 F5
Allen Cft *BIRK/DRI* BD11 57 F5
Allerby Gn *WBSY* BD6 54 A4
Allerton Cl *WIL/AL* BD15 37 E3
Allerton Grange Dr
WIL/AL BD15 37 E3
Allerton La *WIL/AL* BD15 36 D5
Allerton Pl *HFAX* HX1 4 C4
Allerton Rd *GIR* BD8 38 A4
WIL/AL BD15 36 A3
Allison La *ECHL* BD2 29 E5
Alloe Field Vw *LUD/ILL* HX2 50 D4
All Saints Ct *KGHY* BD21 7 E4
All Saints Rd *GTHN* BD7 46 D2
All Saints Ter *KGHY* BD21 7 E4
All Souls' Rd *HIPP* HX3 59 H4
All Souls' St *HIPP* HX3 59 H4
All Souls' Ter *HIPP* HX3 59 H4
Alma Cl *PDSY/CALV* LS28 41 H1
Alma Pl *BFDE* BD3 40 C4
KGHY BD21 14 B1
Alma St *BOW* BD4 48 C3
CUL/QBY BD13 52 A1
HWTH BD22 22 D1
KGHY BD21 14 B2
SHPY BD18 29 E1
YEA LS19 11 H4
Alma Ter *KGHY* BD21 14 B2
Almond St *BFDE* BD3 48 B1
Alpha St *KGHY* BD21 7 G4
Alpine Ri *CUL/QBY* BD13 36 A5
Alston Cl *HTON* BD9 37 G3
Alston Rd *KGHY* BD21 7 G2
Altar Dr *AIRE* BD20 8 B2
HTON BD9 38 B1
Altar La *BGLY* BD16 15 F2
BGLY BD16 16 B3
Althorpe Gv *IDLE* BD10 29 H3
Alton Gv *HTON* BD9 38 A1
SHPY BD18 28 C4
Alum Ct *HTON* BD9 38 B1
Alum Dr *HTON* BD9 38 B1
Alvanley Ct *GIR* BD8 37 G4
Amberley Ct *BFDE* BD3 * 40 B5
Amberley St *BFDE* BD3 40 B5
Ambler Gv *LUD/ILL* HX2 51 E4
Amblers Cft *IDLE* BD10 20 A4
Amblers Ter *HIPP* HX3 59 H4
Ambler St *GIR* BD8 38 D2
KGHY BD21 7 G4
Ambler Wy *CUL/QBY* BD13 51 H3
Ambleside Av *HTON* BD9 38 A2
Ambleside Gdns
PDSY/CALV LS28 41 H5
Ambleton Wy *CUL/QBY* BD13 51 H2
Amelia St *SHPY* BD18 28 A1
America La *BRIG* HD6 78 D1
Amisfield Rd *HIPP* HX3 61 G5
Amos St *HFAX* HX1 4 B3
Amport Cl *BRIG* HD6 78 C2
Amundsen Av *ECHL* BD2 29 H4
Amyroyce Dr *SHPY* BD18 29 F2
Amy St *BGLY* BD16 16 D3
HIPP HX3 59 F3
The Anchorage *BGLY* BD16 16 C2
Anderson St *GIR* BD8 * 38 D3
Andover Gn *BOW* BD4 48 D3
Andrew Cl *HIPP* HX3 69 H4
Angel Pl *BGLY* BD16 16 D1
Angel Rd *HFAX* HX1 4 D2
Angel St *BAIL* BD17 19 E2
Angel Wy *BFD* BD1 2 A5
Angerton Wy *WBSY* BD6 54 B4
Angus Av *LM/WK* BD12 62 D4
Anlaby St *BOW* BD4 48 C2
Anne Ga *BFDE* BD3 3 F4
Annes Ct *HIPP* HX3 69 H4
Anne St *GTHN* BD7 46 A4
Annie St *KGHY* BD21 * 7 F2
RPDN/SBR HX6 67 E3
SHPY BD18 28 D3
Annison St *BFDE* BD3 3 G5
Ann Pl *WBOW* BD5 47 F2
Ann St *CUL/QBY* BD13 34 C3
KGHY BD21 * 7 E5
Anson Gv *GTHN* BD7 46 A5
Anthony La *BGLY* BD16 15 G4
Anvil Ct *CUL/QBY* BD13 24 C4
GIR BD8 38 C3
Anvil St *BRIG* HD6 71 F5
GIR BD8 38 C3
Apperley Gdns *IDLE* BD10 30 D1
Apperley La *IDLE* BD10 30 D1
Apperley Rd *IDLE* BD10 30 C1
Appleby Cl *CUL/QBY* BD13 51 H1
Applehaigh Cl *IDLE* BD10 30 B2
Apple St *HWTH* BD22 13 H3
HWTH BD22 * 32 D2
Appleton Cl *BGLY* BD16 17 E1
LM/WK BD12 55 G5
Apsley Crs *GIR* BD8 38 D3
Apsley St *HWTH* BD22 13 E3
KGHY BD21 14 A1
Apsley Vls *GIR* BD8 38 D3
Aquila Wy *LVSG* WF15 73 G3
Arcadia St *KGHY* BD21 14 A1
Archbell Av *BRIG* HD6 78 C3
Archer Rd *BRIG* HD6 79 E2
Arches St *HFAX* HX1 5 F5
The Arches *HIPP* HX3 * 59 H4
Archibald St *GTHN* BD7 38 D5
Arctic Pde *GTHN* BD7 46 B3
Arctic St *AIRE* BD20 7 E2
HWTH BD22 23 F1
Ardennes Cl *ECHL* BD2 29 G5
Arden Rd *GIR* BD8 37 F5
HFAX HX1 4 E7
Ardsley Cl *BOW* BD4 49 E5
Argent Wy *BOW* BD4 49 E5
Argyle St *BOW* BD4 48 A3
KGHY BD21 7 E4
SHPY BD18 28 C3
Argyll Cl *BAIL* BD17 19 F4
Arkendale Ms *GTHN* BD7 * 45 H4
Arkwright St *BOW* BD4 48 D1
CLAY BD14 45 E3
Arlesford Rd *BOW* BD4 48 D5
Arlington Crs *LUD/ILL* HX2 67 G3
Arlington St *BFDE* BD3 3 J6
Armadale Av *BOW* BD4 56 A2
Armgill La *ECHL* BD2 29 E5
Armidale Wy *ECHL* BD2 39 G1
Armitage Av *BRIG* HD6 78 C3
Armitage Rd *HFAX* HX1 4 A7
LM/WK BD12 63 G1
The Armitage *AIRE* BD20 8 C3
Armstrong St *BOW* BD4 48 C1
Armytage Rd *BRIG* HD6 78 D1
Armytage Wy *BRIG* HD6 79 E2
Arncliffe Av *HWTH* BD22 6 D5
Arncliffe Crs *BRIG* HD6 77 H3
Arncliffe Gv *HWTH* BD22 13 H1
Arncliffe Pl *HWTH* BD22 * 6 D5
Arncliffe Rd *HWTH* BD22 13 H1
Arncliffe Ter *GTHN* BD7 46 C1
Arnford Cl *BFDE* BD3 3 F2
Arnold Pl *GIR* BD8 38 C4
Arnold Royd *BRIG* HD6 77 H4
Arnold St *GIR* BD8 38 D3
HFAX HX1 4 C4
RPDN/SBR HX6 * 67 E4
Arnside Av *AIRE* BD20 7 H2
Arnside Rd *WBOW* BD5 47 E5
Arthington St *GIR* BD8 38 D4
Arthur Av *GIR* BD8 37 G5
Arthur St *BGLY* BD16 * 16 C3
BRIG HD6 78 D1
HWTH BD22 12 C4
IDLE BD10 30 A3
Arum St *WBOW* BD5 46 D4
Arundel St *HFAX* HX1 4 B3
Ascot Av *GTHN* BD7 45 H5
Ascot Dr *GTHN* BD7 45 H5
Ascot Gdns *GTHN* BD7 45 H5
Ascot Gv *BRIG* HD6 77 H3
Ascot Pde *GTHN* BD7 45 H5
Ashbourne Av *CLECK* BD19 73 G2
ECHL BD2 39 G1
Ashbourne Bank *ECHL* BD2 39 G1
Ashbourne Cl *ECHL* BD2 39 G1
Ashbourne Crs *CUL/QBY* BD13 52 A1
ECHL BD2 39 G1
Ashbourne Cft *CLECK* BD19 73 G2
Ashbourne Dr *CLECK* BD19 73 G2
ECHL BD2 39 G1
Ashbourne Gdns *CLECK* BD19 73 G2
ECHL BD2 39 G1
Ashbourne Garth *ECHL* BD2 29 H5
Ashbourne Gv *ECHL* BD2 39 G1
HFAX HX1 4 A4
Ashbourne Hvn *ECHL* BD2 39 G1
Ashbourne Mt *ECHL* BD2 39 G1
Ashbourne Ov *ECHL* BD2 39 G1
Ashbourne Ri *ECHL* BD2 39 G1
Ashbourne Rd *ECHL* BD2 39 G1
HWTH BD22 13 H2
Ashbourne Vw *CLECK* BD19 73 G2
Ashbourne Wy *CLECK* BD19 73 G2
ECHL BD2 39 G1
Ashburn Gv *BAIL* BD17 18 D2
Ashburnham Gv *HTON* BD9 38 C1
Ashby St *BOW* BD4 47 H3
Ash Cl *HIPP* HX3 61 G5
Ash Ct *CLECK* BD19 63 G5
Ash Cft *WBSY* BD6 54 B2
Ashday La *HIPP* HX3 77 F1
Ashdene Ct *CUL/QBY* BD13 24 C3
Ashfield *BOW* BD4 56 C1
Ashfield Av *SHPY* BD18 28 C4
Ashfield Cl *HIPP* HX3 59 E3
Ashfield Crs *BGLY* BD16 16 D4
Ashfield Dr *BAIL* BD17 19 E2
HIPP HX3 59 F3
SHPY BD18 28 C4
Ashfield Gv *SHPY* BD18 28 B4
Ashfield Pl *ECHL* BD2 40 C2
Ashfield Rd *CUL/QBY* BD13 44 A1
GTL/HWG HX4 75 G4
IDLE BD10 20 B5
SHPY BD18 27 H2
Ashfield Ter *GTL/HWG* HX4 75 G3
HWTH BD22 22 D3
Ash Ford Gn *WBSY* BD6 * 54 A1
Ash Ghyll Gdns *BGLY* BD16 * 16 C2
Ash Gv *BGLY* BD16 16 D5
BIRK/DRI BD11 57 F4
BRIG HD6 78 D1
CLECK BD19 65 F4
HWTH BD22 13 H2
Ashgrove *ECHL* BD2 40 B1
GTHN BD7 2 A7
IDLE BD10 30 D2
Ashgrove Av *HIPP* HX3 * 69 F5
Ashgrove Rd *AIRE* BD20 6 D1
Ashington Cl *ECHL* BD2 40 C1
Ashlar Cl *HWTH* BD22 23 E2
Ashlar Gv *CUL/QBY* BD13 52 A3
Ashlea Av *BRIG* HD6 78 C3
Ashlea Cl *BRIG* HD6 78 C3
Ashlea Dr *BRIG* HD6 78 C3
Ashleigh St *KGHY* BD21 7 F3
Ashley Cl *CLECK* BD19 65 F3
Ashley La *BAIL* BD17 28 B1
Ashley Rd *BGLY* BD16 16 D4
LM/WK BD12 62 D3
Ashley St *HFAX* HX1 4 B4
SHPY BD18 28 C1
Ashmews *IDLE* BD10 * 30 D2
Ashmore Gdns *BOW* BD4 * 56 A2
Ashmount *CLAY* BD14 45 G3
Ash Mt *GTHN* BD7 46 C2
KGHY BD21 13 H1
Ash St *CLECK* BD19 73 F1
HWTH BD22 32 D1
Ash Ter *BGLY* BD16 16 C4
Ashtofts Mt *GSLY* LS20 10 D2
Ashton Av *GTHN* BD7 45 H2
Ashton St *BFD* BD1 2 A4
Ashton Wk *IDLE* BD10 29 H2
Ash Tree Av *CUL/QBY* BD13 43 G1
Ash Tree Gdns *LUD/ILL* HX2 50 B5
Ashtree Gv *GTHN* BD7 46 A5
Ash Tree Rd *LUD/ILL* HX2 50 B5
Ashville Cft *LUD/ILL* HX2 58 C4
Ashville Gdns *LUD/ILL* HX2 58 C4
Ashville Gv *LUD/ILL* HX2 58 C4
Ashville St *HIPP* HX3 * 59 F4
Ashwell Rd *GIR* BD8 38 C3
HTON BD9 28 B5
Ashwell St *GIR* BD8 38 C3
Ashwood Dr *AIRE* BD20 8 B2
Ashwood St *BOW* BD4 56 C1
Ashworth Pl *WBSY* BD6 55 E1
Aspect Gdns *PDSY/CALV* LS28 41 H4
Aspen Cl *KGHY* BD21 14 D1
Aspen Ri *WIL/AL* BD15 26 C5
Aspinall St *HFAX* HX1 4 B6
Asprey Dr *WIL/AL* BD15 37 E4
Asquith Ct *LUD/ILL* HX2 * 67 G1
Aston Rd *WBOW* BD5 47 F4
Astral Av *HIPP* HX3 61 G5
Astral Cl *HIPP* HX3 61 G5
Astral Vw *WBSY* BD6 46 B5
Atalanta Ter *LUD/ILL* HX2 67 H4
Atherstone Rd *WIL/AL* BD15 37 E4
Atherton La *BRIG* HD6 78 C3
Athol Gdns *HIPP* HX3 59 F2
Athol Gn *HIPP* HX3 59 F2
Athol Rd *HIPP* HX3 59 F2
HTON BD9 38 C2
Athol St *HIPP* HX3 59 F2
KGHY BD21 7 H2
Atkinson St *SHPY* BD18 28 C1
Atlas Mill Rd *BRIG* HD6 78 B1
Atlas St *GIR* BD8 38 C3
Auckland Rd *WBSY* BD6 54 B1
Austin Av *BRIG* HD6 71 E4
Austin St *KGHY* BD21 7 G3
Autumn St *HFAX* HX1 * 4 B7
Avenel Rd *WIL/AL* BD15 37 E4
Avenel Ter *WIL/AL* BD15 37 E4
Avenham Wy *BFDE* BD3 3 G3
Avenue No 2 *BRIG* HD6 78 B2
Avenue Rd *WBOW* BD5 47 G4
Avenue St *BOW* BD4 56 C1
The Avenue *BGLY* BD16 * 27 E1
CLAY BD14 45 E3
HIPP HX3 61 G5
IDLE BD10 20 D3
IDLE BD10 20 D5
Averingcliffe Rd *IDLE* BD10 30 C3
Avondale *AIRE* BD20 6 D3
Avondale Crs *SHPY* BD18 28 B2
Avondale Gv *SHPY* BD18 28 B2
Avondale Mt *SHPY* BD18 28 B2

Avondale Pl HIPP HX3 ... 68 C4
Avondale Rd SHPY BD18 ... 28 A2
Aydon Wy WBSY BD6 ... 53 H5
Aygill Av HTON BD9 ... 37 G1
Aylesbury St KGHY BD21 ... 13 H2
Aynsley Gv WIL/AL BD15 ... 36 D5
Ayresome Ov WIL/AL BD15 ... 36 D5
Aysgarth Av BRIG HD6 ... 7 F2
Aysgarth Cl LM/WK BD12 ... 62 D3
Ayton Cl BFDE BD3 ... 3 H5
Azealea Ct BFDE BD3 ... 3 J5

B

Back Ada St KGHY BD21 ... 6 D4
Back Aireview Ter KGHY BD21 * ... 7 H5
Back Aireville St AIRE BD20 ... 2 D1
Back Ann St CUL/OBY BD13 ...
Back Ashgrove West GTHN BD7 ... 2 A7
Back Aylesbury St KGHY BD21 ... 13 H2
Back Baker St SHPY BD18 * ... 28 B1
Back Balfour St KGHY BD21 ... 16 C4
   KGHY BD21 * ... 6 D4
Back Beech St BGLY BD16 ... 16 C4
Back Blackwood Gv HFAX HX1 *
Back Blenheim Mt GIR BD8 * ... 38 D2
Back Bower Rd ELL HX5 ... 76 D4
Back Broomfield Rd ... 7 E4
Back Broomfield St
   KGHY BD21 * ... 7 E4
Back Buxton St KGHY BD21 * ... 7 C4
Back Byrl St KGHY BD21 * ... 7 F2
Back Caister St KGHY BD21 * ... 13 H2
Back Caledonia Rd KGHY BD21 * ... 7 G2
Back Cartmel Rd KGHY BD21 ... 6 D4
Back Castle Rd KGHY BD21 * ... 7 E3
Back Cavendish Rd IDLE BD10 ... 30 A2
Back Cavendish St KGHY BD21 * ... 7 F4
Back Cavendish Ter HFAX HX1 ... 4 D5
Back Charles St BRIG HD6 ... 71 F5
Back Clarence St HFAX HX1 ... 4 C4
Back Clarendon Pl HFAX HX1 * ... 4 C4
Back Clock View St AIRE BD20 * ... 7 E1
Back Close Lea BRIG HD6 ... 78 B2
Back Close Lea Dr BRIG HD6 * ... 78 B2
Back Clough HIPP HX3 ... 60 D3
Back Colenso Rd KGHY BD21 * ... 7 E4
Back Croft House La
   AIRE BD20 * ... 6 D1
Back Cromer Av KGHY BD21 * ... 14 A2
Back Cromer Gv KGHY BD21 * ... 14 A1
Back Cromwell Ter HFAX HX1 ... 4 C4
Back Cross La ELL HX5 ... 76 B5
Back Dudley Hill Rd
   ECHL BD2 * ... 40 A2
Back Eaton St KGHY BD21 * ... 13 H2
Back Edensor Rd KGHY BD21 * ... 14 A1
Back Elizabeth St WBOW BD5 ... 47 F2
Back Elmfield Ter HFAX HX1 ... 68 B3
Back Emily St KGHY BD21 ... 7 G3
Back Eric St KGHY BD21 ... 7 F5
Back Eversley Mt LUD/ILL HX2 ... 67 H2
Back Ferguson St HFAX HX1 * ... 5 G5
Back Field Ct CUL/OBY BD13 * ... 44 A1
Back Florist St KGHY BD21 ... 6 A5
Back Fold CLAY BD14 ... 45 E2
Back Foster Rd KGHY BD21 ... 14 A2
Back Foster St KGHY BD21 ... 14 A1
Back Gerrard St HFAX HX1 ... 4 C5
Back Giles St North
   WBOW BD5 ... 47 E2
Back Giles St South
   WBOW BD5 ... 47 E2
Back Girlington Rd GIR BD8 ... 38 B3
Back Gladstone St BGLY BD16 ... 16 C4
Back Gooder La BRIG HD6 * ... 78 C2
Back Grant St HWTH BD22 ... 6 D4
Back Granville Ter CSLY LS20 ... 11 F1
Back Great Russell St
   GTHN BD7 ... 38 D5
Back Greaves St KGHY BD21 ... 47 E4
Back Grosvenor Ter HFAX HX1 ... 4 D4
Back Grouse St KGHY BD21 ... 7 G3
Back Heights Rd
   CUL/OBY BD15 ... 35 C5
Back High St CUL/OBY BD13 ... 44 A1
   YEA LS19 ... 11 G4
Back Hird St KGHY BD21 * ... 7 F5
Backhold Av HIPP HX3 ... 76 B1
Backhold Dr HIPP HX3 ... 76 B1
Backhold La HIPP HX3 ... 76 A1
Backhold Rd HIPP HX3 ... 76 B1
Back Hyde Gv KGHY BD21 * ... 7 F5
Back Irwell St BOW BD4 ... 47 H2
Back John St CUL/OBY BD13 * ... 44 A1
Back Kensington St GIR BD8 ... 38 B4
Back Kirby St KGHY BD21 * ... 7 G3
Back Kirkgate SHPY BD18 * ... 28 B2
Back Laisteridge La GTHN BD7 ... 46 D1
Back La AIRE BD20 ... 9 E2
   CUL/OBY BD13 ... 8 B5
   GSLY LS20 ... 10 C2
   HTON BD9 ... 29 H1
   IDLE BD10 ... 50 C5
   LUD/ILL HX2 ... 50 C5
   WIL/AL BD15 ... 37 E5
   YEA LS19 ... 21 F1
Back Leeming St HWTH BD22 ... 33 E3
Back Lime St KGHY BD21 * ... 14 A2
Back Lindum St GIR BD8 ... 38 D2
Back Lombard St YEA LS19 ... 21 F2
Back Lord St HFAX HX1 * ... 5 F4
Back Lyon St CUL/OBY BD13 * ... 52 C1
Back Mait St HWTH BD22 ... 13 H2
Back Mannville Rd KGHY BD21 ... 6 D5
Back Manor St ECHL BD2 ... 40 A1
Back Market St WBSY BD6 * ... 54 D1
Back Minnie St KGHY BD21 * ... 7 E5
Back Mitchell Ter BGLY BD16 ... 16 C4
Back Moorfield St HFAX HX1 * ... 4 C7
Back Morning St KGHY BD21 * ... 14 A2

Back Muff St BOW BD4 ... 48 A2
Back Myrtle Av BGLY BD16 ... 16 C4
Back North St LM/WK BD12 * ... 63 H1
Back Oak Av BGLY BD16 ... 16 C4
Back O' The Ml BGLY BD16 ... 15 F5
Back Otterburn St KGHY BD21 * ... 7 F3
Back Paget St KGHY BD21 ... 7 G4
Back Park Ter HFAX HX1 ... 4 C4
Back Pleasant St
   RPDN/SBR HX6 ... 67 F3
Back Prospect Pl KGHY BD21 * ... 14 A1
Back Queen St GTL/HWG HX4 ... 75 H5
Back Rhodes St HFAX HX1 ... 4 E4
Back Ribble St KGHY BD21 ... 8 A3
Back Richardson St
   LM/WK BD12 ... 63 H1
Back Ripley St AIRE BD20 ... 8 A2
Back Ripon Ter HIPP HX3 ... 59 G4
Back River St HWTH BD22 ... 25 E2
Back Rd LM/WK BD12 ... 62 D1
Back Rowsley St KGHY BD21 ... 7 G4
Back Rupert St KGHY BD21 ... 7 F5
Back Russell St WBOW BD5 ... 47 E2
Back Rydal St KGHY BD21 ... 7 G4
Back Rylstone St KGHY BD21 ... 7 G3
Back St Paul's Rd SHPY BD18 * ... 28 B2
Back Saltaire Rd North
   SHPY BD18 ... 28 B1
Back Savile Pde HFAX HX1 ... 68 C3
Back Shaw La KGHY BD21 ... 14 C3
Back Simpson St KGHY BD21 ... 6 D4
Back Sladen St KGHY BD21 ... 7 F2
Back Smith Rw WBOW BD5 ... 46 D4
Back Springfield Rd ELL HX5 * ... 77 E4
Back Stone Hall Rd ECHL BD2 ... 30 A5
Back Swinton St KGHY BD21 ... 14 A6
Back Sycamore Av BGLY BD16 ... 16 C4
Back Tamworth St BOW BD4 ... 48 D1
Back Thornhill St
   PDSY/CALV LS28 * ... 31 G3
Back Trinity Ter WBOW BD5 ... 7 G3
Back Unity St North
   BGLY BD16 ... 16 C4
Back Unity St South
   BGLY BD16 ... 16 C4
Back Victoria St KGHY BD21 * ... 5 G3
Back Victor Ter HFAX HX1 ... 4 C1
Back Walnut St KGHY BD21 * ... 14 A1
Back West St RPDN/SBR HX6 ... 67 F4
Back Wharf St RPDN/SBR HX6 ... 67 F4
Back Winterburn St
   KGHY BD21 * ... 7 F5
Back Woodlands Av
   PDSY/CALV LS28 ... 41 H3
Back Woodlands Gv
   PDSY/CALV LS28 * ... 41 H3
Back Woodlands Ter
   PDSY/CALV LS28 ... 41 H3
Back Wood St GIR BD8 ... 38 C4
Back Wright Av HWTH BD22 ... 41 H4
Bacon St CSLY LS20 ... 11 E3
Baddeley Gdns IDLE BD10 ... 19 H5
Baden St HWTH BD22 ... 55 F4
Badgergate Av WIL/AL BD15 ... 25 H5
Badger Hl BRIG HD6 ... 71 H5
Badger La HFAX HX1 ... 70 A1
Badgerstone Cl AIRE BD20 ... 9 E5
Badgers Wy ECHL BD2 ... 29 F5
Bagnall Ter WBSY BD6 ... 54 C1
Baildon Holmes BAIL BD17 ... 18 D4
Baildon Rd BAIL BD17 ... 18 D4
Baildon Wood Ct BAIL BD17 ... 18 D4
Bailey Hall Bank HFAX HX1 ... 5 K2
Bailey Hall Rd HIPP HX3 ... 5 K2
Bailey Hills Rd BGLY BD16 ... 16 B2
Bailey St BOW BD4 ... 48 A2
Bailey Wells Av WBOW BD5 ... 46 D4
Baines St HFAX HX1 ... 4 A5
Baird St WBOW BD5 ... 47 F3
Bairstow Ct LUD/ILL HX2 ... 67 F2
Bairstow La LUD/ILL HX2 ... 67 F2
Bairstow St WIL/AL BD15 ... 36 D1
Baker Fold HFAX HX1 ... 4 D3
Baker St ECHL BD2 ... 40 A2
   SHPY BD18 ... 28 B1
Baker St North LUD/ILL HX2 ... 51 F5
Bakes St GTHN BD7 ... 46 D5
Balbec Av GTHN BD7 ... 37 H5
Baldwin La CLAY BD14 ... 44 D4
Bale Dr IDLE BD10 ... 29 G1
Balfour St BGLY BD16 ... 16 C4
   BOW BD4 ... 47 H3
   KGHY BD21 ... 7 G3
Balk La GTHN BD7 ... 46 C5
Balkram Rd LUD/ILL HX2 ... 50 A5
Ballantyne Rd IDLE BD10 ... 19 H4
Balk St CUL/OBY BD13 ... 44 B1
Balme La LM/WK BD12 ... 63 E2
Balme Rd CLECK BD19 ... 63 F5
Balm St BFD BD1 ... 2 E4
   LM/WK BD12 ... 63 G2
Balme Ter HWTH BD22 * ... 22 D3
Balmoral Pl HFAX HX1 ... 5 F1
Bamlett Brow HWTH BD22 ... 25 E1
Bank IDLE BD10 ... 30 C3
Bank Bottom HFAX HX1 ... 5 K4
Bank Cl IDLE BD10 ... 30 B4
Bank Crest BAIL BD17 ... 18 A3
Bank Crest Ri SHPY BD18 ... 27 G2
Bank Dr WBSY BD6 ... 55 E2
Bank Edge Gdns LUD/ILL HX2 ... 58 C2
Bank Edge Rd LUD/ILL HX2 ... 58 C2
Bankfield Av SHPY BD18 ... 27 G2
Bankfield Dr HWTH BD22 ... 6 B4
   SHPY BD18 ... 27 G2
Bankfield Gdns HIPP HX3 ... 69 G2
Bank Field Gra GTL/HWG HX4 ... 75 H4
Bankfield Mt HWTH BD22 ... 6 B4
Bankfield Rd HWTH BD22 ... 6 B4
   SHPY BD18 ... 27 G2
Bankfield St HWTH BD22 ... 6 B5
Bankfield Ter BAIL BD17 ... 19 E4
Bankfield Vw HIPP HX3 ... 59 G4
Bankfield Wk HWTH BD22 ... 6 B4
Bankfield Yd HIPP HX3 * ... 59 G4

Bankholme Ct BOW BD4 ... 49 E5
Bankhouse La HIPP HX3 ... 76 A1
Bank Rd RPDN/SBR HX6 ... 67 E5
Banks End Rd ELL HX5 ... 77 F5
Banksfield Av YEA LS19 ... 11 G3
Banksfield Cl YEA LS19 ... 11 G3
Banksfield Crs YEA LS19 ... 11 G3
Banksfield Gv YEA LS19 ... 11 G3
Banksfield Mt YEA LS19 ... 11 G3
Banksfield Ri YEA LS19 ... 11 G3
Banks La AIRE BD20 ... 8 A1
Bank St BFD BD1 ... 2 D5
   BRIG HD6 ... 78 B1
   CLECK BD19 ... 73 F1
   SHPY BD18 ... 28 C1
   WBOW BD5 ... 54 D1
Bank Top HIPP HX3 ... 69 F2
Bank Top Dr AIRE BD20 ... 8 A1
Bank Top Wy KGHY BD21 ... 8 A5
Bank Vw BAIL BD17 ... 18 C4
Bank Vw Rd IDLE BD10 ... 30 C4
Bankwell Fold WBSY BD6 ... 55 E1
Bannerman St LM/WK BD12 ... 55 H5
Banner St BFDE BD3 ... 3 H6
Bannockburn Ct BOW BD4 * ... 55 H1
Bantree Ct IDLE BD10 ... 19 H5
Baptist Fold CUL/OBY BD13 ... 52 B1
Baptist Pl BFD BD1 ... 2 B2
Barberry Av BFDE BD3 ... 40 C4
Barber St BRIG HD6 ... 71 F4
Barclay Cl CUL/OBY BD13 ... 24 D4
Barcroft HWTH BD22 ... 25 G1
Barcroft Gv YEA LS19 ... 11 F5
Barden Av WBSY BD6 ... 53 H2
Barden Dr BGLY BD16 ... 17 F2
Barden St GIR BD8 ... 38 C3
Bardsey Crs BFDE BD3 ... 3 H5
Barfield Av YEA LS19 ... 11 F5
Barfield Gv YEA LS19 ... 11 F5
Barfield Rd HIPP HX3 ... 70 B1
Bargrange Av SHPY BD18 ... 28 C3
Barham Ter IDLE BD10 ... 30 C5
Baring Av BFDE BD3 ... 3 J1
Barker Cl HIPP HX3 ... 69 F5
Barkerend Rd BFDE BD3 ... 3 J4
Bar La AIRE BD20 ... 8 A2
Barley Cote Av AIRE BD20 ... 8 A1
Barley Cote Gv AIRE BD20 ... 8 B1
Barley Cote Rd AIRE BD20 ... 8 A1
Barley St HWTH BD22 ... 13 H2
Barlow Rd KGHY BD21 ... 7 E5
Barlow St BFDE BD3 ... 3 J4
Barmby Pl ECHL BD2 ... 40 A5
Barmby Rd ECHL BD2 ... 40 A3
Barmouth Ter BFDE BD3 ... 39 G3
Barnaby Rd BGLY BD16 ... 17 F2
Barnard Rd BOW BD4 ... 48 A4
Barnby Av GIR BD8 ... 37 F5
Barnes Rd GIR BD8 ... 38 A4
Barnsley Beck Gv BAIL BD17 ... 17 G4
Barn St HWTH BD22 ... 32 D2
The Barn LM/WK BD12 ... 55 F4
Barraclough Sq LM/WK BD12 ... 62 D1
Barraclough St LM/WK BD12 ... 54 C4
Barran St BGLY BD16 ... 16 D3
Barrington Cl HIPP HX3 ... 69 H4
Barrington Pde CLECK BD19 ... 65 F5
Barrowclough La HIPP HX3 ... 59 G1
Barr Ter CLAY BD14 ... 44 C3
Barry St BFD BD1 ... 2 C5
Barsey Green La GTL/HWG HX4 ... 74 B5
Barthorpe Cl BOW BD4 ... 49 E5
Bartle Cl GTHN BD7 ... 46 A4
Bartle Fold GTHN BD7 ... 46 B3
Bartle Gill Dr BAIL BD17 ... 19 F2
Bartle Gill Ri BAIL BD17 ... 19 F2
Bartle Gill Vw BAIL BD17 * ... 19 F2
Bartle Gv GTHN BD7 ... 46 A4
Bartle La GTHN BD7 ... 46 A4
Bartle Pl GTHN BD7 ... 46 A4
Bartle Sq GTHN BD7 ... 46 A4
Barton St BRIG HD6 ... 71 F5
   WBOW BD5 ... 46 C4
Barwick Av WBSY BD6 ... 53 H1
Basil St WBOW BD5 ... 54 D1
Baslow Gv HTON BD9 ... 38 A2
Bateman St GIR BD8 ... 38 B5
Bates Av RPDN/SBR HX6 ... 66 C5
Bateson St IDLE BD10 ... 30 D2
Bath Pl CLECK BD19 ... 73 G1
   HIPP HX3 ... 59 G4
Bath Rd CLECK BD19 ... 73 G1
   HIPP HX3 ... 68 D4
Bath St BFDE BD3 ... 3 H5
   ELL HX5 ... 76 C5
   HFAX HX1 * ... 5 J5
   KGHY BD21 ... 7 E4
Batley Ct BAIL BD17 ... 19 E2
Batley St HIPP HX3 ... 59 F4
Batter La YEA LS19 ... 11 G4
Battinson Rd HFAX HX1 ... 4 A2
Battinson St HIPP HX3 ... 69 F3
Battlefield Vw BOW BD4 ... 47 F3
Battye St BOW BD4 ... 48 B1
Bavaria Pl GIR BD8 ... 38 C4
Bawson Ct CLECK BD19 ... 65 F5
Baxandall St WBOW BD5 ... 47 E4
Baxter La HWTH BD22 ... 60 D2
Bayne Dr BOW BD4 ... 56 A2
Bay of Biscay WIL/AL BD15 ... 27 E5
Bayswater Gv ECHL BD2 ... 40 C2
Bayswater Ter HIPP HX3 ... 68 D4
Beacon Brow WBSY BD6 ... 45 G5
Beacon Cl BGLY BD16 ... 17 E3
Beacon Gv WBSY BD6 ... 54 A1
Beacon Hill Rd HIPP HX3 ... 5 J2
Beacon Rd WBSY BD6 ... 53 H1
Beaconsfield Rd CLAY BD14 ... 45 G3
Beaconsfield St HIPP HX3 ... 69 F2
Beacon St GTHN BD7 ... 46 D5
   WBSY BD6 ... 53 H1
Beamsley Gv BGLY BD16 ... 17 E3
Beamsley Rd HTON BD9 ... 28 A4
Beamsley Wk HTON BD9 ... 38 B2

Bean St ELL HX5 ... 77 F5
Beatrice St AIRE BD20 ... 7 F2
   CLECK BD19 ... 3 A5
   HWTH BD22 ... 32 D2
Beaufort Gv ECHL BD2 ... 39 H1
Beaumont Rd GIR BD8 ... 38 C3
Beck Bottom PDSY/CALV LS28 ... 30 D5
Beckenham Pl HFAX HX1 ... 58 D5
Beckett Cl BRIG HD6 ... 71 F5
Beckfield Rd BGLY BD16 ... 26 D2
Beckfoot La BGLY BD16 ... 16 A5
Beck Hl WBSY BD6 ... 53 H5
Beck La BGLY BD16 ... 9 F5
Beck Rd BGLY BD16 ... 9 F5
Beck Side KGHY BD21 ... 7 F6
Beckside La GTHN BD7 ... 46 B2
Beckside Rd GTHN BD7 ... 46 B2
Becks Rd HWTH BD22 ... 6 D5
Beck St KGHY BD21 ... 7 F5
Beckwith Dr IDLE BD10 ... 30 C4
Bedale Av BRIG HD6 ... 77 H5
Bedale Dr WBSY BD6 ... 53 H1
Bede's Cl CUL/OBY BD13 ... 44 A4
Bedford St BOW BD4 ... 2 E7
   ELL HX5 ... 5 F4
   HFAX HX1 ... 5 F4
   KGHY BD21 ... 7 E5
Bedford St North HFAX HX1 ... 5 F3
Bedivere Rd GIR BD8 ... 37 G5
Beech Av CUL/OBY BD13 ... 34 B1
   RPDN/SBR HX6 ... 67 E3
Beech Ct HIPP HX3 ... 53 G4
   IDLE BD10 ... 20 A4
Beech Crs BAIL BD17 ... 18 A5
   BFDE BD3 ... 3 J4
Beech Dr CUL/OBY BD13 ... 34 B1
Beecher St KGHY BD21 ... 59 G3
   KGHY BD21 ... 7 H2
Beech Gv CUL/OBY BD13 ... 34 B1
The Beeches BAIL BD17 ... 7 H5
   BIRK/DRI BD11 ... 57 F5
   GSLY LS20 ... 10 D2
   PDSY/CALV LS28 ... 41 G4
Beech Sq CLAY BD14 ... 44 D5
Beech St BGLY BD16 ... 16 C4
   ELL HX5 ... 76 C5
   HFAX HX1 ... 5 F4
   KGHY BD21 ... 7 H5
Beech Ter BFDE BD3 ... 3 J5
Beechtree Ct BAIL BD17 ... 17 G4
Beech Vw RPDN/SBR HX6 * ... 67 E3
Beech Wk CLECK BD19 ... 65 G1
Beechwood Av AIRE BD20 ... 8 A1
   HIPP HX3 ... 53 G5
   LUD/ILL HX2 ... 51 F5
   RPDN/SBR HX6 ... 66 C4
   SHPY BD18 ... 27 H2
   WBSY BD6 ... 46 B5
Beechwood Cl LUD/ILL HX2 ... 59 E1
   RPDN/SBR HX6 ... 66 C5
   WBSY BD6 ... 46 B5
Beechwood Crs
   RPDN/SBR HX6 ... 66 C5
   WBSY BD6 ... 46 B5
Beechwood Gv LUD/ILL HX2 * ... 59 E1
   SHPY BD18 ... 27 H2
   WBSY BD6 ... 46 B5
Beechwood Pk BRIC HD6 ... 71 G2
Beechwood Rd LUD/ILL HX2 ... 59 E1
   WBSY BD6 ... 46 B5
Beechwood St
   PDSY/CALV LS28 ... 41 H3
Beecroft St KGHY BD21 ... 7 G4
Beehive St WBSY BD6 ... 54 A3
Beehive Yd WBSY BD6 ... 54 A3
Bela Av BOW BD4 ... 55 H1
Belcross Dr HIPP HX3 ... 5 J1
Beldon La GTHN BD7 ... 54 A1
Beldon Park Av GTHN BD7 ... 46 A5
Beldon Park Cl GTHN BD7 ... 46 A5
Beldon Pl ECHL BD2 ... 40 A3
Beldon Rd GTHN BD7 ... 46 B4
Belfast St HFAX HX1 ... 5 H3
The Belfry LS19 ... 11 H5
Belgrave Av HIPP HX3 ... 5 K1
Belgrave Cl HIPP HX3 ... 59 F4
Belgrave Crs HIPP HX3 ... 60 B5
Belgrave Dr HIPP HX3 ... 60 B5
Belgrave Gdns HIPP HX3 ... 60 A4
Belgrave Gv HIPP HX3 ... 60 B5
Belgrave Ms YEA LS19 ... 21 F2
Belgrave Mt HIPP HX3 ... 60 B5
Belgrave Pk HIPP HX3 ... 60 A4
Belgrave Rd BGLY BD16 ... 16 D5
   KGHY BD21 ... 7 H5
Belgrave Rd RPDN/SBR HX6 ... 67 G4
Bell Balk HWTH BD22 ... 16 B2
Bell Dean Rd WIL/AL BD15 ... 37 E4
Belle Isle Rd HWTH BD22 ... 22 D3
Bellerby Brow WBSY BD6 ... 53 F4
Belle View Ri HIPP HX3 ... 53 G5
Belle Vue CUL/OBY BD13 ... 52 B5
   GIR BD8 ... 2 A1
Belle Vue Dr PDSY/CALV LS28 ... 41 H1
Belle Vue Pk HFAX HX1 * ... 4 D4
Belle Vue Ri HFAX HX1 ... 4 D4
Belle Vue Rd HIPP HX3 ... 59 F4
   KGHY BD21 * ... 7 G5
Belle Vue Ter HIPP HX3 ... 69 F5
Bell Hall Mt HFAX HX1 ... 68 B5
Bell Hall Ter HFAX HX1 ... 68 C5
Bell House Av BOW BD4 ... 56 A1
Belle View Ri HIPP HX3 ... 68 B5
Belloe St WBOW BD5 ... 54 D1
Bellshaw St GIR BD8 ... 37 H5
Bell St HIPP HX3 ... 69 F3
   LM/WK BD12 ... 62 D1

Belmont Av BAIL BD17 ... 18 C3
   LM/WK BD12 ... 55 F3
Belmont Ct BAIL BD17 ... 18 C3
Belmont Crs LM/WK BD12 ... 55 F3
   SHPY BD18 ... 28 B1
Belmont Gdns WBSY BD6 ... 55 E3
Belmont Gv WBSY BD6 ... 55 E3
   YEA LS19 ... 21 H1
Belmont Ri BAIL BD17 ... 4 C6
Belmont Rd BAIL BD17 ... 18 C3
   LM/WK BD12 ... 55 F3
Belmont St ECHL BD2 ... 30 B4
   HIPP HX3 ... 60 B5
   RPDN/SBR HX6 ... 67 F4
Belmont Ter LUD/ILL HX2 ... 66 B3
   SHPY BD18 ... 28 B1
Belton Cl GTHN BD7 ... 46 B4
Belvedere Ter GIR BD8 ... 38 C4
Belvoir Gdns HIPP HX3 ... 68 D5
Bempton Ct GTHN BD7 ... 46 C3
Bempton Pl GTHN BD7 ... 46 C3
Bentnow Av IDLE BD10 ... 30 D4
Benn Av GTHN BD7 ... 46 A5
Benn Crs GTHN BD7 ... 46 A5
Bennett St HIPP HX3 ... 5 K6
Bentfield Cottages
   HIPP HX3 ... 45 F2
Bent Lea HUDN HD2 ...
Bentley Av BRIG HD6 ... 71 F1
Bentley Cl BAIL BD17 ... 18 C2
Bentley Mt RPDN/SBR HX6 ... 67 G3
Bentley Royd Cl
   RPDN/SBR HX6 ... 66 D5
Bentley St LM/WK BD12 * ... 63 E2
Benton Park Av YEA LS19 ... 21 G1
Benton Park Crs YEA LS19 ... 21 H1
Benton Park Dr YEA LS19 ... 21 H1
Benton Park Rd YEA LS19 ... 21 H1
Bents La WIL/AL BD15 ... 25 F3
Beresford Rd WBSY BD6 ... 54 B5
Beresford St LM/WK BD12 ... 55 H5
Berrington Wy HWTH BD22 ... 12 C3
Berry La HFAX HX1 ... 5 K4
   KGHY BD21 ... 14 A1
Berry Moor Rd RPDN/SBR HX6 ... 74 C1
Bertie St BOW BD4 ... 48 B4
Bertram Dr BAIL BD17 ... 18 C4
Bertram Rd GIR BD8 ... 38 D2
Berwick St HFAX HX1 ... 5 J4
Bescaby Gv BAIL BD17 * ... 19 F5
Besha Av LM/WK BD12 ... 55 E4
Besha Gv LM/WK BD12 ... 55 E4
Bessingham Gdns WBSY BD6 ... 54 A2
Best La HWTH BD22 ... 32 D2
Beswick Cl BFDE BD3 ... 40 C5
Bethel Rd SHPY BD18 ... 29 E1
Bethel St BRIG HD6 ... 78 C1
   HIPP HX3 ... 59 F5
Beulah Pl LUD/ILL HX2 * ... 66 B3
Bevan Ct GTHN BD7 ... 46 A4
Beverley Av LM/WK BD12 ... 63 E2
Beverley Cl ELL HX5 ... 77 E5
Beverley Dr LM/WK BD12 ... 63 E2
Beverley Pl HIPP HX3 * ... 59 G4
Beverley St BOW BD4 ... 48 C2
Beverley Ter HIPP HX3 ... 59 G4
Bewerley Crs LM/WK BD12 ... 54 B4
Bewick Ct WBSY BD6 ... 45 E5
Bierley Hall Gv BOW BD4 ... 56 A3
Bierley House Av BOW BD4 ... 56 A2
Bierley La BOW BD4 ... 56 B1
Bierley Vw BOW BD4 ... 56 B1
Bilberry Cl CLAY BD14 ... 45 F4
Bilberry Ri HWTH BD22 ... 25 E2
Billing Vw IDLE BD10 ... 30 B2
Bilsdale Gra WBSY BD6 ... 54 A2
Bilsdale Wy BAIL BD17 ... 18 A4
Bilton Pl GIR BD8 ... 38 D4
Binbrook Vw WIL/AL BD15 * ... 37 E3
Bingley Lands GSLY LS20 ... 10 D2
Bingley Rd CUL/OBY BD13 ... 24 D2
   HTON BD9 ... 27 G5
   KGHY BD21 ... 14 A5
   SHPY BD18 ... 27 G1
Bingley St GIR BD8 ... 38 B5
Binnie St BFDE BD3 ... 3 J3
Binns Hill La LUD/ILL HX2 ... 67 E2
Binns La GTHN BD7 ... 46 A2
Binns St BGLY BD16 ... 16 D3
Binns Top La HIPP HX3 ... 70 A5
Birch Av WBOW BD5 ... 47 G5
Birch Cl BRIC HD6 ... 71 H5
Birch Cliff BAIL BD17 ... 18 C3
Birch Cl BRIG HD6 ... 71 H5
   WBOW BD5 ... 47 G5
Birchdale BGLY BD16 ... 9 C5
Birch Gv HWTH BD22 ... 13 H2
   WBOW BD5 ... 55 F1
Birchlands Av WIL/AL BD15 ... 25 G3
Birchlands Gv WIL/AL BD15 ... 25 G3
Birch La WBOW BD5 ... 47 G4
Birch St GIR BD8 ... 38 B4
Birch Tree Gdns KGHY BD21 ... 7 H5
Birch Wy WBOW BD5 ... 47 G5
Birchwood Av AIRE BD20 ... 8 D1
Birchwood Av IDLE BD10 ... 31 E1
Birchwood Rd AIRE BD20 ... 6 D1
Birdcage Hl HIPP HX3 ... 68 B5
Birdcage La HIPP HX3 ... 68 B5
Bird Holme La HIPP HX3 ... 61 E4
Birds Royd La BRIG HD6 ... 78 B3
Birdswell Av BRIC HD6 ... 72 A5
The Birdwalk BGLY BD16 ... 45 F5
Birkby Hvn WBSY BD6 ... 53 H2
Birkby La BRIG HD6 ... 71 H1
Birkby St LM/WK BD12 ... 63 E1
Birkdale Gv LUD/ILL HX2 ... 24 D3
Birkenshaw La BIRK/DRI BD11 ... 57 G5
Birkett St CLECK BD19 ... 64 C5
Birk Hey Cl BRIC HD6 ... 71 G2
Birkhill Crs BIRK/DRI BD11 ... 57 G5
Birkhouse La BRIG HD6 ... 72 A2
Birkhouse Rd BRIG HD6 ... 71 H1

Birklands Moor CLECK BD19 ...65 G2
Birklands Rd SHPY BD18 ...28 C2
Birklands Ter SHPY BD18 ...28 C2
Birk Lea St WBOW BD5 ...47 F5
Birks Av GTHN BD7 ...46 A1
Birks Fold GTHN BD7 ...46 A1
Birkshall La BOW BD3 ...5 K7
Birks Hall St HFAX HX1 ...4 D3
Birks Hall Ter HFAX HX1 ...4 D2
Birksland St BOW BD4 ...48 A2
Birnam Gv BOW BD4 ...47 H5
Birr Rd HTON BD9 ...38 C1
Bishopdale Holme WBSY BD6 ...53 H2
Bishop St HTON BD9 ...38 C1
Bitterne St WBSY BD6 ...45 F5
Blackberry Wy CLAY BD14 ...45 E4
Blackbird Gdns GIR BD8 ...37 E5
Black Brook Wy GTL/HWG HX4 ...75 H5
Blackburn Cl GIR BD8
   HIPP HX3 ...59 E2
Blackburn Rd BRIG HD6 ...71 E4
Black Dyke La CUL/QBY BD13 ...35 G3
Black Edge La CUL/QBY BD13 ...42 B1
Blackett St PDSY/CALV LS28 ...31 G2
Black Hill La AIRE BD20 ...6 A2
Blackledge HFAX HX1 ...4 D3
Blackmires LUD/ILL HX2 ...51 F5
Black Moor Rd HWTH BD22 ...2 A3
Blackshaw Beck La HIPP HX3 ...52 D5
Blackstone Dr WBSY BD6 ...53 G2
Blacksmith GTHN BD7 ...46 B3
Blacksmith Fold GTHN BD7
Blackstone Av LM/WK BD12 ...62 D5
Blackwall HFAX HX1
Blackwall La RPDN/SBR HX6
Blackwall Ri RPDN/SBR HX6 ...67 E3
Blackwood Gv HFAX HX1 ...4 A2
Blacup Moor Vw CLECK BD19 ...73 G1
Blaithroyd La HIPP HX3 ...69 F2
Blake Crs GSLY LS20 ...11 E3
Blake Hl HIPP HX3 ...60 B2
Blakehill Av ECHL BD2 ...40 B2
Blake Hill End HWTH BD22 ...60 C1
Blakehill Ter ECHL BD2 ...40 B2
Blakelaw Dr BRIG HD6 ...72 A5
Blake Law La BRIG HD6 ...79 G1
Blamires Pl GTHN BD7 ...46 A4
Blamires St GTHN BD7 ...46 A4
Blanche St BOW BD4 ...48 C1
Bland St HFAX HX1 ...5 F4
Blantyre Ct CUL/QBY BD13 ...24 C3
Bleak St CLECK BD19 ...65 H5
Bleak St Lower CLECK BD19 ...65 H5
Blenheim St HFAX HX1 *
Blenheim Mt GIR BD8 ...38 D2
Blenheim Pl GIR BD8 ...20 A5
Blenheim Rd GIR BD8 ...38 D3
Blind La BGLY BD16 ...16 A3
   LUD/ILL HX2 ...50 D2
Blucher St BOW BD4
Bluebell Cl SHPY BD18 ...29 E4
   WIL/AL BD15 ...37 E4
Bluebird Wk BGLY BD16 ...17 F2
Blythe Av GIR BD8 ...38 B4
Blythe St GTHN BD7 ...38 D5
Bob La LUD/ILL HX2 ...67 G1
Bodmin Av SHPY BD18 ...29 F2
Boggart La HIPP HX3 ...61 G4
   RPDN/SBR HX6 ...67 E5
Bogthorn HWTH BD22 ...13 F2
Boland Crs HWTH BD22 ...13 F3
Boldron Holt WBSY BD6 ...54 A2
Boldshay St BFDE BD3 ...3 J5
Bolehill Pk BRIG HD6 ...70 D2
Bolingbroke St WBOW BD5 ...47 E5
Bolland St LM/WK BD12 ...55 F5
Bolling Rd BOW BD4 ...3 F7
Boltby La CUL/QBY BD13 ...34 A3
Bolton LUD/ILL HX2 ...50 D5
Bolton Brow RPDN/SBR HX6 ...67 F4
Bolton Dr ECHL BD2 ...30 A5
Bolton Gra YEA LS19 ...11 H5
Bolton Gv ECHL BD2 ...30 A5
Bolton Hall Rd ECHL BD2 ...29 E4
Bolton La ECHL BD2 ...39 G1
Bolton Rd BFD BD1 ...5 F2
   BFDE BD3 ...39 G2
   YEA LS19 ...11 H5
Bolton St BFDE BD3 ...5 H1
Bond St HWTH BD22
   HFAX HX1 *
Bonegate Av BRIG HD6 ...71 G5
Bonegate Rd BRIG HD6 ...71 F5
Bonn Rd HTON BD9 ...38 B2
Bonwick Ml WBSY BD6 ...53 H5
Bosanquet Pk HTON BD9 ...37 G2
Boothman Wk BRAT BD22 ...13 H1
Booth Royd IDLE BD10 ...20 A5
Booth Royd Dr IDLE BD10 ...20 A4
Booth Royd La BRIG HD6 ...77 G3
Booth St CLECK BD19 ...64 C5
   CUL/QBY BD13 ...30 A2
   IDLE BD10 ...30 A2
   SHPY BD18 ...29 E2
Boothtown Rd HIPP HX3 ...59 G2
Borrins Wy BAIL BD17 ...17 H4
Borrowdale Cft YEA LS19 ...11 F4
Boston St HFAX HX1 ...4 B4
   RPDN/SBR HX6 ...67 F4
Boston Wk WBSY BD6 ...54 A2
Bosworth Cl WIL/AL BD15 ...37 E3
Botany Av ECHL BD2 ...29 G5
Botany Dr AIRE BD20 ...9 F1
Bottomley St BRIG HD6 ...71 G4
   WBOW BD5 ...47 E3
   WBSY BD6 ...45 H5
Bottoms HIPP HX3 ...69 G5
Bottoms La BIRK/DRI BD11 ...65 H3
Boundary Cl BAIL BD17 ...19 E2
Boundary Dr BGLY BD16 ...37 H3
The Boundary GIR BD8 ...37 H4
Bourbon Cl WBSY BD6 ...54 A2
Bourne St IDLE BD10 ...20 A4
Bowater Ct BOW BD4 ...48 A4
Bow Beck BOW BD4 ...47 H2
Bowbridge Rd WBOW BD5 * ...47 F4

Bower Gn BFDE BD3 * ...40 B5
Bowers La GTL/HWG HX4 ...74 C5
Bower St WBOW BD5 * ...47 F2
Bowes Nook WBSY BD6 ...53 H5
Bow Gn CLAY BD14 ...45 G3
Bowland St GIR BD8 ...2 B2
Bowler Cl LM/WK BD12 ...54 D4
Bowling Aly BOW BD4 ...78 B3
Bowling Back La BOW BD4 ...47 H2
Bowling Ct BRIG HD6 ...71 E5
Bowling Dyke HIPP HX3 ...5 J2
Bowling Hall Rd BOW BD4 ...47 H4
Bowling Old La WBOW BD5 ...47 E4
Bowling Park Cl BOW BD4 ...47 H3
Bowling Park Dr WBOW BD5 ...47 G4
Bowman Av WBSY BD6 ...54 C5
Bowman Gv HFAX HX1 * ...4 C3
Bowman Pl HFAX HX1 * ...4 C3
Bowman Rd WBSY BD6 ...54 C5
Bowman St HFAX HX1 * ...4 C3
Bowman Ter HFAX HX1 * ...4 D3
Bowness Av IDLE BD10 ...30 C5
Bow St HFAX HX1 ...4 D3
Bowwood Dr AIRE BD20 ...8 A4
Boxhall Rd ELL HX5 ...76 C4
Box Tree Cl GIR BD8 ...37 H5
Box Tree Gv KGHY BD21 * ...7 H5
Box Trees La LUD/ILL HX2 ...58 C2
Boyd Av BFDE BD3 ...40 C5
Boy La BOW BD4
   HIPP HX3 ...58 C4
Boyne St HFAX HX1 ...5 F4
Boynton St WBOW BD5 ...47 E4
Boynton Ter WBOW BD5 ...47 F4
Boys La HIPP HX3 ...69 E5
Bracewell Av WIL/AL BD15 ...36 D4
Bracewell Bank HIPP HX3 ...59 E3
Bracewell Dr HIPP HX3 ...59 E3
Bracewell Gv HIPP HX3 ...59 F4
Bracewell St KGHY BD21 ...7 H6
Bracken Av BRIG HD6 ...71 F5
Bracken Bank Av HWTH BD22 ...13 G5
Bracken Bank Crs HWTH BD22 ...13 G5
Bracken Bank Gv HWTH BD22 ...13 G5
Bracken Bank Wk HWTH BD22 ...13 G5
Brackenbeck Rd GTHN BD7 ...46 A3
Brackendale Gv LUD/ILL HX2 * ...58 D4
Brackenbed La HFAX HX1 ...58 D5
   ELL HX5 ...77 F4
Brackendale IDLE BD10 ...19 G4
Brackendale Av IDLE BD10 ...19 H4
Brackendale Dr IDLE BD10 ...19 G4
Brackendale Gv IDLE BD10 ...19 G4
Brackendale Pde IDLE BD10 ...19 G4
Bracken Edge IDLE BD10 ...30 B2
Brackenhill Dr GTHN BD7 ...45 H4
Brackenholme Royd
   BOW BD4 ...53 H2
Bracken Pk BGLY BD16 ...17 F3
Bracken Rd BRIG HD6 ...71 F5
   HWTH BD22 ...13 H2
Brackens La HIPP HX3 ...53 E3
Bracken Wy ELL HX5 ...7 F4
Bradbeck Rd GTHN BD7 ...38 A5
Bradford La BFDE BD3 ...40 C5
Bradford Old Rd BGLY BD16 ...27 E2
   HIPP HX3 ...59 H2
Bradford Rd AIRE BD20 ...9 E4
   BFDE BD3 ...5 J6
   BGLY BD16 ...16 C5
   BIRK/DRI BD11 ...65 F1
   BRIG HD6 ...71 G4
   CLAY BD14 ...45 G2
   CLECK BD19 ...64 A2
   GSLY LS20 ...11 G5
   HIPP HX3 ...60 D2
   IDLE BD10 ...29 H4
   KGHY BD21 ...7 H2
   SHPY BD18 ...28 C3
Bradford St KGHY BD21 ...7 F5
Bradford & Wakefield Rd
   BOW BD4 ...57 H3
Bradlaugh Rd WBSY BD6 ...54 C1
Bradlaugh Ter WBSY BD6 ...54 D1
Bradley Grange Gdns
   HUDN ...79 G5
Bradley La LUD/ILL HX2 * ...5 F5
   PDSY/CALV LS28 ...41 G5
Bradley Quarry Cl HUDN HD2 * ...79 H5
Bradley St BGLY BD16 ...16 C3
   HTON BD9 ...28 D5
Bradshaw La LUD/ILL HX2 ...51 E2
Bradshaw Vw CUL/QBY BD13 ...51 H1
Brae Av ECHL BD2 ...29 G5
Brafferton Arbor WBSY BD6 ...53 H2
Braithwaite Av HWTH BD22 ...6 C4
Braithwaite Crs HWTH BD22 ...6 C4
Braithwaite Dr HWTH BD22 ...6 C4
Braithwaite Edge Rd
   HWTH BD22 ...6 A3
Braithwaite Gv HWTH BD22 ...6 C4
Braithwaite Rd HWTH BD22 ...6 C4
Braithwaite Wk HWTH BD22 ...6 C4
Bramble Cl CLAY BD14 ...45 E4
Bramble Gv ELL HX5 ...77 F4
Bramble Dr WBSY BD6 ...45 F5
Brambling Dr WBSY BD6 ...45 F5
Bramham Dr BAIL BD17 ...19 E2
Bramham Rd BGLY BD16 ...16 D2
Bramhope Rd CLECK BD19 ...64 B5
Bramley Cl HWTH BD22 ...12 C3
Bramley Fold HIPP HX3 * ...60 B5
Bramley La HIPP HX3 ...61 G5
Bramley St WBOW BD5 ...47 F5
Bramley Vw HIPP HX3 ...61 H5
Bramston Gdns BRIG HD6 ...78 B3
Bramston St BRIG HD6 ...78 B2
Branch Rd CLECK BD19 ...64 D5
   GTL/HWG HX4 ...74 D5
Brander Cl IDLE BD10 ...29 H3
Brandfort St GTHN BD7 ...46 B2
Bransome Ct HTON BD9 * ...38 A2

Bransome Crs HTON BD9 ...38 A2
Bransome Dr SHPY BD18 ...27 C1
Bransome Gv BGLY BD16 ...27 F1
Bransdale Av WBSY BD6 ...10 D3
Bransdale Cl BAIL BD17 ...18 B4
   GSLY LS20 ...10 D5
Bransdale Clough WBSY BD6 ...53 H1
Bransdale Garth GSLY LS20 ...10 D5
Branshaw Dr HWTH BD22 ...13 F1
Branshaw Gv HWTH BD22 ...13 F1
Branshaw Mt HWTH BD22 ...13 F1
Bransdale Ms HWTH BD22 ...13 H2
Brant Av LUD/ILL HX2 ...59 E1
Brantcliffe Dr BAIL BD17 ...18 C2
Brantdale Cl HTON BD9 ...27 F5
Brantdale Rd HTON BD9 ...27 F5
Brantwood Av HTON BD9 ...27 F5
Brantwood Cl HTON BD9 ...27 F5
Brantwood Crs HTON BD9 ...27 F5
Brantwood Dr HTON BD9 ...27 F5
Brantwood Gv HTON BD9 ...27 F5
Brantwood Ov HTON BD9 ...27 F5
Brantwood Rd HTON BD9 ...27 F5
Branwell Ct HTON BD9 ...37 H2
Branwell Dr HWTH BD22 ...22 D1
Brassey Rd BOW BD4 ...47 H3
Brassey St HFAX HX1 ...5 F6
Brassey Ter BOW BD4 ...47 H3
Braybrook Ct GIR BD8 ...38 D1
Bray Cl HFAX HX1 ...45 G5
Brayshaw Dr GTHN BD7 ...45 G5
Break Neck HIPP HX3 ...60 D5
Breaks Rd LM/WK BD12 ...55 E4
Brearcliffe Cl WBSY BD6 ...54 B2
Brearcliffe Dr WBSY BD6 ...54 B2
Brearcliffe Gv WBSY BD6 ...54 B3
Brearcliffe Rd WBSY BD6 ...54 B3
Brearcliffe St WBSY BD6 ...54 B3
Brearton St BFD BD1 ...2 C2
Brecks La CLAY BD14 ...44 B3
Brecon Cl IDLE BD10 ...30 A2
Bredon Av SHPY BD18 ...29 G2
Breighton Adown WBSY BD6 ...53 G2
Brendon Ct BOW BD4 ...48 C4
Brendon Wk BOW BD4 * ...48 C4
Brentford Rd LM/WK BD12 ...54 D4
Brentwood Gdns WBSY BD6 ...54 A2
Bretton St WBSY BD6 * ...54 A2
Brewery La CUL/QBY BD13 ...51 H3
Brewery Rd KGHY BD21 ...51 H3
Brewery St HIPP HX3 ...59 H3
   KGHY BD21
Brian Royd La GTL/HWG HX4 ...75 E4
Briardale Rd HTON BD9 ...27 E5
Briarfield Cl IDLE BD10 ...29 H2
Briarfield Ct IDLE BD10 ...29 H2
Briarfield Gdns SHPY BD18 ...28 C3
Briarfield Gv IDLE BD10 ...29 H2
Briarfield Rd SHPY BD18 ...28 C3
Briarlea Cl YEA LS19 ...11 E5
Briar Rhydding BAIL BD17 ...19 F4
Briar Wd SHPY BD18 ...29 F2
Briarwood Av AIRE BD20 ...8 A2
Briarwood Crs WBSY BD6 ...54 C1
Briarwood Dr WBSY BD6 ...54 C1
Briarwood Gv WBSY BD6 ...46 C5
Brick and Tile Ter BRIG HD6 ...78 B2
Brickfield Gv LUD/ILL HX2 ...51 F5
Brickfield La LUD/ILL HX2 ...51 F5
Brickfield Ter LUD/ILL HX2 ...51 F5
Bridge End BRIG HD6 ...71 G5
Bridgegate Wy IDLE BD10 ...30 C4
Bridgehouse La HWTH BD22 ...22 D3
Bridle Dene HIPP HX3 ...53 F5
Bridle Stile HIPP HX3 ...53 F5
Bridle Stile La CUL/QBY BD13 ...44 B5
Brier Hill Cl CLECK BD19 ...72 D2
Brier La ELL HX5 ...77 G1
Brierley Cl SHPY BD18 ...29 G3
Brier St HIPP HX3 ...14 A2
   KGHY BD21
Briery Fld SHPY BD18 ...28 C1
Briggate BAIL BD17
   BRIG HD6 ...78 B1
   ELL HX5 ...76 C4
Brigg Gdns HWTH BD22 ...6 C4
Briggland Ct WIL/AL BD15 ...25 H4
Brigglands WIL/AL BD15 * ...25 H4
Briggs Av WBSY BD6 ...54 B1
Briggs Gv WBSY BD6 ...54 B1
Briggs Pl WBSY BD6 ...54 B1
Briggs St CUL/QBY BD13 * ...52 B1
Brighouse & Denholme Gate
   Rd HIPP HX3 ...52 D4
Brighouse & Denholme Rd
   CUL/QBY BD13 ...43 F3
Brighouse Rd CUL/QBY BD13 ...52 B1
   CUL/QBY BD13 ...61 H1
   HIPP HX3 ...70 B1
   LM/WK BD12 ...55 E5
Brighouse Wood La BRIG HD6 ...71 E5
Brighouse Wood Rw ...71 E5
Brighton Gv HFAX HX1 ...4 C2
Brighton St BAIL BD17 ...28 C1
   HIPP HX3 ...5 H5
   IDLE BD10 ...19 H5
Brighton Ter CLECK BD19 ...63 G5
Bright St CLAY BD14 * ...45 G1
   CUL/QBY BD13 ...52 C1
   RPDN/SBR HX6 ...67 E3
   WIL/AL BD15 ...37 E3
Brindley Gv GIR BD8 ...37 E5
Brisbane Av ECHL BD2 ...39 F1
Briscoe La GTL/HWG HX4 ...75 G4

Bristol Av AIRE BD20 ...8 C3
Bristol St HIPP HX3 ...69 E5
Britannia St BGLY BD16 ...16 D3
   WBOW BD5
Britannia Ter CLECK BD19 ...64 C5
Broadacre Wy BAIL BD17 ...18 B4
Broadfield Cl BOW BD4 ...56 D1
Broadfolds CLAY BD14 ...45 G1
Broad Ings Wy LUD/ILL HX2 ...53 F5
Broadlands AIRE BD20 ...8 A3
Broadlands St BFDE BD3 ...48 C5
Broad La BOW BD4 ...47 H5
Broadlea Crs WBOW BD5 ...47 G4
Broadley Av LUD/ILL HX2 ...58 B4
Broadley Cl LUD/ILL HX2 ...58 B4
Broadley Crs LUD/ILL HX2 ...58 B4
Broadley Rd LUD/ILL HX2 ...58 B4
Broad Oak La HIPP HX3 ...70 C2
Broad Oak St HIPP HX3 ...70 C2
Broadstone Pk BGLY BD16 * ...17 G3
Broadstone Wy BOW BD4 ...48 D3
Broad St BFD BD1 ...3 G3
   HFAX HX1 * ...5 G3
   PDSY/CALV LS28 ...41 H1
Broad Tree Rd HIPP HX3 ...59 F5
Broadway BFD BD1 ...3 G5
   BGLY BD16 ...16 D3
   GSLY LS20 ...10 B3
   HIPP HX3 ...59 H5
   RPDN/SBR HX6 ...66 A5
Broadway Av WBOW BD5 ...47 E5
Broadway Cl WBOW BD5 ...47 E5
Broadwood Av LUD/ILL HX2 ...58 B4
Brocklebank Cl AIRE BD20
Brockleby Dr WIL/AL BD15 ...37 F3
Brockstones GTL/HWG HX4 * ...75 E4
Brockwell Gdns
   RPDN/SBR HX6
Brodley Cl HIPP HX3 ...61 F5
Broken Wy WBOW BD5 * ...47 F5
Bromet Pl ECHL BD2 ...30 A5
Bromford Rd BOW BD4 ...47 H4
Bromley Gv HWTH BD22 ...13 H2
Bromley Rd BGLY BD16 ...16 C2
   SHPY BD18 ...27 H1
Brompton Av BOW BD4 ...47 H4
Brompton Rd BOW BD4 ...47 H5
Bronshill Gv WIL/AL BD15 ...37 H2
Bronte Cl CLECK BD19 ...65 G4
   HTON BD9 ...37 H2
Bronte Dr HWTH BD22 ...13 H3
Bronte Old Rd CUL/QBY BD13 ...44 B1
Bronte Pl CUL/QBY BD13 ...44 B1
Bronte St HWTH BD22 ...22 C2
   KGHY BD21 ...7 F6
Bronte Vls HWTH BD22 ...23 C1
Bronte Wy BGLY BD16 ...62 C5
   BRIG HD6 ...72 A4
   CUL/QBY BD13 ...44 C1
   HIPP HX3 ...53 F5
   HWTH BD22 ...22 A4
Brooke St BRIG HD6 ...71 H1
   CLECK BD19 ...73 H1
Brookeville Av HIPP HX3 ...70 B1
Brookfield Av CLECK BD19 ...29 E1
Brookfield Rd BFDE BD3 ...29 E1
   SHPY BD18 ...29 E1
Brookfields Av LM/WK BD12 ...63 E4
Brookfield Ter CLECK BD19 ...65 G4
Brookfoot Av BIRK/DRI BD11 ...64 D4
Brookfoot La BIRK/DRI BD11 ...71 G5
Brook Grain Hl BRIG HD6 ...78 B5
Brookhouse Gdns IDLE BD10 ...44 C1
Brooklands Av CUL/QBY BD13 ...44 C1
Brooklands Dr GSLY LS19 ...11 G5
Brooklands Dr YEA LS19 ...11 G5
Brook La LVSG WF15 ...73 F4
Brooklyn Ct CLECK BD19 ...64 C5
Brooklyn Dr CLECK BD19 ...64 C5
Brooklyn Rd CLECK BD19 ...64 C5
Brooklyn St AIRE BD20 ...7 F6
Brooklyn Ter CLECK BD19 ...64 C5
Brook Rw GTL/HWG HX4 * ...75 E4
Brookroyd Av BRIG HD6 ...71 G2
Brooksbank Av GTHN BD7 ...46 A3
Brooksbank Gdns CLECK BD19 ...76 C4
Brookside Fold HWTH BD22 ...22 C2
Brooks Ter CUL/QBY BD13 ...44 C1
Brook St ELL HX5 ...76 D5
   KGHY BD21 ...7 G5
   LM/WK BD12 ...64 A1
Brooks Yd HUDN HD2 ...79 H5
Brookwater CLAY BD14 ...45 E3
Broom Av ECHL BD2 ...48 C1
Broome Av ECHL BD2 ...39 G1
Broomfield CLAY BD14 ...44 D4
   GTL/HWG HX4
Broomfield Av HIPP HX3 ...68 C5
   KGHY BD21 ...7 E4
Broomfield Rd KGHY BD21 ...7 E4
   CUL/QBY BD13 ...52 B1
   KGHY BD21 ...7 E4
Broomfield Ter CLECK BD19 ...64 D5
Broomhill Av KGHY BD21 ...13 H1
   KGHY BD21 ...7 E4
Broomhill Gv KGHY BD21 ...13 H1
Broomhill Mt KGHY BD21 ...13 H1
Broomhill St KGHY BD21 ...13 H1
Broomhill Wk KGHY BD21 ...13 H1
Broomhill Wy KGHY BD21 ...13 H1
Broom St BOW BD4 ...48 C1
Broster Av HWTH BD22 ...6 C4
Brougham Rd HWTH BD22
Brougham St HIPP HX3 ...59 H4
Broughton Av BOW BD4 ...48 C1
Brow Bottom La LUD/ILL HX2 ...50 A4
Browfield Vw HWTH BD22
Browfoot SHPY BD18 ...29 E2
Browfoot Dr LUD/ILL HX2 ...67 G1

Brow Foot Gate La
   LUD/ILL HX2 ...67 G1
Browgate BAIL BD17 ...18 C3
Brow La CLAY BD14 ...44 B4
   HIPP HX3 ...53 G4
   HIPP HX3 ...60 B2
Brownberry Gv HIPP HX3 ...53 G5
Brown Hill Cl BIRK/DRI BD11 ...57 F3
Brown Hill Dr BIRK/DRI BD11 ...57 H4
Browning Av HIPP HX3 ...60 A5
Browning St BFDE BD3 ...5 J5
Brown Lee La WIL/AL BD15 ...25 F5
Brownroyd Hill Rd WBSY BD6 ...54 C1
Brownroyd St GIR BD8 ...38 C5
Brownroyd Wk WBOW BD5 ...46 C5
Brown Springs La HWTH BD22 ...13 F2
Brown St KGHY BD21 * ...7 G3
Brow Rd HWTH BD22 ...23 E5
Browsholme St KGHY BD21 * ...7 F5
Brow St KGHY BD21
Brow Top Rd HWTH BD22 ...23 F2
Brow Wood Crs ECHL BD2 ...39 F1
Brow Wood Ri HIPP HX3 ...53 G4
Brow Wood Rd HIPP HX3 ...53 G4
Browwood Ter WBSY BD6 ...54 A3
Bruce St HFAX HX1 ...4 B6
Brunel Cl HTON BD9 ...59 G3
Brunel St HIPP HX3
Brunswick Gdns HFAX HX1 ...5 F4
Brunswick Pl IDLE BD10 ...30 C2
Brunswick Rd IDLE BD10 ...30 C2
Brunswick St BGLY BD16 ...17 F3
   CLECK BD19 ...65 G4
   CUL/QBY BD13 ...52 C1
Bryan Rd GTL/HWG HX4 ...76 A5
Bryanstone Rd BOW BD4 ...48 C2
Bryan St BRIG HD6 ...78 B2
Bubwith Gv GTL/HWG HX4 * ...67 H2
Buckfast Ct IDLE BD10
Buckingham Crs CLAY BD14 ...45 G2
Buckland Pl HFAX HX1 ...67 H2
Buck La BAIL BD17 ...19 G3
Buckley La LUD/ILL HX2 ...58 B5
Buck Mill La IDLE BD10 ...19 H3
Buck Pk CUL/QBY BD13 * ...34 D2
Buckrose St HUDN HD2 ...79 H5
Buckstone Garth AIRE BD20 ...9 E2
Buck St BFDE BD3 ...3 H7
   CUL/QBY BD13
Bude Rd WBOW BD5 ...55 G1
Bullace Trees La LVSG WF15 ...73 H5
Bull Close La HFAX HX1 ...5 F5
Buller St BOW BD4 ...48 B2
The Bullfield BGLY BD16 ...15 G5
Bull Gn HFAX HX1 ...5 F4
Bull Royd Av GIR BD8 ...37 H4
Bull Royd Crs GIR BD8 ...37 H4
Bull Royd Dr GIR BD8 ...37 H4
Bull Royd La GIR BD8 ...37 H4
Bundria Ct GIR BD8 ...38 D2
The Bungalows HIPP HX3 ...76 B1
Bunker's Hill La HWTH BD22 ...13 E1
Bunting Dr WBSY BD6 ...53 E1
Burberry Cl BOW BD4 ...56 D1
Burdale Pl GTHN BD7 ...46 A3
Burdock Wy HFAX HX1 ...5 F4
Burleigh St HFAX HX1 ...4 B7
Burley St ECHL BD2 ...29 E5
   ELL HX5 ...76 C5
Burlington Av BFDE BD3 ...40 C5
Burlington St GTHN BD7
   HFAX HX1 ...4 B5
Burned Gv HIPP HX3 ...53 G5
Burned Rd HIPP HX3 ...53 G5
Burneston Gdns WBSY BD6 ...53 H2
Burnett Av WBOW BD5 ...47 H4
Burnett Pl WBOW BD5 ...47 E4
Burnett St BFD BD1 ...3 G5
Burnham Av BOW BD4 ...56 A1
Burniston Cl WIL/AL BD15 ...25 H5
Burnley Rd RPDN/SBR HX6 ...66 A5
Burnleyville CLECK BD19 ...65 G4
Burnsall Rd BFDE BD3 ...3 K3
   BRIG HD6 ...77 G3
Burnsdale WIL/AL BD15 ...36 D1
Burns St LUD/ILL HX2 ...59 F2
Burnup Gv CLECK BD19 ...65 H3
Burnwells Av IDLE BD10 ...19 H4
Burrage St BGLY BD16 ...16 C3
Burras Rd BOW BD4 ...48 A5
Burrow St WBOW BD5 ...2 C7
Burton St AIRE BD20 ...7 E2
   BOW BD4
   LUD/ILL HX2 ...51 F5
Busfield St BGLY BD16 ...16 C3
   BOW BD4 ...48 A4
Bush Hill Fold CUL/QBY BD13 ...43 H5
Busy La SHPY BD18 ...19 F5
Butcher St BFD BD1 ...5 G2
Bute Av BRIG HD6 ...71 F5
Bute St BFDE BD3 ...29 E5
Butler La BAIL BD17 ...19 G3
Butler St BFDE BD3 ...3 H5
Butler St West BFDE BD3 ...3 H5
Buttermeade Cl WBSY BD6 ...54 B5
Buttershaw Dr WBSY BD6 ...53 H2
Buttershaw La LVSG WF15 ...73 F5
   WBSY BD6 ...54 C3
Buttholme Ga WBSY BD6 ...54 A2
Button Pk WBSY BD6 ...54 A2
Butts Green La LUD/ILL HX2 ...66 C1
Butts Green Rd LUD/ILL HX2 ...66 C1
Butts Hl CLECK BD19 ...65 F5
Butts Yd CLECK BD19 ...73 G1
Buxton Av HTON BD9 ...28 D5
Buxton La HTON BD9 ...59 F4
   HTON BD9 ...38 C2
   KGHY BD21
Buxton Wy HIPP HX3 ...59 E2
Byeway GSLY LS20 ...10 B2

Byland LUD/ILL HX2 50 C4
Byland Gv WIL/AL BD15 36 C2
Byre Wy HWTH BD22 * 13 F1
Byrl St KGHY BD21 7 G3
Byron Av RPDN/SBR HX6 * 67 E3
Byron Ms BGLY BD16 16 D1
Byron St BFDE BD3 3 J3
HFAX HX1 4 A3
RPDN/SBR HX6 67 E3

C

Cadney Cft HFAX HX1 5 G5
Cain La HIPP HX3 69 H4
Cairn Av GSLY LS20 10 B2
Cairn Cl AIRE BD20 6 D1
Cairns Cl ECHL BD2 39 G1
Caister Gv KGHY BD21 * 13 H2
Caister St KGHY BD21 14 A2
Caister Wy KGHY BD21 14 A2
Calde Ct LM/WK BD12 55 F4
Caldene Av LM/WK BD12 55 F4
Calder Av LUD/ILL HX2 68 A3
Calder Banks CUL/QBY BD13 52 D1
Caldercroft ELL HX5 76 D5
Calderdale Wy BRIG HD6 71 H3
ELL HX5 76 B4
GTL/HWG HX4 75 F3
HIPP HX3 52 D5
Calderstone Av WBSY BD6 53 G2
Calder St BRIG HD6 78 D2
GTL/HWG HX4 76 A4
Calder Ter HIPP HX3 75 F2
Calder Vw BRIG HD6 78 A2
Caledonia Rd KGHY BD21 7 G3
Caledonia St WBOW BD5 47 G2
Calpin Cl IDLE BD10 * 30 A1
Calton Gv KGHY BD21 8 A5
Calton Rd KGHY BD21 7 H5
Calton St KGHY BD21 14 A1
Calver Av KGHY BD21 6 C3
Calver Gv KGHY BD21 6 D3
Calverley Av BFDE BD3 40 C4
Calverley Cutting IDLE BD10 31 E1
Calverley La
PDSY/CALV LS28 31 H3
Calverley Moor Av
PDSY/CALV LS28 41 F3
Calver Rd KGHY BD21 6 D4
Calversyke St HWTH BD22 6 D4
Camargue Fold ECHL BD2 29 G5
Camberley Mt BOW BD4 48 D3
Camborne Wy HWTH BD22 13 F1
Cambrian Bar LM/WK BD12 54 C4
Cambridge Cha CLECK BD19 65 G3
Cambridge Pl BFDE BD3 3 F2
CUL/QBY BD13 52 B1
Cambridge St CLAY BD14 * 45 E3
CUL/QBY BD13 52 C1
GTHN BD7 46 C3
Camden Ter GIR BD8 2 A1
Camellia Ct SHPY BD18 29 E4
Camellia Mt GTHN BD7 45 H1
Cameron Av LM/WK BD12 62 C4
Cameronian Ct KGHY BD21 * 7 F4
Cam La BRIG HD6 72 A5
Camm St BRIG HD6 71 F5
Campbell St CUL/QBY BD13 52 C1
KGHY BD21 7 F4
Campus Rd GTHN BD7 46 D1
Canada Crs YEA LS19 21 H2
Canada Dr YEA LS19 21 H1
Canada Rd YEA LS19 21 H1
Canada Ter YEA LS19 21 H2
Canal Rd AIRE BD20 7 H1
BFD BD1 2 E4
BGLY BD16 16 C1
ECHL BD2 28 D5
RPDN/SBR HX6 67 H4
Canal St BRIG HD6 78 C1
HIPP HX3 5 K6
Canary Dr BGLY BD16 17 F2
Canary St CLECK BD19 64 C5
Canberra Cl HWTH BD22 23 G1
Canberra Dr HWTH BD22 23 G1
Canford Dr WIL/AL BD15 37 E3
Canford Gv WIL/AL BD15 37 F3
Canford Rd WIL/AL BD15 37 E3
Cannon Hall Cl BRIG HD6 79 E1
Cannon Hall Dr BRIG HD6 79 E1
Cannon Mill La GTHN BD7 46 B3
Cannon St BGLY BD16 16 D4
HFAX HX1 * 4 B7
Canterbury Av WBOW BD5 46 D4
Canterbury Crs HIPP HX3 59 G4
Capel Ct PDSY/CALV LS28 31 G3
Capel St BRIG HD6 78 B2
PDSY/CALV LS28 31 G3
Cape St BFD BD1 2 D2
Captain St BFD BD1 2 E4
Carden Rd BOW BD4 48 D2
Cardigan St CUL/QBY BD13 52 C1
Carisbrooke Crs WBSY BD6 54 C2
Cark Rd KGHY BD21 7 F3
Carlby Gv HWTH BD22 6 D5
Carlby St HWTH BD22 6 D5
Carleton St AIRE BD20 7 F2
Carling Cl GTHN BD7 46 A4
Carlisle Av YEA LS19 11 H5
Carlisle Pl GIR BD8 38 D3
Carlisle Rd GIR BD8 38 C3
Carlisle St GIR BD8 38 C3
KGHY BD21 7 G4
LUD/ILL HX2 58 D5
PDSY/CALV LS28 41 H3
Carlisle Ter GIR BD8 38 D3
Carlton Av SHPY BD18 28 A1
Carlton Dr BAIL BD17 18 D2
GSLY LS20 11 E1
HTON BD9 28 B5
Carlton Gv ELL HX5 77 E4
SHPY BD18 28 C4
WBOW BD5 47 E4
Carlton House Ter HFAX HX1 4 D7
Carlton La GSLY LS20 11 E1
Carlton Mt YEA LS19 11 H3
Carlton Pl HFAX HX1 5 G5
Carlton Rd SHPY BD18 27 H1
Carlton St GTHN BD7 2 B6
HFAX HX1 5 G5
HWTH BD22 23 E2
Carlton Ter HFAX HX1 5 G5
Carlton Wk SHPY BD18 28 A1
Carmel Rd HIPP HX3 59 G3
Carmona Av SHPY BD18 28 C4
Carmona Gdns SHPY BD18 28 C4
Carnaby Rd GTHN BD7 45 H5
Carnegie Dr SHPY BD18 28 D1
Carnoustie Gv BGLY BD16 26 D2
Caroline St CLECK BD19 64 C5
SHPY BD18 28 A1
Carperley Crs CUL/QBY BD13 34 D4
Carr Bank AIRE BD20 8 C2
Carr Bottom Av WBOW BD5 46 C5
Carr Bottom Fold
WBOW BD5 54 D1
Carr Bottom Gv WBOW BD5 46 C5
Carr Bottom Rd IDLE BD10 30 D3
WBOW BD5 46 D5
Carr Green Av BRIG HD6 78 A5
Carr Green Cl BRIG HD6 78 A5
Carr Green Dr BRIG HD6 78 A5
Carr Green La BRIG HD6 78 A4
Carr Gv AIRE BD20 8 B2
Carr Hall Rd LM/WK BD12 62 D2
Carr Hill Av PDSY/CALV LS28 31 F3
Carr Hill Dr PDSY/CALV LS28 31 F3
Carr Hill Gv PDSY/CALV LS28 31 F3
Carr Hill Nook
PDSY/CALV LS28 * 31 F3
Carr Hill Ri PDSY/CALV LS28 31 F3
Carr Hill Rd PDSY/CALV LS28 31 F3
Carr House Ga LM/WK BD12 54 C5
Carr House Gv LM/WK BD12 62 D1
Carr House La HIPP HX3 53 G3
LM/WK BD12 54 C5
Carr House Mt
LM/WK BD12 * 62 D1
Carr House Rd HIPP HX3 53 G4
Carriage Dr CLECK BD19 65 G3
The Carriage Dr
GTL/HWG HX4 75 H3
Carricks Cl LM/WK BD12 55 F4
Carrington St BFDE BD3 40 B5
Carrington Ter GSLY LS20 10 C3
Carr La AIRE BD20 8 B2
BGLY BD16 9 F3
CUL/QBY BD13 34 D2
LM/WK BD12 55 E5
SHPY BD18 29 E2
Carroll St BFDE BD3 3 G6
Carr Rd LM/WK BD12 * 62 D2
PDSY/CALV LS28 31 E3
Carr St BRIG HD6 71 F4
CLECK BD19 73 G1
KGHY BD21 7 F4
WBOW BD5 47 E5
Carr Wood Gdns
PDSY/CALV LS28 31 F2
Carter La CUL/QBY BD13 44 A4
Carter St BFD BD1 3 F7
Cartmel Rd KGHY BD21 6 D4
Carver St CLECK BD19 64 C5
Caryl Rd BOW BD4 47 H4
Cashmere St HWTH BD22 6 D4
Castle Av BRIG HD6 78 A3
Castle Cft BGLY BD16 15 F5
Castlefields Crs BRIG HD6 78 A3
Castlefields Dr BRIG HD6 78 A3
Castlefields La BGLY BD16 16 B1
Castlefields Rd BGLY BD16 16 A1
BRIG HD6 78 A3
Castlegate Dr IDLE BD10 30 B3
Castle Gv BGLY BD16 15 F5
Castle Hl BRIG HD6 78 A3
Castle Hill Ct HWTH BD22 * 6 D5
Castlemore Rd BAIL BD17 19 E4
Castle Rd KGHY BD21 7 E3
SHPY BD18 28 B2
Castle St WBOW BD5 47 F2
Cater St BFD BD1 3 F5
Cathcart St HIPP HX3 59 G3
Catherine Slack BRIG HD6 71 E2
Catherine St BRIG HD6 71 F5
ELL HX5 76 C5
KGHY BD21 14 A1
Cat La GTL/HWG HX4 74 D4
Cauldwell Gdns
WBOW BD5 * 47 F3
Causeway HFAX HX1 5 J4
Cavalier Dr IDLE BD10 30 C2
Cave Hl HIPP HX3 60 C1
Cavendish Ct KGHY BD21 * 7 F4
Cavendish Dr BGLY BD16 17 E2
GSLY LS20 10 C3
Cavendish Gv GSLY LS20 10 C3
Cavendish Rd GSLY LS20 10 C3
IDLE BD10 30 A2
Cavendish St HFAX HX1 4 D3
KGHY BD21 7 F4
YEA LS19 11 H4
Cavendish Ter HFAX HX1 4 D4
Cawcliffe Dr BRIG HD6 71 F4
Cawcliffe Rd BRIG HD6 71 F4
Cawood Hvn WBSY BD6 * 53 H2
Caygill Ter HFAX HX1 5 G7
Caythorne Wk IDLE BD10 30 B4
Cecil Av BAIL BD17 18 D2
GTHN BD7 46 C3
HIPP HX3 61 H5
Cecil St HWTH BD22 23 F1
Cedar Dr LM/WK BD12 63 F1
Cedar Gv BRIG HD6 71 G2
GTL/HWG HX4 75 G4
Cedar St HFAX HX1 4 B4
KGHY BD21 14 A2
Cedar Wy CLECK BD19 65 F5
Cemetery La AIRE BD20 7 E1
RPDN/SBR HX6 66 D5
Cemetery Rd BGLY BD16 16 B2
GIR BD8 38 A5
HWTH BD22 22 B2
WBSY BD6 54 C3
YEA LS19 11 H4
Centenary Rd BAIL BD17 19 G2
Central Av BAIL BD17 18 C4
HWTH BD22 13 G3
LVSG WF15 73 E3
SHPY BD18 28 C2
WBOW BD5 46 D3
Central Av East LVSG WF15 73 E3
Central Dr HWTH BD22 13 G3
Central Pk HFAX HX1 5 F7
Central St HFAX HX1 5 G4
Centre St WBOW BD5 * 46 D4
Centurion Wy CLECK BD19 64 B3
Century Pl GIR BD8 38 D3
Century Rd ELL HX5 76 C4
Century St KGHY BD21 * 14 A2
Chadwell Springs BGLY BD16 26 D2
Chaffinch Rd GIR BD8 37 F5
Chain Bar Rd CLECK BD19 64 B4
Chain St BFD BD1 2 B4
Challenge Wy BOW BD4 48 C3
Challis Gv WBOW BD5 47 F4
Chandos St BOW BD4 2 E7
Changegate HWTH BD22 22 C1
Changegate Ct HWTH BD22 22 C2
Change La HIPP HX3 76 B1
Channing Wy BFD BD1 2 C6
Chapel Cft BRIG HD6 78 A4
Chapel Fold LM/WK BD12 62 D5
WBSY BD6 54 C1
Chapel Gv BGLY BD16 16 B1
Chapel Hl YEA LS19 11 G4
Chapel House Rd
LM/WK BD12 55 E3
Chapel La BAIL BD17 20 A1
CUL/QBY BD13 45 E5
CUL/QBY BD13 52 A1
HIPP HX3 70 A4
HIPP HX3 76 A1
KGHY BD21 7 E4
RPDN/SBR HX6 67 G4
WIL/AL BD15 37 F4
YEA LS19 11 G4
Chapel Ms GIR BD8 * 37 F4
Chapel Rd BGLY BD16 16 B1
LM/WK BD12 55 F5
Chapel Rw WIL/AL BD15 25 H3
Chapel St BFD BD1 3 F5
BRIG HD6 70 D3
CLECK BD19 64 D5
CUL/QBY BD13 34 C4
CUL/QBY BD13 44 A1
CUL/QBY BD13 52 A1
ECHL BD2 30 C5
LUD/ILL HX2 * 58 D5
LVSG WF15 73 F3
PDSY/CALV LS28 31 G2
WBOW BD5 * 47 E3
WBSY BD6 54 D1
YEA LS19 21 G2
Chapel St North LUD/ILL HX2 59 E2
Chapel Ter WIL/AL BD15 * 37 E3
Chapeltown HFAX HX1 5 F3
Chapel Wk BGLY BD16 16 C3
ECHL BD2 30 C5
Chapman St BOW BD4 48 C1
Charles Av BFDE BD3 40 C5
HIPP HX3 69 H4
Charles Ct HWTH BD22 * 32 D2
Charles St BAIL BD17 28 C1
BFD BD1 2 D5
BGLY BD16 16 C3
CLECK BD19 65 G5
CUL/QBY BD13 52 A1
ELL HX5 76 C5
HFAX HX1 5 J4
RPDN/SBR HX6 67 E3
Charlestown Rd HIPP HX3 5 J2
Charlesworth Gv LUD/ILL HX2 58 D5
Charlesworth Sq CLECK BD19 65 F5
Charlesworth Ter LUD/ILL HX2 58 D5
Charlotte Ct HWTH BD22 23 E1
Charnock Cl HFAX HX1 68 D3
Charnwood Cl ECHL BD2 * 40 B2
Charnwood Gv ECHL BD2 40 B2
Charnwood Rd ECHL BD2 40 B2
Charterhouse Rd IDLE BD10 20 A5
Charteris Rd GIR BD8 37 G5
The Chase AIRE BD20 6 C3
YEA LS19 21 F2
Chase Wy WBOW BD5 47 F5
Chassum Gv HTON BD9 38 B2
Chatham St BFDE BD3 39 G3
HFAX HX1 4 E3
RPDN/SBR HX6 67 E3
Chat Hill Rd CUL/QBY BD13 44 C2
Chatsworth Av
PDSY/CALV LS28 41 F4
Chatsworth Crs
PDSY/CALV LS28 41 F4
Chatsworth Dr
PDSY/CALV LS28 41 F4
Chatsworth Fall
PDSY/CALV LS28 41 F4
Chatsworth Pl GIR BD8 38 C2
Chatsworth Ri
PDSY/CALV LS28 41 F4
Chatsworth Rd
PDSY/CALV LS28 41 F4
Chatsworth St KGHY BD21 7 G4
Chatts Wood Fold
LM/WK BD12 56 A5
Chaucer St HFAX HX1 4 A5
Cheapside BFD BD1 2 D4
CLECK BD19 73 H1
HFAX HX1 * 5 H4
HIPP HX3 53 F4
Cheddington Gv WIL/AL BD15 37 E4
Chellow Gdns WIL/AL BD15 * 36 D2
Chellow Grange Rd HTON BD9 37 F1
Chellow La HTON BD9 37 F2
Chellow St WBOW BD5 47 E5
Chelmsford Rd BFDE BD3 * 40 B4
Chelmsford Ter BFDE BD3 40 B5
Chelsea Man HIPP HX3 60 D3
Chelsea Rd GTHN BD7 46 A3
Chelsea St KGHY BD21 14 A1
Cheltenham Ct HIPP HX3 * 69 E4
Cheltenham Gdns HIPP HX3 69 E4
Cheltenham Pl HIPP HX3 69 E4
Cheltenham Rd ECHL BD2 29 G4
Chelwood Dr WIL/AL BD15 37 E5
Cheriton Dr CUL/QBY BD13 52 C1
Cherry Ct HFAX HX1 * 4 D2
Cherry Flds ECHL BD2 29 F5
Cherry Lea Ct YEA LS19 21 G2
Cherry St HWTH BD22 23 F1
KGHY BD21 7 H3
Cherry Tree Av IDLE BD10 * 30 C3
Cherry Tree Dr
GTL/HWG HX4 75 G4
Cherry Tree Gdns SHPY BD18 19 G5
Cherry Tree Ri KGHY BD21 14 C1
Cherry Tree Rw BGLY BD16 25 G2
Chervana Ct BOW BD4 48 D3
Cherwell Dr WBSY BD6 54 A3
Chesham St GTHN BD7 46 D1
KGHY BD21 7 G4
Chester Cl HIPP HX3 59 G4
Chester Gv HIPP HX3 59 G4
Chester Pl HIPP HX3 59 G4
Chester Rd HIPP HX3 59 G4
Chester St GTHN BD7 2 B7
HIPP HX3 59 G4
RPDN/SBR HX6 67 E4
Chester Ter HIPP HX3 59 G4
Chestnut Cl GTL/HWG HX4 75 G3
HWTH BD22 6 C5
Chestnut Ct SHPY BD18 27 H2
Chestnut Gv ECHL BD2 29 E5
PDSY/CALV LS28 31 G3
Chestnut St HFAX HX1 4 A6
Chevet Mt WIL/AL BD15 36 D5
Chevinedge Crs HIPP HX3 76 A2
Chevington Ct YEA LS19 * 21 F3
Cheviot Ga LM/WK BD12 54 C4
Cheyne Wk KGHY BD21 6 D5
Childs La SHPY BD18 29 F3
Chiltern Wy LVSG WF15 73 G3
Chilver Dr BOW BD4 49 F5
Chippendale Ri GIR BD8 37 G4
Chislehurst Pl WBOW BD5 46 D4
Chrisharben Pk CLAY BD14 45 F3
Chrismoor IDLE BD10 29 H2
Christopher St WBOW BD5 * 46 D4
Christopher Ter WBOW BD5 46 D4
Church Bank BFD BD1 2 E5
LUD/ILL HX2 67 G2
RPDN/SBR HX6 * 67 F4
Church Cl LUD/ILL HX2 50 C5
Churchcourt AIRE BD20 8 A1
Church Ct GTHN BD7 * 46 A2
YEA LS19 11 G5
Church Crs YEA LS19 11 F5
Church Flds ECHL BD2 40 C2
Churchfields Rd BRIG HD6 71 F5
Church Gn GIR BD8 38 C3
LUD/ILL HX2 * 58 D4
Church Hl BAIL BD17 19 E2
Churchill Rd CUL/QBY BD13 44 C1
Church La BAIL BD17 20 B1
BRIG HD6 71 F5
CLECK BD19 65 H5
ELL HX5 77 G4
HIPP HX3 70 B4
LUD/ILL HX2 58 D4
LVSG WF15 73 E5
WBSY BD6 54 C2
Church Pl HFAX HX1 4 E5
Church Rd WBSY BD6 54 C2
Church Side Cl HIPP HX3 59 H4
Church Side Dr HIPP HX3 59 H4
Church St BGLY BD16 16 D4
BRIG HD6 78 A3
CLECK BD19 73 H1
CUL/QBY BD13 * 24 C3
ELL HX5 76 C4
GIR BD8 38 D3
GSLY LS20 10 D2
GTL/HWG HX4 76 A4
HFAX HX1 5 J5
HWTH BD22 22 C2
HWTH BD22 32 D2
KGHY BD21 7 E5
KGHY BD21 7 G4
LVSG WF15 73 F3
SHPY BD18 29 E1
WBSY BD6 53 H3
YEA LS19 11 F5
Church Ter LUD/ILL HX2 50 C5
Church Vw CLECK BD19 64 A5
RPDN/SBR HX6 67 F4
Church Wk HIPP HX3 60 D3
Church Wy KGHY BD21 7 F5
Churn La LUD/ILL HX2 67 G1
Churn Milk La HIPP HX3 59 F1
Cinderhills La HIPP HX3 69 F5
City La HIPP HX3 58 D4
City Rd GIR BD8 2 A3
Clapham St CUL/QBY BD13 34 D4
Clapton Av HFAX HX1 4 D6
Clara Dr PDSY/CALV LS28 31 F2
Clara Rd ECHL BD2 29 G4
Clara St BRIG HD6 78 B2
Clare Crs LM/WK BD12 62 D3
Clare Hall La HFAX HX1 5 H6
Claremont Av ECHL BD2 29 F3
Claremont Crs ECHL BD2 29 F3
Claremont Gdns BGLY BD16 16 D2
Claremont Gv ECHL BD2 29 F3
Claremont Rd SHPY BD18 29 F3
Claremont St CLECK BD19 64 C5
ELL HX5 76 D5
RPDN/SBR HX6 * 67 F3
Claremont Ter GTHN BD7 2 A7
Claremount Rd HIPP HX3 59 H3
Claremount Ter HIPP HX3 59 H3
Clarence Rd SHPY BD18 28 A1
Clarence St CLECK BD19 73 G1
HFAX HX1 5 F4
Clarendon Pl CUL/QBY BD13 51 H2
HFAX HX1 * 4 C5
Clarendon Rd BGLY BD16 17 E2
Clarendon St HWTH BD22 22 D3
KGHY BD21 14 A1
Clare Rd CLECK BD19 73 F1
HFAX HX1 5 H5
LM/WK BD12 62 D3
Clare Rd Flats HFAX HX1 5 H6
Clare St HFAX HX1 5 H5
Clarges St WBOW BD5 46 D4
Clarke St PDSY/CALV LS28 31 G3
Clayborn Vw CLECK BD19 73 G2
Clayfield Dr GTHN BD7 46 B5
Clay Hill Dr LM/WK BD12 63 E2
Clay House La
GTL/HWG HX4 * 75 H4
Clay Pits La HFAX HX1 4 A2
Clay St HFAX HX1 4 B3
RPDN/SBR HX6 67 F4
Clayton Gv YEA LS19 11 G4
Clayton La CLAY BD14 45 E4
WBOW BD5 47 F3
Clayton Ri AIRE BD20 6 D3
Clayton Rd GTHN BD7 45 H3
Cleckheaton Rd WBSY BD6 55 E3
Cleeve Hl YEA LS19 21 G2
Clegg La GTL/HWG HX4 75 E4
Clement St GIR BD8 38 A4
RPDN/SBR HX6 * 67 E4
Clevedon Pl HIPP HX3 59 F3
Cleveland Av HIPP HX3 69 F4
Cleveland Rd HTON BD9 38 C1
Cleveleys RPDN/SBR HX6 67 E4
Cliff Crs LUD/ILL HX2 67 H3
Cliffe Av BAIL BD17 18 D3
BGLY BD16 15 F5
HIPP HX3 71 F1
Cliffe Crs AIRE BD20 8 C3
Cliffe Dr YEA LS19 21 G4
Cliffe Gdns SHPY BD18 28 B3
Cliffe La BAIL BD17 18 D5
CLECK BD19 64 D4
CUL/QBY BD13 36 B5
YEA LS19 21 H3
Cliffe La South BAIL BD17 18 D5
Cliffe La West BAIL BD17 18 D4
Cliffe Mill Fold AIRE BD20 9 F3
Cliffe Mt CLECK BD19 65 F4
Cliffe Rd BFDE BD3 39 G2
BRIG HD6 78 B1
KGHY BD21 14 A2
Cliffestone Dr AIRE BD20 9 E3
Cliffe St CUL/QBY BD13 36 A5
KGHY BD21 7 E3
Cliffe Ter BAIL BD17 18 D5
GIR BD8 39 E3
KGHY BD21 14 B2
RPDN/SBR HX6 66 D3
Cliffe Vw WIL/AL BD15 36 C2
Cliffe Wood Cl HTON BD9 37 H1
Cliff Gdns LUD/ILL HX2 67 H3
Cliff Hill La LUD/ILL HX2 67 E2
Cliff Hollins La LM/WK BD12 56 C4
Clifford Rd BAIL BD17 18 D4
Clifford St WBOW BD5 47 F2
Cliff St HWTH BD22 23 E2
Cliff Vale Rd SHPY BD18 28 C4
Cliff Wood Av SHPY BD18 28 C3
Clifton Av HFAX HX1 4 A6
Clifton Common BRIG HD6 78 D1
Clifton Pl SHPY BD18 28 C3
Clifton Rd BRIG HD6 78 C1
HIPP HX3 68 D4
Clifton Side HUDN HD2 79 G5
Clifton St GIR BD8 39 E3
HIPP HX3 59 F4
HWTH BD22 6 D5
RPDN/SBR HX6 67 F4
Clifton Vls GIR BD8 39 E3
Clipstone St WBOW BD5 47 F5
Clive Pl GTHN BD7 46 C2
Clive Ter GTHN BD7 46 C2
Clock La CUL/QBY BD13 34 C3
Clock View St AIRE BD20 7 E2
Clog Sole Rd BRIG HD6 71 E4
The Cloisters HFAX HX1 4 C7
Close Head Dr CUL/QBY BD13 43 F1
Close Head La CUL/QBY BD13 35 G5
Close Lea BRIG HD6 78 A2
Close Lea Av BRIG HD6 78 A2
Close Lea Dr BRIG HD6 78 A3
Close Lea Wy BRIG HD6 78 A2
Closes Rd BRIG HD6 78 A2
The Close GSLY LS20 10 B3
Cloudsdale Av WBOW BD5 47 F3
Clough Bank LUD/ILL HX2 50 A5
Clough Ct CUL/QBY BD13 42 D1
Clough Ga HWTH BD22 13 E4
Clough La BRIG HD6 72 A3
BRIG HD6 78 A5
HWTH BD22 12 D3
LUD/ILL HX2 50 B4
LVSG WF15 73 G4
Clough Pl LUD/ILL HX2 50 A5
Clough Rd RPDN/SBR HX6 74 C1
Clough St WBOW BD5 47 F4
Clover Ct PDSY/CALV LS28 31 F3
Clover Crs PDSY/CALV LS28 31 F2
Cloverdale HIPP HX3 53 G3
Clover Hl LVSG WF15 73 G3
Clover Hill Cl HFAX HX1 5 F6
Clover Hill Rd HFAX HX1 68 C3
Clover Hill Ter HFAX HX1 68 C3
Clover Hill Vw HFAX HX1 * 68 C3
Clover Ri KGHY BD21 7 H4
Clover St WBOW BD5 46 C4
Cloverville Ap WBSY BD6 54 D3
Club La LUD/ILL HX2 59 E2
Club Rw YEA LS19 11 H4
Club St GTHN BD7 46 A1
Clydesdale Dr WBSY BD6 54 A3
Clyde St BGLY BD16 16 C3
RPDN/SBR HX6 67 E5

Coach La CLECK BD19 * 64 D5
  CUL/OBY BD13 ......44 C1
Coach Rd BAIL BD17 ......18 B5
  GSLY LS20 ......10 C4
  HIPP HX3 ......71 E1
Coal La CUL/OBY HX2 ......42 D4
Coal Pit La BRIG HD6 ......79 E2
Coalpit La HIPP HX3 ......69 H4
Coates St WBOW BD5 ......47 E3
Coates Ter WBOW BD5 ......47 E3
Cobden Ct HFAX HX1 * 4 C5
Cobden St CLAY BD14 ......45 G5
  CUL/OBY BD13 ......52 C1
  IDLE BD10 ......30 A2
  WIL/AL BD15 ......37 E3
Cock Hill La HIPP HX3 ......52 D4
Cockcroft Gv BFDE BD3 ......3 H4
Cockin La CLAY BD14 ......44 B4
Coldbeck Dr WBSY BD6 ......54 D2
Coldshaw Top HWTH BD22 ......22 D3
Cold St HWTH BD22 ......22 D3
Colehill Wy BOW BD4 ......56 B2
Coleman St BFDE BD3 ......2 E1
Colenso Rd KGHY BD21 * 7 H2
Colenso Wk KGHY BD21 ......7 H2
Colenso Wy KGHY BD21 * 7 H2
Coleridge Gdns BFDE BD10 ......30 B1
Coles Wy AIRE BD20 ......7 G1
Coley Hall La HIPP HX3 ......61 G3
Coley Rd HIPP HX3 ......61 F2
Coley Vw HIPP HX3 ......60 D2
Collbrook Av WBSY BD6 ......54 D2
College Rd BGLY BD16 ......9 H5
College Ter HFAX HX1 * 68 A3
Collier La BAIL BD17 ......18 C2
Colliers Cl SHPY BD18 ......27 H2
Collindale Cl IDLE BD10 ......30 D4
Collinfield Ri WBSY BD6 ......54 B3
Collingham Av WBSY BD6 ......53 G2
Collin Moor La GTL/HWG HX4 ......75 H5
Collins Cl HWTH BD22 ......23 F1
Collinson St CLECK BD19 ......48 A2
Collins St BOW BD4 ......46 B4
  GTHN BD7 ......46 B4
Colne Rd (Goodley)
  HWTH BD22 ......12 D4
Colston Cl GIR BD8 ......37 H3
Columbus St HIPP HX3 * 59 F4
Colyon Mt WIL/AL BD15 ......37 E3
Commerce Ct BFDE BD3 ......48 C3
Commercial Buildings
  LM/WK BD12 ......64 A1
Commercial St BFD BD1 * 64 A1
  BRIG HD6 ......78 B1
  CLECK BD19 ......73 H1
  CUL/OBY BD13 ......34 C4
  CUL/OBY BD13 ......44 B1
  CUL/OBY BD13 ......52 A1
  HFAX HX1 ......5 H5
  SHPY BD18 ......27 G3
Commonedale Wy BOW BD4 ......55 H4
Common La HIPP HX3 ......69 G2
Common Rd ELL HX5 ......77 F5
  LM/WK BD12 ......54 C4
Como Av GIR BD8 ......38 A3
Como Dr GIR BD8 ......38 A3
Como Gdns GIR BD8 ......38 A3
Como Gv GIR BD8 ......38 A3
Compeigne Av AIRE BD20 ......8 F2
Compton St BOW BD4 ......48 B5
  KGHY BD21 ......7 G3
Concrete St HIPP HX3 * 59 F4
Condor Cl WBSY BD6 ......54 C1
Conduit St GIR BD8 ......38 D3
Coney La KGHY BD21 ......6 D6
Coniston Av CUL/OBY BD13 ......52 A1
Coniston Cl CUL/OBY BD13 ......52 A1
Coniston Dr HTON BD9 ......38 A2
Coniston Rd GTHN BD7 ......45 H4
Constance St SHPY BD18 * 28 A1
Constitutional St HFAX HX1 * 4 C5
Conway St HFAX HX1 ......4 C5
Cooke Crs CLECK BD19 ......65 F5
Cooke La KGHY BD21 * 7 H5
Cooke St KGHY BD21 ......7 H5
Cookson St BRIG HD6 ......71 E5
Coombe Hl CUL/OBY BD13 ......45 G5
Co-operative Buildings
  BRIG HD6 ......71 G1
  HIPP HX3 ......59 E3
Cooper Cl BGLY BD16 ......16 D1
Cooperfields LUD/ILL HX2 ......66 B3
Cooper Gv WBSY BD6 ......53 G2
Cooper La HIPP HX3 ......53 G2
Copeland St BOW BD4 ......48 C2
Copgrove Cl BOW BD4 ......48 C2
Copgrove Ct BOW BD4 ......48 C2
Copgrove Rd BOW BD4 ......48 C2
Copley Av LUD/ILL HX2 ......75 G5
Copley Gln HIPP HX3 ......75 G5
Copley Hall St HIPP HX3 ......75 G5
Copley La HIPP HX3 ......75 G1
Copley Mt HIPP HX3 ......75 G5
Copley St WBOW BD5 ......46 C4
Copley Ter HIPP HX3 ......75 G5
Copperas La WIL/AL BD15 ......66 D6
Copperas Rw GTL/HWG HX4 * 74 D4
Coppice Gra YEA LS19 ......11 G5
The Coppice HFAX HX1 ......4 E7
  YEA LS19 ......21 E1
Coppice Vw IDLE BD10 ......29 H1
Coppice Wood Av GSLY LS20 ......11 F2
Coppice Wood Cl GSLY LS20 ......11 F3
Coppice Wood Crs GSLY LS20 ......11 F3
Coppice Wood Gv GSLY LS20 ......11 F3
  GTHN BD7 * ......
Coppice Wood Ri YEA LS19 ......11 G5
The Coppies LM/WK BD12 ......62 C1
Coppy Cl BGLY BD16 ......16 A5
The Copse BGLY BD16 ......17 G5
  CLECK BD19 ......72 C1

Copt Royd Gv YEA LS19 ......11 F4
Corban St BOW BD4 ......48 B4
Cordingley Cl BOW BD4 ......56 D1
Cordingley St BOW BD4 ......56 D1
Corn Market HFAX HX1 ......5 H4
Corn Mill La CLAY BD14 ......44 C2
Corn St HWTH BD22 ......7 J3
Cornwall Crs BAIL BD17 ......18 C2
  BRIG HD6 ......71 G2
Cornwall Pl GIR BD8 ......2 B1
Cornwall Rd BGLY BD16 ......17 E4
  GIR BD8 ......2 B1
Cornwall Ter GIR BD8 ......2 B1
Coronation Av HIPP HX3 ......20 C2
Coronation Mt HWTH BD22 ......6 C4
Coronation Rd HIPP HX3 ......68 D4
Coronation St ELL HX5 ......76 C5
  GTL/HWG HX4 ......76 A3
  LM/WK BD12 ......55 H5
Coronation Wk HWTH BD22 ......6 C5
Coronation Wy HWTH BD22 ......6 B5
Corporal La CUL/OBY BD13 ......52 B4
Corporation St ECHL BD2 ......40 B1
  HIPP HX5 ......5 G2
  RPDN/SBR HX6 ......67 E4
Corrance Rd LM/WK BD12 ......63 E4
Corrie St CUL/OBY BD13 ......44 B1
Cote Farm La IDLE BD10 ......19 G5
Cotefields Av HTON BD9 ......41 H2
Cote Gap CUL/OBY BD13 ......36 B6
Cote La PDSY/CALV LS28 ......41 H2
  WIL/AL BD15 ......36 D3
The Cote PDSY/CALV LS28 ......41 H2
Cotewall Rd WBOW BD5 ......47 E4
Cotswold Av SHPY BD18 ......29 F2
Cotswold Dr LVSG WF15 ......73 G5
Cottage Gn GIR BD8 ......38 A4
Cottage Ms HWTH BD22 * 22 C2
Cottage Rd IDLE BD10 ......30 C2
Cottam Av GTHN BD7 ......46 C1
Cottam Ter GTHN BD7 ......46 C1
Cotterdale WIL/AL BD15 ......36 D1
Cottingley Cliffe Rd
  BGLY BD16 ......27 E5
Cottingley Dr BGLY BD16 ......26 D1
Cottingley Manor Pk
  BGLY BD16 ......26 D4
Cottingley Moor Rd
  BGLY BD16 ......27 E2
Cottingley New Rd
  BGLY BD16 ......27 E2
Cottingley Rd WIL/AL BD15 ......36 D1
Cottingley Ter GIR BD8 * 2 B1
Courtenay Cl BFDE BD10 ......40 D5
Court La LUD/ILL HX2 ......47 H4
Courts Leet LM/WK BD12 ......62 D1
The Court LVSG WF15 ......73 H4
  SHPY BD18 * 27 H2
Cousen Av GTHN BD7 ......46 A2
Cousen Rd GTHN BD7 ......46 C5
Cousin La LUD/ILL HX2 ......66 D4
Coventry St BOW BD4 ......48 A3
  LUD/ILL HX2 * 67 H1
Coverdale Wy BAIL BD17 ......19 F2
Cover Dr WBSY BD6 ......54 B2
Coverley Rd YEA LS19 ......11 E4
The Covet IDLE BD10 ......30 C1
Cow Close La LM/WK BD12 ......63 F5
Cowdray Dr CLECK BD19 ......63 G5
Cowgill St GIR BD8 ......38 D3
Cow Gn HFAX HX1 ......5 G4
Cow Hill Gate La LUD/ILL HX2 ......50 D2
Cow La HIPP HX3 ......75 H1
  HIPP HX3 ......75 H1
Cowley Crs HTON BD9 ......27 F5
Cowling La HIPP HX3 ......52 C5
Cowroyd Pl HIPP HX3 ......5 J1
Crabtree Pl GTHN BD7 ......46 B3
Crabtree St GTHN BD7 ......46 B3
  HFAX HX1 ......4 C4
Crack La WIL/AL BD15 ......26 A4
Cracoe Rd BFDE BD3 ......3 K6
Crag Cl LUD/ILL HX2 ......58 C1
Cragg La CUL/OBY BD13 ......42 D2
Cragg Wood Dr YEA LS19 ......21 F3
Cragg Ter GTHN BD7 ......46 B4
Cragg Top CUL/OBY BD13 ......42 D2
Crag Hill Rd IDLE BD10 ......19 H4
Crag La LUD/ILL HX2 ......58 C1
Crag Pl KGHY BD21 ......7 J3
Crag Rd SHPY BD18 ......28 D3
Crag Vw IDLE BD10 ......30 B2
Craiglands HIPP HX3 ......61 G5
Craiglea Dr LM/WK BD12 ......63 E3
Craigmore Ct BOW BD4 ......49 E5
Crake Dr WBSY BD6 ......53 F1
Cranbourne Rd HTON BD9 ......39 H3
Cranbrook Av WBSY BD6 ......54 D2
Cranbrook Pl WBOW BD5 ......47 F4
Cranbrook St CLAY BD14 ......45 E3
  WBOW BD5 ......47 F4
Cranford Pl WIL/AL BD15 ......35 G4
Cranleigh Mt KGHY BD21 ......13 H1
Cranmer Rd BFDE BD3 ......39 G3
Craven Av CUL/OBY BD13 ......44 B1
Craven Cl CLECK BD19 ......65 H5
Craven Ct GIR BD8 ......38 A4
  HFAX HX1 ......4 C4
Craven Dr CLECK BD19 ......65 H5
Craven Edge HFAX HX1 ......4 C7
Craven La CLECK BD19 ......65 H5
Craven Rd HFAX HX1 ......7 H1
Craven St BFDE BD3 * 3 F5
Craven Ter HFAX HX1 ......4 C7
Crawford Av WBSY BD6 ......54 D2
Crawford St BOW BD4 ......47 H3
Crediton Av WIL/AL BD15 ......37 E4
Crediton Ct WIL/AL BD15 ......37 E4
The Crescent BAIL BD17 ......18 D4
  BGLY BD16 ......16 A5
  BIRK/DRI BD11 ......57 F5
  GSLY LS20 ......10 B3
  HIPP HX3 ......61 G5
  HIPP HX3 ......69 F2
  LVSG WF15 ......73 G3
  WBSY BD6 ......54 B2
Crescent Vw HWTH BD22 ......13 H3
Crescent Wk CLAY BD14 ......45 G2
Creskeld Wy WIL/AL BD15 ......36 C2
Cresswell Av GTHN BD7 ......45 H5
Cresswell Pl GTHN BD7 ......45 H5
Cresswell Ter GTHN BD7 ......45 H5
Crest Av WIL/AL BD15 ......36 C2
Crestfield Dr LUD/ILL HX2 ......62 D4
Crestfield Gv ELL HX5 ......76 B5
Crestfield Dr LUD/ILL HX2 ......45 G2
The Crest HUDN HD2 ......79 F5
Crestville Cl CLAY BD14 ......45 G2
Crestville Rd CLAY BD14 ......45 G2
Crestville Ter CLAY BD14 ......45 G2
Crestwood Cl BOW BD4 ......56 A1
Crib La HIPP HX3 ......5 G1
Cricketers Gn YEA LS19 ......11 G5
Crimshaw La SHPY BD18 ......29 E5
Cripplegate HFAX HX1 ......5 K3
Croft Av BGLY BD16 ......9 G6
Croft Bank BIRK/DRI BD11 ......57 F5
Crofters Gn IDLE BD10 ......29 H1
Crofters Lea YEA LS19 ......11 E5
Croft Fold HIPP HX3 ......59 E5
Croft House Cl WBSY BD6 ......54 C2
Croft House La AIRE BD20 ......6 D1
Croft House Rd WBSY BD6 ......54 C2
Croftlands IDLE BD10 ......29 H1
Crofton Rd HTON BD9 ......39 H3
Croft Pl BRIG HD6 ......71 G4
Croft Ri HIPP HX3 ......59 E5
Croft Rd BGLY BD16 ......9 E5
Croft St BFD BD1 ......2 E7
  BIRK/DRI BD11 ......57 F5
  BRIG HD6 ......78 B1
  HWTH BD22 ......22 D2
  IDLE BD10 ......30 B1
  KGHY BD21 ......7 F5
  RPDN/SBR HX6 * 67 E4
  SHPY BD18 ......28 C2
  WBSY BD6 ......54 D1
Croisdale Cl LVSG WF15 ......73 H4
Cromack Vw PDSY/CALV LS28 ......41 H5
Cromer Av KGHY BD21 ......14 A1
Cromer Gv KGHY BD21 ......14 A1
Cromer Rd KGHY BD21 ......14 A1
Cromer St HFAX HX1 ......14 A7
  KGHY BD21 ......14 A1
Cromwell Bottom Dr
  BRIG HD6 * 71 F4
Cromwell Ct HIPP HX3 ......69 H4
Cromwell Pl BGLY BD16 ......27 E5
Cromwell Rd HIPP HX3 ......69 H4
Cromwell Ter HFAX HX1 * 4 E4
Crooked La IDLE BD10 ......19 G5
Crooke La WIL/AL BD15 ......25 H5
Cropredy Cl CUL/OBY BD13 ......52 C1
Crosby St KGHY BD21 ......7 H5
Croscombe Wk WBOW BD5 ......47 F2
Crosland St KGHY BD21 ......14 A1
Crosley Wood Rd BGLY BD16 ......17 E4
Cross Banks SHPY BD18 ......28 C2
Cross Crown St CLECK BD19 ......73 G1
Crossdale Av WBSY BD6 ......53 G1
Cross Emily St KGHY BD21 ......7 F5
Cross Farm Ct HWTH BD22 ......32 C1
Crossfield Cl HWTH BD22 ......32 C1
Crossfield Rd HWTH BD22 ......32 C1
Cross Gates La BGLY BD16 ......15 H3
Cross Hl GTL/HWG HX4 ......75 H4
  HIPP HX3 ......5 H2
Crosshills Mt GTL/HWG HX4 ......75 H4
Cross House Ct LM/WK BD12 ......63 H1
Cross La BGLY BD16 ......16 C3
  BIRK/DRI BD11 ......79 F2
  CUL/OBY BD13 ......45 E5
  ELL HX5 ......76 B5
  GTHN BD7 ......46 B4
  HIPP HX3 ......52 D4
  HWTH BD22 ......32 D1
  WIL/AL BD15 ......26 A2
Cross Leeds St KGHY BD21 ......7 E4
Crossley Gdns HFAX HX1 ......4 A5
Crossley Hall Ms GIR BD8 ......37 H5
Crossley Hl HIPP HX3 ......69 E5
Crossley St BRIG HD6 ......78 C2
  CUL/OBY BD13 ......46 C2
  HFAX HX1 ......5 G4
Crossley Ter North
  LUD/ILL HX2 ......59 F1
Crossley Ter South
  LUD/ILL HX2 ......59 F1
Cross River St KGHY BD21 * 7 H2
Cross Rd GIR BD8 ......38 C3
  IDLE BD10 ......30 B1
  LM/WK BD12 ......55 H5
Cross Rosse St SHPY BD18 * 28 C1
Cross Rydal St KGHY BD21 * 7 E5
Cross St West LUD/ILL HX2 * 58 D5
Cross Sun St BFD BD1 ......2 E3
Crossway BGLY BD16 ......26 C2
Crowgill Rd SHPY BD18 ......28 C1
Crown Dr LM/WK BD12 ......62 D1
Crownest La BGLY BD16 ......16 D3
Crown Rd HIPP HX3 ......59 G3
Crown St BFD BD1 ......2 D5
  BRIG HD6 ......71 F5
  CLECK BD19 ......73 G1
  ELL HX5 ......76 C5
  HFAX HX1 ......5 G4
  LM/WK BD12 ......62 D1
Crowther Av PDSY/CALV LS28 ......31 G3
Crowther Fold BGLY BD16 ......15 G5
Crowther La BOW BD4 ......56 B1

Crowther St CLECK BD19 ......64 C5
  IDLE BD10 ......30 B1
  LM/WK BD12 ......62 D1
Crowther Wk WBOW BD5 * 47 F2
Crow Tree Cl BAIL BD17 ......19 E3
Crow Tree La GIR BD8 ......37 H3
Crowtrees Ct YEA LS19 ......21 E5
Crowtrees Crs BRIG HD6 ......78 A5
Crowtrees La BRIG HD6 ......77 H5
Crowtrees Pk BRIG HD6 ......78 A4
Crow Trees Pk YEA LS19 ......21 E5
Crow Wood Pk LUD/ILL HX2 ......67 E3
Croydon Rd GTHN BD7 ......46 A5
Crumack La HWTH BD22 ......33 F1
Crystal Ct HFAX HX1 ......4 C5
Crystal Ter BOW BD4 ......48 B4
Cullingworth Rd
  CUL/OBY BD13 ......24 C4
Culver St HFAX HX1 * 5 G5
Cumberland Cl LUD/ILL HX2 ......58 D1
Cumberland Rd HTON BD9 ......46 B2
Cunliffe La BAIL BD17 ......20 A1
Cunliffe Rd GIR BD8 ......38 D2
Cunliffe Ter GIR BD8 ......38 D2
Cunliffe Vis HTON BD9 ......39 E1
Cupstone Cl BAIL BD17 ......20 A2
Cure Hl HWTH BD22 ......12 C3
Curlew St WBOW BD5 ......46 D4
Currer Av BOW BD4 ......56 A1
Currerbell Ms CUL/OBY BD13 ......44 C1
Currer St BFD BD1 ......3 H6
Curtis Cl CUL/OBY BD13 * 24 C5
Curzon Rd BFDE BD3 ......3 H5
Cuthberts Cl CUL/OBY BD13 ......52 A2
Cutler Heights La BOW BD4 ......48 C3
Cutler Pl BOW BD4 ......48 C3
Cyprus Av IDLE BD10 ......19 G5
Cyprus Dr IDLE BD10 ......19 G5

D

Daffels Wood Cl BOW BD4 ......56 A2
Daffodil Ct WIL/AL BD15 ......37 E4
Dagenham Rd BOW BD4 ......48 B4
Daisy Bank HFAX HX1 ......5 F7
Daisy Hl LM/WK BD12 ......55 H5
Daisy Hill Back La HTON BD9 ......37 H2
Daisy Hill Gv HTON BD9 ......37 H2
Daisy Hill La HTON BD9 ......37 H2
Daisy Mt RPDN/SBR HX6 ......66 D5
Daisy Rd BRIG HD6 ......78 C3
Daisy St BRIG HD6 ......78 C3
  GTHN BD7 ......46 B4
  HWTH BD22 ......23 H1
Dalby Av BFDE BD3 ......40 A2
Dalby St BFDE BD3 * 40 B4
Dalcross Gv WBOW BD5 ......47 G3
Dalcross St WBOW BD5 ......47 G3
Dale Cl GSLY LS20 ......10 A3
Dale Croft Ri WIL/AL BD15 ......36 B3
Dale Garth BAIL BD17 ......18 C3
Dale Gv WBSY BD6 ......54 D2
Dales Dr GSLY LS20 ......10 A3
Daleside GTL/HWG HX4 ......75 F4
Daleside Av PDSY/CALV LS28 ......41 H4
Daleside Cl PDSY/CALV LS28 ......41 H4
Daleside Gv LM/WK BD12 ......63 G1
  PDSY/CALV LS28 ......41 H4
Daleside Rd AIRE BD20 ......8 B2
  BFDE BD3 ......19 E5
  SHPY BD18 ......29 F2
Daleside Wk WBOW BD5 ......47 G5
Daleson Cl HIPP HX3 ......60 D2
Dale St BFD BD1 ......3 F3
  RPDN/SBR HX6 ......67 E4
  SHPY BD18 ......27 H2
Dalesway BGLY BD16 ......17 E1
Dales Way GSLY LS20 ......10 A3
Dales Way Link BAIL BD17 ......17 H1
Dalewood CI BFDE BD3 ......40 A2
Daleview Ct BAIL BD17 ......18 D4
Dale View Gv KGHY BD21 ......7 H5
Dale View Rd KGHY BD21 ......7 H5
Dallam Av SHPY BD18 ......27 H1
Dallam Dr SHPY BD18 ......27 H1
Dallam Gv SHPY BD18 ......28 A1
Dallam Wk SHPY BD18 ......28 A1
Dalton La KGHY BD21 ......7 H5
Dalton Rd KGHY BD21 ......7 H5
Dalton St RPDN/SBR HX6 ......67 E4
  KGHY BD21 ......7 H5
Damask St HFAX HX1 * 5 J2
Damems La HWTH BD22 ......13 G4
Dam Head Rd RPDN/SBR HX6 ......67 F5
Damon Av IDLE BD10 ......30 D2
Damside HFAX HX1 ......5 H4
Damson Ct CLAY BD14 ......45 E2
Danby Av BOW BD4 ......56 A2
Danebury Rd BRIG HD6 ......78 C2
Danecourt Rd BOW BD4 ......48 C4
Dane Hill Dr BOW BD4 ......49 E5
Daniel Ct BOW BD4 ......49 E5
Dan La WBSY BD6 ......53 F1
Danum Dr BAIL BD17 ......66 A1
Darcey Hey La LUD/ILL HX2 ......67 H3
Darfield St GIR BD8 ......2 B3
Dark La HWTH BD22 ......32 D1
  HWTH BD22 ......32 D1
Darley St BFD BD1 ......2 D3
  BFD BD1 ......2 D3
Darnes Av LUD/ILL HX2 ......67 G3
Darren St BOW BD4 ......48 B4
Darryl Dr LUD/ILL HX2 ......66 C3
Dartmouth Ter GIR BD8 ......38 B2
Darwin St WBOW BD5 ......46 D4
Dawnay Rd WBSY BD6 ......54 D2
Dawson Av WBSY BD6 ......54 D2
Dawson La BOW BD4 ......56 B1

Dawson Mt BOW BD4 ......56 B1
Dawson Pl BOW BD4 ......56 B1
  KGHY BD21 ......14 B1
Dawson Rd KGHY BD21 ......14 B1
Dawsons Meadow
  PDSY/CALV LS28 ......41 H2
Dawson St BOW BD4 ......48 B5
  IDLE BD10 ......20 A4
Dawson Ter BOW BD4 ......56 B1
Dawson Wy KGHY BD21 ......14 B1
Deacon Cl BFDE BD3 * 40 C2
Dealburn Rd LM/WK BD12 ......63 H1
Deal St HFAX HX1 ......5 J5
  KGHY BD21 ......7 H3
Dean Beck Av WBSY BD6 ......55 F2
Dean Beck Ct WBSY BD6 * 55 G2
Dean Cl GIR BD8 ......37 G3
Dean Clough HIPP HX3 ......5 G2
Dean Clough Office Pk
  HIPP HX3 ......5 G1
Dean Ct HIPP HX3 ......75 F1
Dean End GTL/HWG HX4 ......76 A3
Deanery Gdns IDLE BD10 ......30 B4
Dean Lane Head
  CUL/OBY BD13 * 35 H3
Dean Rd WBSY BD6 ......55 E2
Dean's Laithe KGHY BD21 * 36 A3
Deanstones Crs CUL/OBY BD13 ......52 B2
Deanstones La CUL/OBY BD13 ......52 B2
  GTL/HWG HX4 ......76 A4
  HWTH BD22 ......23 E2
Deanwood Av WIL/AL BD15 ......36 C2
Deanwood Crs WIL/AL BD15 ......36 D2
Deanwood Wk WIL/AL BD15 ......36 C2
Dearden St RPDN/SBR HX6 ......67 E3
Dee Ct HWTH BD22 ......12 D4
Deepdale Cl BAIL BD17 ......18 B4
Deep La BRIG HD6 ......79 F1
  CLAY BD14 ......45 F2
  HIPP HX3 ......43 F5
  LUD/ILL HX2 ......66 C1
Defarge Ct WBOW BD5 ......47 F4
De Lacey Ms BOW BD4 ......48 B5
De Lacy Av BOW BD4 * 56 A2
Delamere St WBOW BD5 ......47 G5
Delaware Ct BOW BD4 ......56 A2
Delf Hl BRIG HD6 ......77 H4
Delius Av IDLE BD10 ......30 C4
Dellside Fold CUL/OBY BD13 ......24 C3
The Dell CUL/OBY BD13 ......24 D3
Delph Crs CLAY BD14 ......45 E3
Delph Croft Vw KGHY BD21 * 7 G5
Delph Dr CLAY BD14 ......44 D3
Delph Gv CLAY BD14 ......45 E3
Delph Hl BAIL BD17 ......18 D2
Delph Hill Castle LUD/ILL HX2 * 67 G2
Delph Hill La LUD/ILL HX2 ......68 A4
Delph Hill Ter LUD/ILL HX2 ......68 A4
Delph St HFAX HX1 ......5 J5
Delph Ter CLAY BD14 ......45 E3
Delph Wood Cl BGLY BD16 ......17 F5
Delverne Gv ECHL BD2 ......40 B1
Denbrook Cl BOW BD4 ......57 E2
Denbrook Ct BOW BD4 ......57 E1
Denbrook Cl BOW BD4 ......57 E1
Denbrook Wk BOW BD4 ......57 E1
Denbrook Wy BOW BD4 ......57 E1
Denbury Mt BOW BD4 ......48 D5
Denby Cl HWTH BD22 ......12 C5
Denby Dr BAIL BD17 ......18 C5
Denby Hill Rd HWTH BD22 ......12 C5
Denby La HWTH BD22 ......13 E5
Denby Mt HWTH BD22 ......32 D2
Denby Pl RPDN/SBR HX6 ......67 E3
Denby St GIR BD8 ......14 B1
Dence Gn BOW BD4 * 38 D4
Dendrum Cl HWTH BD22 ......12 D3
Dene Back BGLY BD16 ......9 H5
Dene Crs GTHN BD7 ......45 H3
Dene Hl BAIL BD17 ......18 A3
Denehill HTON BD9 ......37 G2
Dene Mt WIL/AL BD15 ......37 E3
Dene Pk HFAX HX1 ......1 F2
Dene Rd WBSY BD6 ......53 C1
Deneside WBOW BD5 ......54 D1
Deneside Ter WBOW BD5 ......47 E5
Deneway PDSY/CALV LS28 ......41 H2
Denfield Av HIPP HX3 ......59 E3
Denfield Crs HIPP HX3 ......59 E3
Denfield Edge HIPP HX3 ......59 E3
Denfield Gdns HIPP HX3 ......59 E3
Denfield La HIPP HX3 ......59 E3
Denfield Sq HIPP HX3 ......59 E3
Denham St BRIG HD6 ......78 C1
Denholme Gate Rd HIPP HX3 ......61 F4
Denholme Rd HWTH BD22 ......33 E5
Denison St YEA LS19 ......11 G4
Dennison Fold BOW BD4 ......48 D2
Denton Dr BGLY BD16 ......17 F2
Derby Pl BFDE BD3 * 40 D5
  YEA LS19 ......21 G2
Derby St CLAY BD14 * 45 E3
  CUL/OBY BD13 ......52 A1
  GTHN BD7 ......46 C5
  RPDN/SBR HX6 ......67 F3
Derwent Av WIL/AL BD15 ......37 E3
Derwent Rd ECHL BD2 ......39 H1
Derwent St KGHY BD21 ......8 A3
Devonshire Cl HIPP HX3 ......7 F4
Devonshire St West
  KGHY BD21 ......6 D4
Devon St GIR BD8 ......38 D2
Devon St HFAX HX1 ......4 A6
Devon Wy BRIG HD6 ......71 G2
Dewhirst Cl BAIL BD17 ......19 E4
Dewhirst Pl BFDE BD3 ......19 E4
Dewhirst Rd BAIL BD17 ......19 E4
  HIPP HX3 ......25 H4
Dewsbury Rd CLECK BD19 ......65 G3
  CLECK BD19 ......73 H1
  ELL HX5 ......77 F5

Diamond St BFD BD1 ....2 E6
HFAX HX1 ....4 C2
HWTH BD22 ....13 H2
Diamond Ter HFAX HX1 ....4 C2
Dibb La YEA LS19 ....11 E4
Dicken's St LUD/ILL HX2 ....67 H1
WBOW BD5 ....4 F7
Dick La BFDE BD3 ....41 E4
BOW BD4 ....48 D2
Dimples La AIRE BD20 ....9 E3
HWTH BD22 ....22 D2
Dirkhill Rd GTHN BD7 ....46 B2
Dirkhill St GTHN BD7 ....46 C2
Discovery Rd HFAX HX1 ....5 J4
Dispensary Wk HFAX HX1 ....5 J4
Dixon Av GTHN BD7 ....46 A2
Dixon St CTL/HWG HX4 ....75 F3
Dob La RPDN/SBR HX6 ....66 A5
Dockfield Rd BAIL BD17 ....28 D1
Dockfield Rd BAIL BD17 ....28 D1
Dockfield Ter BAIL BD17 ....18 D5
Dock La SHPY BD18 ....28 D1
Dockroyd La HWTH BD22 ....12 D4
Doctor Hl IDLE BD10 ....29 H3
LUD/ILL HX2 ....58 C4
Doctor La IDLE BD10 ....30 C3
Dodgeholme Cl
LUD/ILL HX2 ....58 C1
Dodge Holme Gdns
LUD/ILL HX2 ....58 C1
Dodge Holme Rd LUD/ILL HX2 ....58 C1
Dog Kennel La HIPP HX3 ....69 F3
Dog La GTL/HWG HX4 ....74 D4
Dole St CUL/QBY BD13 ....84 B1
Doll La CUL/QBY BD13 ....24 D4
Dombey La HFAX HX1 ....4 D4
Donald Av WBSY BD6 ....54 D3
Doncaster St HIPP HX3 ....69 E5
Donisthorpe St WBOW BD5 ....47 F4
Don St KGHY BD21 ....7 E3
Dorchester Ct BOW BD4 * 48 D4
Dorchester Crs BAIL BD17 ....19 G2
BOW BD4 ....48 D4
Dorchester Dr LUD/ILL HX2 ....67 H5
YEA LS19 ....11 H5
Dorian Cl IDLE BD10 ....30 C3
Dorothy St KGHY BD21 ....13 H5
Dorset Cl WBOW BD5 ....47 E4
Dorset St WBOW BD5 ....47 E4
Douglas Dr BOW BD4 ....48 B3
Douglas Rd BOW BD4 ....48 B3
Douglas St HIPP HX3 ....59 G3
HWTH BD22 ....23 F1
Dovedale Cl HWTH BD22 ....53 E4
Dover St BFDE BD3 ....3 H7
Dovesdale Gv WBOW BD5 ....06 D5
Dovesdale Rd WBOW BD5 ....47 E5
Dove St SHPY BD18 ....28 A1
Dowker St HFAX HX1 ....4 C6
Dowley Gap La BGLY BD16 ....17 E5
Downham St BFDE BD3 ....3 H6
Downing Ct BFDE BD3 ....3 J6
Downside Crs WIL/AL BD15 ....36 D3
Dracup Av GTHN BD7 ....45 H2
Dracup Rd GTHN BD7 ....46 A4
Drakes HIPP HX3 ....59 F1
Drake St KGHY BD21 ....7 G5
Draughton Gv WBOW BD5 ....55 E1
Draughton St WBOW BD5 ....55 E1
Drewry Rd KGHY BD21 ....7 E4
Drewton Rd BFD BD1 ....2 B4
Drill Pde GIR BD8 ....2 A1
Drill St HWTH BD22 ....22 D3
KGHY BD21 ....7 F1
The Drive BGLY BD16 ....9 F5
HIPP HX3 ....61 G5
IDLE BD10 ....30 C3
Drovers Wy ECHL BD2 ....72 D5
Drub La CLECK BD19 ....64 D3
Druids St CLAY SD14 ....65 E5
Drummond Rd GIR BD8 ....38 D5
Dryclough Cl HIPP HX3 ....68 D5
Dryclough La HIPP HX3 ....68 D5
Dryden St BFD BD1 ....3 F7
BGLY BD16 * 16 C3
Dubb La BGLY BD16 ....16 D5
Duchy Av HTON BD9 ....37 H1
Duchy Crs HTON BD9 ....37 H1
Duchy Dr HTON BD9 ....37 H2
Duchy Gv HTON BD9 ....37 H1
Duchy Vls HTON BD9 ....37 H1
Duchywood HTON BD9 ....37 H1
Ducie St IDLE BD10 ....20 A5
Duckett Gv PDSY/CALV LS28 ....41 E4
Ducking Pond Cl HWTH BD22 ....22 D3
Duckworth Gv HTON BD9 ....38 A2
Duckworth La HTON BD9 ....37 H5
Duckworth Ter HTON BD9 ....38 A2
Dudley Crs LUD/ILL HX2 ....50 C5
Dudley Gv BOW BD4 ....48 D2
Dudley Hill Rd ECHL BD2 ....40 A1
Dudley St BOW BD4 ....48 D2
BOW BD4 ....48 D2
Dudwell Av HIPP HX3 ....76 A1
Dudwell Gv HIPP HX3 ....75 H1
Dudwell La HIPP HX3 ....75 H1
Duich Rd WBSY BD6 ....53 H4
Duinen St WBOW BD5 ....47 F2
Duke St AIRE BD20 ....7 E2
BFD BD1 ....6 C5
ELL HX5 ....76 C5
HWTH BD22 ....23 E2
Dulverton Gv BOW BD4 ....48 C4
Dunbar Cft CUL/QBY BD13 ....52 C1
Duncan St WBOW BD5 ....47 F2
Duncombe Rd GIR BD8 ....38 A5
Duncombe St GIR BD8 ....38 B5
Duncombe Wy GTHN BD7 ....38 B5
Dundas St HFAX HX1 ....4 B7
KGHY BD21 ....7 G5
Dunkhill Cft IDLE BD10 * 30 A2
Dunkirk Crs HFAX HX1 ....4 A6
Dunkirk La HFAX HX1 ....4 A6
Dunkirk Ri AIRE BD20 ....7 H1
Dunkirk St HFAX HX1 ....67 H2
Dunkirk Ter HFAX HX1 ....4 A6

Dunlin Wy GIR BD8 ....37 F5
Dunmore Av
CUL/QBY BD13 ....51 H1
Dunnington Wk
LM/WK BD12 ....54 B4
Dunnock Av WBSY BD6 ....55 E1
Dunsford Av BOW BD4 ....56 A2
Dunstan Gv CLECK BD19 ....64 D5
Durham Rd GIR BD8 ....38 B3
Durham St LUD/ILL HX2 ....58 D5
Durham Ter GIR BD8 ....38 B3
Durkheim Ct BFDE BD3 * 40 B5
Durley Av HTON BD9 ....38 A1
Durling Dr SHPY BD18 ....27 G2
Durlston Gv LM/WK BD12 ....63 E1
Durlston Ter LM/WK BD12 ....63 E1
Durrance St HWTH BD22 ....6 C5
Dye House Dr CLECK BD19 ....64 B5
Dyehouse La BRIC HD6 ....76 B2
Dye House La WIL/AL BD15 ....25 C4
Dyehouse La LM/WK BD12 ....63 G5
Dyer La HIPP HX3 ....59 E4
Dyson St HIPP HX3 * 69 E5
Dyson St BFD BD1 ....2 A4
BRIC HD6 ....71 F5
HTON BD9 ....28 B5

E

Eaglesfield Dr WBSY BD6 ....54 A4
Eagle St HWTH BD22 ....23 F2
KGHY BD21 ....7 E4
Earls Ter HIPP HX3 ....59 F3
Earl St HWTH BD22 ....22 D3
KGHY BD21 ....7 E3
WBOW BD5 ....47 F2
Earlswood LM/WK BD12 ....63 C2
Earl Ter HIPP HX3 ....59 F3
Easby Rd WBOW BD5 ....2 B7
East Av KGHY BD21 ....7 F3
East Bolton LUD/ILL HX2 ....50 D3
Eastbourne Rd HTON BD9 ....28 C4
Eastbury Av WBSY BD6 ....53 G1
East Byland LUD/ILL HX2 ....50 D4
Eastcliffe HIPP HX3 ....69 F2
Eastfield Gdns BOW BD4 ....48 D3
Eastgate ELL HX5 ....76 C4
Easthorpe Ct ELL HX5 ....30 C5
Eastleigh Gv WBOW BD5 ....47 E4
East Mt BRIC HD6 ....71 F5
East Pde BAIL BD17 ....19 E2
BFD BD1 ....2 F4
KGHY BD21 ....7 G4
RPDN/SBR HX6 ....67 G3
East Park Rd HIPP HX3 * 59 F4
East Rd LM/WK BD12 ....55 E4
East Royd HWTH BD22 ....13 E4
East Squire La GIR BD8 ....38 B3
East St BRIC HD6 ....78 B2
HIPP HX3 ....71 F1
East Ter HWTH BD22 ....23 F1
WBSY BD6 ....45 F5
East Vw LSI9 ....11 H5
East View Rd YEA LS19 ....11 H5
East View Ter LM/WK BD12 ....63 E1
Eastwick Vw WIL/AL BD15 * 37 E3
Eastwood Av LUD/ILL HX2 ....50 D3
Eastwood Cl LUD/ILL HX2 ....50 D3
Eastwood Gv LUD/ILL HX2 ....50 D3
Eastwood St BOW BD4 ....48 D2
BRIC HD6 ....71 G5
HIPP HX3 ....59 F3
Eaton St KGHY BD21 ....13 H2
Ebenezer Pl BFDE BD1 ....46 B3
Ebenezer St BFD BD1 ....2 A5
Ebor La HWTH BD22 ....23 E1
Eccles Ct GIR BD8 ....30 A5
Edale Gv CUL/QBY BD13 ....51 H2
Edderthorpe St BFDE BD3 ....3 H6
Eden Cl LM/WK BD12 ....63 E2
Edensor Rd KGHY BD21 ....7 E4
Ederoyd Av PDSY/CALV LS28 ....41 G3
Ederoyd Crs PDSY/CALV LS28 ....41 G3
Ederoyd Dr PDSY/CALV LS28 ....41 G3
Ederoyd Gv PDSY/CALV LS28 ....41 G3
Ederoyd Mt PDSY/CALV LS28 ....41 G3
Ederoyd Ri PDSY/CALV LS28 ....41 G3
Edgar St CLAY SD14 ....65 G3
Edgebank Av WBOW BD5 ....55 E1
Edge End Gdns WBSY BD6 ....53 H5
Edge End Rd WBSY BD6 ....53 H5
Edgehill Cl CUL/QBY BD13 ....52 C1
Edgeholme La LUD/ILL HX2 ....57 E1
Edgemoor Cl BOW BD4 ....56 D2
HIPP HX3 ....68 C4
Edlington Cl BOW BD4 ....48 D4
Edmund St GTHN BD7 ....2 B7
Edrich Cl LM/WK BD12 ....55 F4
Edroyd St PDSY/CALV LS28 ....69 H1
Edward Cl HIPP HX3 ....69 H1
Edwards Rd LUD/ILL HX2 ....58 D5
Edward St BOW BD4 ....2 E7
BOW BD4 ....56 D1
BRIC HD6 ....71 F5
BOW BD4 ....56 D1
RPDN/SBR HX6 ....66 C5
SHPY BD18 ....28 A1
Edward Turner Cl
LM/WK BD12 ....54 D4
Edwin Av GSLY LS20 ....10 C2
Eel Holme View St AIRE BD20 ....7 F1
Effingham Rd WILY LS16 ....11 H1
Egerton Gv WIL/AL BD15 ....35 E4
Egerton St RPDN/SBR HX6 ....67 E4
Eggleston St BOW BD4 ....48 D5
Egremont Crs WBSY BD6 ....54 A4
Egremont St RPDN/SBR HX6 ....66 D5
Egypt Rd CUL/QBY BD13 ....35 H3
Eider Cl WBSY BD6 ....55 F1
Eighth Av LVSG WF15 ....73 E3

Elbow La ECHL BD2 ....40 A2
Elderberry Cl BFDE BD20 ....8 C2
Elder St AIRE BD20 ....6 D1
IDLE BD10 ....30 D2
Elderwood Gdns IDLE BD10 ....30 D4
Eldon Pl BFD BD1 ....2 B3
CLECK BD19 ....64 D5
Eldon St HIPP HX3 ....5 H1
Eldroth Mt HFAX HX1 ....68 B5
Eldroth Rd HFAX HX1 ....68 B5
Eldwick Cft BGLY BD16 ....17 F1
Eleanor Dr PDSY/CALV LS28 ....31 E2
Eleanor St BRIC HD6 ....78 B2
Eleventh Av LVSG WF15 ....73 E3
Elia St KGHY BD21 ....7 G3
Eliot Gv GSLY LS20 ....11 E3
Eli St WBOW BD5 ....47 G4
Elizabeth Av LM/WK BD12 ....62 D1
Elizabeth Ct LM/WK BD12 ....63 E1
Elizabeth Crs LM/WK BD12 ....63 E1
Elizabeth Dr LM/WK BD12 ....63 E1
Elizabeth Frances St ELL HX5 ....76 C5
Elizabeth St BGLY BD16 * 16 D3
ELL HX5 ....76 C5
CTL/HWG HX4 ....76 A4
KGHY BD21 ....7 E3
LM/WK BD12 ....62 D1
LVSG WF15 ....73 H4
WBOW BD5 ....47 F2
Elland Br ELL HX5 ....76 C4
Elland Hall ELL HX5 ....76 C4
Elland Riorges Link ELL HX5 ....76 B4
Elland Rd BRIC HD6 ....78 B1
ELL HX5 ....77 F2
Elland Wood Bottom ELL HX5 ....76 A2
Ellar Carr Rd CUL/QBY BD13 ....24 B2
Ellen Royd St HIPP HX3 ....5 H1
Ellen St BGLY BD16 ....16 D5
Ellenthorpe Rd BAIL BD17 ....17 H4
Ellercroft Av GTHN BD7 ....46 B1
Ellercroft Rd GTHN BD7 ....46 B1
Ellercroft Ter GTHN BD7 ....46 B1
Ellerton St BFDE BD3 ....40 B5
Ellinthorpe St BOW BD4 ....48 A2
Elliott St SHPY BD18 ....28 B1
Ellis St WBOW BD5 ....47 E4
Ellistones Gdns GTL/HWG HX4 ....75 F4
Ellistones La GTL/HWG HX4 ....75 F5
Ellistones Pl GTL/HWG HX4 ....75 F5
Elm Av WBSY BD6 ....54 B1
Elm Av RPDN/SBR HX6 ....67 E3
Elm Ct CLECK BD19 ....65 C1
Elm Crs AIRE BD20 ....9 E3
Elmfield BAIL BD17 ....19 E2
Elmfield Ct BIRK/DRI BD11 ....65 F1
Elmfield Dr WBSY BD6 ....54 D2
Elmfield Ter HFAX HX1 ....68 C3
Elm Gdns HFAX HX1 ....68 D3
Elm Gv AIRE BD20 ....9 E3
CLECK BD19 ....65 F5
HIPP HX3 ....53 C4
HWTH BD22 ....23 F2
SHPY BD18 ....29 F2
Elm Pl RPDN/SBR HX6 ....67 E3
Elm Rd SHPY BD18 ....29 E2
Elmsall St GIR BD8 ....2 B2
The Elms GSLY LS20 ....10 C2
Elm St GIR BD8 ....2 B2
Elm Tree Av WBSY BD6 ....54 D2
Elm Tree Cl KGHY BD21 ....7 G5
WBSY BD6 ....54 D2
Elm Tree Gdns WBSY BD6 ....54 D2
Elmwood Dr BRIC HD6 ....71 E5
HWTH BD22 ....13 G2
Elmwood Pl BFDE BD3 ....40 B3
Elmwood Rd HWTH BD22 ....13 G3
Elm Wood St BRIC HD6 ....71 E4
Elmwood Ter HFAX HX1 ....68 B3
Elmwood Ter HWTH BD22 ....13 G2
Elsdon Gv WBOW BD5 ....47 F2
Elsie St AIRE BD20 ....7 E1
HWTH BD22 ....23 E1
Elsinore Av ELL HX5 ....76 B5
Elsinore Ct ELL HX5 ....76 B5
Elsworth Av BFDE BD3 ....40 A3
Eltham Gv WBSY BD6 ....54 B2
Elvey Cl ECHL BD2 ....30 C5
Elwell Cl WBSY BD5 ....53 G5
Elwyn Gv WBOW BD5 ....47 F4
Elwyn Rd WBOW BD5 ....47 G4
Ely St CTL/HWG HX4 ....75 F4
Emblem Ct CUL/QBY BD13 ....52 A2
Emerald St HWTH BD22 ....13 H2
Emerson Av HTON BD9 ....37 G1
Emily Hall Gdns WIL/AL BD15 ....25 H4
Emily St KGHY BD21 ....7 F3
Emmeline Cl IDLE BD10 * 30 A1
Emmet Cl BIRK/DRI BD11 ....57 G5
Emmfield Dr HTON BD9 ....28 B5
Emm La HTON BD9 ....38 B1
Emmott Farm Fold
HWTH BD22 ....22 D3
Emscote Av HFAX HX1 ....4 D7
Emscote Gdns HFAX HX1 ....4 D7
Emscote Gv HFAX HX1 ....4 D7
Emscote Pl HFAX HX1 ....4 D7
Emscote St South HFAX HX1 ....4 D7
Emsley Cl BOW BD4 ....56 A2
Enderby Cl HIPP HX3 ....69 H1
Enderley Rd CUL/QBY BD13 ....44 H1
Endsleigh Pl CLAY SD14 ....45 E3
Enfield LSI9 ....11 G5
Enfield Av WBSY BD6 ....54 B1
Enfield Dr WBSY BD6 ....54 B1
Enfield Pde WBSY BD6 ....54 B1
Enfield Rd KGHY BD21 ....18 C4
Enfield St KGHY BD21 ....7 E4
Englefield Cl BOW BD4 ....48 D5
Englefield Crs BOW BD4 ....48 D5
Ennerdale Dr ECHL BD2 ....40 A1
ELL HX5 ....77 H4
Ennerdale Rd ECHL BD2 ....40 A1
Enterprise Wy IDLE BD10 ....30 A3
Epworth Pl HWTH BD22 ....12 C3

Eric St KGHY BD21 ....7 F3
Escroft Cl LM/WK BD12 ....63 E4
Esholt Av GSLY LS20 ....10 C4
Esholt La BAIL BD17 ....18 D4
Eshton Av LM/WK BD12 ....55 G5
Eskdale Av HIPP HX3 ....53 E5
Eskdale Ri WIL/AL BD15 ....37 E4
Eskine Pde WBSY BD6 ....54 A4
Esmond St GTHN BD7 ....46 A4
Essex St BFDE BD3 ....3 H7
BOW BD4 ....47 H2
HFAX HX1 ....4 A5
Estcourt Av GTHN BD7 ....46 A3
Estcourt Gv GTHN BD7 ....46 A3
Estcourt Rd GTHN BD7 ....46 B2
Ethel St AIRE BD20 ....7 F2
Etna St GTHN BD7 ....46 A4
Eton St HFAX HX1 ....4 B4
Evelyn Av BFDE BD3 ....40 B3
Evens Ter WBOW BD5 ....47 F5
Everest Av SHPY BD18 ....29 F2
Eversley Dr BOW BD4 ....48 D5
Eversley Ldg LUD/ILL HX2 * 67 H2
Eversley Mt LUD/ILL HX2 * 67 H2
Evesham Gv IDLE BD10 ....30 A2
Ewart Pl GTHN BD7 ....46 B3
Ewart St CUL/QBY BD13 * 52 B1
GTHN BD7 ....46 B4
Exchange Sq BFD BD1 * 2 E6
Exchange St CLECK BD19 ....64 A5
GTL/HWG HX4 ....76 A5
Exe St WBOW BD5 ....47 F5
Exeter St HIPP HX3 ....69 E5
RPDN/SBR HX6 ....67 F4
Exhibition Rd SHPY BD18 ....28 A1
Exley Av KGHY BD21 ....13 H2
Exley Bank HIPP HX3 ....76 A1
Exley Bank Top HIPP HX3 ....76 A1
Exley Crs KGHY BD21 ....13 H1
Exley Dr KGHY BD21 * 13 H1
Exley Gdns HIPP HX3 ....76 A1
Exley Gv KGHY BD21 ....13 H1
Exley Head HWTH BD22 ....13 C1
Exley La ELL HX5 ....76 B2
Exley Mt GTHN BD7 ....46 A1
KGHY BD21 ....13 H1
Exley Rd KGHY BD21 ....13 H1
Exley St KGHY BD21 ....6 C5
Exley Wy KGHY BD21 * 13 H1
Exmoor St HFAX HX1 ....4 A6
Exmouth Pl BFDE BD3 ....39 G3

F

Factory La BOW BD4 ....48 A5
Factory St BOW BD4 ....48 B5
Fagley Crs ECHL BD2 ....40 B2
Fagley Cft ECHL BD2 ....40 C2
Fagley Dr ECHL BD2 ....40 B2
Fagley La ECHL BD2 ....40 C1
Fagley Pl ECHL BD2 ....40 B3
Fagley Rd ECHL BD2 ....40 B3
Fagley Ter ECHL BD2 ....40 B3
Fair Bank SHPY BD18 ....28 C3
Fairbank Rd GIR BD8 ....38 B3
Fairbanks RPDN/SBR HX6 ....67 F4
Fairbank Ter GIR BD8 ....38 B3
Fairburn Ct HIPP HX3 ....69 H4
Fairburn Gdns ECHL BD2 ....30 B5
Fairclough Gv LUD/ILL HX2 ....59 E2
Fairfax Av BOW BD4 ....56 B1
HIPP HX3 ....69 H3
Fairfax Crs YEA LS19 ....11 G1
Fairfax Rd BGLY BD16 ....16 C1
CUL/QBY BD13 ....24 C2
Fairfax St BGLY BD16 ....16 C3
HWTH BD22 ....23 E2
Fairfax Vw BOW BD4 ....57 E3
Fairfield CUL/QBY BD13 ....34 C4
Fairfield Dr BAIL BD17 ....19 F2
Fairfield Rd BGLY BD16 ....16 C1
Fairfield St BOW BD4 ....56 C1
Fairhaven Gn IDLE BD10 ....30 B2
Fair Isle Ct KGHY BD21 ....7 E1
Fairless Av HIPP HX3 ....71 F1
Fairmount HTON BD9 ....38 B2
Fairmount Pk SHPY BD18 ....27 H5
Fairmount Ter KGHY BD21 ....8 A5
Fair Rd WBSY BD6 ....54 B1
Fairview Cft BAIL BD17 ....18 C5
Fairview Ter HIPP HX3 ....59 F4
Fairway GSLY LS20 ....10 B2
GTHN BD7 ....54 A2
IDLE BD10 ....21 E5
SHPY BD18 ....27 H4
Fairway Av GTHN BD7 ....54 A3
Fairway Cl GSLY LS20 ....10 B3
GTHN BD7 ....53 H3
Fairway Crs WBSY BD6 ....38 A5
Fairway Dr GTHN BD7 ....53 H3
Fairway Gv GTHN BD7 ....54 A3
The Fairways HTON BD9 ....27 H4
The Fairway LUD/ILL HX2 ....50 A4
PDSY/CALV LS28 ....41 G3
Fairway Wk GTHN BD7 ....53 H3
Fairweather Ms GIR BD8 * 37 H5
Fairy Dell BGLY BD16 ....26 D2
Falcon Ms GIR BD8 * 37 H5
Falcon Rd BGLY BD16 ....16 C1
Falcon St CTHN BD7 ....46 B4
HIPP HX3 ....5 H9
Falkland Rd IDLE BD10 ....30 D5
Fall Brow Cl CLAY SD14 ....44 D4
Fall La RPDN/SBR HX6 ....66 B5
Fallowfield Cl BOW BD4 ....56 B1
Fallowfield Dr BOW BD4 ....56 B1
Fallowfield Gdns BOW BD4 ....56 B1
Fall Wood St HWTH BD22 ....23 E3
Falmouth Av BFDE BD3 ....3 F1
Falsgrave Av ECHL BD2 ....40 C4

Faltis IDLE BD10 ....30 B4
Fanny St KGHY BD21 ....7 E5
SHPY BD18 ....28 A1
Farcliffe Pl GIR BD8 ....38 C3
Farcliffe Rd GIR BD8 ....38 C3
Farcliffe Ter GIR BD8 ....38 C3
Far Crook IDLE BD10 ....19 G5
Farfield Av BRIC HD6 ....71 H5
Farfield Crs WBSY BD6 ....54 A3
Farfield Gv PDSY/CALV LS28 ....41 H1
WBSY BD6 ....54 A3
Farfield Ri PDSY/CALV LS28 ....41 H1
Farfield Rd BAIL BD17 ....19 E5
SHPY BD18 ....28 B2
WBSY BD6 ....54 B3
Farfield St CLECK BD19 ....64 C4
HTON BD9 ....38 B2
Farfield Ter HTON BD9 ....38 B2
Farlea Dr ECHL BD2 ....40 C2
Farleton St HFAX HX1 ....40 C2
Farley Crs HWTH BD22 ....12 C3
Farm Hill Rd IDLE BD10 ....30 A4
Farm Pond Dr BRIC HD6 ....70 D3
Farmstead Rd IDLE BD10 ....30 A4
Farmdale Rd BAIL BD17 ....18 B4
WIL/AL BD15 ....25 H5
Farnham Cl BAIL BD17 ....19 E2
Farnham Ct GIR BD8 ....46 C2
Farrar Mill La HIPP HX3 ....69 E5
Farriers Cft ECHL BD2 ....30 B5
Farringdon Cl BOW BD4 ....48 D4
Farringdon Dr BOW BD4 ....48 D4
Farringdon Gv WBSY BD6 ....54 B3
Farside Gn WBOW BD5 ....46 D4
Farway BOW BD4 ....48 D5
Faversham Wk BOW BD4 * 48 D5
Farm Pond Dr BRIC HD6 ....56 B2
Faxfleet St WBOW BD5 ....55 E1
Faye Gdns BOW BD4 ....56 C1
Fearnley Cft CLECK BD19 ....65 G5
Fearnsides St GIR BD8 ....38 C4
Fearnsides Ter GIR BD8 ....38 C4
Fearnville Dr BOW BD4 ....48 D5
Featherbed Ct GTL/HWG HX4 ....76 A5
Feather Bed La ELL HX5 ....76 A5
Feather Rd BFDE BD3 ....3 J4
Federation St WBOW BD5 ....47 G5
Felbrigg Av HWTH BD22 ....6 C5
Felcourt Dr BOW BD4 ....48 D5
Felcourt Fold BOW BD4 ....48 D5
Fell Crs HWTH BD22 ....13 F1
Fell Gv HWTH BD22 ....6 B5
Fell La HWTH BD22 ....6 B5
Fellside Ct WBOW BD5 ....47 G5
Fellwood Av HWTH BD22 ....13 F1
Fellwood Cl HWTH BD22 ....23 F1
Fenby Av BOW BD4 ....48 A3
Fenby Cl BOW BD4 ....48 A3
Fenby Gdns BOW BD4 ....48 A3
Fencote Crs ECHL BD2 ....40 C4
Fender Rd WBSY BD6 ....54 A1
Fenton Rd HFAX HX1 ....19 F2
Fenton Rd HFAX HX1 ....4 A7
Fenwick Dr WBSY BD6 ....54 A4
Ferguson St BFDE BD3 ....5 G5
Fernbank Av HWTH BD22 ....13 G2
Fernbank Dr BAIL BD17 ....18 C5
BGLY BD16 ....16 D5
Fernbank Rd BFDE BD3 ....3 C1
BAIL BD17 ....18 C5
Ferncliffe Dr AIRE BD20 ....8 C1
Ferncliffe Rd BGLY BD16 ....16 D5
SHPY BD18 * 28 B2
Ferndale Av CLAY SD14 ....44 D4
Ferndale Gv HTON BD9 ....28 D5
Ferndene BGLY BD16 ....17 E3
Ferndown Gn WBOW BD5 ....47 G5
Fernfield Ter HIPP HX3 * 59 G3
Fernhill BGLY BD16 ....16 D1
Fern Hill Av SHPY BD18 ....28 A2
Fern Hill Gv SHPY BD18 ....28 A2
Fern Hill Mt SHPY BD18 ....28 A2
Fern Hill Rd SHPY BD18 ....28 A2
Fern Lea St RPDN/SBR HX6 ....66 C5
Fernley Gdns LM/WK BD12 ....62 D1
Fern Ri HX5 ....77 E4
Fern St BOW BD4 ....48 C4
HFAX HX1 ....59 G5
HIPP HX3 ....7 F3
Fern Ter AIRE BD20 ....2 A3
GIR BD8 ....38 D2
Ferrand Av BOW BD4 ....56 B2
Ferrand La BGLY BD16 ....16 C3
CLECK BD19 ....65 F4
Ferrands Ct BGLY BD16 ....40 C1
Ferrands Park Wy BGLY BD16 ....15 G5
Ferriby Ct ECHL BD2 ....40 C1
Festival Av SHPY BD18 ....29 E3
Feversham St BFDE BD3 ....3 G6
Field Cl HIPP HX3 ....77 H1
Fieldedge La AIRE BD20 ....8 B1
Fieldfare Dr WBSY BD6 ....53 C1
Field Head La HWTH BD22 ....22 B4
LUD/ILL HX2 ....50 C3
Fieldhead Dr GSLY LS20 ....10 B3
GTHN BD7 ....46 C1
Fieldhouse Gv
PDSY/CALV LS28 ....41 H2
Field Hurst CLECK BD19 ....72 C1
Fieldhurst Ct BOW BD4 ....56 A2
Field La BRIC HD6 ....78 A3
Fieldside CUL/QBY BD13 ....24 C1
Field Side HFAX HX1 ....4 B3
Fields Rd LM/WK BD12 ....55 F5
Field St BFD BD1 ....2 F4
Field Top Rd BRIC HD6 ....78 A3
Fieldway AIRE BD20 ....8 B1
Fieldway CLAY SD14 ....45 F3
Fifth Av BFDE BD3 ....40 B5
Fifth Av West LVSG WF15 ....73 E4

Filey St BFDE BD3 ...... 3 F6
Filey Royd CLECK BD19 ...... 73 G2
Finch Cl BGLY BD16 ...... 17 F2
Finchley St WBOW BD5 ...... 47 E4
Finch St WBOW BD5 ...... 47 E3
Findon Ter IDLE BD10 ...... 30 D5
Finkil St BRIG HD6 ...... 70 D3
Finkle St LUD/ILL HX2 ...... 64 C5
Finsbury Dr AIRE BD20 ...... 29 G5
Firbank Gn ECHL BD2 * 40 C2
Firbeck BGLY BD16 ...... 25 G1
Firethorn Cl GIR BD8 * 38 B4
First Av BFDE BD3 ...... 40 B3
   HIPP HX3 ...... 68 C4
   KGHY BD21 ...... 7 F3
   LVSC WF15 ...... 73 F3
   YEA LS19 ...... 21 H1
Fir St HWTH BD22 ...... 22 D3
   KGHY BD21 ...... 7 F4
First St LM/WK BD12 ...... 55 F4
Firth Av BRIG HD6 ...... 71 F5
Firth House La BRIG HD6 ...... 78 C4
Firth La WIL/AL BD15 ...... 25 H4
Firth Rd HTON BD9 ...... 38 B1
Firth St BRIG HD6 ...... 78 B2
   HFAX HX1 ...... 17 F5
Fir Tree Gdns IDLE BD10 ...... 30 C5
Fitzgerald St WBOW BD5 ...... 47 E2
Fitzroy Rd BFDE BD3 ...... 3 K5
Fitzwilliam St BOW BD4 ...... 47 G2
Five Oaks BAIL BD17 ...... 18 B4
Fixby Av LUD/ILL HX2 ...... 67 H3
Flasby St KGHY BD21 ...... 7 F5
Flat Nook BGLY BD16 * 17 G3
Flawith Dr ECHL BD2 ...... 40 C2
Flaxen Ct WBSY BD6 ...... 55 E1
Flaxton Gn ECHL BD2 ...... 40 C2
Flaxton Pl GTHN BD7 ...... 46 C4
Fleece St KGHY BD21 ...... 7 F4
   WBSY BD6 ...... 54 A3
Fleet La CUL/OBY BD13 ...... 52 A2
Fletcher Crs BRIG HD6 ...... 77 H5
Fletcher La 29 E4
Fletcher St WBSY BD6 * 54
Fletton Ter ECHL BD2 ...... 40 A2
Flinton Cv BOW BD4 ...... 40 C1
Flockton Av BOW BD4 ...... 47 H5
Flockton Cl BOW BD4 ...... 47 H5
Flockton Crs BOW BD4 ...... 47 H5
Flockton Dr BOW BD4 ...... 47 H5
Flockton Gv BOW BD4 ...... 47 H5
Flockton Rd BOW BD4 ...... 47 H5
Florence Av WIL/AL BD15 ...... 25 G3
Florence St BFDE BD3 ...... 48 B1
   HFAX HX1 ...... 4 D4
Florida Rd WIL/AL BD15 ...... 26 D5
Florist St KGHY BD21 ...... 7 E5
Flower Acre ELL HX5 ...... 76 C5
Flower Bank ECHL BD2 ...... 29 G5
   RPDN/SBR HX6 ...... 66 C5
Flower Cl YEA LS19 ...... 11 F4
Flower Ct ECHL BD2 ...... 40 C3
Flower Cft HWTH BD22 ...... 13 G1
Flower Garth IDLE BD10 ...... 30 C4
Flower Hvn HTON BD9 ...... 27 G5
Flower Hl HTON BD9 ...... 28 A5
Flowerlands HIPP HX3 ...... 61 H4
Floyd St WBOW BD5 ...... 46 C4
Foldings Av CLECK BD19 ...... 63 F5
Foldings Cl CLECK BD19 ...... 63 F5
Foldings Ct CLECK BD19 ...... 63 F5
Foldings Gv CLECK BD19 ...... 63 F5
Foldings Pde CLECK BD19 ...... 63 F5
Foldings Rd CLECK BD19 ...... 63 F5
Folkestone St BFDE BD3 ...... 3 K4
Folkton Holme ECHL BD2 ...... 40 C2
Folly Hall Av WBSY BD6 ...... 54 A3
The Folly Hall Gdns WBSY BD6 ...... 54 A2
Folly Hall Wk WBSY BD6 ...... 54 A2
Folly View Rd HWTH BD22 * 13 F3
Fontmell Cl BOW BD4 ...... 41 H5
Football YEA LS19 ...... 11 H5
Forber Gv BOW BD4 ...... 48 D2
Ford CUL/OBY BD13 ...... 51 H2
Ford Hl CUL/OBY BD13 ...... 51 H2
Ford St KGHY BD21 ...... 7 H2
Fore La RPDN/SBR HX6 ...... 66 C5
Foreside Bottom La
   CUL/OBY BD13 ...... 42 C3
Forest Av LUD/ILL HX2 ...... 58 D2
Forest Crs LUD/ILL HX2 ...... 58 D2
Forest Gn LUD/ILL HX2 ...... 58 D2
Forster St BFD BD1 5
Foster Av CUL/OBY BD13 ...... 44 C1
Foster Gdns HWTH BD22 ...... 6 C4
Foster Park Gv CUL/OBY BD13 ...... 34 D3
Foster Park Rd CUL/OBY BD13 ...... 34 D3
Foster Park Vw CUL/OBY BD13 ...... 34 D3
Foster Rd KGHY BD21 ...... 14 A1
Foston Cl ECHL BD2 ...... 52 A1
Foston La ECHL BD2 ...... 40 D2
Foulds' Ter BGLY BD16 ...... 16 D3
Foundry Hl BGLY BD16 ...... 16 C3
Foundry La BOW BD4 ...... 48 A2
Foundry St BRIG HD6 ...... 78 D2
   CLECK BD19 ...... 64 C5
   HFAX HX1 ...... 5 H4
   RPDN/SBR HX6 ...... 67 E5
Fountain St North
   LUD/ILL HX2 * 59 E2
Fountain Cl CUL/OBY BD13 ...... 44 A1
Fountain St CUL/OBY BD13 ...... 52 B1
   HFAX HX1 ...... 5 F5
   LM/WK BD12 ...... 54 D4
Fountain Ter LM/WK BD12 ...... 54 D4
Fountain Wy SHPY BD18 ...... 28 C2
Fourlands Crs IDLE BD10 ...... 30 B1
Fourlands Dr IDLE BD10 * 30 B1
Fourlands Gdns IDLE BD10 * 30 B1
Fourlands Gv IDLE BD10 * 30 B1
Fourlands Rd IDLE BD10 ...... 30 B1

Fourth Av BFDE BD3 ...... 40 B3
   KGHY BD21 ...... 6 D5
   LVSC WF15 ...... 73 E3
Fourth St LM/WK BD12 ...... 55 F4
Fowlers Garth HWTH BD22 ...... 13 E5
Fowler St BOW BD4 * 48 A2
Fox Ct GTL/HWG HX4 ...... 76 A4
Foxcroft Cl CUL/OBY BD13 ...... 51 H5
Foxcroft Dr BRIG HD6 ...... 77 H5
Foxhill BAIL BD17 ...... 18 B5
Foxhill Av CUL/OBY BD13 ...... 52 A1
Foxhill Cl CUL/OBY BD13 ...... 52 A1
Foxhill Dr CUL/OBY BD13 ...... 52 A1
Foxhill Cv CUL/OBY BD13 ...... 52 A1
Foxhole La PDSY/CALV LS28 ...... 31 C3
Foxstone Ri BAIL BD17 ...... 19 F5
Fox St BGLY BD16 ...... 16 C3
   CLECK BD19 ...... 73 E1
   WBOW BD5 * 5 D4
Fraisthorpe Md ECHL BD2 ...... 40 C2
Frances St AIRE BD20 ...... 6 D3
   BRIG HD6 ...... 71 F5
Francis Cl HFAX HX1 ...... 4 D4
Francis St BFDE BD3 ...... 47 H2
   HFAX HX1 ...... 4 D5
Franklin St HFAX HX1 ...... 4 D4
Frank Pl GTHN BD7 ...... 46 C3
Frank St GTHN BD7 ...... 46 C3
   HFAX HX1 ...... 4 D5
Fraser Rd PDSY/CALV LS28 ...... 31 E3
Fraser St GIR BD8 ...... 38 D4
Frederick Cl IDLE BD10 ...... 19 G5
Frederick St KGHY BD21 ...... 7 G4
   PDSY/CALV LS28 ...... 41 H1
Fred's Pl BOW BD4 ...... 48 B4
Fred St KGHY BD21 ...... 7 H3
Freeman Rd HIPP HX3 ...... 69 H5
Free School La HFAX HX1 ...... 68 C5
Fremantle Gv BOW BD4 ...... 48 D2
Frensham Dr GTHN BD7 ...... 45 G4
Frensham Gv GTHN BD7 ...... 45 G5
Frensham Wy GTHN BD7 ...... 45 G4
Freshfield Gdns WIL/AL BD15 ...... 37 E3
Friar Ct IDLE BD10 ...... 30 B3
Friendly Av CUL/OBY BD13 ...... 66 D3
Friendly Fold Rd HIPP HX3 ...... 59 F3
Friendly St CUL/OBY BD13 ...... 44 A1
   HIPP HX3 ...... 59 F3
Frimley Dr WBOW BD5 ...... 46 A4
Frith St HWTH BD22 ...... 23 F1
Frizinghall Rd ECHL BD2 ...... 28 D4
   HTON BD9 ...... 38 D1
Frizley Gdns HTON BD9 ...... 28 D5
Frodingham Vls ECHL BD2 ...... 40 C2
Frogmoor Av LM/WK BD12 * 55 G5
Fruit St KGHY BD21 ...... 7 H1
Fulford Wk ECHL BD2 ...... 40 C2
Fullerton St BFDE BD3 ...... 3 G6
Fulmar Ms GIR BD8 ...... 37 F5
Fulton St BFD BD1 ...... 2 B5
Furnace Ca LM/WK BD12 ...... 55 G5
Furnace Inn St BOW BD4 ...... 48 C2
Furnace La BIRK/DRI BD11 ...... 57 F4
Furnace Rd BOW BD4 ...... 55 H4
Furness Av LUD/ILL HX2 ...... 58 D1
Furness Crs LUD/ILL HX2 ...... 50 C5
Furness Gdns LUD/ILL HX2 ...... 58 D1
Furness Dr LUD/ILL HX2 ...... 58 D1
Furness Pl LUD/ILL HX2 ...... 58 D1
Fusden La CLECK BD19 ...... 65 F4
Fyfe Cv BAIL BD17 ...... 19 E4
Fyfe Gn BAIL BD17 ...... 19 F4
Fyfe La BAIL BD17 ...... 19 F4

G

The Gables BAIL BD17 ...... 19 F3
   HWTH BD22 ...... 6 D4
Gainest LUD/ILL HX2 ...... 68 A3
Gain La BFDE BD3 ...... 40 D3
Gainsborough Cl BFDE BD3 ...... 39 H2
Gaisby La ECHL BD2 ...... 28 D5
   SHPY BD18 ...... 29 E4
Gaisby Mt SHPY BD18 ...... 29 E4
Gaisby Pl SHPY BD18 ...... 29 E5
Gaisby Ri SHPY BD18 ...... 29 E5
Galefield Gn WBSY BD6 ...... 54 A4
Gale St KGHY BD21 ...... 7 F5
Galloway Ct PDSY/CALV LS28 ...... 41 F4
Galloway La PDSY/CALV LS28 ...... 41 F4
Galloway Rd IDLE BD10 ...... 30 C2
Galsworthy Av HTON BD9 ...... 37 G1
Gannerthorpe Cl
   LM/WK BD12 ...... 62 D2
Ganny Rd BRIG HD6 ...... 78 C1
Gaol La HFAX HX1 ...... 5 H3
Garden Cl LM/WK BD12 ...... 62 D1
Gardener's Sq HIPP HX3 ...... 61 F5
Garden Fld LM/WK BD12 ...... 62 D2
Garden Fold HIPP HX3 ...... 61 F5
Garden La HTON BD9 ...... 38 A1
Garncroft Dr BRIG HD6 ...... 71 E4
Gardens St HTON BD9 ...... 28 B5
The Gardens BGLY BD16 ...... 17 G3
   HFAX HX1 ...... 68 D3
   PDSY/CALV LS28 ...... 41 H1
Garden St HWTH BD22 ...... 23 F1
Garden St North HIPP HX3 ...... 5 J2
Garden Ter HTON BD9 ...... 38 B1
Garden Vw BGLY BD16 ...... 17 F3
Gardiner Rw BOW BD4 ...... 48 A5
Garfield Av GIR BD8 ...... 38 C3
Garfield St HIPP HX3 ...... 59 F4
   WIL/AL BD15 ...... 36 C5
Garforth Rd KGHY BD21 ...... 7 H3
Garforth St WIL/AL BD15 ...... 37 E3
Gargrave Cl BRIG HD6 ...... 77 G4
Garibaldi St BFDE BD3 ...... 40 D5
Garlick St BRIG HD6 ...... 71 F5
Garnet St BFDE BD3 ...... 3 G5
Garsdale Av IDLE BD10 ...... 30 B2

Garsdale Crs BAIL BD17 ...... 19 F2
Garth Barn Cl HTON BD9 ...... 38 B1
Garth Land Wy BOW BD4 ...... 48 B4
Garth St KGHY BD21 ...... 7 F3
Garthwaite Mt WIL/AL BD15 ...... 37 E2
Garton Dr IDLE BD10 ...... 30 C4
Garvey Vw WBOW BD5 ...... 47 F5
Garwick Ter GTL/HWG HX4 ...... 76 A4
Gas St HWTH BD22 * 23 E2
Gas Works Rd ECHL BD2 ...... 29 E5
Gas Works Rd KGHY BD21 ...... 8 A4
   RPDN/SBR HX6 ...... 67 G4
Gatefield Mt LM/WK BD12 ...... 54 C4
Gate Head La GTL/HWG HX4 ...... 75 E5
Gateway BGLY BD16 ...... 15 F5
Gate Way Dr YEA LS19 ...... 11 F5
The Gateways LM/WK BD12 ...... 54 D5
Gathorne St BRIG HD6 ...... 71 G5
   WBOW BD5 * 47 G4
Gaukroger La HFAX HX1 ...... 5 J7
Gavin Cl BFDE BD3 ...... 40 C3
Gawthorpe Dr BGLY BD16 ...... 16 C1
Gawthorpe St WIL/AL BD15 ...... 25 F2
Gayle Cl LM/WK BD12 ...... 62 D3
Gaynor St BFD BD1 ...... 2 A4
Gaythorne Rd ECHL BD2 ...... 40 B2
   WBOW BD5 ...... 47 F4
Gaythorne St HIPP HX3 ...... 45 F3
Gaythorn Ter HIPP HX3 ...... 61 F4
Geelong Cl ECHL BD2 ...... 39 G1
George Sq HFAX HX1 * 5 G4
George's Sq CUL/OBY BD13 ...... 24 C3
   KGHY BD21 ...... 7 F5
George's St LUD/ILL HX2 ...... 59 E2
George St BAIL BD17 * 18 D5
   BFD BD1 ......
   BRIG HD6 ...... 78 B1
   BRIG HD6 ...... 78 D1
   CLECK BD19 ...... 64 C5
   CUL/OBY BD13 * 34 D3
   CUL/OBY BD13 ...... 44 A1
   GTL/HWG HX4 ...... 76 A4
   HFAX HX1 ...... 5 G4
   HIPP HX3 ...... 70 C1
   RPDN/SBR HX6 ...... 67 E4
   SHPY BD18 ...... 28 A1
   YEA LS19 ...... 21 G2
Geraldton Av ECHL BD2 ...... 39 F1
Gerrard St HFAX HX1 ...... 5 G4
Ghyll Dr HWTH BD22 ...... 22 D5
Ghyll Mt YEA LS19 ...... 11 E5
Ghyll Royd GSLY LS20 ...... 10 D4
Ghyllroyd Av BIRK/DRI BD11 ...... 57 G5
Ghyllroyd Dr BIRK/DRI BD11 ...... 57 G5
The Ghyll BGLY BD16 ...... 16 D1
Ghyll Wood Dr BGLY BD16 ...... 26 D1
Gibbet St HFAX HX1 ...... 4 A6
Gibb La LUD/ILL HX2 ...... 58 A2
Gibraltar Av HFAX HX1 ...... 67 H1
Gibraltar St HFAX HX1 ...... 67 H1
   PDSY/CALV LS28 ...... 41 F1
Gibson St BFDE BD3 ...... 3 K6
Giles Hill La HIPP HX3 ...... 52 D5
Giles St WBOW BD5 ...... 47 G4
   WBSY BD6 ...... 54 B1
Gill Beck Cl BAIL BD17 ...... 19 F2
Gillingham Dr BOW BD4 ...... 48 D2
Gill La BAIL BD17 ...... 12 B2
   HWTH BD22 ...... 22 D2
   YEA LS19 ...... 21 F1
Gillroyd Ri GTHN BD7 ...... 38 C5
Gill St HFAX HX1 ...... 5 G4
Gillstone Dr HWTH BD22 ...... 23 E3
Gilpin St BFDE BD3 ...... 3 K4
Gilstead Ct BGLY BD16 ...... 17 F3
Gilstead Dr BGLY BD16 ...... 17 F3
Gilstead La BGLY BD16 ...... 17 F3
Gilynda Cl GIR BD8 ...... 37 H5
Gipsy St BFDE BD3 ...... 40 D4
Girlington Rd GIR BD8 ...... 38 A4
Gisburn St KGHY BD21 ...... 7 E3
The Glade PDSY/CALV LS28 ...... 41 F2
Gladstone Crs YEA LS19 ...... 21 G1
Gladstone Rd HFAX HX1 * 4 A5
   YEA LS19 ...... 21 G2
Gladstone St BFDE BD3 ...... 40 B5
   BGLY BD16 * 16 C4
   CLECK BD19 ...... 73 G1
   CUL/OBY BD13 ...... 52 C1
   KGHY BD21 ...... 7 F5
   WIL/AL BD15 ...... 37 E3
Gladstone Vw HIPP HX3 ...... 69 F5
Glaisdale Ct WIL/AL BD15 ...... 36 D1
Glaisdale Cv LUD/ILL HX2 ...... 67 E1
Glaisdale Vw HIPP HX3 ...... 70 C1
Glazier Rd CUL/OBY BD13 ...... 43 H5
Gleanings Av LUD/ILL HX2 ...... 58 B4
Gleanings Dr LUD/ILL HX2 ...... 67 E1
Gledcliffe HIPP HX3 * 5 H2
Gleddings Cl HIPP HX3 ...... 68 B5
Gledhill Rd BFDE BD3 ...... 3 K6
Gledhow Dr HWTH BD22 ...... 22 D5
Glenaire Dr SHPY BD18 ...... 27 H5
Glenaire Ter BAIL BD17 ...... 18 D5
Glenbrook Dr GTHN BD7 ...... 37 H5
Glen Dl BGLY BD16 ...... 26 C2
Glendale Cl WBSY BD6 ...... 54 B3
Glendale Dr WBSY BD6 ...... 54 B3
Glendare Av GTHN BD7 ...... 46 A1
Glendare Rd GTHN BD7 ...... 46 A1
Glendare Ter GTHN BD7 ...... 46 A1
Glen Dene BGLY BD16 ...... 26 C2
Gleneagles Cl BOW BD4 ...... 48 B5
Glenfield BGLY BD18 ...... 19 F5
Glenfield Av WBSY BD6 * 54 A3
Glen Garth KGHY BD21 ...... 14 C1
Glenholme SHPY BD18 ...... 19 F5
Glenholme Heath HFAX HX1 ...... 59 F4
Glenholme Pk CLAY BD14 ...... 45 F3
Glenholme Rd GIR BD8 ...... 38 C5
   PDSY/CALV LS28 ......
Glenhurst BOW BD4 ...... 56 C1
Glenhurst Av KGHY BD21 ...... 14 B1
Glenhurst Dr KGHY BD21 ...... 14 C1

Glenhurst Gv KGHY BD21 ...... 14 C1
Glenhurst Rd SHPY BD18 ...... 27 H1
Glen Lee La KGHY BD21 ...... 14 C2
Glenlee Rd GTHN BD7 ...... 46 A1
Glenlyon Av AIRE BD20 ...... 6 D2
Glenlyon Dr AIRE BD20 ...... 6 D2
Glenmore Ct ECHL BD2 ...... 40 B5
Glen Mt BGLY BD16 ...... 26 C2
   HIPP HX3 ...... 58 D3
Glen Mount Cl HIPP HX3 ...... 58 D5
Glen Ri BAIL BD17 ...... 18 B4
Glen Rd BGLY BD16 ...... 17 F1
Glenrose Dr GTHN BD7 ...... 45 H1
Glenroyd SHPY BD18 ...... 19 F5
Glenroyd Av WBSY BD6 ...... 55 E3
Glenroyd Cl PDSY/CALV LS28 ...... 41 F5
Glenside Av SHPY BD18 ...... 19 F5
Glenside Rd SHPY BD18 ...... 19 F5
Glenstone Gv GTHN BD7 ...... 38 A5
Glen Ter HFAX HX1 ...... 68 C3
Glenton Sq HTON BD9 ...... 38 B2
Glen Vw BGLY BD16 ...... 15 G5
   HFAX HX1 ...... 5 F7
Glenview Av GTHN BD7 ...... 37 H1
Glenview Cl SHPY BD18 ...... 27 H2
Glenview Dr BGLY BD16 ...... 27 F3
Glenview Gv SHPY BD18 ...... 27 G2
Glen View Rd SHPY BD18 ...... 27 G2
Glenview Ter KGHY BD21 ...... 14 C1
Glenwood Av BAIL BD17 ...... 28 A1
Globe Fold GIR BD8 ...... 38 D4
Gloucester Ct BFDE BD3 ...... 40 C3
Gloucester Rd BGLY BD16 ...... 17 E4
Glover Ct WBOW BD5 ...... 47 F3
Glydegate WBOW BD5 ...... 78 C5
Glyndon Ct BRIG HD6 ...... 6 D2
Glynn Ter GIR BD8 ...... 38 C4
Gobind Marg BFDE BD3 ...... 3 G5
Godfrey Rd HIPP HX3 ...... 75 H1
Godfrey St GIR BD8 ...... 37 G5
Godley Branch Rd HIPP HX3 ...... 60 B5
Godley Gdns HIPP HX3 ...... 60 C4
Godley La HIPP HX3 ...... 60 C4
Godley Rd HIPP HX3 ...... 5 K2
Godwin St BFD BD1 ...... 2 E3
Goff Well La KGHY BD21 ...... 14 B4
Goit Side BFD BD1 ...... 2 B5
Goit Stock La BGLY BD16 ...... 15 G1
Goit Stock Ter BGLY BD16 ...... 25 G1
Coldcrest Av GIR BD8 ...... 37 E5
Golden View Dr BAYLD HX5 ...... 75 F3
Goldfields Av GTL/HWG HX4 ...... 75 G3
Goldfields Cl GTL/HWG HX4 ...... 75 G3
Goldfields Vw GTL/HWG HX4 ...... 75 G3
Golf Av LUD/ILL HX2 ...... 67 F1
Golf Crs LUD/ILL HX2 ...... 67 F1
Gondal Ct WBOW BD5 ...... 46 D4
Gooder La BRIG HD6 ...... 78 B2
Gooder St BRIG HD6 ...... 78 B2
Goodfellow Cl BGLY BD16 ...... 27 E3
Goose Cote La HWTH BD22 ...... 13 F4
Goose Cote Wy HWTH BD22 ...... 13 F4
Goosedale Ct BOW BD4 ...... 57 F1
Goosegate LUD/ILL HX2 ...... 67 E1
Goose West La RPDN/SBR HX6 ...... 74 A1
Gordon St CLAY BD14 * 76 C5
   ELL HX5 ...... 76 C5
   HIPP HX3 ...... 59 G3
   HWTH BD22 ...... 23 F1
   KGHY BD21 ...... 7 F4
   RPDN/SBR HX6 ...... 66 D5
Gordon Ter IDLE BD10 ...... 20 A5
Gorse Av BAIL BD17 ...... 17 H4
Gothic St CUL/OBY BD13 ...... 52 B1
Gott's Ter HIPP HX3 ...... 6 D1
Gott St HWTH BD22 ...... 23 G1
Goulbourne St KGHY BD21 ...... 7 F3
Gower St WBOW BD5 ...... 47 F3
Gracechurch St GIR BD8 ...... 2 A3
Grace St KGHY BD21 ...... 7 H4
Gracey La WBSY BD6 ...... 54 A1
Grafton Cl BAIL BD17 ...... 19 F2
Grafton Pl HIPP HX3 ...... 59 F2
Grafton Rd KGHY BD21 ...... 13 H1
Grafton St KGHY BD21 ...... 7 H4
   WBOW BD5 ...... 47 F2
Graham St HTON BD9 ...... 38 B2
Grain St WBOW BD5 ...... 46 C4
Grammar School St BFD BD1 ...... 2 E1
Gramary Ct ECHL BD2 ...... 40 A2
Granby Dr AIRE BD20 ...... 8 A2
Granby La AIRE BD20 ...... 8 A2
Granby St BOW BD4 * 47 G2
   CUL/OBY BD13 ...... 52 B1
Grandage Ter GIR BD8 ...... 38 B4
Grandsmere Pl HIPP HX3 ...... 68 C4
Grange Av BFDE BD3 ...... 40 B4
   BOW BD4 ...... 48 F2
   LUD/ILL HX2 ...... 51 E5
   SHPY BD18 ...... 37 F4
   WIL/AL BD15 ...... 37 E4
   YEA LS19 ...... 11 H4
Grange Bank HIPP HX3 ...... 53 F4
Grange Ct BGLY BD16 ...... 16 C3
   HIPP HX3 ...... 69 H5
Grange Crs AIRE BD20 ...... 7 H2
Grange Dr GIR BD8 ...... 37 H4
Grange Gv AIRE BD20 ...... 7 H2
   BFDE BD3 ...... 41 E4
Grange Hts LM/WK BD12 ...... 79 F1
Grange La BRIG HD6 ...... 79 F1
Grange Ms YEA LS19 ...... 11 H5
Grange Pk BAIL BD17 ...... 19 F3
   HIPP HX3 ...... 68 C3
Grange Park Dr BGLY BD16 ...... 26 D1
Grange Park Rd BGLY BD16 ...... 26 D1
Grange Rd BAIL BD17 ...... 28 B2
   BGLY BD16 16
   CLECK BD19 ...... 64 B5
   WIL/AL BD15 ...... 37 F4
   YEA LS19 ...... 11 H5

Grange St HIPP HX3 ...... 59 F4
   KGHY BD21 ...... 7 F3
Grange Ter SHPY BD18 ...... 28 C3
   WIL/AL BD15 ...... 37 F4
Grange Vw BFDE BD3 ...... 41 E4
Grangeway GIR BD8 ...... 37 F4
Granny Hall Gv BRIG HD6 ...... 71 E4
Granny Hall La BRIG HD6 ...... 71 E4
Granny Hall Pk BRIG HD6 ...... 71 E3
Granny Hill Ter HFAX HX1 ...... 4 H5
Grantham Pl GTHN BD7 ...... 46 B2
   HIPP HX3 ...... 59 G3
Grantham Rd GTHN BD7 ...... 46 D2
   HIPP HX3 ...... 59 G3
Grantham Ter CTHN BD7 ...... 46 B2
Granton St BFDE BD3 ...... 40 B5
Grant St BFDE BD3 ...... 3 H4
   HWTH BD22 ...... 22 D2
   KGHY BD21 ...... 7 F3
Granville Pl WIL/AL BD15 ...... 37 E3
Granville Rd WBOW BD5 ...... 28 C4
Granville St ELL HX5 ...... 76 C5
   KGHY BD21 * 41 H4
   PDSY/CALV LS28 ...... 41 H4
Granville Ter BGLY BD16 ...... 16 D3
   SHPY BD18 ...... 28 C4
   YEA LS19 ...... 11 H4
Grape St BFDE BD3 ...... 3 H7
   HFAX HX1 ...... 5 H5
   KGHY BD21 ...... 7 F3
Grasleigh Av WIL/AL BD15 ...... 35 D2
Grasleigh Wy WIL/AL BD15 ...... 36 D1
Grasmere Dr ELL HX5 ...... 75 E4
Grasmere Rd ECHL BD2 ...... 39 H1
   LM/WK BD12 ...... 54 D5
Gratrix La RPDN/SBR HX6 ...... 67 F4
Grattan Rd BFD BD1 ...... 2 B5
Gray Av SHPY BD18 ...... 29 E4
Grayshon Dr WBSY BD6 ...... 54 D1
Gray St LVSC WF15 ...... 73 F3
Graywood Crs BOW BD4 ...... 48 C5
Graywood Dr BOW BD4 ...... 48 C3
Great Albion St HFAX HX1 ...... 5 G3
Great Cross St BFD BD1 ...... 2 E6
Great Edge Rd LUD/ILL HX2 ...... 66 C2
Great Horton Rd GTHN BD7 ...... 45 H5
Great Northern Rd
   KGHY BD21 ...... 7 F5
Great Russell Ct GTHN BD7 ...... 38 C5
Great Russell St GTHN BD7 ...... 38 C5
Greave House Dr LUD/ILL HX2 ...... 64 A1
Greave House Pk 66 A1
Greaves St WBOW BD5 ...... 47 E4
Grebe Cl WBSY BD6 ...... 53 E1
Greenacre Av LM/WK BD12 ...... 63 E3
Greenacre Cl LM/WK BD12 ...... 63 E3
Greenacre Pk YEA LS19 ...... 21 G1
Greenacre Park Av YEA LS19 ...... 21 G1
Greenacre Park Ms YEA LS19 ...... 21 H1
Greenacre Park Ri YEA LS19 ...... 21 G1
Greenacres AIRE BD20 ...... 53 G4
Greenacres Av HIPP HX3 ...... 53 G4
Greenacres Dr AIRE BD20 ...... 6 C2
   HIPP HX3 ...... 53 G4
Greenacre Wy LM/WK BD12 ...... 63 E3
Greenbank Rd WIL/AL BD15 ...... 37 E3
Greencliffe Av BAIL BD17 ...... 18 C5
Green Cl GIR BD8 ...... 38 C5
Green Ct CLECK BD19 ...... 63 G5
   GTHN BD7 ...... 46 A2
Greencroft Av HIPP HX3 ...... 61 E2
Green End BRIG HD6 ...... 78 D2
   CLAY BD14 ...... 45 E3
Green End Rd BAIL BD17 ...... 9 F2
   WBSY BD6 ...... 54 C2
Greenfield Cl HWTH BD22 ...... 10 A1
Greenfield Gv GSLY LS20 ...... 71 F4
   HIPP HX3 ...... 59 D3
Greenfield Cl HIPP HX3 ...... 60 D2
Greenfield Ct HWTH BD22 ...... 6 D4
Greenfield Crs CUL/OBY BD13 ...... 43 G5
Greenfield Dr CLECK BD19 ...... 63 G5
Greenfield La BOW BD4 ...... 56 A4
   GTHN BD7 ...... 46 A2
   IDLE BD10 ...... 20 A5
Greenfield Pl GIR BD8 * 38 D3
   HIPP HX3 ...... 71 F1
Greenfield Ter HWTH BD22 ...... 13 F5
Greenfinch Wy WIL/AL BD15 ...... 37 E5
Greengate Rd KGHY BD21 ...... 7 F5
Greengates Av LM/WK BD12 ...... 62 D4
Green Hall Pk HIPP HX3 ...... 53 G5
Green Head Av AIRE BD20 ...... 6 D1
Green Head La AIRE BD20 ...... 6 D1
Green Hl LUD/ILL HX2 ...... 67 E2
Green Head Rd AIRE BD20 ...... 7 E1
Greenhill Dr BGLY BD16 ...... 9 F4
Greenhill La BFDE BD3 ...... 40 B5
   BGLY BD16 ...... 9 G5
Greenhills YEA LS19 ...... 11 F5
Greenholme St SBFD BD3 ...... 48 B1
Greenhome Ct BOW BD4 ...... 49 E5
Greenland Av CUL/OBY BD13 ...... 44 C5
Greenland Vls CUL/OBY BD13 ...... 52 B2
Green La BAIL BD17 ...... 18 C5
   BRIG HD6 ...... 70 D3
   BRIG HD6 ...... 79 C1
   CLECK BD19 ...... 73 F1
   CUL/OBY BD13 ...... 43 G4
   CUL/OBY BD13 ...... 43 H3
   CUL/OBY BD13 ...... 52 B3
   ECHL BD2 ...... 40 C1
   GTHN BD7 ...... 46 B2
   GTL/HWG HX4 ...... 75 H4

HIPP HX3 52 B5
HIPP HX3 53 H5
HIPP HX3 69 F2
HWTH BD22 12 A2
HWTH BD22 13 E4
IDLE BD10 29 H1
IDLE BD10 30 B1
LM/WK BD12 62 D3
LM/WK BD12 63 G1
LUD/ILL HX2 50 D2
LUD/ILL HX2 67 H3
LVSG WF15 73 G5
YEA LS19 21 H1
Greenlea Av YEA LS19 11 E5
Greenlea Cl YEA LS19 21 E1
Greenlea Mt YEA LS19 11 E5
Greenlea Rd YEA LS19 11 E5
Green Meadow WIL/AL BD15 26 A5
Green Mt BOW BD4 * 48 C4
Green Mount Rd
CUL/QBY BD13 44 B1
Green Park Av HIPP HX3 75 H1
Green Park Dr HIPP HX3 75 H1
Green Park Rd HIPP HX3 75 H1
Green Park St HIPP HX3 68 D5
Green Pl ECHL BD2 * 40 A2
Green Rd BAIL BD17 18 C4
Green Royd GTL/HWG HX4 75 H5
Greenroyd Av CLECK BD19 64 C3
HIPP HX3 68 C5
Greenroyd Cl HIPP HX3 75 G1
Greenroyd Crs HFAX HX1 * 59 E4
Greenroyd La LUD/ILL HX2 58 D4
Greenside CLECK BD19 73 H1
LM/WK BD12 63 H1
Greenside La CUL/QBY BD13 24 C3
GIR BD8 38 A5
Green's Sq LUD/ILL HX2 58 D5
Green St BFD BD1 3 F5
HWTH BD22 22 D3
HWTH BD22 32 D2
Green Ter ECHL BD2 40 A2
Green Terrace Sq HFAX HX1 68 B3
The Green BGLY BD16 9 F4
BGLY BD16 9 H5
BGLY BD16 * 17 G3
BOW BD4 57 E3
GSLY LS20 10 D3
Greenthwaite Cl AIRE BD20 6 D2
Greenton Av CLECK BD19 63 F4
Greenton Crs CUL/QBY BD13 52 A2
Green Top St GIR BD8 37 H5
Greenups Ter RPDN/SBR HX6 67 E4
Greenville Dr LM/WK BD12 55 F3
Greenway GSLY LS20 10 B4
Green Wy LUD/ILL HX2 50 D2
Greenway Dr WIL/AL BD15 37 E5
Greenway Rd WBOW BD5 47 F5
The Greenway BFDE BD3 3 J2
Greenwell Rw CLAY BD14 45 E3
Greenwood Av ECHL BD2 29 H4
Greenwood Dr ECHL BD2 29 H5
Greenwood Mt ECHL BD2 29 H5
Greenwood Rd BAIL BD17 18 C5
Gregory Ct CLAY BD14 45 F3
Gregory Crs GTHN BD7 45 H5
Grenfell Dr BFDE BD3 40 C4
Grenfell Rd BFDE BD3 40 C4
Grenfell Ter BFDE BD3 40 C4
Gresham Av ECHL BD2 29 G5
Gresley Rd KGHY BD21 7 F4
Greycourt Cl ECHL BD2 29 H3
HFAX HX1 4 C6
Greyfriar Wk GTHN BD7 45 H4
Greystone Ct BRIG HD6 78 B4
Greystone Crs IDLE BD10 30 B3
Greystones Dr HWTH BD22 13 G3
Greystones Mt HWTH BD22 13 G4
Greystones Ri HWTH BD22 13 G3
Greystones Rd LUD/ILL HX2 66 B1
Griffe Dr LM/WK BD12 62 D4
Griffe Gdns HWTH BD22 12 C4
Griffe Head Crs LM/WK BD12 * 62 D3
Griffe Head Rd LM/WK BD12 62 D3
Griffe Rd LM/WK BD12 62 D3
Grisedale Cl GTHN BD7 46 A4
LUD/ILL HX2 58 C4
Grosvenor Av SHPY BD18 28 A1
Grosvenor Rd GIR BD8 2 A1
SHPY BD18 28 A2
Grosvenor St ELL HX5 76 C5
Grosvenor Ter GIR BD8 2 A1
HFAX HX1 4 D4
Grouse Moor La
CUL/QBY BD13 43 H5
Grouse St KGHY BD21 * 7 F3
Grove Av HIPP HX3 59 E3
SHPY BD18 28 C4
Grove Cl CLECK BD19 65 G4
ECHL BD2 29 H5
Grove Ct HIPP HX3 59 F3
Grove Crs LUD/ILL HX2 66 A1
Grove Cft HIPP HX3 59 E3
Grove Dr HIPP HX3 59 E2
Grove Edge HIPP HX3 59 E3
Grove Gdns HIPP HX3 59 F3
Grove House Crs ECHL BD2 29 H5
Grove House Dr ECHL BD2 39 H1
Grove House Rd ECHL BD2 29 H5
Grovelands ECHL BD2 39 H1
Grove La CLECK BD19 65 G4
Grove Pk HIPP HX3 59 E2
Grove Rd ELL HX5 76 D4
SHPY BD18 28 C4
Grove Royd HIPP HX3 59 F3
Grove Sq CLECK BD19 * 65 G4
HIPP HX3 59 E3
Grove St BRIG HD6 78 C1
RPDN/SBR HX6 67 G4
Grove St South HFAX HX1 * 4 B4
Grove Ter GTHN BD7 * 2 B6
The Grove BAIL BD17 18 D2
BGLY BD16 9 F5
HIPP HX3 61 F5
IDLE BD10 30 A2
IDLE BD10 30 C2
SHPY BD18 27 H2
YEA LS19 11 G5
YEA LS19 21 F2
Groveville HIPP HX3 61 F4
Groveway ECHL BD2 29 H5
Guard House Av HWTH BD22 6 D4
Guard House Dr HWTH BD22 6 D4
Guard House Gv HWTH BD22 6 C4
Guard House Rd HWTH BD22 6 D4
Guild Wy LUD/ILL HX2 67 E2
Guiseley Dr ILK LS29 10 A1
Gurbax Ct BFDE BD3 40 D5
Gurney Cl WBOW BD5 47 E4
Guy St BOW BD4 2 E7
Gwynne Av BFDE BD3 40 D3

H

Hadassah St HIPP HX3 69 E4
Haddon Av HIPP HX3 68 D5
Haddon Cl CLECK BD19 65 G5
Hag La HIPP HX3 59 H2
Haigh Beck Vw IDLE BD10 30 B2
Haigh Cnr IDLE BD10 30 C2
Haigh Fold ECHL BD2 40 B1
Haigh Hall IDLE BD10 30 C2
Haigh La HIPP HX3 69 E5
Haigh St BOW BD4 48 A4
BRIG HD6 71 F5
GTL/HWG HX4 75 F4
HFAX HX1 4 B2
Haincliffe Rd KGHY BD21 14 A2
Hainsworth Moor Crs
CUL/QBY BD13 52 A2
Hainsworth Moor Dr
CUL/QBY BD13 52 A2
Hainsworth Moor Garth
CUL/QBY BD13 52 A2
Hainsworth Moor Gv
CUL/QBY BD13 52 A2
Hainsworth Moor Vw
CUL/QBY BD13 52 A2
Hainworth Crag Rd
KGHY BD21 13 H4
Hainworth La KGHY BD21 14 A3
Hainworth Rd KGHY BD21 14 B2
Hainworth Wood Rd
KGHY BD21 14 A2
Hainworth Wood Rd North
KGHY BD21 14 B1
Halcyon Wy WBOW BD5 46 D4
Halesworth Crs BOW BD4 48 D4
Haley Ct HIPP HX3 5 G1
Haley Hl HIPP HX3 5 G1
Half Acre Rd CUL/QBY BD13 35 G5
Half House La BRIG HD6 70 C3
Half St KGHY BD21 7 E3
Halifax Old Rd HIPP HX3 61 E5
Halifax Rd BRIG HD6 78 B1
CLECK BD19 72 B1
CUL/QBY BD13 24 C3
CUL/QBY BD13 51 H4
ELL HX5 76 B4
HIPP HX3 61 E1
HIPP HX3 61 E5
HWTH BD22 23 G2
KGHY BD21 13 H5
LUD/ILL HX2 42 C3
LVSG WF15 73 F3
WBSY BD6 54 A3
Hallas La CUL/QBY BD13 24 D4
Hall Av IDLE BD10 30 C4
Hallbank Cl WBOW BD5 55 E1
Hall Bank Dr BGLY BD16 16 C2
Hallbank Dr WBOW BD5 55 E1
Hallcliffe BAIL BD17 19 E2
Hall Cl HIPP HX3 60 D2
Hallfield Dr BAIL BD17 18 D3
Hallfield Pl BFD BD1 2 C2
Hallfield Rd GIR BD8 2 B3
Hallfield St BFD BD1 2 C3
Hall Ings BFD BD1 2 E5
HIPP HX3 69 H5
Hall La BOW BD4 47 G2
HIPP HX3 60 C1
SHPY BD18 28 D1
Hallowes Gv CUL/QBY BD13 24 C4
Hallowes Park Rd
CUL/QBY BD13 24 C4
Hallows Rd KGHY BD21 7 H2
The Hallows AIRE BD20 6 D3
Hall Rd IDLE BD10 30 C4
Hall Royd SHPY BD18 28 C2
Hallside Cl BAIL BD17 19 G2
Hall Stone Ct HIPP HX3 * 53 F5
Hall St BRIG HD6 78 C1
HWTH BD22 13 E3
HWTH BD22 22 D3
WBSY BD6 54 D1
Hall St North HIPP HX3 59 G3
Hall Ter AIRE BD20 * 8 A2
Hallwood Gn IDLE BD10 30 D4
Halstead Pl GTHN BD7 46 B4
Halton Pl WBOW BD5 46 C4
Hambledon Av BOW BD4 56 A1
Hambleton Bank LUD/ILL HX2 50 A5
Hambleton Crs LUD/ILL HX2 50 A5
Hambleton Dr LUD/ILL HX2 50 A5
Hammerstones Rd ELL HX5 76 A5
Hammerton St BFDE BD3 3 G6
Hammond Pl HTON BD9 38 B1
Hammond St HFAX HX1 4 B5
Hamm Strasse BFD BD1 2 D3
Hampden Pl HFAX HX1 4 E4
WBOW BD5 47 E3
Hampden St WBOW BD5 47 E3
Hampton Pl IDLE BD10 30 A1
Hampton St HFAX HX1 4 A7
Hamworth Dr HWTH BD22 13 E4
Handel St GTHN BD7 38 D5
Hanging Gate La HWTH BD22 22 B4
Hanging Wood Wy
CLECK BD19 64 B3
Hannah Ct LM/WK BD12 62 D2
Hanover Cl GIR BD8 38 B3
Hanover Gdns WBOW BD5 * 47 E2
Hanover Sq BFD BD1 2 B2
Hanover St HFAX HX1 5 F5
KGHY BD21 7 F4
RPDN/SBR HX6 67 G3
Hanson Ct LM/WK BD12 62 C3
Hanson Fold LM/WK BD12 62 D2
Hanson La HFAX HX1 4 A3
Hanson Mt LM/WK BD12 62 D3
Hanson Rd BRIG HD6 77 H3
Hanworth Rd LM/WK BD12 54 D4
Harbeck Dr BGLY BD16 25 G1
Harbour Crs WBSY BD6 54 B2
Harbour Pk WBSY BD6 54 A3
Harbour Rd WBSY BD6 54 B3
Harclo Rd KGHY BD21 7 H3
Harcourt Av CUL/QBY BD13 36 A5
Harcourt St BOW BD4 48 A4
Hardaker La BAIL BD17 18 B4
Hardaker St GIR BD8 2 A3
Harden Brow La BGLY BD16 15 F5
Harden Gv IDLE BD10 40 D1
KGHY BD21 14 D1
Harden La BGLY BD16 25 G1
Harden Rd BGLY BD16 15 H5
KGHY BD21 15 E2
Hardgate La HWTH BD22 23 G3
Hard Ings Rd KGHY BD21 7 F2
Hardings Rd KGHY BD21 7 F2
Hardknot Cl GTHN BD7 45 H4
Hard Nese La HWTH BD22 32 A3
Hardwick St KGHY BD21 6 D5
Hardy Av WBSY BD6 54 D2
Hardy Pl BRIG HD6 70 D3
Hardy St BOW BD4 2 E7
BRIG HD6 71 G5
Harehill Cl IDLE BD10 20 A5
Harehill Rd IDLE BD10 20 A5
Hare Park Av LVSG WF15 73 F4
Hare Park Cl LVSG WF15 73 F4
Harepark Dr LVSG WF15 73 F4
Hare Park La LVSG WF15 73 F4
Hare St HFAX HX1 4 B4
Harewood Av LUD/ILL HX2 58 C5
Harewood Crs HWTH BD22 13 F3
Harewood Pl LUD/ILL HX2 67 H2
Harewood Ri HWTH BD22 13 G3
Harewood Rd HWTH BD22 13 F4
Harewood St BFDE BD3 3 K5
Harker Rd WBSY BD6 54 D3
Harland Cl ECHL BD2 39 F2
Harley St BRIG HD6 78 B2
Harlow Rd GTHN BD7 46 B2
Harmon Cl BOW BD4 56 B2
Harold St BGLY BD16 16 B2
Harper Av IDLE BD10 20 A5
Harper Crs IDLE BD10 20 B5
Harper Ga BOW BD4 49 E3
Harper Gv IDLE BD10 20 A5
Harper La YEA LS19 11 G5
Harper Royd La
RPDN/SBR HX6 74 A1
Harrier Cl GIR BD8 37 E5
Harriet St BRIG HD6 71 F4
GIR BD8 38 C4
Harris Ct GTHN BD7 46 B4
Harrison Rd HFAX HX1 5 G5
Harrison St BGLY BD16 16 D4
Harris St BFD BD1 3 G5
BGLY BD16 16 D4
Harrogate Av BFDE BD3 39 H2
Harrogate Pl BFDE BD3 39 H2
Harrogate Rd ECHL BD2 40 B1
IDLE BD10 30 C3
YEA LS19 21 H1
Harrogate St BFDE BD3 39 H2
Harrogate Ter BFDE BD3 39 H2
Harrop La WIL/AL BD15 35 G1
Harrow St HFAX HX1 4 B5
Harry La CLAY BD14 45 E3
HWTH BD22 32 D1
Harry St BOW BD4 48 B4
Hartington St KGHY BD21 7 F3
Hartington Ter GTHN BD7 46 B2
Hartland Rd BOW BD4 48 D3
Hartley's Sq AIRE BD20 9 E2
Hartley St BOW BD4 47 H2
HFAX HX1 4 C2
Hartlington Ct BAIL BD17 * 19 F3
Hartman Pl HTON BD9 * 38 A2
Hart St GTHN BD7 46 B3
Harvest Ct HFAX HX1 * 4 E4
Harvest Mt IDLE BD10 29 G1
Haslam Cl BFDE BD3 3 H3
Haslam Gv SHPY BD18 29 F3
Haslemere Cl BOW BD4 48 C4
Haslingden Dr HTON BD9 38 A2
Hastings Av WBOW BD5 47 E5
Hastings Pl WBOW BD5 47 E5
Hastings St WBOW BD5 47 E5
Hastings Ter WBOW BD5 47 E5
Hatchet La LM/WK BD12 63 H1
Hatfield Rd ECHL BD2 40 A2
Hathaway Av HTON BD9 37 G1
Hatton Cl WBSY BD6 55 E2
Haugh Shaw Cft HFAX HX1 4 D7
Haugh Shaw Rd HFAX HX1 4 C7
Haugh Shaw Rd West
HFAX HX1 68 A3
Hauxwell Dr YEA LS19 11 G5
Havelock Sq CUL/QBY BD13 44 B1
Havelock St CUL/QBY BD13 44 B1
GTHN BD7 46 A3
The Haven IDLE BD10 30 B3
Haw Av YEA LS19 11 H3
Hawes Av WBOW BD5 46 D5
Hawes Crs WBOW BD5 46 D5
Hawes Dr WBOW BD5 46 D5
Hawes Gv WBOW BD5 46 D5
Hawes Mt WBOW BD5 46 D5
Hawes Rd WBOW BD5 46 D5
Hawes Ter WBOW BD5 46 D5
Hawke Wy LM/WK BD12 55 F4
Hawkhill Av GSLY LS20 10 C3
Hawksbridge La HWTH BD22 32 A1
Hawkshead Cl WBOW BD5 47 F2
Hawkshead Dr WBOW BD5 47 F2
Hawkshead Wk WBOW BD5 * 47 F2
Hawkshead Wy WBOW BD5 * 47 F2
Hawkstone Av GSLY LS20 10 B4
Hawkstone Dr AIRE BD20 6 D2
Hawkstone Vw GSLY LS20 10 B4
Hawk St KGHY BD21 * 7 G3
Hawkswood Av HTON BD9 38 A1
Hawksworth Av GSLY LS20 10 C4
Hawksworth Rd BAIL BD17 18 D1
Haw La YEA LS19 11 H3
Hawley Ter IDLE BD10 30 D5
Haworth Gv HTON BD9 37 H1
Haworth La YEA LS19 11 G4
Haworth Rd HTON BD9 37 H1
HWTH BD22 23 F1
WIL/AL BD15 25 F5
WIL/AL BD15 27 E5
Haworth to Hebden Bridge Wk
HWTH BD22 22 A5
Hawthorn Av BFDE BD3 40 D4
YEA LS19 11 G4
Hawthorn Cl BRIG HD6 71 H5
Hawthorn Crs YEA LS19 11 G4
Hawthorn Dr IDLE BD10 30 B2
YEA LS19 11 H3
Hawthorne Av SHPY BD18 29 E4
Hawthorn Rd YEA LS19 11 G4
Hawthorn St BFDE BD3 40 D4
HFAX HX1 * 4 C7
HIPP HX3 * 61 G5
Hawthorn Ter HFAX HX1 * 4 C7
Hawthorn Vw BAIL BD17 19 E3
Haycliffe Av GTHN BD7 46 B5
Haycliffe Dr GTHN BD7 46 A5
Haycliffe Gv GTHN BD7 46 B5
Haycliffe Hill Rd WBOW BD5 46 C5
Haycliffe La WBOW BD5 46 C5
Haycliffe Rd WBOW BD5 46 C4
Haycliffe Ter WBOW BD5 46 C4
Hay Cft IDLE BD10 29 G1
Hayden St BFDE BD3 3 J7
Hayfields Cl HWTH BD22 13 F1
The Hayfields HWTH BD22 22 D1
Haynes St KGHY BD21 7 G5
Hays La LUD/ILL HX2 50 A3
Hazel Beck BGLY BD16 26 D1
Hazel Cl BIRK/DRI BD11 57 F4
Hazelcroft IDLE BD10 30 C5
Hazel Cft SHPY BD18 29 E2
Hazeldene CUL/QBY BD13 52 A2
Hazel Gv HIPP HX3 71 F1
Hazelheads BAIL BD17 18 D1
Hazelhurst Av BGLY BD16 26 C1
Hazelhurst Brow HTON BD9 37 G2
Hazelhurst Ct BFDE BD3 40 B5
Hazel Hurst Gv
CUL/QBY BD13 52 A3
Hazel Hurst Rd
CUL/QBY BD13 52 A3
Hazelhurst Rd HTON BD9 37 G2
Hazelhurst Ter HTON BD9 37 G2
Hazelmere Av BGLY BD16 26 D1
Hazel Mt SHPY BD18 28 D2
Hazel Wk HTON BD9 37 G2
Hazelwood Av AIRE BD20 8 A2
Hazelwood Rd HTON BD9 37 F1
Headland Gv WBSY BD6 54 A1
Headley La CUL/QBY BD13 44 B2
Healey Av BGLY BD16 16 D4
Healey La BGLY BD16 17 E5
Healey Wood Crs BRIG HD6 78 B3
Healey Wood Gdns BRIG HD6 78 B3
Healey Wood Gv BRIG HD6 78 C3
Healey Wood Rd BRIG HD6 78 B3
Heap La BFDE BD3 3 G3
Heap St BFDE BD3 3 G4
HIPP HX3 59 H3
Heath Av HIPP HX3 68 C4
Heathcliff HWTH BD22 22 C2
Heathcote Ri HWTH BD22 23 E1
Heatherbank Av HWTH BD22 13 G2
Heather Bank Cl
CUL/QBY BD13 24 C4
Heather Gv HTON BD9 37 E1
KGHY BD21 6 C3
Heatherlands Av
CUL/QBY BD13 34 C2
Heather Rd BAIL BD17 * 19 E2
Heather Side BAIL BD17 18 C2
Heatherstones HIPP HX3 68 C4
Heather Vw BGLY BD16 17 G1
Heathfield Av ELL HX5 77 E4
Heathfield Cl BGLY BD16 16 D2
Heathfield Gv GTHN BD7 45 H3
HIPP HX3 * 68 D4
Heathfield Pl HIPP HX3 * 68 D4
Heathfield St ELL HX5 76 D5
Heathfield Ter HFAX HX1 68 D3
Heath Gdns HIPP HX3 68 D4
Heath Gv AIRE BD20 9 E3
PDSY/CALV LS28 41 H5
Heath Hall HFAX HX1 68 D3
Heath Hall Av BOW BD4 56 A1
Heath La HIPP HX3 68 D4
Heath Lea HFAX HX1 5 G6
Heathmoor Cl IDLE BD10 29 H2
LUD/ILL HX2 50 C4
Heathmoor Mt LUD/ILL HX2 50 C4
Heathmoor Park Rd
LUD/ILL HX2 50 C4
Heathmoor Wy LUD/ILL HX2 50 C4
Heath Mt HFAX HX1 68 C4
Heath Mount Rd BRIG HD6 78 B3
Heath Park Av HFAX HX1 68 D3
Heath Rd BFDE BD3 3 J1
HFAX HX1 68 D3
Heath Royd HIPP HX3 68 D4
Heath St BFDE BD3 40 B5
BGLY BD16 16 D3
HIPP HX3 68 D4
Heath Ter BFDE BD3 3 K5
Heath Vw HFAX HX1 * 5 H6
Heath View St HFAX HX1 5 H6
Heathy Av LUD/ILL HX2 51 F5
Heathy La LUD/ILL HX2 51 E4
Heaton Av AIRE BD20 8 D4
CLECK BD19 73 F1
Heaton Cl BGLY BD16 17 E2
Heaton Crs BGLY BD16 * 17 E2
Heaton Dr BAIL BD17 18 C2
BGLY BD16 17 E2
Heaton Gv CLECK BD19 * 73 F1
HTON BD9 28 C5
SHPY BD18 28 D2
Heaton Hl WBSY BD6 53 H3
Heaton Park Dr HTON BD9 38 A1
Heaton Park Rd HTON BD9 38 A1
Heaton Rd HTON BD9 38 B1
Heaton Royds SHPY BD18 * 28 A4
Heaton Royds La SHPY BD18 28 A4
Heaton St BOW BD4 47 H2
BRIG HD6 78 B1
CLECK BD19 64 C5
Hebble Brook Cl LUD/ILL HX2 58 B1
Hebble Gdns LUD/ILL HX2 58 D4
Hebble La HFAX HX1 59 E4
Hebble Vale Dr LUD/ILL HX2 58 D3
Hebb Vw GTHN BD7 45 H5
Hebden Rd HWTH BD22 23 E2
Heber St KGHY BD21 7 E5
Hector Cl WBSY BD6 54 D1
Heddon Cl WBOW BD5 47 F2
Heddon Gv WBOW BD5 47 F2
Heddon Wk WBOW BD5 * 47 F2
Hedge Cl GIR BD8 37 G3
Hedge Side GIR BD8 37 H4
Hedge Top La HIPP HX3 60 D2
Hedge Wy GIR BD8 37 H3
Heidelberg Rd HTON BD9 38 B2
Height Gn RPDN/SBR HX6 67 E4
Height La HWTH BD22 33 E2
Heights Ct LVSG WF15 73 E3
Heights La BGLY BD16 9 H4
HTON BD9 37 G1
Helena Wy BOW BD4 56 B2
Helen Rose Ct SHPY BD18 19 F5
Helen St SHPY BD18 28 A1
Hellewell St WBSY BD6 54 A3
Helmsley St BOW BD4 47 H3
Hemingway Rd IDLE BD10 30 C1
Hemsby Gv KGHY BD21 * 13 H2
Hemsby St KGHY BD21 13 H2
Henacrewood Ct
CUL/QBY BD13 52 B3
Henderson Pl WBSY BD6 54 D1
Hendford Dr BFDE BD3 3 H4
Henley Av WBOW BD5 47 F5
Henley Ct WBOW BD5 47 G5
Henley Dr YEA LS19 21 H3
Henley Gv WBOW BD5 47 F5
Henley Hl YEA LS19 21 H3
Henley Rd WBOW BD5 47 G5
Henry St BRIG HD6 71 F4
CLAY BD14 45 F3
CUL/QBY BD13 44 A1
HFAX HX1 5 F5
KGHY BD21 7 F4
Henry Ter YEA LS19 11 E4
Henshaw Av YEA LS19 11 G5
Henshaw Crs YEA LS19 11 G5
Henshaw La YEA LS19 11 G5
Henshaw Ov YEA LS19 11 G5
Herbert Pl BFDE BD3 40 D4
Herbert St BGLY BD16 16 D3
CLAY BD14 45 F3
HFAX HX1 4 A5
SHPY BD18 28 A1
WBOW BD5 47 E3
Hereford Wy BOW BD4 * 47 H3
Heritage Ms HFAX HX1 * 5 J5
Heritage Pk BGLY BD16 9 H5
Heritage Wy HWTH BD22 12 D4
Hermit St HWTH BD22 13 H4
Hermon Av HFAX HX1 4 C5
Hermon Gv HFAX HX1 4 C5
Heron Cl BGLY BD16 15 F5
CUL/QBY BD13 43 H5
Herschel Rd GIR BD8 37 F5
Heshbon St BOW BD4 48 B4
Hetton Dr BFDE BD3 48 C1
Hew Clews GTHN BD7 45 H4
Hew Royd IDLE BD10 29 G1
Heybeck Wk BOW BD4 49 E5
Heyford Ct ECHL BD2 39 E1
Heygate Cl BAIL BD17 19 E2
Heygate La BAIL BD17 19 E2
Heys Av CUL/QBY BD13 44 C1
Heys Crs CUL/QBY BD13 44 D1
Heysham Dr BOW BD4 49 E4
Hey St BRIG HD6 71 G4
GTHN BD7 2 A5
Heywood Cl HIPP HX3 60 D3
Heywood Ct HIPP HX3 60 D3
Heywood Pl HFAX HX1 4 D3
Heywood St HFAX HX1 4 D3
Hick St BFD BD1 * 3 F5
Higgin La HIPP HX3 69 F3
High Ash SHPY BD18 29 F2
High Ash Pk WIL/AL BD15 36 C3
High Bank Cl ELL HX5 77 F4
High Bank La SHPY BD18 27 G3
High Banks Cl AIRE BD20 8 A1
Highbridge Ter WBOW BD5 55 G1
High Bury Cl CUL/QBY BD13 51 H2
High Busy La IDLE BD10 29 G1
Highcliffe Ct HIPP HX3 53 E5
Highcliffe Dr LUD/ILL HX2 67 G1
High Cl GSLY LS20 10 A3
YEA LS19 21 G3
High Cft CUL/QBY BD13 52 B1
HIPP HX3 59 E3
Highcroft Cl PDSY/CALV LS28 41 H4
Highcroft Gdns KGHY BD21 8 A5
High Cross La HIPP HX3 52 D3
Highdale Cft IDLE BD10 30 A1
Higher Brockwell
RPDN/SBR HX6 66 C5
Higher Coach Rd BGLY BD16 17 F4
Higher Downs GIR BD8 37 G4

Higher Intake Rd ECHL BD2 ....40 B3
Higher School St SHPY BD18 * ...28 A1
Higherwood Cl KGHY BD21 ....7 H4
High Fernley Ri HWTH BD22 ....13 F1
High Fernley Ct LM/WK BD12 * 7 H4
High Fernley Rd LM/WK BD12....62 B2
Highfield BOW BD4 ....56 C1
　HIPP HX3 ....53 E5
Highfield Ri HWTH BD6 ....62 C5
　GTL/HWG HX4 ....29 G1
　HIPP HX3 ....53 G5
　IDLE BD10 ....29 H2
Highfield Cl AIRE BD20 ....8 D2
Highfield Ct HWTH BD22 ....12 D4
Highfield Crs BAIL BD17 ....18 D2
Highfield Dr HTON BD9 ....27 G5
　LVSG WF15 ....73 H4
　YEA LS19 ....LS19
Highfield Gdns HTON BD9 ....37 G1
Highfield Gv ELL HX5 ....76 B3
High Field La HWTH BD22 ....12 D3
Highfield La KGHY BD21 ....6 D3
Highfield Ms AIRE BD20 ....3 J2
　BAIL BD17 ....18 D2
Highfield Pl GIR BD8 ....38 D3
　HFAX HX1 ....4 C5
Highfield Rd BRIG HD6 ....77 H5
　CLECK BD19 ....73 F1
　ELL HX5 ....76 C5
　HTON BD9 ....28 D4
　IDLE BD10 ....29 H3
　PDSY/CALV LS28 ....41 H4
High Flds LUD/ILL HX2 ....67 H4
Highfield St KGHY BD21 ....7 E4
　PDSY/CALV LS28 ....41 H4
Highfield Ter HFAX HX1 * 4 B6
　PDSY/CALV LS28 ....41 H4
　SHPY BD18 ....29 G3
High Fold HWTH BD22 ....13 G1
Highfold YEA LS19 ....21 F1
High Fold La AIRE BD20 ....6 D1
Highgate HTON BD9 ....38 B3
Highgate Cl CUL/QBY BD13 ....45 F5
Highgate Gdns LUD/ILL HX2 ....58 D5
Highgate Gv CLAY BD14 ....45 F5
Highgate Rd CUL/QBY BD13 ....45 E5
　HTON BD9 ....38 B5
High Grove La HIPP HX3 ....69 F3
High Holly Garth HWTH BD22 * 7 G5
High House Av ECHL BD2 ....29 H5
High House Rd ECHL BD2 ....29 H5
Highlands Cl HTON BD9 ....45 H4
Highlands Gv GTHN BD7 ....45 H4
Highlands La LUD/ILL HX2 ....51 E4
The Highlands LVSG WF15 ....73 G3
Highland Ville HIPP HX3 ....70 C1
High La LUD/ILL HX2 ....66 B5
Highlea Cl YEA LS19 ....21 E1
High Lees Rd LUD/ILL HX2 ....50 A5
High Level Wy HFAX HX1 * 4 E3
Highley Hall Cft BRIG HD6 ....79 E1
Highley Pk BRIG HD6 ....79 F1
High Meadow AIRE BD20 ....3 J3
High Mdw GTL/HWG HX4 ....25 G4
　WIL/AL BD15 ....25 G4
Highmoor BAIL BD17 ....18 B3
Highmoor Crs BRIG HD6 ....76 A5
Highmoor La BRIG HD6 ....72 A5
Highmoor Wk BAIL BD17 ....18 B4
Highoak Garth HWTH BD22 ....12 D4
High Park Crs HTON BD9 ....37 H1
High Park Dr HTON BD9 ....37 G1
High Park Gv HTON BD9 ....37 H1
High Pastures HWTH BD22 ....13 F1
High Poplars ECHL BD2 ....29 G5
Highroad Well La LUD/ILL HX2 ...67 F1
High Spring Gardens La
　AIRE BD20 ....6 D2
High Spring Rd KGHY BD21 ....8 A1
High St BRIG HD6 ....71 G5
　CLECK BD19 ....71 G5
　CUL/QBY BD13 ....44 A1
　CUL/QBY BD13 ....52 B1
　GTL/HWG HX4 * 76 A4
　HFAX HX1 ....4 C5
　IDLE BD10 ....30 A1
　KGHY BD21 ....7 E4
　WBSY BD6 ....69 G1
　YEA LS19 ....11 H4
Highthorne Av BFDE BD3 ....40 B5
Hightown Rd CLECK BD19 ....73 G1
Hightown Vw LVSG WF15 ....73 F3
High Trees La GTL/HWG HX4 ....76 A5
Highway GSLY LS20 ....10 A2
High Wicken Cl CUL/QBY BD13 ...43 H1
Hilda St ECHL BD2 ....39 E1
Hillam St WBOW BD5 ....55 G3
Hillam Rd SHPY BD18 ....29 F2
Hillbro Ct BAIL BD17 * 19 E2
Hill Brow Cl WIL/AL BD15 ....36 D3
Hill Cl BAIL BD17 ....18 C4
Hillcote Dr WBOW BD5 ....47 F5
Hill Crs HIPP HX3 ....69 F3
Hill La AIRE BD20 ....21 H1
Hill Crest Av CUL/QBY BD13 ....34 C3
Hillcrest Av CUL/QBY BD13 ....54 C3
Hill Crest Dr CUL/QBY BD13 ....34 C3
Hillcrest Dr CUL/QBY BD13 ....54 C2
Hill Crest Mt CLECK BD19 ....73 C1
Hill Crest Mt CUL/QBY BD13 ....54 B3
Hill Crest Rd CUL/QBY BD13 ....54 B3
　CUL/QBY BD13 ....36 A5
Hillcrest Rd CUL/QBY BD13 ....34 C3
Hill Cft CUL/QBY BD13 ....36 B5
Hill End Cl HIPP HX3 ....62 B5
Hill End Gv GTHN BD7 ....45 H3
Hill End La CUL/QBY BD13 ....24 D1
　CUL/QBY BD13 ....52 A2
Hill Foot SHPY BD18 ....27 G2
Hillfoot Crs PDSY/CALV LS28 .....41 G4
Hillfoot Dr PDSY/CALV LS28 ......41 G4

Hillfoot Ri PDSY/CALV LS28 ....41 G4
Hill House Edge La
　HWTH BD22 ....32 C4
Hill House La HWTH BD22 ....32 D5
Hill Lands LM/WK BD12 ....62 C1
Hill Park Av HIPP HX3 ....59 E4
Hillside Av HWTH BD22 ....12 C4
　LUD/ILL HX2 ....66 A1
Hillside Gv HWTH BD22 ....12 C4
Hillside Gv CSLY LS20 ....10 C1
Hill Side Rd BFDE BD3 ....3 C4
　BGLY BD16 ....16 C5
Hillside Ter BAIL BD17 ....28 D5
Hillside Ter BAIL BD17 * 18 D2
Hillside Vw RPDN/SBR HX6 ....67 E5
Hill St BOW BD4 ....48 C1
　CLECK BD19 ....73 F1
　HFAX HX1 ....5 F6
　HWTH BD22 ....22 D3
　WBSY BD6 ....54 B1
Hill Top HFAX HX1 ....67 H5
Hill Top Cottages HTON BD9 ....37 H2
Hill Top Gv WIL/AL BD15 ....36 D2
Hill Top La BGLY BD16 ....9 H5
　WIL/AL BD15 ....36 D3
Hill Top Rd CUL/QBY BD13 ....35 C5
　HTON BD9 ....12 C4
　HWTH BD22 ....13 H5
Hill Top Wy HWTH BD22 * 6 C4
Hill Vw LM/WK BD12 ....51 E3
Hillview Gdns HIPP HX3 ....60 D4
Hillway CSLY LS20 ....10 B4
Hilton Av SHPY BD18 ....28 C4
Hilton Crs BAIL BD17 ....18 C4
Hilton Dr SHPY BD18 ....28 C4
Hilton Gv GTHN BD7 ....46 C1
　SHPY BD18 ....28 C4
Hilton Rd GTHN BD7 ....46 B1
Hinchliffe St BFDE BD3 ....3 J2
Hinchliffe Av BAIL BD17 ....19 E4
Hindley Wk GTHN BD7 ....45 C5
Hind St GIR BD8 ....38 D4
Hinton La GIR BD8 ....62 D3
Hions Cl BRIG HD6 ....78 B5
Hipswell St BFDE BD3 ....40 B4
Hird Av WBSY BD6 ....54 D2
Hird Rd LM/WK BD12 ....55 E4
Hird St BAIL BD17 ....28 C1
　KGHY BD21 ....14 A1
Hirst Cl SHPY BD18 * 29 G5
Hirst Lodge Ct ECHL BD2 ....29 G5
Hirst Mill Crs SHPY BD18 ....17 H5
Hirst Wood Crs SHPY BD18 ....27 H1
Hirst Wood Rd SHPY BD18 ....27 G1
Hive St HWTH BD22 ....6 D5
Hob Cote La HWTH BD22 ....13 F1
Hob La RPDN/SBR HX6 ....74 A2
Hockney Rd GIR BD8 ....38 C4
Hodgson Av WBSY BD6 ....40 C4
Hodgson La BIRK/DRI BD11 ....57 G3
Holborn Ct WBSY BD6 ....54 D4
Holden La BAIL BD17 ....18 C4
Holdsworth Ct CLECK BD19 ....73 C1
Holdsworth Rd LUD/ILL HX2 ......51 F3
Holdsworth St BFD BD1 * 2 E3
　CLECK BD19 ....64 C5
　SHPY BD18 ....28 D3
Holdsworth Ter HFAX HX1 ....69 E5
Holker St GIR BD8 ....38 C4
Hollas La RPDN/SBR HX6 ....74 D1
Hollin Close La HIPP HX3 ....39 F1
Hollin Greaves La HIPP HX3 ....59 H4
Hollings HWTH BD22 * 32 B2
Hollings La RPDN/SBR HX6 ....74 A2
Hollings Sq GIR BD8 ....38 C4
Hollings St GIR BD8 ....38 C4
　PDSY/CALV LS28 ....31 G2
Hollings Ter GIR BD8 ....38 C4
Hollingwood Av GTHN BD7 ....45 H4
Hollingwood Dr GTHN BD7 ....45 H5
Hollingwood La GTHN BD7 ....45 H4
Hollingwood Mt GTHN BD7 ....45 H4
Hollin Hall Rd SHPY BD18 ....27 H5
Hollin Head BAIL BD17 ....19 G2
Hollin La RPDN/SBR HX6 ....74 A2
　SHPY BD18 ....29 E3
Hollin Park Ct
　PDSY/CALV LS28 ....31 F3
Hollin Park Dr
　PDSY/CALV LS28 ....31 F3
Hollin Park Rd
　PDSY/CALV LS28 ....31 F3
Hollin Ri SHPY BD18 * 28 D3
Hollins Bank RPDN/SBR HX6 .....67 E4
Hollins Cl AIRE BD20 ....6 C1
Hollins Gv PDSY/CALV LS28 ....41 G4
Hollins La LUD/ILL HX2 ....50 B5
　RPDN/SBR HX6 ....74 A2
Hollins Mill La RPDN/SBR HX6 ...66 D4
Hollin Ter SHPY BD18 ....28 D3
Hollin Wood Cl SHPY BD18 ....27 H2
Hollinwood Vw ECHL BD20 ....9 G4
Hollowfield Cft
　LM/WK BD12 ....56 A1
Holly Bank Dr HIPP HX3 ....61 C5
Hollybank Gdns GTHN BD7 ....45 H4
Hollybank Gv GTHN BD7 ....45 H4
Holly Bank Pk BRIG HD6 ....78 H5
Holly Bank Rd BRIG HD6 ....71 H5
Hollybank Rd GTHN BD7 ....45 H4
Holly Gv HFAX HX1 ....4 C5
Holly Hall La LM/WK BD12 ....62 D1
Hollynsmill GTL/HWG HX4 ....76 A4
Holly Rd Park Dr GTHN BD7 ....45 H3
Holly Park Dr GTHN BD7 * 45 H3
Holly Park Mills
　PDSY/CALV LS28 ....31 F3
Holly St WBSY BD6 ....45 G5
Holme Dr LUD/ILL HX2 ....67 E2
Holme Farm Cl WBSY BD6 ....53 C1
Holmefield Vw BOW BD4 ....48 D5

Holme House La
　HWTH BD22 ....12 D1
Holme La BOW BD4 ....48 E4
　BOW BD4 ....56 D1
Holme Rd LUD/ILL HX2 ....67 E2
Holmes Rd RPDN/SBR HX6 ....67 F4
Holmes St BOW BD4 ....2 A3
Holmes Ter LUD/ILL HX2 ....58 C5
Holme St BRIG HD6 ....71 F1
　HWTH BD22 ....47 E3
　WBOW BD5 ....47 E3
Holme Top La WBOW BD5 ....55 E3
Holme Top St WBOW BD5 ....55 E3
Holme Wood Rd BOW BD4 ....48 C4
　HWTH BD22 ....6 C5
Holroyd Hl WBSY BD6 ....54 D1
Holroyd Mill La AIRE BD20 ....9 F3
Holsworthy Rd BOW BD4 ....48 D4
Holtby Gv BRIG HD6 ....71 F1
Holt Gdns IDLE BD10 ....29 G1
Holts La CLAY BD14 ....45 E2
Holts Ter HFAX HX3 ....69 E4
The Holt HIPP HX3 ....20 D3
Holybrook Av IDLE BD10 ....29 E1
Holycroft St KGHY BD21 ....7 E5
Holyoake Av BGLY BD16 ....16 C5
Holywell Ash La GIR BD8 ....28 B1
Home Vine Ter GIR BD8 ....38 C3
Honey Pot La BAIL BD17 * 18 C3
The Hoods BRIG HD6 ....78 A4
Hoopoe Ms WIL/AL BD15 ....37 E4
Hopbine Av WBOW BD5 ....55 F4
Hopbine Rd WBOW BD5 ....47 F5
Hope Av WBOW BD5 ....29 E1
　WBOW BD5 ....55 F4
Hopefield Wy BOW BD4 ....56 A1
Hope Hall St HFAX HX1 ....5 H6
Hope Hall Ter HFAX HX1 * 5 H6
Hope La CLAY BD14 ....18 C3
Hope Pl KGHY BD21 * 14 A1
Hope St HFAX HX1 ....4 E3
　RPDN/SBR HX6 ....67 F5
Hope Vw SHPY BD18 ....28 D2
Hopkinson Dr BOW BD4 ....56 A1
Hopkinson St LUD/ILL HX2 ....59 E2
Hopkin St BOW BD4 ....56 B1
Hops La HIPP HX3 ....58 D3
Hopton Av BOW BD4 ....56 A1
Hopwood La HFAX HX1 ....4 A5
Horley Green La HIPP HX3 ....60 B4
Hornbeam Cl WIL/AL BD15 ....26 C5
Hornby St HFAX HX1 ....4 B7
Hornby Ter HFAX HX1 * 4 B6
Horncastle St CLECK BD19 ....73 H1
Horne St HFAX HX1 ....4 E5
Hornsea Dr WIL/AL BD15 ....25 H5
Horseshoe Ct WIL/AL BD15 ....25 H5
Horsfall St HFAX HX1 ....68 B3
Horsham Ct HWTH BD22 ....13 F1
Horsham Rd BOW BD4 * 48 D5
Horsley St WBSY BD6 ....48 D5
Horsman St BOW BD4 ....56 B1
Horton Grange Rd
　GTHN BD7 ....46 C1
Horton Hl LV WBOW BD5 ....47 E2
Horton Park Av GTHN BD7 ....46 C2
Horton St HFAX HX1 ....5 H5
Hospital Rd AIRE BD20 ....8 B2
Hough HIPP HX3 ....60 D3
Houghton Pl BFD BD1 * 2 B3
Houghton St BRIG HD6 ....71 G5
Hoults La GTL/HWG HX4 ....76 A5
Howards Dean HWTH BD22 ....13 C5
Howard St HFAX HX1 ....4 C5
　WBOW BD5 ....2 E7
Howarth Av ECHL BD2 ....29 H4
Howarth Crs ECHL BD2 * 29 H4
Howbeck Av AIRE BD20 ....8 B2
Howbeck Dr AIRE BD20 ....8 B3
Howcans La HIPP HX3 ....59 F1
Howden Av AIRE BD20 ....6 D1
Howdenbrook HIPP HX3 ....53 C3
Howden Cl BOW BD4 ....48 D5
Howes La HIPP HX3 ....60 C2
Howgate IDLE BD10 ....30 B1
Howgate Hl HIPP HX3 ....46 A5
Howgill Gn WBSY BD6 ....54 B4
Howson Ct CSLY LS20 ....11 E3
Hoxton St GIR BD8 ....38 A4
Hoyle Court Av BAIL BD17 ....19 F3
Hoyle Court Dr BAIL BD17 ....19 F3
Hoyle Court Rd BAIL BD17 ....19 F3
Hoyle Fold HWTH BD22 ....13 C1
Hoyle Ing Rd CUL/QBY BD13 .....44 C1
Hubert St BFDE BD3 ....3 K7
　LUD/ILL HX2 ....68 B2
Huddersfield Rd BRIG HD6 ....78 C1
　ELL HX5 ....76 B2
　HFAX HX3 ....68 D5
　LM/WK BD12 ....62 B2
　WBSY BD6 ....54 B1
Hud Hl HIPP HX3 ....61 E1
Hudson Av CUL/QBY BD13 ....46 C3
Hudson Cl GTHN BD7 ....48 A4
Hudson Crs GTHN BD7 ....46 C3
Hudson Gdns GTHN BD7 ....46 C3
Hudson St BFDE BD3 ....46 D4
The Hudson LM/WK BD12 ....62 D2
Hughenden Dr
　CUL/QBY BD13 ....44 D1
Hughendon Wk
　CUL/QBY BD13 ....44 D1
Hugill St CUL/QBY BD13 ....44 A1
Hulbert St BGLY BD16 ....16 D4
Hullenedge Gdns ELL HX5 ....76 A5
Hullenedge La GTL/HWG HX4 ....76 A5
Hullenedge Rd ELL HX5 ....76 A5
Hullen Rd ELL HX5 ....76 A5
Humboldt St BFD BD1 ....3 G5
Hunger Hl HFAX HX1 ....5 H6
Hunsworth La BIRK/DRI BD11 ....56 D4
　CLECK BD19 ....57 E5
Huntercombe Ct BGLY BD16 ......17 G1
Hunters Ct HTON BD9 ....27 H5

Hunters Gn CUL/QBY BD13 ....24 C2
Hunters Park Av CLAY BD14 ....45 G2
Huntington Rd BRIG HD6 ....78 D2
Huntock Pl BRIG HD6 ....7 H5
Huntsmans Cl AIRE BD20 ....6 D3
　BGLY BD16 ....17 F1
Hurstville Av BIRK/DRI BD11 ......37 E5
Hustlergate BFD BD1 ....2 D5
Hustler St BFDE BD3 ....1 J4
Hutson St WBOW BD5 ....47 E5
Hutton Rd WBOW BD5 ....46 D5
Hutton Ter IDLE BD10 ....30 C4
Hydale Cl KGHY BD21 ....14 D1
Hydale Ct LM/WK BD12 ....54 D4
Hyde Gv KGHY BD21 ....7 G5
Hyde Pk HFAX HX1 ....4 D6
Hyde Park Rd HFAX HX1 ....4 C7
Hyde St IDLE BD10 ....20 A5
Hyne Av BOW BD4 ....56 B1

I

Ida St WBOW BD5 ....46 D4
Iddesleigh St BOW BD4 ....48 B1
Idlecroft Rd IDLE BD10 ....30 A1
Idle Rd ECHL BD2 ....29 H4
Idlethorp Wy IDLE BD10 ....30 B2
Ilbert Av BOW BD4 ....56 B1
Ilkley Rd AIRE BD20 ....8 A1
Illingworth Av LUD/ILL HX2 ....50 D5
Illingworth Cl LUD/ILL HX2 ....50 D5
　YEA LS19 ....21 H1
Illingworth Crs LUD/ILL HX2 ....60 B4
Illingworth Dr LUD/ILL HX2 ....50 D5
Illingworth Gdns
　LUD/ILL HX2 ....50 D4
Illingworth Gv LUD/ILL HX2 ....50 D5
Illingworth Rd LM/WK BD12 ....63 G1
　LUD/ILL HX2 ....50 D5
Illingworth Wy LUD/ILL HX2 ....50 D5
The Incline HIPP HX3 ....5 K2
Independent St
　WBOW BD5 ....46 D4
Industrial Rd
　RPDN/SBR HX6 ....67 E4
Industrial St BGLY BD16 ....16 C3
　BRIG HD6 ....71 G5
　HWTH BD22 ....22 D3
　LVSG WF15 ....73 H4
Industrial Ter HFAX HX1 * 68 C3
Infirmary St BFD BD1 ....2 B4
Ing Fld LM/WK BD12 ....63 H1
Ingham La LUD/ILL HX2 ....51 E2
Ingham La LUD/ILL HX2 ....58 C3
Ingham's Av
　PDSY/CALV LS28 ....41 G4
Inghams Ct HIPP HX3 * 59 H4
Inghams Ter
　PDSY/CALV LS28 ....41 G4
Ingham's Vw
　PDSY/CALV LS28 ....41 G4
Inghead Gdns HIPP HX3 ....61 E1
Ingleborough Cl BOW BD4 ....48 D4
Ingleby Pl GTHN BD7 ....46 B1
Ingleby Rd GIR BD8 ....38 B5
Ingleby St GIR BD8 ....38 B5
Ingram Sq HFAX HX1 * 68 B3
Ingram St HFAX HX1 ....68 B3
　WBOW BD5 ....2 C7
Ingrow Br KGHY BD21 ....14 A2
Ingrow La HWTH BD22 ....13 G2
Ingrow Wk HFAX HX1 * 68 B3
Ings Av GSLY LS20 ....10 C1
Ings Crs CSLY LS20 ....10 B2
Ings Crs GSLY LS20 ....10 C1
Ings La GSLY LS20 ....10 B1
The Ings BRIG HD6 ....71 F1
Ings Mill Av CLECK BD19 ....73 C1
Ings St BFDE BD3 ....40 C5
Ings Wy GIR BD8 ....38 A3
Ingwell Ter CLECK BD19 ....73 H1
Inkerman St BOW BD4 ....48 C3
　ECHL BD2 ....30 C5
Inkersley Rd BFD BD1 ....1 K1
Innovad Rd BFDE BD3 ....57 G5
The Innings IDLE BD10 ....29 H1
Institute Rd ECHL BD2 ....30 B5
Intake Gv ECHL BD2 ....40 B2
Intake Rd BFD BD2 ....40 A2
Intercity Wy ECHL BD2 ....30 A4
Invertrees Av YEA LS19 ....21 H2
Iona Av ECHL BD2 ....30 A5
Iona St HIPP HX3 ....59 G4
Iqbal Ct BFDE BD3 * 3 K7
Ireland St BGLY BD16 ....16 B3
Ireland Ter BGLY BD16 ....16 B3
Ireton St GTHN BD7 ....46 C1
Iron St CLECK BD19 ....73 F1
Irving St HFAX HX1 ....68 A3
Irving Ter CLAY BD14 ....45 F4
Irwell St BOW BD4 ....47 H2
Isaac St GIR BD8 ....38 A4
Isles St GIR BD8 ....38 B3
Ivanhoe Rd GTHN BD7 ....46 C1
Ivegate BFD BD1 ....2 C5
Iveson Gdns 11 G5
Iver Wy SHPY BD18 ....28 B2
Ivy Bank La HWTH BD22 ....13 G2
Ivy Gdns HIPP HX3 ....70 D1
Ivy Gv SHPY BD18 ....28 B2
Ivy House Rd WBOW BD5 ....55 F1
Ivy La LUD/ILL HX2 ....50 D5
　WIL/AL BD15 ....37 F5
Ivy St BRIG HD6 ....71 E5
　HFAX HX1 ....4 C5
　KGHY BD21 ....7 E5
Ivy Ter BRIG HD6 ....71 E5
　HIPP HX3 ....70 D1
　KGHY BD21 ....8 A5

J

Jacana Wy WBSY BD6 ....53 F1
Jackdaw Cl WIL/AL BD15 ....37 E5
Jackie Smart Rd WBOW BD5 ......54 D3
Jackson Hill La CUL/QBY BD13 ...52 C3
Jackson St BFDE BD3 ....3 H7
Jacky La HWTH BD22 ....22 D3
Jacobs Cft CLAY BD14 ....45 E3
Jacobs La HWTH BD22 ....23 E1
Jacob St WBOW BD5 ....47 E3
James Ga BFD BD1 ....2 C4
James St BFD BD1 ....2 C4
　BIRK/DRI BD11 * 57 F4
　BRIG HD6 ....71 F4
　CUL/QBY BD13 ....36 A5
　ELL HX5 ....76 C5
　HWTH BD22 ....12 C4
　WIL/AL BD15 ....37 F5
　YEA LS19 ....21 G2
Jamie St IDLE BD10 ....30 C3
Jane St CUL/QBY BD13 ....34 C3
　IDLE BD10 ....28 A1
Janet St HWTH BD22 ....32 B5
Japonica Wy BFDE BD5 ....40 B5
Jardine Rd BGLY BD16 ....16 D3
Jarratt St GIR BD8 ....38 C3
Jarratt St East GIR BD8 ....38 C3
Jarrom Cl BOW BD4 ....48 C3
Jasmine Gdns HFAX HX1 * 4 B6
Jasmin Ter GIR BD8 ....38 D4
Jasper St HFAX HX1 ....4 B4
　IDLE BD10 ....30 A1
Javelin Cl IDLE BD10 ....30 A3
Jay House La BRIG HD6 ....72 A3
Jay St HWTH BD22 ....23 E3
Jennings Pl GTHN BD7 ....46 B5
Jennings St GTHN BD7 ....46 B5
Jenny La BAIL BD17 ....19 E2
Jepson La ELL HX5 ....76 C5
Jer Gv GTHN BD7 ....45 H5
Jer La GTHN BD7 ....45 H5
Jermyn St BFD BD1 ....2 E4
Jerry Fields Rd LUD/ILL HX2 ......66 A2
Jerry La RPDN/SBR HX6 ....66 D5
Jervaulx Crs GIR BD8 ....38 D4
Jerwood Hill Cl HIPP HX3 ....60 A4
Jesmond Av HTON BD9 ....38 A2
Jesmond Gv HTON BD9 ....38 A2
Jesse St GIR BD8 ....37 G5
　WBOW BD5 ....47 F2
Jew La HWTH BD22 ....32 D2
Jim Laker Pl SHPY BD18 ....28 A2
Joba Av BFDE BD3 ....3 K5
John Escritt Rd BGLY BD16 ....16 C5
John Hanson Ct
　CUL/QBY BD13 ....42 D1
John Naylor La LUD/ILL HX2 ......66 B3
Johnson St BFDE BD3 ....40 C5
　BOW BD4 ....56 B1
John St BAIL BD17 ....18 D5
　BFD BD1 ....2 C4
　BOW BD4 ....56 B1
　BRIG HD6 ....71 F5
　CLAY BD14 ....45 G5
　CUL/QBY BD13 ....24 C3
　CUL/QBY BD13 ....34 C4
　CUL/QBY BD13 ....44 A1
　ELL HX5 ....76 C5
　GTL/HWG HX4 ....75 H5
　HFAX HX1 ....15 E4
　HWTH BD22 ....14 B2
　SHPY BD18 ....28 B1
　YEA LS19 ....21 G2
John St West RPDN/SBR HX6 .....67 E4
John William St CLECK BD19 ......64 C5
　ELL HX5 ....76 C5
Jordan Wy ECHL BD2 ....30 A5
Joseph Av HIPP HX3 ....60 D5
Joseph St BFD BD1 ....3 G5
　BOW BD4 ....56 B1
Jowett Park Crs IDLE BD10 ....19 H4
Jowett St BFD BD1 ....38 D5
Jubilee Ct HFAX HX1 ....12 B1
Jubilee Dr KGHY BD21 ....13 H1
Jubilee Rd HIPP HX3 ....76 A1
Jubilee St BFD BD1 ....2 B1
　HIPP HX3 ....5 K6
Jubilee St North LUD/ILL HX2 .....59 F2
Jubilee Ter HIPP HX3 * 5 K6
Jubilee Wy SHPY BD18 ....29 E1
Julian Dr CUL/QBY BD13 ....45 F5
Jumble Dyke BRIG HD6 ....78 A3
Jumples LUD/ILL HX2 ....58 C1
Jumples Cl LUD/ILL HX2 ....58 C1
Junction Rd BAIL BD17 ....28 D1
June St KGHY BD21 ....7 E3
Juniper Cl GIR BD8 * 38 D3
Jureshi Vw GIR BD8 ....38 D3

K

Katherine St SHPY BD18 ....28 A1
Kaycell St BOW BD4 ....48 A5
Kaye Hl CUL/QBY BD13 ....43 C4
Kay St HTON BD9 ....28 D4
Keedar Ct GTHN BD7 ....46 C4
Keelham Dr YEA LS19 ....21 H2
Keelham La AIRE BD20 ....6 D1
Keighley Cl LUD/ILL HX2 ....50 C4
Keighley Dr LUD/ILL HX2 ....50 C4
Keighley Rd BGLY BD16 ....15 F3
　CUL/QBY BD13 ....24 C1
　HTON BD9 ....38 D3
　HWTH BD22 ....13 F3
　LUD/ILL HX2 ....50 D2
Kelburn Gv HWTH BD22 ....12 C3

Kelcliffe Av *GSLY* LS20 ....10 D2
Kelcliffe La *GSLY* LS20 ....10 D1
Kell La *HIPP* HX3.........60 C3
Kelloe St *CLECK* BD19 ....64 B4
Kell St *BGLY* BD16 ....16 D3
Kenmore Gv *WBSY* BD6 ....53 H4
Kelsey St *HFAX* HX1 ....6 B2
Kelvin Av *LUD/ILL* HX2 ....67 C1
Kelvin Crs *LUD/ILL* HX2 ....67 C2
Kelvin Rd *ELL* HX5 ....76 B5
Kelvin Wy *ECHL* BD2 ....40 B2
Kendall Av *SHPY* BD18 ....27 H1
Kendal Mellor Ct *KGHY* BD21 ....7 E4
Kendal St *KGHY* BD21 ....7 E4
Kenilworth Av *BRIG* HD6 ....71 F2
Kenilworth St *BOW* BD4 ....47 H3
Kenley Av *WBSY* BD6 ....54 B1
Kenley Mt *WBSY* BD6 ....46 B5
Kenley Pde *GTHN* BD7 ....46 B5
Kenmore Av *CLECK* BD19 ....64 B5
Kenmore Cl *CLECK* BD19 ....64 B5
Kenmore Crs *CLECK* BD19 ....64 B5
WBSY BD6 ....46 B5
Kenmore Dr *CLECK* BD19 ....64 B5
WBSY BD6 ....46 B5
Kenmore Gv *CLECK* BD19 ....64 B5
WBSY BD6 ....46 B5
Kenmore Rd *CLECK* BD19 ....64 B5
WBSY BD6 ....46 B5
Kenmore Vw *CLECK* BD19 ....64 B5
Kenmore Wk *WBSY* BD6 ....46 B5
Kenmore Wy *CLECK* BD19 ....64 B5
Kennion St *HIPP* HX3 ....47 E2
Kenstone Crs *IDLE* BD10 ....29 H2
Kentmere *IDLE* BD10 ....29 C3
Kentmere Av *LM/WK* BD12 ....63 F4
Kent Ms *BGLY* BD16 ....17 E4
Kenton Wy *BOW* BD4 * 48 D4
Kent Rd *BGLY* BD16 ....17 F3
Kent St *HFAX* HX1 ....5 F5
Kenya Mt *HWTH* BD22 ....6 C3
Kenyon La *LUD/ILL* HX2 ....67 C1
Kershaw Crs *LUD/ILL* HX2 ....66 A1
Kershaw St *BFDE* BD3 ....40 C5
Kesteven Cl *BOW* BD4 ....49 E5
Kesteven Ct *BOW* BD4 ....48 D5
Kesteven Rd *BOW* BD4 ....48 D5
Kestrel Dr *ECHL* BD2 ....29 H5
Kestrel Mt *ECHL* BD2 ....29 H5
Kestrel Vw *CLECK* BD19 ....64 C4
Keswick Cl *HIPP* HX3 ....69 F5
Keswick St *BOW* BD4 ....5 H5
Kettlewell Dr *WBOW* BD5 ....46 C4
Khalaq Ct *BFDE* BD3 ....3 K3
Khus Wk *KGHY* BD21 ....14 B2
Kildare Crs *WIL/AL* BD15 ....36 D3
Killinghall Av *ECHL* BD2 ....40 A3
Killinghall Dr *ECHL* BD2 ....40 A3
Killinghall Gv *ECHL* BD2 ....40 A3
Killinghall Rd *BFDE* BD3 ....40 B3
Kilner Rd *WBSY* BD6 * 54 B1
Kiln Fold *BRIG* HD6 ....72 A5
Kilnsea St *BOW* BD4 ....48 C3
Kilnsey Ms *BAIL* BD17 ....18 C4
Kilnsey Rd *BFDE* BD3 ....3 K6
Kilroyd Av *CLECK* BD19 ....64 C3
Kilroyd Dr *CLECK* BD19 ....64 D3
Kimberley Pl *HIPP* HX3 ....59 F1
Kimberley St *BFDE* BD3 ....48 B1
BRIG HD6 ....71 F2
HIPP HX3 ....59 F1
Kinara Cl *HWTH* BD22 ....7 H3
King Cross Rd *HFAX* HX1 ....4 B7
King Cross St *HFAX* HX1 ....4 C7
King Edward Rd
CUL/OBY BD13 ....44 A1
King Edward St *HFAX* HX1 * 5 H4
Kingfield *GSLY* LS20 ....11 E1
Kingfisher Ct *KGHY* BD21 * 7 G4
Kingfisher Gv *GIR* BD8 ....37 F5
Kingsbury Pl *HFAX* HX1 ....4 E5
Kings Ct *HFAX* HX1 ....4 E5
Kingsdale Av *ECHL* BD2 ....39 H1
Kingsdale Ct *ECHL* BD2 ....39 H1
Kingsdale Dr *ECHL* BD2 ....39 H1
Kingsdale Gv *ECHL* BD2 ....39 G1
Kings Ga *BFDE* BD3 ....3 H5
Kings Gv *BGLY* BD16 ....16 D2
Kings Lea *HIPP* HX3 ....75 C1
Kingsley Av *BIRK/DRI* BD11 ....65 C1
ECHL BD2 ....39 F1
RPDN/SBR HX6 ....66 C5
Kingsley Crs *BAIL* BD17 ....18 C4
BIRK/DRI BD11 ....65 C1
Kingsley Dr *BIRK/DRI* BD11 ....65 C1
Kingsley Pl *HFAX* HX1 ....4 B6
Kingsmark Fwy *LM/WK* BD12 ....55 G4
King's Rd *BGLY* BD16 ....16 D2
ECHL BD2 ....29 G4
ECHL BD2 ....39 F2
Kingston Cl *HFAX* HX1 ....4 B5
WIL/AL BD15 ....25 H5
Kingston Ct *HFAX* HX1 ....4 B6
Kingston Dr *HFAX* HX1 ....4 B5
Kingston Gv *IDLE* BD10 ....20 A5
Kingston Rd *IDLE* BD10 ....20 A5
Kingston St *HFAX* HX1 ....4 B5
King St *BRIG* HD6 ....78 C1
CLECK BD19 ....64 C5
HFAX HX1 ....5 J4
IDLE BD10 ....30 B4
RPDN/SBR HX6 * 66 B5
YEA LS19 ....11 H4
Kings Vw *HIPP* HX3 ....69 H4
Kingsway *AIRE* BD20 ....21 F2
BGLY BD16 ....16 D4
ECHL BD2 ....29 G3
Kingswood Gn *HIPP* HX3 ....60 C4

Kingswood Pl *GTHN* BD7 ....46 B3
Kingswood St *HIPP* HX3 ....46 B3
Kingswood Ter *GTHN* BD7 * 46 B3
Kinnaird Cl *ELL* HX5 ....76 C1
Kipling Ct *IDLE* BD10 ....30 C2
Kipling La *CUL/OBY* BD13 ....44 A1
Kipping Pl *CUL/OBY* BD13 ....44 A1
Kirby St *KGHY* BD21 ....7 G3
Kirkbourne Gv *BAIL* BD17 ....19 F4
Kirkburn Pl *GTHN* BD7 ....5 G6
Kirkby Leas *HFAX* HX1 ....5 G6
Kirkdale Wy *BOW* BD4 ....57 E1
Kirk Dr *BAIL* BD17 ....19 F3
Kirkfields *BAIL* BD17 ....19 F2
Kirkgate *BFD* BD1 ....2 C5
SHPY BD18 ....28 B2
Kirkham Rd *GTHN* BD7 ....46 C1
Kirklands Av *BAIL* BD17 ....19 F3
Kirklands Cl *BAIL* BD17 ....19 F4
YEA LS19 ....11 F4
Kirklands Gdns *BAIL* BD17 ....19 F3
Kirklands La *BAIL* BD17 ....19 F3
Kirklands Rd *BAIL* BD17 ....19 F3
Kirklands Vls *BAIL* BD17 * 19 F3
Kirk La *HIPP* HX3 ....60 C5
YEA LS19 ....11 F4
Kirklees Rd *WIL/AL* BD15 ....37 G5
Kirklees Wy *BIRK/DRI* BD11 ....57 G5
CLECK BD19 ....63 H2
HUDN HD2 ....79 E5
Kirkley Av *LM/WK* BD12 ....62 D4
Kirkstall Gv *GIR* BD8 ....37 C5
Kirkstone Dr *CLECK* BD19 ....65 C5
LUD/ILL HX2 ....58 A5
Kirkwall Dr *BOW* BD4 ....38 B4
Kismet Gdns *BFDE* BD3 ....40 B4
Kitson La *RPDN/SBR* HX6 ....74 C5
Kitson St *SHPY* BD18 ....28 B2
Kliffen Pl *HIPP* HX3 ....69 E4
Knightsbridge Wk *BOW* BD4 ....56 A2
Knight's Fold *GTHN* BD7 ....46 B3
Knight St *HFAX* HX1 ....4 B7
Knoll Park Dr *BAIL* BD17 ....18 C5
The Knoll *PDSY/CALV* LS28 ....41 F1
Knowle La *LM/WK* BD12 ....63 C5
Knowles Av *BOW* BD4 ....48 C5
Knowles Cft *BOW* BD4 * 48 C5
CLECK BD19 ....65 G2
Knowle Spring Rd
KGHY BD21 * 14 A1
Knowles Rd *BRIG* HD6 ....78 B3
Knowles St *BOW* BD4 ....56 B1
BFD BD1 ....34 C4
Knowles Vw *BOW* BD4 ....48 C5
Knowle Top Dr *HIPP* HX3 ....61 H5
Knowle Top Rd *HIPP* HX3 ....61 H5
Knowsley St *BFDE* BD3 ....3 H6
Knutsford Gv *BOW* BD4 ....48 D5
Knutsford Ms *BOW* BD4 * 48 D5
Komla Cl *BFD* BD1 ....3 F4
Kyffin Pl *BOW* BD4 ....48 D2

L

Laburnum Dr *BAIL* BD17 ....19 E2
Laburnum Gv *BRIG* HD6 ....71 F2
CLECK BD19 ....65 F4
HWTH BD22 ....23 F1
Laburnum Pl *GIR* BD8 ....38 C5
IDLE BD10 ....30 D1
Laburnum Rd *SHPY* BD18 ....29 F2
Laburnum St *GIR* BD8 ....38 C5
PDSY/CALV LS28 ....41 H4
Laceby Cl *IDLE* BD10 ....30 D1
Lacy Wy *ELL* HX5 ....76 D5
Ladbroke Gv *BOW* BD4 ....56 D1
Ladderbanks La *BAIL* BD17 ....19 E2
Lady La *BGLY* BD16 ....9 H5
Lady Park Av *BGLY* BD16 ....9 H5
Ladyroyd Dr *BIRK/DRI* BD11 ....56 D4
Ladysmith Rd *CUL/OBY* BD13 ....51 H2
Ladywell Cl *WBOW* BD5 ....47 H4
Ladywell La *LVSG* WF15 ....73 E5
Ladywood Ter *HFAX* HX1 ....4 C1
Lake Rw *BOW* BD4 ....48 A2
Lakeside *AIRE* BD20 ....21 F2
Lakeside Cha *YEA* LS19 ....21 H2
Lakeside Gdns *YEA* LS19 ....21 H2
Lakeside Ter *YEA* LS19 ....21 H2
Lakeside Vw *YEA* LS19 ....21 H2
Lake St *BOW* BD4 ....48 A2
KGHY BD21 ....7 H2
Lake Vw *HIPP* HX3 ....59 G2
Lamb Cote Rd *HUDN* HD2 ....79 E5
Lambert Cl *GTL/HWG* HX4 ....74 D5
Lambert Pl *ECHL* BD2 ....40 A2
Lambert St *GTL/HWG* HX4 ....74 A4
Lambourne Av *IDLE* BD10 ....30 B1
Lamb Springs La *BAIL* BD17 ....19 H1
Lampards Cl *WIL/AL* BD15 ....36 A2
Lancaster Ct *KGHY* BD21 ....14 A1
Landor St *KGHY* BD21 * 7 G5
Landscove Av *BOW* BD4 ....49 F5
Lands Head La *HIPP* HX3 ....60 C1
Lands La *GSLY* LS20 ....10 B4
IDLE BD10 ....30 B4
Landsmoor Gv *BGLY* BD16 ....17 G2
Lane End *CUL/OBY* BD13 ....44 A1
Lane Ends *LUD/ILL* HX2 ....58 D3
Lane Ends Cl *BOW* BD4 ....48 D5
Lane Ends Gn *HIPP* HX3 ....61 G5
Lane Head La *LUD/ILL* HX2 ....58 B5
Lane Side *CUL/OBY* BD13 ....52 B5
WIL/AL BD15 ....25 G5
Lane Side *LM/WK* BD12 ....62 D4
Lane Top *BRIG* HD6 * 71 H4
Langbar Av *HTON* BD9 ....37 G1

Langdale Av *GIR* BD8 ....37 H4
LM/WK BD12 ....63 F4
Langdale Ct *BGLY* BD16 ....16 C2
Langdale Crs *LUD/ILL* HX2 ....58 C5
Langdale Dr *CUL/OBY* BD13 ....52 A1
Langdale Rd *BGLY* BD16 ....16 D5
Langdale Rd *RPDN/SBR* HX6 ....66 B5
Langdale St *ELL* HX5 ....76 C5
Langlands Rd *BGLY* BD16 ....26 D2
Langley Av *BGLY* BD16 ....16 D1
BOW BD4 ....56 A1
Langley Cl *BAIL* BD17 ....19 F3
Langley Crs *BAIL* BD17 ....19 F3
Langley Gv *BAIL* BD17 ....19 F2
Langley La *BAIL* BD17 ....19 F2
Langport Ct *CUL/OBY* BD13 ....52 C1
Langton Av *BOW* BD4 ....56 A1
Langton Ct *CLECK* BD19 ....65 F3
Langton St *RPDN/SBR* HX6 ....67 E5
Lansdowne Cl *BAIL* BD17 ....19 G3
Lansdowne Pl *WBOW* BD5 ....2 B7
Lapage St *BFDE* BD3 ....40 B5
Lapage Ter *BFDE* BD3 * 40 B5
Lapwing Ct *GIR* BD8 ....37 G5
Larch Cl *HWTH* BD22 ....13 G4
Larch Dr *BOW* BD4 ....54 D3
Larch Gv *BGLY* BD16 ....16 C1
Larch Hill *WBSY* BD6 ....55 E5
Larch Hill Crs *WBSY* BD6 ....55 E5
Larchmont *CLAY* BD14 ....45 F3
Larch Rd *HUDN* HD2 ....78 D5
Larchwood *BAIL* BD17 ....14 A2
Larkfield Av *YEA* LS19 ....21 H2
Larkfield Crs *YEA* LS19 ....21 H2
Larkfield Dr *YEA* LS19 ....21 H2
Larkfield Mt *YEA* LS19 ....21 H2
Larkfield Rd *YEA* LS19 ....21 H2
Larkfield Ter *KGHY* BD21 ....7 H5
Lark Hill Av *CLECK* BD19 ....73 E2
Lark Hill Dr *CLECK* BD19 ....73 E1
Larkfield Cl *CLECK* BD19 ....16 C3
HWTH BD22 ....13 E4
KGHY BD21 ....7 E4
Lark V *BGLY* BD16 ....17 F2
Larwood Av *IDLE* BD10 ....30 C5
Lastingham Gn *WBSY* BD6 * 53 H1
Latham Ct *CLECK* BD19 ....65 G3
Latham La *CLECK* BD19 ....65 F2
Latham La *CLECK* BD19 ....65 G3
Latimer St *BFDE* BD3 ....48 C1
Launceston Dr *BOW* BD4 ....48 D5
Launton Wy *WBOW* BD5 ....47 E3
Laura St *BRIG* HD6 ....78 B2
HFAX HX1 ....59 H4
Laurel Bank *BGLY* BD16 * 17 G2
Laurel Bank Cl *LUD/ILL* HX2 ....51 F4
Laurel Cl *ELL* HX5 ....76 B5
HFAX HX1 ....53 F5
Laurel Crs *KGHY* BD21 ....7 E5
Laurel Gv *BGLY* BD16 ....16 B1
WIL/AL BD15 ....25 H5
Laurel Mt *HFAX* HX1 * 4 D7
Laurel Pk *WIL/AL* BD15 ....25 H5
The Laurels *BGLY* BD16 * 17 E3
Laurel St *BFDE* BD3 ....48 B1
HFAX HX1 ....4 D7
Lavender Ct *SHPY* BD18 ....29 E3
Lavender Hill *IDLE* BD10 ....30 B4
Laverhills *LVSG* WF15 ....73 G3
Laverock Crs *BRIG* HD6 ....71 E3
Laverock La *BRIG* HD6 ....71 E3
Laverton Rd *BOW* BD4 ....48 A3
Lawcliffe Crs *HWTH* BD22 ....23 E1
Lawkholme Crs *KGHY* BD21 ....7 F4
Lawkholme La *KGHY* BD21 ....7 F4
Law La *HIPP* HX3 ....69 H5
Lawnswood Rd *KGHY* BD21 ....13 H1
Lawrence Ct *HWTH* BD22 * 23 F1
Lawrence Dr *CUL/OBY* BD13 ....68 C5
Lawrence St *HIPP* HX3 * 59 F4
Lawson Rd *BRIG* HD6 ....78 C1
Lawson St *BFDE* BD3 ....3 F2
CLECK BD19 ....64 B5
Lea Av *HIPP* HX3 ....68 D5
Leach Crs *AIRE* BD20 ....7 H1
Leache's Br *AIRE* BD20 ....7 G1
Leach Ri *AIRE* BD20 ....7 H1
Leach Rd *AIRE* BD20 ....7 H1
Lea Ct *BRIG* HD6 ....71 F4
Lea Ct *GTHN* BD7 ....45 H5
Leadenhall St *HFAX* HX1 ....4 D7
Leafield Av *ECHL* BD2 ....40 B1
Leafield Crs *ECHL* BD2 ....40 A1
Leafield Dr *ECHL* BD2 ....30 B5
Leafield Gv *ECHL* BD2 ....40 A1
Leafield Ter *ECHL* BD2 ....40 A1
Leafield Wy *ECHL* BD2 ....40 B1
Leafland St *HFAX* HX1 ....4 D7
Lea Mill Park Cl *YEA* LS19 ....11 F4
Lea Mill Park Dr *YEA* LS19 ....11 F4
Leamington Dr *IDLE* BD10 ....30 D1
Leamington St *HTON* BD9 ....38 C2
Leamside Wk *BOW* BD4 ....48 D5
Leaside Dr *CUL/OBY* BD13 ....36 A5
Leaventhorpe Av *GIR* BD8 ....37 C5
Leaventhorpe Cl *GIR* BD8 ....37 G5
Leaventhorpe Gv
CUL/OBY BD13 ....45 F1
Leaventhorpe La
CUL/OBY BD13 ....45 F1
Leaventhorpe Wy *GIR* BD8 ....37 G5
Leavington Cl *LM/WK* BD12 ....54 C4
Ledbury Pl *BOW* BD4 ....47 H3
Lee Bank *HIPP* HX3 ....59 G4
Lee Br *HFAX* HX1 ....5 F1
Leech La *BGLY* BD16 ....25 E1
Lee Cl *WIL/AL* BD15 ....25 H5
Lee Ct *KGHY* BD21 ....8 A5
Leeds Country Wy

PDSY/CALV LS28 ....21 F5
PDSY/CALV LS28 ....41 E1
Leeds Old Rd *BFDE* BD3 ....40 C4
Leeds Rd *BFD* BD1 ....3 F5
GSLY LS20 ....10 D3
HIPP HX3 ....60 D4
SHPY BD18 ....29 H3
YEA LS19 ....21 H3
Leeds St *KGHY* BD21 ....7 F5
Lee La *BGLY* BD16 ....25 H2
BGLY BD16 ....26 D4
HIPP HX3 ....60 A2
HWTH BD22 ....32 A1
Leeming St *BFD* BD1 ....2 E3
Lee Mount Gdns *HIPP* HX3 ....59 F4
Lee Mount Rd *HIPP* HX3 ....59 F4
Lees Bank Av *HWTH* BD22 ....23 F1
Lees Bank Dr *HWTH* BD22 * 23 F1
Lees Bank Hl *HWTH* BD22 ....23 F1
Lees Bank Rd *HWTH* BD22 ....23 F1
Lees Cl *CUL/OBY* BD13 ....24 B3
Lees La *HWTH* BD22 ....23 F1
Lees Moor Rd *CUL/OBY* BD13 ....24 B3
Lee St *BFD* BD1 ....2 C6
BRIG HD6 ....71 F4
CUL/OBY BD13 ....52 C6
Leesworth Ct *HWTH* BD22 * 23 F1
Legrams Av *GTHN* BD7 ....46 A2
Legrams La *GTHN* BD7 ....46 B1
Legrams Mill La *GTHN* BD7 ....38 D5
Legrams St *GTHN* BD7 ....38 D5
Leicester St *BOW* BD4 ....47 H5
Leicester Ter *HIPP* HX3 ....68 C4
Leigh St *RPDN/SBR* HX6 ....67 F3
Leith St *KGHY* BD21 ....7 F5
Le Mar Vw *HIPP* HX3 ....69 F2
Lemington Av *HFAX* HX1 ....4 D6
Lemon St *HFAX* HX1 ....4 C4
WBOW BD5 ....46 D4
Lennie St *KGHY* BD21 ....7 F5
Lennon Dr *GIR* BD8 ....38 C3
Lens Dr *BAIL* BD17 ....18 D2
Lentilfield St *HIPP* HX3 ....59 F5
Lentilfield Ter *HIPP* HX3 ....59 F5
Lenton Vls *IDLE* BD10 ....20 A5
Leonard's Pl *BGLY* BD16 ....16 C4
Leonard St *BGLY* BD16 ....16 D4
LM/WK BD12 ....63 E2
Leslie Av *YEA* LS19 ....11 G5
Lesmere Gv *GTHN* BD7 ....46 A5
Lessarna Ct *BOW* BD4 ....48 B2
Lever St *WBSY* BD6 ....54 B1
Levita Gv *BOW* BD4 ....48 C3
Levita Pl *BOW* BD4 ....48 C3
Lewis Cl *CUL/OBY* BD13 ....52 A1
Lewis St *HFAX* HX1 ....5 F2
Lexington Cl *BOW* BD4 ....56 A2
Leyburn Av *HIPP* HX3 ....59 E2
Leyburn Gv *BGLY* BD16 ....16 D2
Leyden Ri *WIL/AL* BD15 ....37 E4
Leyfield *BAIL* BD17 ....18 B3
Ley Fleaks Rd *IDLE* BD10 ....30 A2
Leyland Cft *HUDN* HD2 ....79 F5
Leylands Av *GIR* BD8 ....38 A1
Leylands Gv *HTON* BD9 ....38 A1
Leylands La *HTON* BD9 ....38 A1
KGHY BD21 ....7 G5
Leylands Ter *HTON* BD9 ....38 A1
Leys Cl *IDLE* BD10 ....19 H5
Leyside Dr *WIL/AL* BD15 ....37 E2
Leyton Crs *IDLE* BD10 * 30 A2
Leyton Dr *IDLE* BD10 ....30 A2
Leyton Gv *IDLE* BD10 ....30 A2
Leyton Ter *IDLE* BD10 ....30 A2
Ley Top La *WIL/AL* BD15 ....37 F4
Libbey St *GIR* BD8 ....38 C3
Lichen Cl *GTHN* BD7 ....46 A3
Lichfield Mt *ECHL* BD2 ....29 F5
Lidget Av *GTHN* BD7 ....46 A2
Lidget Pl *GTHN* BD7 ....46 A2
Lidget Ter *CLAY* BD14 ....45 G3
GTHN BD7 ....46 A2
Lightcliffe Rd *BRIG* HD6 ....71 F4
Lightcliffe Royd La
GTL/HWG HX4 ....74 B5
Lightowler Cl *HFAX* HX1 ....4 D3
Lightowler Rd *HFAX* HX1 ....4 D3
Lightowler St *WBSY* BD6 ....54 D1
Lilac Cl *BRIG* HD6 ....71 H5
Lilac Gv *BOW* BD4 ....54 C4
CLECK BD19 ....65 F4
SHPY BD18 ....29 E3
The Lilacs *GSLY* LS20 ....10 D2
Lilac St *HIPP* HX3 ....60 A2
Lilian St *BOW* BD4 ....48 B4
Lillands Av *BRIG* HD6 ....71 E1
Lillands La *BRIG* HD6 ....71 E1
Lillands Ter *BRIG* HD6 ....78 A1
Lilly La *HIPP* HX3 ....5 J5
Lilly St *RPDN/SBR* HX6 ....67 E5
Lily Cft *GIR* BD8 ....38 C2
Lilycroft Rd *GIR* BD8 ....38 D2
Lilycroft Wk *HTON* BD9 ....38 D2
Lily St *GIR* BD8 ....38 C3
Lilythorne Av *IDLE* BD10 ....30 B1
Lime Gv *AIRE* BD20 ....21 F2
Lime Gv *YEA* LS19 ....21 F2
Limes Av *HIPP* HX3 ....59 G4
Lime St *BGLY* BD16 ....16 C3
GTHN BD7 ....46 B3
HWTH BD22 ....22 D3
KGHY BD21 ....7 E4
Lime Tree Gv *BIRK/DRI* BD11 * 57 F3
Lime Tree Sq *SHPY* BD18 ....27 E5
Lincoln Ct *GIR* BD8 ....38 D3
Lincoln Rd *GIR* BD8 ....38 D3
Lincoln Wy *HIPP* HX3 ....59 G4
Lincs Wold *LVSG* WF15 ....73 G4
Linden Av *BFDE* BD3 ....40 D4
Linden Cl *GIR* BD8 ....25 E1
Linden Rd *KGHY* BD21 ....14 D1
Linden Rd *ELL* HX5 ....76 B5
HIPP HX3 ....68 D4

Lindisfarne Rd *SHPY* BD18 ....28 A2
Lindley Dr *GTHN* BD7 ....46 A5
Lindley Rd *WBOW* BD5 ....47 F4
Lindrick Gv *LUD/ILL* HX2 ....51 E3
Lindrick Wk *LUD/ILL* HX2 ....51 E3
Lindwell Av *GTL/HWG* HX4 ....75 H4
Lindwell Gv *GTL/HWG* HX4 ....75 H4
Lingard St *BFD* BD1 ....3 F3
Ling Bob *LUD/ILL* HX2 ....58 C5
BGLY BD16 ....26 D4
HIPP HX3 ....60 A2
HWTH BD22 ....32 A1
Lingdale Rd *LM/WK* BD12 ....54 B4
Lingfield Crs *WBSY* BD6 ....45 F5
Lingfield Dr *HWTH* BD22 ....13 H5
Lingfield Gv *WIL/AL* BD15 ....26 A4
Lingfield Rd *WIL/AL* BD15 ....25 H5
Lingfield Ter *WBSY* BD6 ....45 F5
Ling Park Ap *WIL/AL* BD15 ....25 H5
Ling Park Av *WIL/AL* BD15 ....25 H5
Ling Royd Av *LUD/ILL* HX2 ....58 C5
Lingwood Av *GIR* BD8 ....38 A4
Lingwood Rd *GIR* BD8 ....38 A4
Links Av *CLECK* BD19 ....64 C4
Linkway *BGLY* BD16 ....26 D2
Linnet Cl *GIR* BD8 * 37 F4
Linnet St *KGHY* BD21 ....7 F5
Linnhe Av *WBSY* BD6 ....54 A1
Linton Gv *BRIG* HD6 ....77 H3
Linton St *BOW* BD4 ....47 G3
HWTH BD22 ....13 G1
Lismore Rd *AIRE* BD20 ....21 E1
Lister Av *BOW* BD4 ....48 A4
Lister Dr *GIR* BD8 * 5 G4
Lister Gdns *GIR* BD8 ....38 D2
Listerhills Rd *BFD* BD1 ....2 A5
GTHN BD7 ....2 B5
Lister La *ECHL* BD2 ....39 H1
HFAX HX1 ....4 D4
Lister's Rd *HIPP* HX3 ....60 B5
Lister St *BOW* BD4 ....48 B4
BRIG HD6 ....71 F5
HFAX HX1 ....5 G2
Lister Vw *GIR* BD8 ....38 D3
Little Baines St *HFAX* HX1 ....4 C3
Littlebeck Dr *BGLY* BD16 ....17 F3
Little Bradley *GTL/HWG* HX4 ....75 H5
Little Cote *IDLE* BD10 ....19 H5
Little Cross St *WBOW* BD5 ....54 C2
Littlefield Wk *WBSY* BD6 ....54 C2
Little Hew Royd *IDLE* BD10 ....29 H2
Little Horton Gn *WBOW* BD5 ....46 D2
Little Horton La *WBOW* BD5 ....2 C7
Littlelands *BGLY* BD16 ....26 D2
Littlelands Ct *BGLY* BD16 * 26 D2
Little La *AIRE* BD20 ....20 A2
HTON BD9 ....38 A2
Littlemoor Gdns *LUD/ILL* HX2 ....50 D4
Littlemoor Rd *LUD/ILL* HX2 ....50 D4
Little Pk *IDLE* BD10 ....30 A1
Little Wood Dr *WBSY* BD6 ....54 D3
Little Wood St *CUL/OBY* BD13 ....68 C2
Little Woodhouse *BRIG* HD6 ....78 B2
Littondale Cl *BAIL* BD17 ....19 F2
Litton Rd *HWTH* BD22 ....13 G4
Livingstone Cl *ECHL* BD2 ....29 E5
Livingstone Rd *ECHL* BD2 ....29 E5
Livingstone St *HIPP* HX3 ....59 F4
Livingstone St North
LUD/ILL HX2 ....51 F5
Lloyds Dr *LM/WK* BD12 ....55 F4
Locarno Av *HTON* BD9 ....37 H2
Locherbie Gn *WIL/AL* BD15 * 36 D3
Lochy Rd *WBSY* BD6 ....54 A1
Locksley Rd *BRIG* HD6 ....79 E2
The Locks *BGLY* BD16 ....16 C2
Lock St *HIPP* HX3 * 5 K6
Lock Vw *ELL* HX5 ....76 D3
Lockwood St *LM/WK* BD12 ....55 F5
SHPY BD18 ....28 B1
WBSY BD6 ....54 B1
Lode Pit La *BGLY* BD16 ....17 G2
Lodge Av *ELL* HX5 ....76 C4
Lodge Dr *ELL* HX5 ....77 F4
Lodge Ga *GIR*
CUL/OBY BD13 ....36 C5
Lodge Hl *BAIL* BD17 ....18 A3
Lodge Pl *ELL* HX5 * 77 F4
Lodge St *CUL/OBY* BD13 ....24 C3
Lodore Pl *ECHL* BD2 ....40 A1
Lodore Rd *ECHL* BD2 ....39 H1
Lombard St *HFAX* HX1 * 4 B2
YEA LS19 ....21 F2
London La *YEA* LS19 ....11 H4
London Rd *RPDN/SBR* HX6 ....67 G5
London St *YEA* LS19 ....11 H4
Longacre La *HWTH* BD22 ....23 E1
Longacres *HWTH* BD22 ....23 E1
Longbottom Av
RPDN/SBR HX6 ....66 B5
Longbottom Ter *HIPP* HX3 * 69 F4
Long Cl *LM/WK* BD12 ....63 C1
Longcroft *KGHY* BD21 ....7 F5
Longcroft Pl *BFD* BD1 ....3 F3
Long Fallas Crs *BRIG* HD6 ....78 B4
Longfield Av *HIPP* HX3 ....60 D4
Longford Dr *BOW* BD4 ....48 B4
Longford Ter *GTHN* BD7 ....46 A3
Long Heys *GTL/HWG* HX4 ....75 H5
Longhouse Dr *CUL/OBY* BD13 ....34 C4
Longhouse La *CUL/OBY* BD13 ....34 C4
Long House Rd *LUD/ILL* HX2 ....50 B4
Longlands Dr *HWTH* BD22 ....23 E1
Longlands Dr *HWTH* BD22 ....23 E1
Longlands St *BFD* BD1 ....2 E3
Long La *BGLY* BD16 ....15 F5
CUL/OBY BD13 ....58 D3
HIPP HX3 ....68 D5
HTON BD9 ....37 C2
WIL/AL BD15 ....36 A5
Long Lee La *KGHY* BD21 ....14 C1

Long Lee Ter KGHY BD21 ....14 D1
Long Mdw ECHL BD2 ....29 F5
Long Preston Cha IDLE BD10 * 30 D2
Long Rdg BRIG HD6 ....78 B4
Long Rw LM/WK BD12 ....55 E5
Longroyd IDLE BD10 ....29 G1
Long Royd Dr BAIL BD17 ....19 F2
Longroyde Cl BRIG HD6 ....78 A3
Longroyde Gv BRIG HD6 ....78 A3
Longroyde Rd BRIG HD6 ....78 A2
Longside La GTHN BD7 ....46 D1
Long St BOW BD4 ....48 A2
Long Wall ELL HX5 ....76 B5
Longwood Av BGLY BD16 ....16 B1
Longwood Cl HIPP HX3 ....68 B5
Longwood Vw BGLY BD16 ....16 B1
Lonsdale St BFDE BD3 ....3 J3
Lord La HWTH BD22 ....22 C1
Lordsfield Pl BOW BD4 ....56 C1
Lord's La BRIG HD6 ....78 C2
Lord St HFAX HX1 ....5 F4
KGHY BD21 ....7 F4
RPDN/SBR HX6 ....67 F3
Loris St BOW BD4 ....56 C1
Lorne St BOW BD4 ....48 A4
HWTH BD22 ....23 G1
KGHY BD21 ....7 H3
Loughrigg St WBOW BD5 ....47 F4
Louisa St IDLE BD10 * 30 A1
Louis Av WBOW BD5 ....46 D3
Love La HFAX HX1 ....5 F6
Low Ash Av SHPY BD18 ....29 E2
Low Ash Crs SHPY BD18 ....29 F2
Low Ash Dr SHPY BD18 ....29 E2
Low Ash Gv SHPY BD18 ....29 E2
Low Ash Rd SHPY BD18 ....29 F2
Low Bank Dr HWTH BD22 ....12 C3
Low Bank La HWTH BD22 ....12 C3
Low Banks AIRE BD20 * 8 A1
Low Bank St PDSY/CALV LS28 ....41 H1
Low Cl BGLY BD16 ....17 E4
Lowell Av GTHN BD7 ....46 A2
Lower Ashgrove WBOW BD5 ....2 B7
Lower Clifton St
RPDN/SBR HX6 * 67 F4
Lower Clyde St RPDN/SBR HX6 ....67 E5
Lower Cow Cl LM/WK BD12 * 63 G3
Lower Cross St HFAX HX1 ....5 J2
Lower Crow Nest Dr BRIG HD6 ....71 G1
Lower Edge Rd ELL HX5 ....77 E4
Lower Ellistones
GTL/HWG HX4 * 75 F4
Lower Finkil St BRIG HD6 ....70 D3
Lower Fold BRIG HD6 ....78 A5
Lower George St WBSY BD6 * 54 C1
Lower Globe St GIR BD8 ....38 D4
Lower Gra HUDN HD2 ....79 F5
Lower Grattan Rd BFD BD1 ....2 A5
Lower Green Av CLECK BD19 ....63 G5
Lower Heights Rd
CUL/QBY BD13 ....35 H4
Lower Holme BAIL BD17 ....18 D5
Lower House Cl IDLE BD10 ....19 G5
Lower Kipping La
CUL/QBY BD13 ....44 A1
Lower Kirkgate HFAX HX1 ....5 K4
BFD BD1 ....2 D5
Lower La BIRK/DRI BD11 ....56 C5
BOW BD4 ....48 B3
Lower Lark Hl CLECK BD19 ....73 E1
Lower Newlands BRIG HD6 ....78 C2
Lower Quarry Rd HUDN HD2 ....79 H4
Lower Range HIPP HX3 ....59 H4
Lower Rushton Rd BFDE BD3 ....40 D5
Lower School St LM/WK BD12 ....54 D4
SHPY BD18 * 28 A1
Lowertown HWTH BD22 ....32 D2
Lower Westfield Rd GIR BD8 * 38 B3
Lower Wyke Gn LM/WK BD12 ....62 C5
Lower Wyke La LM/WK BD12 ....62 D5
Loweswater Av WBSY BD6 ....54 A4
Lowfield Cl LM/WK BD12 ....55 F5
Lowfields Cl ELL HX5 ....76 D3
Lowfields Wy ELL HX5 ....76 D3
Low Fold CLECK BD19 ....63 G5
ECHL BD2 ....39 G2
Low Gn GTHN BD7 ....46 B4
YEA LS19 ....21 H3
Low Green Ter GTHN BD7 ....46 C4
Low Laithes RPDN/SBR HX6 ....66 D5
Low La BRIG HD6 ....71 H2
CLAY BD14 ....44 D2
CUL/QBY BD13 ....43 H4
Low Mill La KGHY BD21 ....7 G4
Low Mills GSLY LS20 * 10 D3
Low Moor St LM/WK BD12 * 55 E4
Low Moor Ter LUD/ILL HX2 ....67 G2
Lowry Vw KGHY BD21 ....7 F5
Low Spring Rd KGHY BD21 ....7 H5
Low St KGHY BD21 ....7 F4
Lowther St ECHL BD2 ....40 A3
Low Well Rd WBOW BD5 * 47 E4
Low Wd WIL/AL BD15 ....26 A5
Lucy Hall Dr BAIL BD17 ....17 H4
Lucy St HIPP HX3 ....5 K1
Luddenden La LUD/ILL HX2 ....66 A1
Ludlam St WBOW BD5 ....47 F2
Luke Rd WBOW BD5 ....46 D3
Lulworth Gv BOW BD4 ....48 C5
Lumb La GIR BD8 ....38 D3
HIPP HX3 ....59 G3
Lumbrook Cl HIPP HX3 ....61 F2
Lumby St IDLE BD10 * 30 A1
Lund St BGLY BD16 ....16 D3
GIR BD8 ....37 H5
KGHY BD21 ....7 F3
Lupton St GIR BD8 ....2 B1
Lustre St KGHY BD21 ....6 D4
Luther Wy ECHL BD2 ....39 G1
Luton St HFAX HX1 ....4 B3
KGHY BD21 ....7 E4
Lydbrook Pk HIPP HX3 ....75 F1
Lydgate HIPP HX3 ....60 D2
Lydgate Pk HIPP HX3 ....70 D1
Lydgate Pl PDSY/CALV LS28 ....31 F2
Lydgate St PDSY/CALV LS28 ....31 F2
Lydget Ct AIRE BD20 ....6 D2
Lymington Dr BOW BD4 ....48 D3
Lynch Av GTHN BD7 ....46 A4
Lyncroft ECHL BD2 ....29 G5
Lyndale Dr SHPY BD18 ....29 G2
Lyndale Rd BGLY BD16 ....17 F1
Lyndean Gdns IDLE BD10 ....29 H2
Lynden Av SHPY BD18 ....29 F1
Lynden Ct WBSY BD6 ....54 B3
Lyndhurst BGLY BD16 * 16 C2
Lyndhurst Av BRIG HD6 ....78 B4
Lyndhurst Cv WIL/AL BD15 ....37 F3
Lyndhurst Grove Rd BRIG HD6 ....78 B4
Lyndhurst Rd BRIG HD6 ....78 B3
Lyndon Ter BGLY BD16 ....16 D3
Lynfield Dr HTON BD9 ....37 G1
LVSG WF15 ....73 E3
Lynfield Mt SHPY BD18 ....29 F1
Lynmoor Ct IDLE BD10 ....29 H2
Lynnwood Gdns
PDSY/CALV LS28 ....49 H1
Lynsey Gdns BOW BD4 ....56 A3
Lynthorne Rd HTON BD9 ....28 D5
Lynton Av HTON BD9 ....38 A1
Lynton Dr AIRE BD20 ....8 A2
HTON BD9 ....37 H2
SHPY BD18 ....28 B2
Lynton Gv LUD/ILL HX2 ....51 E1
Lynton Ter CLECK BD19 * 64 C5
Lynton Vls HTON BD9 ....38 A2
Lynwood Av SHPY BD18 ....29 F1
Lynwood Cl BIRK/DRI BD11 ....57 G5
Lynwood Ct HWTH BD22 ....13 F1
Lynwood Crs HFAX HX1 ....4 A7
Lynwood Ms BOW BD4 ....49 E5
Lyon St CUL/QBY BD13 ....36 A5
CUL/QBY BD13 ....52 C1
Lysander Wy BGLY BD16 ....27 E3
Lytham Dr CUL/QBY BD13 ....45 E5
Lytton Rd GIR BD8 ....38 A4
Lytton St HIPP HX3 * 59 H4

M

Mabel Royd GTHN BD7 ....46 A2
Mackingstone Dr HWTH BD22 ....12 C3
Mackingstone La HWTH BD22 ....12 C3
Mackintosh Homes
LUD/ILL HX2 ....68 B4
Macturk Gv GIR BD8 * 38 B3
Maddocks St SHPY BD18 ....28 B1
Madison Av BOW BD4 ....56 D1
Madni Cl HFAX HX1 ....4 E4
Magnolia Dr WIL/AL BD15 ....26 C5
Magpie Cl WBSY BD6 ....53 F1
Maidstone St BFDE BD3 ....40 B5
Maidwell Wy WBSY BD6 ....54 B4
Main Rd AIRE BD20 ....9 E3
CUL/QBY BD13 ....34 C4
Mainspring Rd WIL/AL BD15 ....25 H4
Main St BAIL BD17 ....20 B1
BGLY BD16 ....16 C3
BGLY BD16 ....27 E3
HWTH BD22 ....22 D2
LM/WK BD12 ....55 F4
LM/WK BD12 ....62 D1
WIL/AL BD15 ....25 H5
Maister Pl HWTH BD22 ....12 C3
Maitland Cl WIL/AL BD15 ....37 E5
Maize St HWTH BD22 * 13 H2
Malham Av BRIG HD6 ....77 H3
HTON BD9 ....37 F1
Malham Rd BRIG HD6 ....77 H4
Mallard Cl IDLE BD10 ....30 B4
Mallard Ct GIR BD8 ....37 F5
Mallard Vw HWTH BD22 ....32 D2
Mallory Cl GTHN BD7 ....38 A5
Malmesbury Cl BOW BD4 ....48 D5
Malsis Crs KGHY BD21 * 6 D5
Malsis Rd KGHY BD21 ....6 D5
Maltings Rd LUD/ILL HX2 ....58 C3
Malt Kiln La CUL/QBY BD13 ....43 G2
Malton St HIPP HX3 ....59 H3
RPDN/SBR HX6 ....67 E3
Malt St HWTH BD22 * 13 H2
Malvern Brow HTON BD9 ....37 G2
Malvern Gv HTON BD9 ....37 G3
Malvern Rd HTON BD9 ....37 G3
Manchester Rd WBOW BD5 ....47 E4
Mandale Gv WBSY BD6 ....53 G2
Mandale Rd WBSY BD6 ....53 G2
Mandeville Crs WBSY BD6 ....54 A2
Manley St BRIG HD6 ....71 F5
Mannheim Rd HTON BD9 ....38 B2
Manningham La GIR BD8 ....38 D2
Mannville Gv HWTH BD22 ....6 D5
Mannville Pl HWTH BD22 ....6 D5
Mannville Rd KGHY BD21 ....13 H1
Mannville St HWTH BD22 ....6 D5
Mannville Ter GTHN BD7 ....2 B7
Mannville Wk HWTH BD22 * 6 D5
Mannville Wy HWTH BD22 * 6 D5
Manor Cl GIR BD8 ....37 G4
HIPP HX3 ....68 C4
YEA LS19 ....11 G4
Manor Ct BGLY BD16 * 26 D2
Manor Dr BGLY BD16 ....26 D2
HIPP HX3 ....68 C4
Manor Farm Cl BGLY BD16 ....27 E3
Manor Fold BGLY BD16 ....27 E3
Manor Gdns CUL/QBY BD13 ....24 C4
Manor Gv AIRE BD20 ....8 B3
Manor Heath Rd HIPP HX3 ....68 C4
Manor House Rd WIL/AL BD15 ....25 H3
Manor La SHPY BD18 ....28 C2
Manorley La HIPP HX3 ....53 H4
Manor Pk GIR BD8 ....37 G4
HWTH BD22 ....12 D4
Manor Park Gdns CLECK BD19 ....65 F2
Manor Rd AIRE BD20 ....6 D1
BGLY BD16 ....27 E2
Manor Rw BFD BD1 ....2 C3
WBSY BD6 ....54 D3
Manor Sq YEA LS19 ....11 G4
Manor St CLECK BD19 ....72 C2
ECHL BD2 ....40 A1
Manor Ter ECHL BD2 ....40 A1
Manscombe Rd WIL/AL BD15 ....37 F3
Mansel Ms BOW BD4 ....56 D1
Manse St BFDE BD3 ....40 B5
Mansfield Av BGLY BD16 ....17 F1
Mansfield Rd GIR BD8 ....38 D2
Mansion La HIPP HX3 ....68 D4
Manywells Brow
CUL/QBY BD13 ....24 B5
Manywells Crs CUL/QBY BD13 ....24 C4
Manywells La CUL/QBY BD13 ....24 A4
Maple Av BFDE BD3 ....40 D4
HWTH BD22 ....13 E4
Maple Gv AIRE BD20 ....6 D2
CLECK BD19 ....65 F4
Maple St HFAX HX1 ....4 B7
Marbridge Ct WBSY BD6 ....46 C5
Marchbank Rd BFDE BD3 ....40 B4
March Cote La BGLY BD16 ....26 D3
Marchwood Gv CLAY BD14 ....45 G2
Marcia Cl IDLE BD10 ....30 B3
Margaret St AIRE BD20 ....6 D3
HFAX HX1 ....4 E4
Margate Rd BOW BD4 ....47 H3
Margate St RPDN/SBR HX6 ....66 D5
Marion Dr SHPY BD18 ....28 D2
Marion St BGLY BD16 * 16 D3
BRIG HD6 ....71 F4
GTHN BD7 ....38 D5
Mark Cl IDLE BD10 ....30 B1
Market Ar CLECK BD19 * 73 H1
Market Balcony HFAX HX1 * 5 H4
Market Ct CUL/QBY BD13 ....44 B1
Market Pl CLECK BD19 ....73 H1
KGHY BD21 ....7 F4
Market Sq SHPY BD18 ....28 C1
Market St BFD BD1 ....2 D5
BGLY BD16 ....16 C3
BRIG HD6 ....78 C1
CLECK BD19 ....73 H1
CUL/QBY BD13 ....44 B1
HFAX HX1 ....5 H4
KGHY BD21 ....7 F5
SHPY BD18 ....28 C2
Markfield Av LM/WK BD12 ....54 D5
Markfield Cl LM/WK BD12 ....54 D5
Markfield Crs LM/WK BD12 ....54 D5
Markfield Dr LM/WK BD12 ....54 D5
Markham Av YEA LS19 ....21 H1
Markham Crs YEA LS19 ....21 H1
Markham Cft YEA LS19 ....21 H1
Mark St WBOW BD5 ....47 F4
Marland Rd KGHY BD21 ....7 H3
Marlborough Av HIPP HX3 ....68 C4
Marlborough Rd GIR BD8 ....38 D3
SHPY BD18 ....28 B2
Marlborough St KGHY BD21 ....7 G3
Marldon Rd HIPP HX3 ....60 D4
Marley Cl GIR BD8 ....37 H4
Marley Ct BGLY BD16 ....9 E4
Marley La CUL/QBY BD13 ....44 B4
Marley Rd KGHY BD21 ....8 A3
Marley St BFDE BD3 ....3 G5
KGHY BD21 ....7 E5
Marley Vw BGLY BD16 ....9 E4
Marlott Rd SHPY BD18 ....29 E1
Marlow St KGHY BD21 ....7 H3
Marmion Av GIR BD8 ....37 F5
Marne Av CLAY BD14 ....45 F4
Marne Crs IDLE BD10 ....30 A2
Marquis Av LM/WK BD12 ....56 A5
Marriner Rd KGHY BD21 ....7 F5
Marriner's Dr HTON BD9 ....28 C5
Marriner's Wk KGHY BD21 ....14 B1
Marriner Wk KGHY BD21 ....14 B1
Marsh PDSY/CALV LS28 ....41 H5
Marshall St AIRE BD20 ....7 E2
YEA LS19 ....11 G4
Marsh Ct PDSY/CALV LS28 ....41 H5
Marsh Delves La HIPP HX3 ....69 G2
Marshfield Pl WBOW BD5 ....47 E4
Marshfield St WBOW BD5 ....47 E4
Marsh Gv WBOW BD5 ....46 D4
Marsh La BIRK/DRI BD11 ....57 F5
HIPP HX3 ....69 G2
HWTH BD22 ....22 D5
Marsh St CLECK BD19 ....73 H2
WBOW BD5 ....47 E5
Marsh Ter PDSY/CALV LS28 ....41 H5
Marshway HFAX HX1 ....4 D2
Marsland Ct CLECK BD19 ....64 C3
Marsland Pl BFDE BD3 ....40 C5
Marston Cl CUL/QBY BD13 ....52 C1
Marten Rd WBOW BD5 ....46 D4
Martin Ct WBSY BD6 ....53 F1
Martin Green La GTL/HWG HX4 ....75 F4
Martin St BRIG HD6 * 71 G5
Martlett Dr WBOW BD5 ....47 G5
Marton Ct BFDE BD3 ....40 C5
Mary St BOW BD4 ....48 B2
BRIG HD6 ....71 F4
CUL/QBY BD13 ....34 D3
CUL/QBY BD13 ....44 A1
HWTH BD22 ....32 D2
LM/WK BD12 ....62 D1
SHPY BD18 ....28 A1
Mary St Caravan Site
BOW BD4 ....48 B2
Maryville Av BRIG HD6 ....71 E3
Masefield Av HTON BD9 ....37 F1
Masefield St GSLY LS20 ....11 E3
Masham Pl HTON BD9 ....38 A2
Masonic St HFAX HX1 ....67 H2
Massey Flds HWTH BD22 ....23 E1
Master La LUD/ILL HX2 ....68 A4
Matlock St HIPP HX3 ....59 F4
Matthew Cl AIRE BD20 ....7 H2
Maude Av BAIL BD17 ....18 D4
Maude Crs RPDN/SBR HX6 ....66 B5
Maude St GTL/HWG HX4 ....76 A4
HIPP HX3 ....59 F1
Maudsley St BFDE BD3 ....3 H5
Maud St BFDE BD3 ....3 J6
Maurice Av BRIG HD6 ....71 E4
Mavis St BFDE BD3 ....3 J4
Mawcroft Cl YEA LS19 ....21 F1
Mawcroft Grange Dr YEA LS19 ....21 F1
Mawson St SHPY BD18 ....28 A1
Maw St BOW BD4 ....47 G2
Maxwell Rd WBSY BD6 ....54 A2
May Av CUL/QBY BD13 ....44 B1
Mayfair WBOW BD5 ....47 E3
Mayfair Wy BOW BD4 ....48 C2
Mayfield Av BRIG HD6 ....62 C5
HFAX HX1 ....4 C6
LM/WK BD12 ....62 D2
Mayfield Dr AIRE BD20 ....8 D3
HFAX HX1 ....4 C6
Mayfield Gdns HFAX HX1 ....4 C6
Mayfield Gv BAIL BD17 ....19 E3
BRIG HD6 ....62 C5
HFAX HX1 ....4 C6
WIL/AL BD15 ....25 G3
Mayfield Mt HFAX HX1 * 4 C6
Mayfield Pl LM/WK BD12 ....62 D2
Mayfield Ri LM/WK BD12 ....63 E2
Mayfield Rd KGHY BD21 ....7 E3
Mayfield St HFAX HX1 ....4 D6
Mayfield Ter CLAY BD14 ....45 F3
HFAX HX1 ....4 B3
LM/WK BD12 ....63 E2
Mayfield Ter South HFAX HX1 * 4 D6
Mayfield Vw LM/WK BD12 ....63 E2
Mayo Av WBOW BD5 ....47 E5
Mayo Crs WBOW BD5 ....55 F1
Mayo Dr WBOW BD5 ....55 F1
Mayo Gv WBOW BD5 ....55 F1
Mayo Rd WBOW BD5 ....55 F1
Mayster Gv BRIG HD6 ....77 H4
Mayster Rd BRIG HD6 ....77 H4
May St CLECK BD19 ....64 C5
HWTH BD22 ....23 E3
KGHY BD21 ....7 F3
Maythorne Crs CLAY BD14 ....45 G3
Maythorne Dr CLAY BD14 ....45 H3
May Tree Cl CLAY BD14 ....45 G2
Mayville Av AIRE BD20 ....8 C3
Mazebrook Av CLECK BD19 ....64 D3
Mazebrook Crs CLECK BD19 ....64 D3
McMahon Dr CUL/QBY BD13 ....45 F5
McMillan Gdns WBSY BD6 ....55 E3
Meadowbank Av
WIL/AL BD15 ....37 E3
Meadow Cl BGLY BD16 ....15 G5
HIPP HX3 ....53 G4
Meadow Ct BRIG HD6 ....79 F1
WIL/AL BD15 ....26 D5
Meadow Crs HIPP HX3 ....58 D3
Meadow Cft HWTH BD22 ....6 B5
Meadow Croft Cl IDLE BD10 ....29 G1
Meadowcroft Ri BOW BD4 ....56 B2
Meadow Dr HIPP HX3 ....58 D3
Meadowlands CLECK BD19 ....63 F4
Meadow La HIPP HX3 ....58 D3
Meadow Park Crs
PDSY/CALV LS28 ....41 G2
Meadow Park Dr
PDSY/CALV LS28 ....41 G2
Meadow Rd IDLE BD10 ....30 D1
The Meadows WBOW BD5 ....54 D1
Meadow Vw HWTH BD22 ....13 E4
LM/WK BD12 ....62 D4
Meadow Wk HIPP HX3 ....58 D3
Mead Vw BOW BD4 * 48 D4
Meadway WBSY BD6 ....53 H4
Mearclough Rd
RPDN/SBR HX6 ....67 G4
Medeway PDSY/CALV LS28 ....41 H2
Medley La HIPP HX3 ....60 C1
Medway CUL/QBY BD13 ....52 C2
Meggison Gv WBOW BD5 ....46 D3
Megnaway WBOW BD5 ....47 F3
Melba Rd WBOW BD5 ....46 C4
Melbourne Gv BFDE BD3 ....40 D4
Melbourne Pl WBOW BD5 ....47 E2
Melbourne St HIPP HX3 ....59 F4
SHPY BD18 ....28 B1
Melbourne Ter WBOW BD5 ....47 E2
Melcombe Wk BOW BD4 ....48 D3
Meldon Wy WBSY BD6 ....53 F1
Melford St BOW BD4 ....48 B5
Mellor St BRIG HD6 * 78 C1
HFAX HX1 ....68 B3
Melrose St GTHN BD7 ....46 B3
HIPP HX3 ....59 F4
Melrose Ter ELL HX5 * 76 C5
Melton Ms HWTH BD22 ....23 E2
Melton Ter IDLE BD10 ....30 D4
Melville St GTHN BD7 ....38 D5
Mendip Wy LM/WK BD12 ....54 C4
Menin Dr BAIL BD17 ....18 D1
Menstone St GIR BD8 ....38 D4
Merchants Ct BOW BD4 ....47 H2
Merlin Ct KGHY BD21 ....14 A1
Merlin Gv GIR BD8 ....37 F5
Merlinwood Dr BAIL BD17 ....19 E2
Merrivale Rd WIL/AL BD15 ....36 D4
Merrydale Rd BOW BD4 ....55 H4
Merton Dr PDSY/CALV LS28 ....41 H2
Merton Fold WBOW BD5 ....47 F3
Merton Gdns PDSY/CALV LS28 ....41 H2
Merton Rd GTHN BD7 ....46 D2
Merville Av BAIL BD17 ....18 D1
Metcalfe St BOW BD4 ....48 A3
Methuen Ov LM/WK BD12 ....62 D4
Miall St HFAX HX1 ....4 C2
Mickledore Cl GTHN BD7 * 45 H4
Mickledore Rdg GTHN BD7 ....45 H4
Micklefield Ct YEA LS19 ....21 G2
Micklefield La YEA LS19 ....21 F2
Micklefield Ms YEA LS19 * 21 F2
Micklefield Rd YEA LS19 ....21 G2
Micklemoss Dr CUL/QBY BD13 ....43 H5
Micklethwaite Dr
CUL/QBY BD13 ....52 B2
Micklethwaite La BGLY BD16 ....9 F5
Middlebrook Cl GIR BD8 ....37 H5
Middlebrook Crs GIR BD8 ....45 G1
Middlebrook Dr GIR BD8 ....37 G5
Middlebrook Hl GIR BD8 ....37 G5
Middlebrook Ri GIR BD8 ....37 G5
Middlebrook Vw GIR BD8 ....37 H5
Middlebrook Wk GIR BD8 ....37 H5
Middlebrook Wy GIR BD8 ....45 G1
Middle Dean St
GTL/HWG HX4 ....75 H4
Middlegate Ct BOW BD4 ....56 A2
Middleham Ct BOW BD4 * 48 D4
Middle La CLAY BD14 ....45 F2
Middleton Ct LVSG WF15 ....73 H4
Middleton St GIR BD8 ....38 C3
Midgeham Gv BGLY BD16 ....15 F5
Midgeley Rd BAIL BD17 ....18 B5
Midland Hl BGLY BD16 ....16 C3
Midland Rd BAIL BD17 ....19 E4
GIR BD8 ....39 E2
HTON BD9 ....28 D4
Midland Ter ECHL BD2 ....39 E2
HTON BD9 ....28 D4
KGHY BD21 ....7 F3
Mid Point BFDE BD3 ....41 E4
Midway Av BGLY BD16 ....26 D2
Mile Cross Gdns HFAX HX1 ....67 H2
Mile Cross Pl HFAX HX1 ....67 H2
Mile Cross Rd HFAX HX1 ....67 H2
Mile Cross Ter HFAX HX1 ....67 H2
Miles Hill Crs BOW BD4 ....56 B1
Miles Hill Dr BOW BD4 ....56 B1
Mile Thorn St HFAX HX1 ....4 B4
Milford Gv CLECK BD19 ....65 F2
Milford Pl HTON BD9 ....38 B1
Millbeck Cl GIR BD8 ....45 F1
Millbeck Dr BGLY BD16 ....15 F5
Mill Carr Hill Rd BOW BD4 ....56 A4
Mill Ct HWTH BD22 ....32 D2
Millergate BFD BD1 ....2 C5
Millersdale Cl BOW BD4 ....55 H3
Mill Field Rd BGLY BD16 ....27 E2
Millgate ELL HX5 ....76 C4
Mill Gv BRIG HD6 ....71 E4
Millhaven Ms GIR BD8 ....38 D2
Mill Hey HWTH BD22 ....23 E2
Mill Hl HWTH BD22 ....22 D2
Mill Hill La BRIG HD6 ....70 D4
BRIG HD6 ....79 G2
Mill Hill Top BGLY BD16 ....25 G1
Mill House Ri BOW BD4 * 56 A1
Milligan Av ECHL BD2 * 29 G4
Milligan Ct BGLY BD16 ....15 F5
Mill La BIRK/DRI BD11 ....57 F4
BRIG HD6 ....78 C1
CLECK BD19 ....64 C2
CUL/QBY BD13 ....43 H5
HIPP HX3 ....59 G3
HWTH BD22 ....12 C4
HWTH BD22 ....32 D1
LUD/ILL HX2 ....50 B3
WBOW BD5 ....47 F2
Millmoor Cl HTON BD9 ....37 G2
Mill Royd St BRIG HD6 ....78 C1
Millside Wy HIPP HX3 ....69 E5
Millstream Cl AIRE BD20 ....8 B2
Mill St BFD BD1 ....2 E3
CUL/QBY BD13 ....24 C3
HIPP HX3 ....75 F2
WBSY BD6 ....54 B1
Milner Cl GTL/HWG HX4 ....75 H4
Milner Ing LM/WK BD12 ....62 D1
Milner La GTL/HWG HX4 ....75 H4
Milner Rd BAIL BD17 ....18 C5
Milner's Rd YEA LS19 ....11 E5
Milner St HFAX HX1 ....4 E3
Milne St GTHN BD7 * 38 D5
Milton Av RPDN/SBR HX6 ....67 F3
Milton Pl HFAX HX1 ....4 E4
Milton St CUL/QBY BD13 ....34 D4
GTHN BD7 ....38 D5
RPDN/SBR HX6 ....67 E3
Milton Ter CLECK BD19 ....64 B5
HFAX HX1 * 4 E4
Minnie St HWTH BD22 ....22 D3
KGHY BD21 ....7 E5
Minorca Mt CUL/QBY BD13 ....34 C3
Minster Dr BOW BD4 ....48 C2
Mint St ECHL BD2 ....40 A2
Mirfield Av ECHL BD2 ....29 H4
Miry La LVSG WF15 ....73 F4
YEA LS19 ....11 G4
Mission St BRIG HD6 ....78 D2
The Mistal IDLE BD10 ....29 G1
Mistral Cl LM/WK BD12 ....62 D3
Mistral Gv LVSG WF15 ....73 E3
Mitcham Dr HTON BD9 ....38 B2
Mitchell Cl IDLE BD10 ....20 B5
Mitchell La IDLE BD10 ....20 B5
Mitchell Sq WBOW BD5 ....47 F3
Mitchell St BRIG HD6 ....71 F5
KGHY BD21 ....7 G3
RPDN/SBR HX6 ....67 F4
Mitchell Ter BGLY BD16 ....16 C4
Mitre Ct BOW BD4 ....48 C4
Mitton St WBOW BD5 ....46 D4
Mixenden Cl LUD/ILL HX2 ....50 B5
Mixenden La LUD/ILL HX2 ....50 C4
Mixenden Rd LUD/ILL HX2 ....50 B5
Moat Crs IDLE BD10 ....30 B1
Moffat Cl WBSY BD6 ....54 A3
Moffatt Cl LUD/ILL HX2 ....59 E2
Mond Av BFDE BD3 ....40 C3
Monk Barn Cl BGLY BD16 * 16 D2
Monk Ings Av BTLY WF17 ....65 H4
Monk St GTHN BD7 ....38 D5
Monson Av PDSY/CALV LS28 ....31 G3
Montague St RPDN/SBR HX6 ....66 D5
WBOW BD5 ....46 D4
Monterey Dr WIL/AL BD15 ....36 C1
Montrose St ECHL BD2 ....29 E5
Montserrat Rd BOW BD4 ....57 E1
Moody St BOW BD4 ....47 G2
Moorbottom CLECK BD19 ....73 E2
Moor Bottom La BGLY BD16 ....16 D3
GTL/HWG HX4 ....75 F2
KGHY BD21 ....14 A4
Moor Bottom Rd LUD/ILL HX2 ....51 E4
Moor Close Av CUL/QBY BD13 ....51 H2

Moor Close Farm Ms
CUL/QBY BD13.....................51 F4
Moor Close La CUL/QBY BD13 ..51 H2
Moor Close Pde
CUL/QBY BD13.....................51 H1
Moor Cls Rd CUL/QBY BD13 ....51 H1
Moor Cft BGLY BD16...................17 E1
Moorcroft Av BFDE BD3.............40 C3
HWTH BD22 ....13 E3
Moorcroft Dr BOW BD4..............57 E1
Moorcroft Rd BOW BD4..............57 E2
Moorcroft Ter BOW BD4.............57 E2
Moor Dr HWTH BD22 ....12 D3
Moore Av HTON BD9 ....46 A5
Moore St KGHY BD21.................. 7 F5
Moore Vw HWTH BD22 ....13 E3
Moorfield Crs YEA LS19.............11 H5
Moorfield Dr BAIL BD17 ....18 D1
HWTH BD22 ....13 E3
Moorfield Gdns
PDSY/CALV LS28......................49 H1
Moorfield Gv PDSY/CALV LS28...49 H1
Moorfield Pl IDLE BD10..............30 A1
Moorfield Rd BGLY BD16............26 D2
Moorfield St HFAX HX1 .... 4 D7
Moorfield Wy CLECK BD19.........72 B1
Moorgate BAIL BD17..................40 C3
Moorgate Av BFDE BD3.............40 C3
Moorgate St HFAX HX1*............. 4 B7
Moor Gv HIPP HX3....................53 F3
Moorhead Crs SHPY BD18..........27 H2
Moorhead La SHPY BD18............27 H2
Moorhead Ter SHPY BD18..........27 H2
Moorhouse Av ECHL BD2...........29 H4
Moorhouse Cl BOW BD4.............57 E3
HWTH BD22 ....32 D1
Moorhouse La BIRK/DRI BD11....57 F3
GSLY LS20 ....10 D1
The Moorings IDLE BD10...........30 C1
Moorland Av BAIL BD17 ....19 E2
GSLY LS20 ....10 D2
Moorland Crs BAIL BD17............19 E3
ILK LS29 ....10 A1
Moorland Dr BIRK/DRI BD11......57 G5
CSLY LS20 ....10 D1
PDSY/CALV LS28......................41 F4
Moorland Gv PDSY/CALV LS28...41 F4
Moorland Pl LM/WK BD12 ....55 F5
Moorland Rd PDSY/CALV LS28...41 F3
Moorlands Av BFDE BD3............40 C3
BIRK/DRI BD11.........................57 F3
HWTH BD22 ....13 G2
LUD/ILL HX2 ....58 D2
Moorlands Ct GTL/HWG HX4 *...75 C3
Moorlands Dr LUD/ILL HX2........58 D3
Moorlands Pl HFAX HX1 ....68 C3
GTL/HWG HX4 ....75 C3
Moorlands Rd BIRK/DRI BD11....57 F3
GTL/HWG HX4 ....75 C3
Moorland Ter KGHY BD21.......... 8 A5
Moorland Vw LM/WK BD12 ....55 F5
RPDN/SBR HX6 ....66 C5
Moor La CLECK BD19.................10 D1
GSLY LS20 ....10 D1
Moorlea Dr BAIL BD17...............19 E3
Moor Park Dr BFDE BD3.............40 C4
Moor Park Rd BFDE BD3 *..........40 B4
Moor Royd HIPP HX5.................54 B1
Moorside BAIL BD17..................19 E3
CLECK BD19 ....72 D2
HTON BD9 ....37 H2
Moorside Av BIRK/DRI BD11......57 F3
ECHL BD2 ....40 C2
Moorside Cl ECHL BD2...............40 B1
Moorside Cft ECHL BD2.............40 B1
Moorside Gdns ECHL BD2..........40 B1
LUD/ILL HX2 ....59 E1
Moorside Gv BFDE BD3..............40 B2
Moor Side La HWTH BD22..........22 A4
Moorside Pl BFDE BD3...............40 C5
Moorside Ri CLECK BD19...........73 E1
Moorside Rd BFDE BD3..............40 C5
ECHL BD2 ....30 B5
WIL/AL BD15 ....54 C4
Moorside St LM/WK BD12 ....54 C4
Moorside Ter ECHL BD2..............40 C2
Moor Stone Pl HIPP HX3 *..........53 F5
Moor St CUL/QBY BD13 *............52 B1
HWTH BD22 ....13 E3
Moor Ter ECHL BD2...................40 B2
Moorthorpe Av BFDE BD3...........40 C5
Moor Top Gdns LUD/ILL HX2.....50 D5
Moor Top Rd LM/WK BD12 ....54 A5
LUD/ILL HX2 ....58 A5
Moor Vw BOW BD4....................57 E1
Moor View Av SHPY BD18...........28 B1
Moor View Ct AIRE BD20 ....8 D4
IDLE BD10 * 19 H5
Moorview Dr SHPY BD18............29 C2
Moorview Gv SHPY BD21............14 C1
Moorville Av BFDE BD5...............40 D4
Moorville Dr BIRK/DRI BD11 ......57 F3
Moorway GSLY LS20...................10 D2
Moor Wy HWTH BD22.................12 D5
Moorwell Pl ECHL BD2...............40 A3
Moravian Pl WBOW BD5 * 47 E5
Moresby Rd WBOW BD5.............48 C5
Morley Av BFDE BD3..................40 C5
Morley Carr Rd LM/WK BD12.....55 E5
Morley St GTHN BD7................... 2 C6
Morningside GIR BD8.................38 C3
Morning St KGHY BD21..............14 A2

Mornington Rd BGLY BD16.........16 D3
Mornington St HWTH BD22........ 7 E3
Mornington Vls GIR BD8.............39 E3
Morpeth St CUL/QBY BD13 ....52 B1
GTHN BD7 ....38 D5
Mortimer Av BFDE BD3..............40 C3
Mortimer Rw BFDE BD3.............48 C1
Mortimer St CLECK BD19 *.........73 G1
GIR BD8 ....38 A4
Morton Gv AIRE BD20.................. 9 E5
Morton La AIRE BD20.................. 9 E4
Morton Rd BOW BD4..................48 C2
Morton Sq HIPP HX5..................46 D5
Mosley Cl HIPP HX3...................29 H4
Moser Av ECHL BD2...................29 H4
Moser Crs ECHL BD2..................29 H4
Moss Carr Av KGHY BD21...........15 E1
Moss Carr Gv KGHY BD21..........15 E1
Moss Carr Rd KGHY BD21..........15 E1
Mossdale Av HTON BD9.............37 F1
Moss Dr LUD/ILL HX2................50 D4
Moss La LUD/ILL HX2................50 D4
Moss Rw WIL/AL BD15...............25 H5
Moss Side CUL/QBY BD13...........35 H5
Mosstree Ct CUL/QBY BD13 *.....34 C4
Mossy Bank Cl CUL/QBY BD13...44 B5
Mostyn Gv WBSY BD6................54 B2
Mostyn Mt HIPP HX3..................59 F2
Motley La LUD/ILL HX2 ....10 D1
Moulson Ct WBOW BD5..............47 F4
Mountain Vw LUD/ILL HX2..........51 F4
SHPY BD18 ....29 E3
Mount Av ECHL BD2..................30 A4
LUD/ILL HX2 ....67 F1
Mount Crs CLECK BD19..............64 C5
ECHL BD2 ....67 F1
Mountfields HIPP HX3................61 H5
Mount Gdns CLECK BD19...........64 C5
Mount La BRIG HD6...................77 H4
Mountleigh Cl BOW BD4.............55 H4
Mount Pellon LUD/ILL HX2......... 4 A1
Mount Pellon Rd LUD/ILL HX2....58 D5
Mount Pl SHPY BD18.................29 E2
Mount Pleasant AIRE BD20.......... 8 D4
CUL/QBY BD13........................34 C4
GIR BD8 * 38 D2
GSLY LS20 ....10 D2
WBSY BD6 ....53 H3
Mount Pleasant Av HFAX HX1.... 4 C2
Mount Rd ECHL BD2..................30 A4
WBSY BD6 ....54 B1
Mount Royd GIR BD8.................38 D2
Mount St BFDE BD3...................... 3 E5
CLECK BD19 ....64 C5
ECHL BD2 ....30 A4
HFAX HX1 .... 5 F4
HWTH BD22 ....13 E3
RPDN/SBR HX6 ....67 E4
Mount St West LUD/ILL HX2 * 58 D5
Mount Tabor St
PDSY/CALV LS28 *...................41 H5
Mount Ter ECHL BD2..................30 A4
LUD/ILL HX2 ....58 D5
Mount Vernon Rd YEA LS19........21 H2
Mount Vw HWTH BD22..............12 C4
Mount Vw CLECK BD19 * 64 B5
Mowat Ct LVSG WF15................73 E5
Mowbray Cl CUL/QBY BD13........24 B4
Mozley Dr LUD/ILL HX2.............51 E4
Muffit La CLECK BD19................65 H5
Muff St BOW BD4......................48 A2
Muirhead Dr BOW BD4...............48 D5
Muirhead Dr BOW BD4...............48 D5
Muirhead Fold BOW BD4............48 D5
Mulberry St KGHY BD21 *............ 7 J3
Mulcture Hall Rd HFAX HX1 * 5 J3
Mulgrave St BFDE BD3 *.............. 3 J7
Mumford St WBOW BD5.............47 F4
Munby St GIR BD8.....................37 H5
Munster St BOW BD4.................48 A4
Munton Cl WBSY BD6 *...............53 H4
Murdoch St KGHY BD21.............. 8 A3
Murgatroyd St SHPY BD18..........28 C1
WBOW BD5 ....47 F5
Murray St WBOW BD5 * 46 D4
Museum Ct ECHL BD2................40 B2
Musgrave Dr ECHL BD2..............40 B2
Musgrave Mt ECHL BD2.............40 B2
Musgrave Rd ECHL BD2..............40 B2
Musselburgh St GTHN BD7.........38 D5
Mutton La WIL/AL BD15.............36 A2
Myers La ECHL BD2...................29 H5
Myers La ECHL BD2...................29 H5
Myrtle Av BGLY BD16 *...............16 C4
LUD/ILL HX2 ....58 D1
Myrtle Ct BGLY BD16.................16 C4
Myrtle Dr HWTH BD22 ....13 G5
LUD/ILL HX2 ....58 D1
Myrtle Gdns LUD/ILL HX2..........58 D1
Myrtle Gv BGLY BD16.................16 C4
LUD/ILL HX2 ....58 D1
Myrtle Pl BGLY BD16..................16 C4
LUD/ILL HX2 ....58 D1
Myrtle St BFDE BD3.................... 3 D5
BGLY BD16 ....16 D3
Mytholmes La HWTH BD22........22 D2

Nab End La ELL HX5...................76 B5
Nab La SHPY BD18.....................27 G2
Nab Wood Bank SHPY BD18.......27 H2
Nab Wood Cl SHPY BD18 *..........27 H2
Nab Wood Crs SHPY BD18..........27 H2
Nab Wood Dr BGLY BD16...........27 H2
Nab Wood Gdns SHPY BD18.......27 H2
Nab Wood Gv SHPY BD18...........27 H2
Nab Wood Mt SHPY BD18...........27 G2
Nab Wood Pl SHPY BD18............27 G2
Nab Wood Ri SHPY BD18............27 G2

Nab Wood Rd SHPY BD18...........27 G3
Nab Wood Ter SHPY BD18..........27 G2
Napier Rd BFDE BD3..................40 C5
ELL HX5 ....76 B5
Napier St BFDE BD3...................52 C1
ELL HX5 ....76 B5
Napier Ter BFDE BD3.................40 C5
Naples St GIR BD8.....................38 C3
Nares St HWTH BD22.................23 F1
KGHY BD21 .... 7 E4
Nares St Upper KGHY BD21*....... 7 E4
Narrow La KGHY BD21................15 G5
The Narrows BGLY BD16............15 G5
Naseby Rd CUL/QBY BD13.........52 C1
Nashville Rd HWTH BD22........... 6 D5
Nashville St HWTH BD22............ 6 D5
Nashville Ter HWTH BD22........... 6 D5
Natty Fields Cl LUD/ILL HX2.......50 D5
Natty La LUD/ILL HX2................50 D5
Nature Wy WBSY BD6.................53 H5
Navigation Cl ELL HX5...............76 D3
Navigation Rd HIPP HX3............. 5 K5
Naylor St HFAX HX1................... 4 A3
Nearcliffe Rd HTON BD9............37 G5
Near Crook IDLE BD10................19 C5
Necropolis Rd GTHN BD7...........46 A2
Ned Hill Rd LUD/ILL HX2............42 D5
Ned La BOW BD4......................49 E3
Nelson Pl LUD/ILL HX2..............58 D2
Nelson St BFD1 BD13.................12 B8
CUL/QBY BD13........................52 B1
HWTH BD22 ....23 F1
RPDN/SBR HX6 ....67 G4
WIL/AL BD15 ....37 F3
Nesfield St BFD1 BD1................. 2 B2
Nessfield Dr HWTH BD22...........13 G1
Nessfield Gv HWTH BD22...........13 G1
Nessfield Rd HWTH BD22...........13 G1
Netherby St BFDE BD3................ 3 K5
Nethercliffe Rd GSLY LS20..........10 C2
Netherfield Cl YEA LS19..............11 G4
Netherfield Gv CLECK BD19........10 C1
Netherfield Pl CLECK BD19........73 H1
Netherfield Rd CLECK BD19........10 C1
Netherhall Rd BAIL BD17............19 E3
Netherlands Av WBSY BD6..........54 D5
Netherlands Sq WBSY BD6.........54 D5
Nether Moor Vw BGLY BD16.......16 C5
Nettle Gv HIPP HX3...................60 C4
Neville Av BOW BD4...................56 A1
Neville Rd BOW BD4..................48 A3
Neville St CLECK BD19...............73 H2
KGHY BD21 * 7 G3
Nevill Gv HTON BD9..................37 G1
Newall St WBOW BD5................47 E3
Newark Rd BGLY BD16...............16 B1
Newark St BOW BD4..................47 H2
New Augustus St BFD1 BD1........ 3 F6
New Bank HIPP HX3.................... 5 K2
New Bank Ri BOW BD4...............48 C4
New Bbrighton BGLY BD16.........27 F5
New Bond St HFAX HX1.............. 5 F3
New Brunswick St HFAX HX1...... 5 F3
Newburn Rd GTHN BD7.............46 C2
Newbury Rd BRIG HD6...............78 A4
Newbury St HWTH BD22............ 7 E4
New Cl SHPY BD18....................27 G2
New Close Rd SHPY BD18..........27 G2
New Clough Rd
RPDN/SBR HX6 ....74 C1
New Cross St LM/WK BD12.........56 A5
WBOW BD5 * 47 F5
New Fold WBSY BD6...................53 H5
Newforth Gv WBOW BD5 *..........46 D5
Newhall Mt WBSY BD6...............55 C2
Newhall Rd ECHL BD2................40 A4
New Hey Rd BOW BD4................47 H3
New Holme Rd HWTH BD22.......23 E5
New House La CUL/QBY BD13....53 E2
Newill Cl WBOW BD5..................47 G5
New John St BFD1 BD1*.............. 2 C5
New Kirkgate SHPY BD18 *.........28 C1
New Laithe Rd WBSY BD6 *.........54 B5
Newlands YEA LS19...................11 F3
Newlands Av BFDE BD3..............40 C3
HIPP HX3 ....60 D1
RPDN/SBR HX6 ....66 B5
YEA LS19 ....11 F4
Newlands Cl BRIG HD6...............78 A1
Newlands Dr BGLY BD16............16 B1
HIPP HX3 ....60 D2
Newlands Gv HIPP HX3...............60 D2
Newlands Pl BFDE BD3................ 3 H2
Newlands Ri YEA LS19................11 F4
Newlands Rd LUD/ILL HX2.........67 E4
New La BOW BD4......................48 C1
BOW BD4 ....49 C5
CLECK BD19 ....72 D2
HIPP HX3 ....69 E4
HIPP HX3 ....75 C1
Newlay Cl IDLE BD10.................30 D2
New Line IDLE BD10..................30 D2
Newlyn Rd AIRE BD20................. 8 B2
Newman St BOW BD4.................48 A5
New Market Pl BFD1 BD1............ 2 D5
New Occupation La
PDSY/CALV LS28......................49 H1
New Otley Rd BFD3 BD3............. 3 G3
New Park Rd CUL/QBY BD13......32 A1
New Popplewell La
CLECK BD19 ....63 C5
Newport Pl GTHN BD7...............38 D4
Newport Rd GIR BD8..................38 D5
New Pudsey Sq
PDSY/CALV LS28......................41 H3
New Rd CUL/QBY BD13..............34 C4
GTL/HWG HX4.........................75 F4
HWTH BD22 .... 5 H5
New Rd East WBOW BD5............47 H1
New Rd Side YEA LS19...............21 G2
New Road Sq BRIG HD6 *...........77 H5

New Rw HTON BD9....................37 H2
Newroyd Rd WBOW BD5.............47 F5
Newsholme New Rd
HWTH BD22 ....12 B2
Newstead Av HFAX HX1..............67 H1
Newstead Cl HFAX HX1..............67 H1
Newstead Gv HFAX HX1..............67 H1
Newstead Heath HFAX HX1.........67 H1
Newstead Pl HFAX HX1..............67 H1
Newstead Ter HFAX HX1.............67 H1
Newstead Wk WBOW BD5 *........47 E3
New St BOW BD4.......................56 A2
BRIG HD6 ....71 C1
BRIG HD6 ....79 E1
CUL/QBY BD13........................34 C4
HIPP HX3 ....69 H4
HWTH BD22 ....30 A1
LM/WK BD12 ....56 A5
LUD/ILL HX2 ....67 E1
Newton Pk BRIG HD6.................71 E2
Newton Pl HFAX HX1.................67 H1
Newton St RPDN/SBR HX6 *.......67 E4
Newton Wy BAIL BD17 *.............18 D2
New Wy GSLY LS20....................10 D2
New Works Rd LM/WK BD12.......54 D5
Nibshaw La CLECK BD19............65 F5
Nibshaw Rd CLECK BD19...........65 F5
Nicholas Ct LUD/ILL HX2............65 F5
Nidderdale Wk BAIL BD17...........19 F2
Nidd St BFDE BD3...................... 3 K6
Nightingale La KGHY BD21 *....... 7 F3
Nightingale Wk BGLY BD16........17 F2
Nile Crs HWTH BD22.................23 F1
Nile St HWTH BD22...................23 F1
HWTH BD22 ....23 F1
Nina Rd GTHN BD7...................38 A7
Ninth Av LVSG WF15.................73 E5
Noble St GTHN BD7..................46 C2
Nog La HTON BD9.....................28 B5
The Nook CLECK BD19...............64 D5
RPDN/SBR HX6 ....67 E5
Norbeck Dr HWTH BD22............23 F1
Norbury Rd IDLE BD10...............30 D4
Norcliffe La HIPP HX3................69 H2
Norcroft Brow GTHN BD7............ 2 D6
Norcroft St BFD1 BD1.................38 D5
Norfolk Gdns BFD1 BD1.............. 2 B6
Norfolk Pl HFAX HX1.................. 4 C3
Norfolk St BGLY BD16................16 D3
Norham Gv LM/WK BD12............55 H4
Norland Rd RPDN/SBR HX6........67 E5
Norland St GTHN BD7................46 A4
Norland Town Rd
RPDN/SBR HX6 ....74 C1
Norland Vw RPDN/SBR HX6........74 C1
Norman Av ECHL BD2................30 A4
ELL HX5 ....76 D5
Norman Crs ECHL BD2...............30 A4
Norman Gv ECHL BD2...............30 A4
ELL HX5 * 76 D5
Norman La ECHL BD2................30 A4
Norman Mt ECHL BD2................30 A4
Norman St BGLY BD16 *.............16 D3
ELL HX5 ....76 D5
HFAX HX1 .... 4 A1
SHPY BD18 ....29 E2
Norman Ter ECHL BD2...............30 A4
ELL HX5 ....76 D5

Oak Av BGLY BD16....................16 C5
GIR BD8 ....38 D2
RPDN/SBR HX6 ....67 E3
Oak Bank BGLY BD16.................16 D4
SHPY BD18 ....29 E4
Oak Bank Broadway
HWTH BD22 ....13 G2
Oakbank Ct HWTH BD22............13 G2
Oakbank Crs HWTH BD22..........13 G1
Oakbank Dr HWTH BD22............13 G1
Oakbank Gv HWTH BD22............13 G1
Oakbank La HWTH BD22............13 G2
Oakbank Mt HWTH BD22...........13 G1
Oakdale Av SHPY BD18..............29 E3
Oakdale Dr IDLE BD10................30 C5
SHPY BD18 ....29 E3
Oakdale Gv SHPY BD18..............29 E3
Oakdale Rd SHPY BD18..............29 E3
Oakdale Ter WBSY BD6...............54 C1
Oakdene Cl LM/WK BD12............22 C2
Oakenshaw Ct LM/WK BD12.......63 H2
Oakenshaw La CLECK BD19........63 H2
Oakfield Av BGLY BD16...............17 F4
Oakfield Cl ELL HX5...................76 B5
Oakfield Dr BAIL BD17...............19 E4
Oakfield Gv HTON BD9...............38 D2
Oakfield Ter SHPY BD18.............29 E2
Oak Gv HWTH BD22 ....13 H2
Oakhall Pk CUL/QBY BD13.........44 A1
Oakhall Park Av
CUL/QBY BD13........................36 A5
Oakham Wy BOW BD4...............47 H5
Oak Hill Rd BRIG HD6................78 A2
Oaklands BRIG HD6...................78 A2
IDLE BD10 ....29 H1
SHPY BD18 ....27 G2
Oaklands Av HIPP HX3...............60 D2
Oak La GIR BD8........................38 D2
HFAX HX1 .... 4 C3
Oakleigh Av CLAY BD14.............45 E4
HIPP HX3 ....68 D5
Oakleigh Cl CLAY BD14..............45 E4
Oakleigh Gdns CLAY BD14*........45 E4
Oakleigh Gv CLAY BD14.............45 E4
Oakleigh Rd CLAY BD14.............45 E4
Oakleigh Ter CLAY BD14.............45 E4
Oakleigh Vw BAIL BD17..............18 C3
Oak Mt GIR BD8.......................39 E2
Oak Pl HIPP HX3.......................70 D1
HIPP HX3 ....68 D5
Oak Pl HFAX HX1*..................... 4 B4
RPDN/SBR HX6 .... 4 B4
Oakridge Ct BGLY BD16.............16 D2
Oak Ri CLAY BD14 ....64 C3
Oakroyd Av WBSY BD6...............54 D2
Oakroyd Cl BIRK/DRI BD11.........57 F5
Oakroyd Ct BRIG HD6................71 G3
Oakroyd Dr BIRK/DRI BD11........65 F1
BRIG HD6 ....71 G5
Oakroyd Rd WBSY BD6...............71 G5

Oakroyd Ter BAIL BD17 19 E4
GIR BD8 39 E2
Oakroyd Vls GIR BD8 39 E2
Oaks Dr GIR BD8 37 F4
Oaks Fold WBOW BD5 47 F2
Oaks Green Mt BRIG HD6 78 A4
Oaks La GIR BD8 37 G5
Oak St CLAY BD14 45 E3
ELL HX5 76 C5
HWTH BD22 23 E2
HWTH BD22 32 D1
PDSY/CALV LS28 41 H4
RPDN/SBR HX6 67 E3
Oak Ter HFAX HX1 * 4 C3
Oak Vls GIR BD8 39 E2
Oakway BIRK/DRI BD11 65 G1
Oakwell Cl GTHN BD7 46 C4
Oakwood Av BIRK/DRI BD11 57 F5
ECHL BD2 29 E5
Oakwood Ct GIR BD8 38 D4
Oakwood Dr BGLY BD16 16 C1
Oakwood Gv GIR BD8 38 B3
Oakworth Hall HWTH BD22 12 D4
Oakworth Rd HWTH BD22 13 G2
Oasby Cft BOW BD4 56 D1
Oastler Pl LM/WK BD12 55 E4
Oastler Rd PDSY/CALV LS28 31 G3
SHPY BD18 28 A1
Oat St HWTH BD22 * 13 H2
Oberon Wy BGLY BD16 27 E3
Occupation La HWTH BD22 13 G2
LUD/ILL HX2 50 D4
PDSY/CALV LS28 49 H1
Octagon Ter LUD/ILL HX2 67 H4
Oddfellows' Ct BFD BD1 2 C6
Oddfellows St BRIG HD6 71 G5
CLECK BD19 63 G5
Oddy Fold HIPP HX3 59 G4
Oddy Pl WBSY BD6 54 C1
Oddy St BOW BD4 56 D1
Odsal Pl WBSY BD6 55 E2
Odsal Rd WBSY BD6 55 E2
Ogden Crs CUL/QBY BD13 34 C2
Ogden La BRIG HD6 78 A3
CUL/QBY BD13 34 C2
LUD/ILL HX2 42 C5
Ogden St RPDN/SBR HX6 66 D5
Ogden View Cl LUD/ILL HX2 50 C3
Old Allen Rd CUL/QBY BD13 35 F1
Old Bank HIPP HX3 5 K3
Old Bell Ct HFAX HX1 * 5 G6
Old Canal Rd BFD BD1 2 D1
Old Cawsey RPDN/SBR HX6 67 F4
Old Cock Yd HFAX HX1 * 5 H4
Old Corn Mill La GTHN BD7 * 46 B3
Old Dalton La KGHY BD21 7 G4
Old Earth ELL HX5 77 E4
Old Farm Crs BOW BD4 * 48 A4
Oldfield La HWTH BD22 22 B2
Oldfield St HIPP HX3 * 59 F1
Old Godley La HIPP HX3 60 B5
Old Guy Rd CUL/QBY BD13 43 H5
Old Hall Cl HWTH BD22 * 22 D3
Old Haworth La YEA LS19 11 G4
Old Hollings Hl BAIL BD17 10 B5
Old La BIRK/DRI BD11 57 G5
BRIG HD6 71 G5
CUL/QBY BD13 24 C3
HIPP HX3 59 F2
Old Langley La BAIL BD17 19 F2
Old Lee Bank HIPP HX3 59 F4
Old Main St BGLY BD16 16 C3
Old Manse Cft HWTH BD22 * 32 D1
Old Market HFAX HX1 5 H4
Old Marsh PDSY/CALV LS28 41 H5
Old Mill Rd BAIL BD17 * 28 B1
Old Oxenhope La HWTH BD22 22 C4
Old Park Rd IDLE BD10 30 B2
Old Popplewell La CLECK BD19 63 F5
Old Power Wy ELL HX5 76 D3
Old Rd CUL/QBY BD13 34 C4
CUL/QBY BD13 44 C1
GTHN BD7 45 H5
Old Schools Gdns HIPP HX3 59 H4
Old Side Ct AIRE BD20 9 F2
Old Souls Wy BGLY BD16 9 F5
Old Station Rd LUD/ILL HX2 66 A1
Old Vicarage Cl BGLY BD16 27 E3
Old Well Head HFAX HX1 5 G6
Old Whack House La YEA LS19 11 E5
Olive Gv GIR BD8 37 H4
Oliver Cl RPDN/SBR HX6 67 E4
Oliver Mdw ELL HX5 76 D3
Oliver St BOW BD4 * 47 H2
Ollerdale Av WIL/AL BD15 36 D1
Ollerdale Cl WIL/AL BD15 36 D2
Olympic Pk LM/WK BD12 55 F5
Onslow Crs BOW BD4 48 A5
Opal St HWTH BD22 13 H2
Orange St BFDE BD3 48 B1
HFAX HX1 5 G3
Orchard Cl LUD/ILL HX2 67 G2
Orchard Gv IDLE BD10 30 C2
The Orchards BGLY BD16 16 D1
CLECK BD19 65 H5
The Orchard KGHY BD21 8 A4
Orchard Wy BRIG HD6 71 F4
Orchid Cl SHPY BD18 29 E4
Orleans St WBSY BD6 54 A3
Ormonde Dr WIL/AL BD15 36 D4
Ormond Rd WBSY BD6 54 C2
Ormondroyd Av WBSY BD6 54 D2
Ormond St GTHN BD7 46 B3
Osborne St HFAX HX1 4 B2
WBOW BD5 47 E2
Osbourne Dr CUL/QBY BD13 52 B1
Osprey Ct GIR BD8 * 37 F5
Osterley Gv IDLE BD10 30 D4
Oswald Cl GSLY LS20 10 C2
Oswald St SHPY BD18 29 E2
Oswaldthorpe Av BFDE BD3 40 C3
Otley La YEA LS19 11 G4
Otley Mt AIRE BD20 * 9 E3
Otley Rd BAIL BD17 19 G3
BFDE BD3 3 F4
BGLY BD16 9 H2
GSLY LS20 10 B2
SHPY BD18 28 C3
Otley St HFAX HX1 4 A3
KGHY BD21 7 E5
Otterburn Cl WBOW BD5 47 E2
Otterburn St KGHY BD21 * 7 F2
Oulton Ter GTHN BD7 46 D2
Ounsworth St BOW BD4 48 A3
Outlands Ri IDLE BD10 30 C1
Outside La HWTH BD22 32 A2
The Oval BGLY BD16 17 E4
GIR BD8 37 H4
GSLY LS20 10 B3
LVSG WF15 73 F3
Ovenden Av HIPP HX3 59 F4
Ovenden Cl HIPP HX3 * 59 F4
Ovenden Crs HIPP HX3 59 F3
Ovenden Gn HIPP HX3 59 E3
Ovenden Pk LUD/ILL HX2 * 59 E1
Ovenden Rd HIPP HX3 59 G4
Ovenden Road Ter HIPP HX3 59 F3
Ovenden Ter HIPP HX3 59 F3
Ovenden Wy HIPP HX3 59 E3
Ovenden Wood Rd
LUD/ILL HX2 58 B3
Overdale Dr SHPY BD18 19 G5
Overdale Mt LUD/ILL HX2 67 G3
Overdale Ter HWTH BD22 * 22 D2
Overland Crs IDLE BD10 30 C1
Over La YEA LS19 21 H3
Overton Dr WBSY BD6 45 G5
Ovington Dr BOW BD4 48 D5
Owen Ct BGLY BD16 9 H5
Owlcotes Dr PDSY/CALV LS28 41 H4
Owlcotes Gdns
PDSY/CALV LS28 41 H4
Owlcotes Garth
PDSY/CALV LS28 41 G4
Owlcotes La PDSY/CALV LS28 41 H4
Owlcotes Rd PDSY/CALV LS28 41 G4
Owlcotes Ter PDSY/CALV LS28 41 H4
Owler Ings Rd BRIG HD6 78 B1
Owlet Rd SHPY BD18 28 D2
Owl St KGHY BD21 * 7 G3
Oxford Av GSLY LS20 10 C2
Oxford Cl CLECK BD19 65 G5
CUL/QBY BD13 51 H3
Oxford Crs CLAY BD14 45 E3
HIPP HX3 69 E4
Oxford Dr CLECK BD19 65 G5
Oxford La HIPP HX3 69 E4
Oxford Pl BAIL BD17 19 E4
BFDE BD3 3 F2
Oxford Rd CLECK BD19 65 G3
CUL/QBY BD13 * 51 H2
ECHL BD2 39 H2
GSLY LS20 10 C2
HFAX HX1 5 G6
Oxford St CLAY BD14 45 E3
GSLY LS20 10 D2
KGHY BD21 6 D5
RPDN/SBR HX6 67 G3
Oxford Wk CLECK BD19 65 G5
Ox Heys Mdw CUL/QBY BD13 44 D1
Oxley Gdns WBSY BD6 54 D3
Oxley St GIR BD8 38 D4

P

Padan St HIPP HX3 69 E4
Paddock HTON BD9 28 C5
Paddock Cl LM/WK BD12 62 D4
Paddock La LUD/ILL HX2 58 B5
Paddock Rd HIPP HX3 52 B5
Paddocks Church BRIG HD6 79 F1
The Paddock BAIL BD17 19 G2
CLECK BD19 * 63 G5
CUL/QBY BD13 24 C3
Padgum BAIL BD17 18 D2
Padma Cl GTHN BD7 38 C5
Page Hl LUD/ILL HX2 58 D3
Paget St KGHY BD21 6 D4
Pagewood Ct IDLE BD10 19 H5
Pakington St WBOW BD5 47 E3
Paley Rd BOW BD4 47 H3
Paley Ter BOW BD4 47 H3
Palin Av BFDE BD3 40 C3
Palm Cl WBSY BD6 54 C2
Palmer Rd BFDE BD3 3 K3
Palmerston St ECHL BD2 * 40 A2
Palm St HIPP HX3 59 G3
Panelagh Av IDLE BD10 30 D4
Pannal St GTHN BD7 46 B4
The Parade BGLY BD16 26 D2
YEA LS19 * 11 E5
Paradise La LUD/ILL HX2 67 E2
Paradise Rd HTON BD9 * 28 A5
Paradise St BFD BD1 2 A4
HFAX HX1 5 F5
Park Av BGLY BD16 16 C4
ELL HX5 76 B5
HWTH BD22 13 E4
IDLE BD10 20 A4
KGHY BD21 7 E5
SHPY BD18 28 B1
YEA LS19 11 F4
Park Cliffe Rd ECHL BD2 39 H2
Park Cl BGLY BD16 16 D2
CUL/QBY BD13 52 A1
HIPP HX3 70 D1
IDLE BD10 30 B4
KGHY BD21 * 14 B1
LUD/ILL HX2 58 A4
Park Crs BFDE BD3 39 H2
GSLY LS20 10 B3
HIPP HX3 59 F4
Park Dene HFAX HX1 * 4 C5
Park Dr BGLY BD16 17 E1
HTON BD9 28 C5
Park Drive Rd KGHY BD21 14 B1
Parkfield Av ELL HX5 76 C5
Parkfield Dr CUL/QBY BD13 52 A1
Parkfield Rd GIR BD8 39 E2
SHPY BD18 27 H1
Park Flds LUD/ILL HX2 58 A3
Park Gdns LUD/ILL HX2 67 G3
Park Ga BFDE BD3 3 F4
Park Ga West HIPP HX3 * 76 B1
Park Gv CUL/QBY BD13 52 A1
HIPP HX3 60 C4
HTON BD9 28 D5
SHPY BD18 28 A1
YEA LS19 11 F4
Park Hl HUDN HD2 79 G5
Park Hill Cl GIR BD8 37 G3
Park Hill Dr GIR BD8 37 G3
Park House Cl LM/WK BD12 55 F3
Park House Crs LM/WK BD12 55 F3
Park House Gv LM/WK BD12 * 55 F3
Park House Rd LM/WK BD12 55 F3
Park House Wk LM/WK BD12 55 F3
Parkin La IDLE BD10 31 E1
Parkinson Rd CUL/QBY BD13 34 D4
Parkinson St WBOW BD5 47 E3
Parkin St LVSG WF15 73 F3
Parkland Dr IDLE BD10 30 B2
Parkland Vw YEA LS19 11 G5
Park La BAIL BD17 19 G2
CLAY BD14 45 E3
CUL/QBY BD13 52 C1
GSLY LS20 10 B4
HIPP HX3 76 B1
KGHY BD21 7 F5
WBOW BD5 47 E3
Park Lea HUDN HD2 79 H5
Park Md IDLE BD10 20 A4
Parkmere Cl BOW BD4 56 A3
Park Mount Av BAIL BD17 19 F3
Park Pl HFAX HX1 * 4 C6
IDLE BD10 20 A4
Park Pl East HIPP HX3 70 D1
Park Pl West HIPP HX3 70 D1
Park Rd BGLY BD16 16 D2
ELL HX5 76 C3
GSLY LS20 10 C4
HFAX HX1 4 E5
IDLE BD10 20 A4
IDLE BD10 30 C4
RPDN/SBR HX6 67 F4
SHPY BD18 28 D2
WBOW BD5 47 F2
WBSY BD6 54 D3
YEA LS19 11 F4
YEA LS19 21 G2
Park Rw BRIG HD6 * 78 C1
Parkside BGLY BD16 16 D2
CLECK BD19 73 G1
Parkside Av CUL/QBY BD13 52 A1
Parkside Ct HWTH BD22 23 F1
Parkside Gv HTON BD9 38 B1
Parkside Rd WBOW BD5 47 F5
Parkside Ter CUL/QBY BD13 24 C3
Park Sq WBSY BD6 54 A2
Parkstone HUDN HD2 79 G5
Parkstone Dr IDLE BD10 30 B4
Park Stone Ri HIPP HX3 53 E4
Park St BRIG HD6 78 C1
CLECK BD19 65 H5
CLECK BD19 73 E2
HWTH BD22 23 E2
RPDN/SBR HX6 67 F4
SHPY BD18 28 B1
YEA LS19 11 F4
Park Ter HFAX HX1 * 4 C4
HIPP HX3 60 C4
KGHY BD21 7 G4
SHPY BD18 28 B1
The Park Towngate
HIPP HX3 69 H5
Park Vw CLECK BD19 64 B5
HFAX HX1 4 C5
Park View Av HIPP HX3 60 D4
HWTH BD22 23 F1
Parkview Ct SHPY BD18 * 28 B2
Park View Rd HTON BD9 38 C2
Park View Ter HTON BD9 38 C1
YEA LS19 21 G2
Park Wy BAIL BD17 18 A5
Parkway CUL/QBY BD13 52 A1
KGHY BD21 14 B1
WBOW BD5 55 G1
Park Willow HIPP HX3 53 G4
Parkwood Gdns
PDSY/CALV LS28 31 G3
Parkwood Ri KGHY BD21 14 B1
Parkwood Rd PDSY/CALV LS28 31 G3
SHPY BD18 28 A2
Parkwood St KGHY BD21 7 G5
Parma St WBOW BD5 47 F2
Parratt Rw BFDE BD3 40 C5
Parrott St BOW BD4 56 C1
Parry Cl BGLY BD16 * 15 F5
Parry La BOW BD4 48 B2
Parsonage La BRIG HD6 71 F5
Parsonage Rd BOW BD4 48 C2
WBOW BD5 47 F4
Parsonage St HIPP HX3 60 A4
Parsons Rd HTON BD9 28 B5
Parson St KGHY BD21 7 F3
Partridge Dr WBSY BD6 53 F1
Paslew Ct AIRE BD20 8 C2
Pasture Av HWTH BD22 12 D5
Pasture Cl CLAY BD14 45 G3
Pasture La CLAY BD14 45 G3
Pasture Ri CLAY BD14 45 G3
Pasture Rd BAIL BD17 19 E4
Pasture Side Ter East
CLAY BD14 45 G3
Pasture Side Ter West
CLAY BD14 45 F3
Pasture Wk CLAY BD14 45 F3
Patent St HTON BD9 38 C2
Paternoster La GTHN BD7 46 B3
Patricia Gdns RPDN/SBR HX6 66 D3
RPDN/SBR HX6 * 68 A4
Pattie St AIRE BD20 7 E2
Pavement La LUD/ILL HX2 50 D3
Pavilion Ct BOW BD4 56 B2
Paw La CUL/QBY BD13 52 C3
Pawson St BOW BD4 48 C1
Peabody St HIPP HX3 59 F4
Peace St BOW BD4 48 B2
Peacock Ct YEA LS19 11 H5
Pearl St HWTH BD22 13 H2
Pearson La HTON BD9 37 G3
Pearson Rd WBSY BD6 55 E2
Pearson Rw LM/WK BD12 63 E2
Pearson St BFDE BD3 48 B1
CLECK BD19 73 E2
PDSY/CALV LS28 31 G2
Pear St HFAX HX1 4 A5
HWTH BD22 13 H3
HWTH BD22 * 32 D2
Peasehill Cl YEA LS19 21 H2
Peasehill Pk YEA LS19 21 H2
Peaseland Av CLECK BD19 73 F1
Peaseland Cl CLECK BD19 73 G1
Peaseland Rd CLECK BD19 73 G1
Peckover Dr PDSY/CALV LS28 41 F4
Peckover St BFD BD1 3 F5
Peel Cl BOW BD4 48 D2
Peel Park Dr ECHL BD2 40 A2
Peel Park Ter ECHL BD2 39 H2
Peel Park Vw BFDE BD3 39 H3
Peel Rw GTHN BD7 46 B4
Peel Sq BFD BD1 2 B3
Peel St BGLY BD16 17 E3
CUL/QBY BD13 44 A1
CUL/QBY BD13 52 C1
RPDN/SBR HX6 * 67 E4
WIL/AL BD15 25 H5
Peep Green Rd LVSG WF15 73 F5
Pelham Ct ECHL BD2 40 A1
Pelham Rd ECHL BD2 40 A1
Pellon La HFAX HX1 4 A1
Pellon New Rd LUD/ILL HX2 58 D5
Pellon Ter IDLE BD10 20 A5
Pellon Wk IDLE BD10 20 A5
Pemberton Dr GTHN BD7 2 A7
Pembroke St WBOW BD5 47 F3
Pendle Ct CUL/QBY BD13 52 B3
Pendle Rd BGLY BD16 17 E3
Pendragon ECHL BD2 * 39 H1
Pendragon La ECHL BD2 40 A1
Penfield Gv CLAY BD14 45 F3
Pengarth BGLY BD16 17 E1
Penistone Ms HWTH BD22 * 22 D2
Penn Cl ECHL BD2 40 A1
Penn Dr CLECK BD19 73 G2
Penn Gv CLECK BD19 73 G2
Pennine Cl CUL/QBY BD13 52 A3
Pennington Ter WBOW BD5 * 46 D3
Pennithorne Av BAIL BD17 18 D2
Penn St HFAX HX1 4 C2
Penny Hill Dr CLAY BD14 45 G3
Pennythorne Ct YEA LS19 21 F1
Pennythorne Dr YEA LS19 21 F1
Penrose Dr GTHN BD7 46 A4
Pentland Av CLAY BD14 45 G3
Pentland Cl HWTH BD22 6 D5
Penzance Ct GIR BD8 38 C4
Percival St BFDE BD3 3 H5
Percy St BGLY BD16 16 D3
KGHY BD21 14 A2
Peregrine Wy WBSY BD6 53 F1
Per La LUD/ILL HX2 50 C3
Perry Cl HWTH BD22 13 H3
Perseverance La GTHN BD7 46 B4
Perseverance Rd
CUL/QBY BD13 43 F4
Perseverance St BAIL BD17 * 19 E2
LM/WK BD12 62 D1
PDSY/CALV LS28 41 H5
Perseverance Ter HFAX HX1 68 B3
Perth Av ECHL BD2 39 F1
Peterborough Pl ECHL BD2 40 A2
Peterborough Rd ECHL BD2 40 A2
Peterborough Ter ECHL BD2 40 A1
Peter La LUD/ILL HX2 67 E1
Petrel Cl WBSY BD6 53 F1
Petrie Gv BFDE BD3 40 D5
Petrie Rd BFDE BD3 40 D5
Peverell Cl BOW BD4 48 D4
Peveril Mt ECHL BD2 40 B2
Pheasant St KGHY BD21 7 G3
Phoebe La HIPP HX3 69 E4
Phoenix St BRIG HD6 78 C1
Phoenix Wy BOW BD4 48 D1
Piccadilly BFD BD1 2 D4
The Pickerings
CUL/QBY BD13 52 B2
Pickles La GTHN BD7 46 A4
Pickles St KGHY BD21 14 A1
Pickwood La RPDN/SBR HX6 74 D2
Picton St GIR BD8 2 A1
Pictureville BFD BD1 2 C6
Piggott St BRIG HD6 71 F5
Pinebury Cl CUL/QBY BD13 51 H1
Pine Cft AIRE BD20 6 D2
Pinedale BGLY BD16 16 C1
Pine St BFD BD1 3 F4
HFAX HX1 5 G5
HWTH BD22 22 D3
Pinfold Cft CLAY BD14 45 F3
Pinfold La ELL HX5 77 G5
RPDN/SBR HX6 66 A4
Pink St HWTH BD22 22 D3
Pinnar La HIPP HX3 69 G3
Pintail Av WBSY BD6 53 F1
Pipercroft WBSY BD6 53 H4
Pirie Cl ECHL BD2 39 G1
Pitcliffe Wy BOW BD4 47 G2
Pit Hl HIPP HX3 5 K6
Pit La CLECK BD19 65 G3
CUL/QBY BD13 34 B3
CUL/QBY BD13 43 H3
Pits La CLECK BD19 72 B2
Pitts St BOW BD4 48 C3
Pitt St KGHY BD21 7 G4
Pitty Beck Vw WIL/AL BD15 37 E5
Plains La ELL HX5 76 C2
Plane Tree Nest La
LUD/ILL HX2 67 H2
Plane Tree Rd
RPDN/SBR HX6 67 E3
Plane Trees LUD/ILL HX2 58 C5
Plane Trees Cl CLECK BD19 64 C2
Planetrees Rd BFDE BD3 48 B1
Planetrees St WIL/AL BD15 36 D3
Plantation Pl BOW BD4 48 B3
Plantation Wy BAIL BD17 19 E3
Pleasant St GTHN BD7 46 B3
Plevna Ter BGLY BD16 16 C2
Plimsoll St BOW BD4 47 H3
Ploughcroft La HIPP HX3 59 G3
Ploughmans Cft ECHL BD2 29 F5
Plover St KGHY BD21 7 F3
WBOW BD5 46 D4
Plumpton Av ECHL BD2 29 G3
Plumpton Cl ECHL BD2 29 H4
Plumpton Dr SHPY BD18 29 G3
Plumpton End ECHL BD2 29 H3
Plumpton Gdns ECHL BD2 29 G3
Plumpton Lea ECHL BD2 29 G3
Plumpton Md ECHL BD2 29 G3
Plumpton St GIR BD8 38 B4
Plumpton Wk ECHL BD2 29 G3
Plum St HFAX HX1 4 B6
HWTH BD22 13 H3
Plymouth Gv HFAX HX1 * 4 C1
Pochard Cl WBSY BD6 53 F1
Pohlman St HFAX HX1 * 4 B7
Pollard Av BGLY BD16 17 E1
CLECK BD19 65 G4
Pollard Cl CLECK BD19 65 G4
Pollard La BFDE BD3 40 A3
Pollard St BOW BD4 47 G2
Pollard Wy CLECK BD19 65 G4
Pollit Av RPDN/SBR HX6 66 C5
Pond St KGHY BD21 7 F3
Pool Ct BFDE BD3 3 H3
Pool St KGHY BD21 * 7 H2
Pope St KGHY BD21 7 G3
Poplar Av GTHN BD7 46 A5
RPDN/SBR HX6 67 E3
SHPY BD18 28 D4
Poplar Ct ELL HX5 * 76 C5
Poplar Crs LUD/ILL HX2 51 E3
SHPY BD18 28 D4
Poplar Dr AIRE BD20 8 D4
SHPY BD18 28 D4
Poplar Gv BGLY BD16 15 F5
CLECK BD19 73 F2
GTHN BD7 46 A5
SHPY BD18 28 D4
Poplar Rd GTHN BD7 46 B5
SHPY BD18 28 D4
Poplars Park Rd ECHL BD2 29 E5
The Poplars GSLY LS20 10 D1
HIPP HX3 * 62 B3
Poplar St HIPP HX3 5 G1
Poplar Ter AIRE BD20 8 D4
Poplar Vw BRIG HD6 71 F2
GTHN BD7 45 H5
Poplarwood Gdns
IDLE BD10 30 D4
Popples Dr LUD/ILL HX2 51 E3
Popple Wells La LUD/ILL HX2 66 C1
Poppy Ct WBSY BD6 * 54 A4
Porritt St CLECK BD19 * 64 C4
Portland Pl BGLY BD16 16 D4
HFAX HX1 5 H6
Portland Rd HIPP HX3 5 H1
Portland St HFAX HX1 5 H3
HWTH BD22 23 E2
WBOW BD5 2 D7
Portman St PDSY/CALV LS28 31 G3
Portsmouth Av BFDE BD3 3 F1
Portwood St HTON BD9 37 G2
Post Office Rd IDLE BD10 30 B4
Pothouse Rd WBSY BD6 54 C2
Potter Cl LM/WK BD12 55 F5
Powell Av WBOW BD5 46 D3
Powell Rd BGLY BD16 16 D3
SHPY BD18 29 E4
Powell St HFAX HX1 5 G4
Pratt La SHPY BD18 28 D3
Premier Wy ELL HX5 76 D3
Prescott St HFAX HX1 5 H6
Prescott Ter WIL/AL BD15 37 E3
Preston La LUD/ILL HX2 58 B3
Preston Pl HFAX HX1 4 D4
Preston St GTHN BD7 38 D5
Priesthorpe Av
PDSY/CALV LS28 41 G2
Priesthorpe La
PDSY/CALV LS28 41 G1
Priesthorpe Rd
PDSY/CALV LS28 31 H5
Priestley Av WBSY BD6 54 C2
Priestley Pl RPDN/SBR HX6 66 D5
Priestley St CUL/QBY BD13 44 A1
Priestley Ter WBSY BD6 54 D1
Priestman Cl GIR BD8 38 D3
Priestman St GIR BD8 38 D3
Priestthorpe Cl BGLY BD16 16 D2
Priestthorpe La BGLY BD16 16 D2
Priestthorpe Rd BGLY BD16 16 D3
Primrose Bank BGLY BD16 17 E4
Primrose Dr BGLY BD16 17 F4
Primrose Gv KGHY BD21 7 H4
Primrose La BGLY BD16 17 E5
ECHL BD2 29 E5
Primrose St GIR BD8 38 D4
KGHY BD21 7 H4
Primrose Wy HIPP HX3 53 G3
Princeroyd Wy GTHN BD7 38 B5
Prince's Crs ECHL BD2 39 F1
Prince's Ga HIPP HX3 68 C4
Princess St BRIG HD6 78 C1
GTL/HWG HX4 76 A4
HFAX HX1 5 H3
RPDN/SBR HX6 67 F4
YEA LS19 21 F2
Prince's St WBSY BD6 53 H3
WBSY BD6 54 C2
Prince St BOW BD4 56 B1
HWTH BD22 23 E2
Prince's Wy WBOW BD5 2 C6
Princeton Cl LUD/ILL HX2 58 D4
Princeville Rd GTHN BD7 38 B5

Princeville St GTHN BD7 ....38 C5
Prior St KGHY BD21 ....7 H3
Priory Cl BGLY BD16 ....16 D2
Priory Ct GIR BD8 * ....A A2
Priory Gv BGLY BD16 ....16 D2
Priory Rd BRIG HD6 ....78 D2
Proctor St BOW BD4 ....56 C1
Prod Ga BAIL BD17 * 18 A4
Prod La BAIL BD17 ....17 H4
Progress Av BGLY BD16 ....15 F5
Prospect Av CUL/QBY BD13 .....67 H4
SHPY BD18 ....28 D2
Prospect Cl LUD/ILL HX2 ....67 H4
SHPY BD18 ....28 D2
Prospect Crs LUD/ILL HX2 ......58 A5
Prospect Crs HWTH BD22 ....13 F1
Prospect Dr HWTH BD22 ....13 F1
Prospect Gv SHPY BD18 ....28 D2
Prospect La BIRK/DRI BD11 ....57 G5
Prospect Mt HWTH BD22 ....13 F1
SHPY BD18 ....28 D2
Prospect Pl BFDE BD3 ....70 B1
ECHL BD2 ....40 B2
HTON BD9 ....38 A3
LUD/ILL HX2 ....59 E2
RPDN/SBR HX6 * 66 A5
Prospect Rd BFDE BD3 ....2 E2
BGLY BD16 ....17 F1
CLECK BD19 ....64 C5
Prospect St BOW BD4 ....47 G2
CUL/QBY BD13 * 73 G1
HIPP HX3 * 5 J3
HWTH BD22 ....13 F1
HWTH BD22 ....22 D5
IDLE BD10 ....30 B4
PDSY/CALV LS28 * 41 H4
SHPY BD18 ....28 D2
WBSY BD6 ....74 C3
YEA LS19 ....21 H3
Prospect Ter CLECK BD19 ....64 C5
WIL/AL BD15 ....37 F3
Prospect Wk SHPY BD18 ....28 D2
Prospect Wy BRIG HD6 ....71 G1
Providence Av BAIL BD17 ....18 D2
Providence La HWTH BD22 ....12 D4
Providence Pl BRIG HD6 * 78 D2
Providence Rw BAIL BD17 ....18 D2
LUD/ILL HX2 ....59 E2
Providence St BFD BD1 ....2 B5
CLECK BD19 * 63 F5
CLECK BD19 * 64 D5
ELL HX5 ....75 H4
Providence Ter CUL/QBY BD13 ..44 A1
Prune Park La WIL/AL BD15 .....36 B1
Pule Green La HIPP HX3 ....59 G2
Pullan Av ECHL BD2 ....30 B5
Pullan Dr ECHL BD2 ....30 B5
Pullan Gv ECHL BD2 ....30 B5
Pullan La ECHL BD2 ....30 B5
Pullan St WBOW BD5 ....47 E2
Punch Bowl Yd CLECK BD19 ....73 F1
Purbeck Ct BOW BD4 * 48 D5
Purley Wk BOW BD4 ....54 C2
Pye Nest Av LUD/ILL HX2 ....67 G3
Pye Nest Dr LUD/ILL HX2 ....67 H4
Pye Nest Gdns LUD/ILL HX2 ....67 H3
Pye Nest Gv LUD/ILL HX2 ......67 G4
Pye Nest Ri LUD/ILL HX2 ....67 G3
Pye Nest Rd RPDN/SBR HX6 ....67 G4
Pyrah Rd LM/WK BD12 * 55 E3
Pyrah St LM/WK BD12 ....65 E1

Queensway BGLY BD16 ....17 E4
GSLY LS20 ....11 E2
HWTH HX1 ....A A2
Queen Victoria Crs HIPP HX3 ...61 E2
Quincy Cl ECHL BD2 ....30 B5

R

Race Moor La HWTH BD22 ....12 C3
Radcliffe Av ECHL BD2 ....29 H4
Radfield Dr WBSY BD6 ....55 F2
Radnor St BFDE BD3 ....40 B5
Radwell Dr WBOW BD5 ....47 F2
Raeburn Dr WBSY BD6 ....54 B3
Rae Rd SHPY BD18 ....28 B3
Raglan Av HWTH BD22 ....6 C5
Raglan Ct HFAX HX1 * 29 H4
Raglan St BFDE BD3 ....40 C5
CUL/QBY BD13 ....52 E1
HFAX HX1 ....4 D5
HWTH BD22 ....6 C5
Raglan Ter BFDE BD3 ....40 D5
Raikes La BOW BD4 ....49 F5
BOW BD4 ....56 D5
Raikes Wood Dr BOW BD4 ....56 D5
Railway Av IDLE BD10 ....30 A1
Railway St BOW BD4 ....56 B1
BRIG HD6 ....78 C2
CLECK BD19 ....73 G1
KGHY BD21 * 7 F2
Railway Ter HIPP HX3 ....75 F1
Rainbow Ms WBSY BD6 * 54 A4
Raistrick Wy SHPY BD18 ....29 E1
Raleigh St HFAX HX1 * 4 C7
Ramsden Av GTHN BD7 ....45 H2
Ramsden Ct GTHN BD7 ....45 H2
Ramsden Pl CLAY BD14 ....45 E2
Ramsden St HIPP HX3 ....58 D5
Ramsey St WBOW BD5 ....47 E4
Ramsgate St HFAX HX1 ....4 A3
Randall Pl HTON BD9 ....38 B1
Randall Well St BFD BD1 ....2 B6
Randolph St BFDE BD3 ....40 D4
HIPP HX3 * 5 G1
Ranelagh Av IDLE BD10 ....30 D4
Range Bank HIPP HX3 ....59 H4
Range Bank Top HIPP HX3 ....59 H4
Range Gdns HIPP HX3 ....59 H4
Range La HIPP HX3 ....5 H1
Ransdale Dr WBOW BD5 ....47 E4
Ransdale Gv WBOW BD5 ....47 E4
Ransdale Rd WBOW BD5 ....47 E4
Rastrick Common BRIG HD6 .....78 B3
Rathmell St WBOW BD5 * 55 E1
Ravenscliffe Av IDLE BD10 ....30 D4
Ravenscliffe Cl HIPP HX3 * 73 H1
Ravenscliffe Rd
PDSY/CALV LS28 ....30 D3
Ravenstone Dr GTL/HWG HX4 ..75 H5
Raven St BGLY BD16 ....16 D3
HFAX HX1 ....4 B5
KGHY BD21 ....7 E4
Ravenswood GTL/HWG HX4 * ...75 E4
Raven Ter GIR BD8 ....37 F5
Rawdon Dr YEA LS19 ....21 G3
Rawdon Hall Dr YEA LS19 ....21 G3
Rawdon Rd HWTH BD22 ....22 D2
Rawdon St HWTH BD22 ....6 D5
Rawfolds Wy CLECK BD19 ....73 H2
Raw Hi BRIG HD6 * 78 A3
Raw La LUD/ILL HX2 ....50 C5
Rawling St KGHY BD21 ....14 A1
Rawnsley Av BFDE BD3 ....40 C4
HIPP HX3 ....66 D5
Rawson Rd BFD BD1 ....2 C4
RPDN/SBR HX6 ....66 D5
Rawson Sq BFD BD1 ....2 B4
IDLE BD10 ....20 A5
Rawson St North HIPP HX3 ......59 G4
Rayleigh St WBOW BD5 * 60 C4
Raymond Dr WBOW BD5 ....47 F5
Raymond St WBOW BD5 ....47 F5
Raynbron Crs WBOW BD5 ....47 G5
Rayner Av GIR BD8 ....38 A5
Rayner Dr BRIG HD6 ....71 F4
Rayner Mt WIL/AL BD15 ....37 E4
Rayner Rd BRIG HD6 ....71 F4
Rayners Av LVSG WF15 ....73 F4
Raynham Crs AIRE BD20 ....6 B5
Raywood Cl YEA LS19 ....11 F3
Rebecca St GIR BD8 ....2 A3
Recreation La ELL HX5 ....76 B5
Recreation Rd RPDN/SBR HX6 ..67 E4
Rectory Rw KGHY BD21 ....7 E4
Red Beck Rd HIPP HX3 ....60 C4
Red Beck V SHPY BD18 ....28 B4
Redburn Av SHPY BD18 ....28 B4
Redburn Dr SHPY BD18 ....28 B4
Redburn Rd SHPY BD18 ....28 B4
Redcar Rd IDLE BD10 ....30 D3
Redcar St HFAX HX1 ....A A5
Redcliffe Av KGHY BD21 ....6 D4
Redcliffe Gv KGHY BD21 ....6 D4
Redcliffe St KGHY BD21 ....6 D4
Redhill Cl BOW BD4 ....56 D4
Red La PDSY/CALV LS28 ....41 H1
Redman Garth HWTH BD22 ......12 C4
Redmire St BFDE BD3 ....40 D5
Redpoll Wy WBSY BD6 ....53 F1
Redshank Cl WBSY BD6 ....53 F1
Red V CLECK BD19 ....65 G3
Redwald Dr GSLY LS20 ....10 B2
Redwood Cl YEA LS19 ....21 H1
Redwood Wy YEA LS19 ....11 E4
Rees Wy BFDE BD3 ....3 F2

Queensway Sq
CUL/QBY BD13 * 52 B1
Queens Cl BGLY BD16 ....17 E4
Queens Dr HIPP HX3 ....69 H4
Queensgate BFD BD1 ....2 D5
Queen's Ga HIPP HX3 ....68 C4
Queens Gv KGHY BD21 ....6 C4
Queens Mt HIPP HX3 * 60 D2
Queens Pl SHPY BD18 ....28 A1
Queen's Ri ECHL BD2 ....39 G1
Queen's Rd BGLY BD16 ....9 F5
ECHL BD2 ....39 F2
HFAX HX1 ....A A5
HIPP HX3 ....62 A3
KGHY BD21 ....13 H2
WBOW BD5 ....28 A1
Queen St BAIL BD17 ....18 D5
BGLY BD16 ....16 C3
CLECK BD19 ....73 H2
GTL/HWG HX4 ....75 H5
IDLE BD10 ....30 C2
RPDN/SBR HX6 ....66 B5
WBSY BD6 ....53 H3
WIL/AL BD15 ....35 H1
YEA LS19 ....21 G2

Queensway BGLY BD16 ....17 E4

Quail Av WBSY BD6 ....53 F1
Quail St KGHY BD21 ....7 G3
Quaker La CLECK BD19 ....75 G2
Quakers La YEA LS19 ....21 G1
Quarry Mt RPDN/SBR HX6 ....67 E5
Quarry Pl ECHL BD2 ....40 A2
Quarry St HFAX HX1 ....73 F1
HIPP HX3 ....58 D3
Quarry St HTON BD9 ....28 B5
KGHY BD21 * 7 G4
Quayside BAIL BD17 ....28 C1
Quebec St ELL HX5 ....76 D5
KGHY BD21 ....7 E5
Queen's Av ECHL BD2 ....39 C1
Queensbury Rd HIPP HX3 ....51 G5

Reeth Rd BRIG HD6 ....77 H5
Reevy Av WBSY BD6 ....54 A2
Reevy Crs WBSY BD6 ....53 H5
Reevy Dr WBSY BD6 ....54 B2
Reevylands Dr WBSY BD6 ....54 A2
Reevy Rd West WBSY BD6 ....53 H2
Reevy St WBSY BD6 ....54 B1
Reform St CLECK BD19 ....65 G4
Regency Ct GIR BD8 ....84 B4
Regency Vw BFDE BD3 ....59 H2
Regent Cl BRIG HD6 ....77 H5
Regent Pde RPDN/SBR HX6 * ...67 E4
Regent Pl IDLE BD10 ....19 H5
RPDN/SBR HX6 ....66 A5
Regent St CUL/QBY BD13 ....52 C1
HFAX HX1 ....5 F5
IDLE BD10 ....19 H5
IDLE BD10 * 30 C2
Reginald St WBOW BD5 ....47 E4
Reighton Cft IDLE BD10 ....30 D5
Reins Av BAIL BD17 ....18 C5
Reins Rd BRIG HD6 ....77 H5
Renee Cl BOW BD4 ....56 B2
Renshaw St IDLE BD10 ....20 A5
Renton Av GSLY LS20 ....10 C2
Renton Dr GSLY LS20 ....10 C2
Reservoir Pl CUL/QBY BD13 .....43 H5
Reservoir Rd LUD/ILL HX2 ....58 D5
Reservoir Vw CUL/QBY BD13 ...66 A5
Retford Pl GTHN BD7 ....46 D2
Reva Cl BGLY BD16 ....17 E2
Reva Syke Rd CLAY BD14 ....45 E3
Reydon Wk WBSY BD6 ....54 A1
Reyhill Gv WBOW BD5 ....47 F2
Reyner House Ms WBOW BD5 ..47 F2
Reynolds Av GTHN BD7 ....45 H2
Rhine St BOW BD4 ....47 H2
Rhodesia Av HIPP HX3 ....68 D5
WIL/AL BD15 ....37 F4
Rhodes Pl SHPY BD18 ....28 C1
Rhodes St HFAX HX1 ....4 E4
SHPY BD18 ....28 B1
Rhodes Wy GIR BD8 ....37 G3
Rhodesway GIR BD8 ....37 F3
Rhondda Pl HFAX HX1 ....67 H1
Rhum Cl WBSY BD6 ....54 A4
Rhylstone Mt GTHN BD7 ....38 A5
Ribble St KGHY BD21 ....7 K6
Ribbleton Gv BFDE BD3 ....3 G5
Riccall Nook IDLE BD10 ....30 C5
Richardson Av WBSY BD6 ....54 B2
Richardson St LM/WK BD12 .....63 H1
Richard St BFDE BD3 ....3 G6
BRIG HD6 ....71 F4
Richmond Av
RPDN/SBR HX6 ....66 C5
Richmond Gdns
RPDN/SBR HX6 ....66 C5
Richmond Gv CLECK BD19 ....65 G5
Richmond Ms SHPY BD18 ....28 A1
Richmond Pl SHPY BD18 ....28 A1
Richmond Rd GTHN BD7 ....38 D5
HFAX HX1 ....5 F7
PDSY/CALV LS28 ....41 H2
SHPY BD18 * 28 A1
Richmond St CLECK BD19 ....73 G1
HFAX HX1 ....5 F7
HIPP HX3 ....7 F3
Riddlesden St AIRE BD20 * 8 A2
Ridge Cl GSLY LS20 ....10 B3
Ridge Hi BRIG HD6 ....78 A2
Ridge Lea BRIG HD6 ....78 A2
Ridgemount Rd AIRE BD20 ....7 H1
Ridge Vw Gdns IDLE BD10 ......30 B2
Ridge View Rd BRIG HD6 ....78 B2
Ridgeway CUL/QBY BD13 ....52 C2
GSLY LS20 ....10 B3
SHPY BD18 ....29 F3
Ridgeway Gdns BRIG HD6 ....70 D5
Ridgeway Mt HWTH BD22 ....13 G1
Ridgewood Cl BAIL BD17 ....13 F4
Riding Hi HIPP HX3 * 53 H4
Riding La LUD/ILL HX2 ....58 B2
Ridings Wy WBSY BD6 ....53 H2
Rievaulx Av GIR BD8 ....38 D4
Rigby Cl WIL/AL BD15 ....35 H2
Riley La LUD/ILL HX2 ....57 E4
Rillington Md IDLE BD10 ....30 C5
Rilston St GTHN BD7 ....46 C1
Rimswell Holt IDLE BD10 ....30 D3
Ringby Ter HIPP HX3 * 59 G3
Ring Hay Rd BOW BD4 ....57 F1
Ring Rd Farsley
PDSY/CALV LS28 ....41 H1
Ringwood Edge GTL/HWG HX4 ..75 H5
Ringwood Rd WBOW BD5 ....46 C4
Ripley La GSLY LS20 ....10 D1
Ripley Rd BOW BD4 ....56 A1
Ripley St AIRE BD20 ....8 A2
HIPP HX3 ....47 F3
WBOW BD5 ....47 F3
WIL/AL BD15 ....36 D2
Ripon St HFAX HX1 ....67 H2
HIPP HX3 ....59 G3
The Rise HIPP HX3 ....62 C5
Rishworthian Ct HIPP HX3 * 75 F2
Rishworth St HWTH BD22 ....6 C5
Roslyn Pl GTHN BD7 * 46 C1
River Bank Wy ELL HX5 ....77 E2
River Mt AIRE BD20 ....8 A3
Riverside AIRE BD20 ....7 E1
Riverside Dr CLECK BD19 ....64 C4
Riverside Est BAIL BD17 ....28 B1
River St BRIG HD6 ....78 D2
HWTH BD22 * 13 E4
KGHY BD21 * 7 F2
Riverwood Dr HIPP HX3 ....75 F2
Rivock Gv AIRE BD20 ....6 C1
Roans Brae IDLE BD10 ....30 D1
Roberson Ter CLECK BD19 ....65 F5
Robertson Av BRIG HD6 ....78 A4
Roberts Pl BFD BD1 ....2 B4
Robert's St CLECK BD19 ....73 H2
Robert St BFDE BD3 ....3 G6

HIPP HX3 ....59 F3
HWTH BD22 ....23 C1
Robert St North HIPP HX3 ....59 H3
Robin Cl ECHL BD2 ....30 B5
Robin Dr ECHL BD2 ....30 B5
Robin Hood Wy BRIG HD6 ....79 F1
Robinson Ct GTHN BD7 ....46 A1
Robin St WBOW BD5 * 46 D5
Robin Wk SHPY BD18 ....28 C3
Rochdale Rd GTL/HWG HX4 .....74 D4
LUD/ILL HX2 ....67 G3
Rochester St ELL HX5 * 76 C5
Rochester St BFDE BD3 ....40 B5
SHPY BD18 ....28 D2
Rockcliffe Av BAIL BD17 ....18 D5
Rockfield Ter YEA LS19 ....11 H4
Rockhill La BOW BD4 ....55 H3
Rockland Crs GTHN BD7 ....45 H2
Rocklands Av BAIL BD17 ....18 D2
Rocklands Pl BAIL BD17 ....18 D2
Rock La CUL/QBY BD13 ....50 C2
Rocks La LUD/ILL HX2 ....66 C4
Rocks Rd HIPP HX3 ....68 B5
Rock St BRIG HD6 ....71 F5
Rocks Vw LUD/ILL HX2 ....68 B4
Rock Ter CUL/QBY BD13 ....44 A1
Rockville Ter HFAX HX1 ....68 B5
Rockwell La IDLE BD10 ....30 B3
Rockwood Cl HUDN HD2 ....79 F5
Rockwood Crs
PDSY/CALV LS28 ....41 F1
Rockwood Gv PDSY/CALV LS28 ..41 G1
Rockwood Hill Ct
PDSY/CALV LS28 ....41 F2
Rockwood Rd PDSY/CALV LS28 ..41 F2
Rodin Av GIR BD8 ....37 G5
Rodley La PDSY/CALV LS28 .....31 H3
Rodmell Rd AIRE BD20 ....8 C2
Roger Ct ECHL BD2 ....40 A3
Rogerson Sq BRIG HD6 ....71 F5
Roils Head Rd LUD/ILL HX2 .....67 E1
Rokeby Gdns IDLE BD10 ....30 C3
Romanby Shaw IDLE BD10 ....30 C3
Rombalds Dr BGLY BD16 ....15 F5
Romsey Gdns BOW BD4 ....48 C4
Romsey Ms BOW BD4 ....48 C4
Ronald Dr GTHN BD7 ....38 B5
Ronalds Cft YEA LS19 ....11 G4
Rookery La HIPP HX3 ....69 E5
Rookes Av WBSY BD6 ....54 B2
Rookes La HIPP HX3 ....62 B4
Rook La BOW BD4 ....48 A5
Rooks Av CLECK BD19 ....64 B5
Rook St BGLY BD16 ....16 C3
Rookwith Pde IDLE BD10 ....30 C3
Rooley Av WBSY BD6 ....55 F1
Rooley Banks RPDN/SBR HX6 ..66 B5
Rooley Cl WBOW BD5 ....55 F1
Rooley La BOW BD4 ....48 A5
WBOW BD5 ....55 F1
Roper Ln LUD/ILL HX2 ....58 C1
Roper La CUL/QBY BD13 ....43 G5
Roper St KGHY BD21 ....7 E4
Rose Bank GIR BD8 ....38 D2
KGHY BD21 ....62 D1
Rose Bank Pl GIR BD8 ....37 H5
Roseberry Av HWTH BD22 ....13 E4
SHPY BD18 ....28 D2
Rosebery Mt SHPY BD18 ....28 D2
Rosebery Rd GIR BD8 ....38 C2
Rosebery St ELL HX5 ....76 C5
PDSY/CALV LS28 ....41 H4
Rosebery Ter HFAX HX1 ....4 C1
Rosechapel Cl WBSY BD6 ....54 A4
Rosedale Av WIL/AL BD15 ....36 C2
Rosedale Gv BAIL BD17 ....18 D4
Rosedale Ct BOW BD4 ....56 D3
Rose Gv RPDN/SBR HX6 ....66 C3
Rose Heath LUD/ILL HX2 ....50 C5
Rosehill Crs LM/WK BD12 ....62 D1
Roship Ri CLAY BD14 ....45 E4
Roselee Cl HIPP HX3 ....60 C4
Rosemary La BRIG HD6 ....78 B3
Rosemary Ms HWTH BD22 * 6 C5
Rose Mdw HWTH BD22 ....13 F1
Rosemont La BAIL BD17 ....19 E4
Rose Mt BOW BD4 ....57 F2
ECHL BD2 ....39 H1
LUD/ILL HX2 ....67 G3
Rosemount Av ELL HX5 ....76 D5
Rosemount Cl KGHY BD21 * 7 E4
Rosemount Wk KGHY BD21 * ...7 E4
Rose Pl LUD/ILL HX2 ....58 C3
Rose St GIR BD8 ....38 C2
HFAX HX1 ....4 B4
KGHY BD21 ....7 E5
Rose Ter HFAX HX1 ....4 C3
LUD/ILL HX2 ....68 B4
Rosetta Dr GIR BD8 ....38 A5
Rosewood Av AIRE BD20 ....8 C2
Rosewood Gv BOW BD4 ....48 C2
Rosley Mt WBSY BD6 ....54 A4
Roslyn Pl GTHN BD7 ....46 C1
Rossefield Pk HTON BD9 ....28 C5
Rossefield Rd HTON BD9 ....28 B5
Rossendale Pl SHPY BD18 ....28 B2
Rosse St GIR BD8 ....38 C1
SHPY BD18 ....28 C1
Rosslyn Gv HWTH BD22 ....22 D3
Rossmore Dr WIL/AL BD15 ....37 F3
Rosy St HWTH BD22 ....23 C1
Rothbury HFAX HX1 * 4 C2
Rothesay Ter GTHN BD7 ....46 D2
Roth St HWTH BD22 ....23 F1
Rothwell Mt HFAX HX1 ....4 E7
Rothwell Rd HFAX HX1 ....4 E7
Roundell Av BOW BD4 ....56 A2
Roundhead Fold IDLE BD10 ......30 D1
Roundhill Av BGLY BD16 ....27 E2

HIPP HX3 ....59 F3
Robert St North HIPP HX3 ....59 H3

Round Hill Cl CUL/QBY BD13 ...45 E5
Roundhill Cl BGLY BD16 ....27 E2
Roundhill Pl BFD BD1 ....2 B4
Roundhill St WBOW BD5 ....47 E5
Round St WBOW BD5 ....47 F4
Round Thorn Pl GIR BD8 * 38 B4
Roundwell Rd LVSG WF15 ....73 F3
Roundwood SHPY BD18 ....27 H2
Roundwood Av BAIL BD17 ....19 C3
IDLE BD10 ....30 C4
Roundwood Gln BAIL BD17 ....30 D3
Roundwood Rd BAIL BD17 ....19 F3
Roundwood Vw IDLE BD10 ....30 D3
Rouse Fold BOW BD4 ....47 G2
Rowan Av BFDE BD3 ....40 D5
Rowanberry Cl ECHL BD2 ....30 A5
Rowan Ct ECHL BD2 * 40 B3
YEA LS19 ....21 G1
Rowan Dr BRIG HD6 ....71 H5
The Rowans BAIL BD17 ....18 A4
Rowan St AIRE BD20 ....6 D1
Rowantree Av BAIL BD17 ....18 C2
Rowantree Dr IDLE BD10 ....30 A3
Rowanwood Gdns IDLE BD10 * ..30 D4
Row La RPDN/SBR HX6 ....66 A5
Rowlestone Ri IDLE BD10 ....30 D4
Rowan Av BFDE BD3 ....40 D5
Rowton Thorpe IDLE BD10 ....30 D5
Roxburgh Gv WIL/AL BD15 ....37 H4
Roxby St WBOW BD5 ....47 F4
Royal Cl GTHN BD7 ....46 A4
Royd Av BGLY BD16 ....17 E3
Royd Crs HFAX HX1 * 4 A2
Royden Gv HTON BD9 ....38 D2
Royd House Gv KGHY BD21 ......14 D1
Royd House Rd KGHY BD21 ......14 D1
Royd House Wk KGHY BD21 .....14 D1
Royd House Wy KGHY BD21 .....14 D1
Royd Ings Av KGHY BD21 ....7 G2
Roydlands St HIPP HX3 ....61 G5
Royd La AIRE BD20 ....7 E2
HIPP HX3 ....59 D3
LUD/ILL HX2 ....50 D3
Royd Moor Rd BOW BD4 ....57 E1
Royd Mt HIPP HX3 ....59 H2
Roydon Gv HTON BD9 ....38 B2
Royd Pl HIPP HX3 ....59 H3
Royds Av BIRK/DRI BD11 ....57 G5
LM/WK BD12 ....62 C5
Roydscliffe Dr HTON BD9 ....28 A5
Roydscliffe Rd HTON BD9 ....37 H1
Royds Crs BRIG HD6 ....71 G1
Roydsdale Wy BOW BD4 ....55 H4
Royds Hall Av WBOW BD5 ....54 D2
Royds Hall La LM/WK BD12 ......54 B5
Royds Park Crs LM/WK BD12 ....63 E1
Roydstone Rd BFDE BD3 ....40 C4
Roydstone Ter BFDE BD3 ....40 C4
Royst St AIRE BD20 ....7 E1
CUL/QBY BD13 ....43 H1
WIL/AL BD15 ....25 H4
Royd Wy KGHY BD21 ....7 F2
Roydwood Ter CUL/QBY BD13 ..24 C3
Roydwood Ter Back
CUL/QBY BD13 ....24 C3
Roy Rd WBSY BD6 ....53 G1
Ruby St HWTH BD22 ....13 H2
Rudding Av WIL/AL BD15 ....36 D3
Rudding Dr WIL/AL BD15 ....36 D3
Rudd St GTHN BD7 ....46 B4
Ruffield Side LM/WK BD12 ....54 D5
Rufford Av YEA LS19 ....11 G5
Rufford Bank YEA LS19 ....11 H5
Rufford Cl YEA LS19 ....11 H5
Rufford Crs YEA LS19 ....11 H5
Rufford Dr YEA LS19 ....11 H5
Rufford Pl ELL HX5 * 68 C4
Rufford Rdg YEA LS19 ....11 C5
Rufford Ri YEA LS19 ....11 G5
Rufford Rd ELL HX5 ....76 B5
HIPP HX3 ....59 G3
Rufford St BFDE BD3 ....40 B5
Rufford Vls HIPP HX3 ....68 C4
Rufus St KGHY BD21 ....7 F3
WBOW BD5 ....46 C4
Rugby Av HIPP HX3 ....59 E2
Rugby Dr HIPP HX3 ....59 E2
Rugby Gdns HIPP HX3 ....59 E2
Rugby Mt HIPP HX3 ....59 E2
Rugby Pl GTHN BD7 ....28 C1
Rugby Ter HIPP HX3 ....59 E2
Runswick Gv WBOW BD5 ....55 E1
Runswick St WBOW BD5 ....55 E1
Runswick Ter WBOW BD5 ....55 E1
Rupert St HWTH BD22 ....23 C1
KGHY BD21 * 7 F3
Rush Cft IDLE BD10 ....19 G5
Rushdene Ct LM/WK BD12 ....62 D4
Rushmoor Rd BOW BD4 ....48 C5
Rusholme Dr PDSY/CALV LS28 ..41 H1
Rushton Av BFDE BD3 ....40 D4
Rushton Hill Cl LUD/ILL HX2 ....58 B4
Rushton Rd BFDE BD3 ....40 C4
Rushton St HFAX HX1 ....4 B2
LUD/ILL HX2 ....68 B4
Ruskin Av HTON BD9 ....38 B2
Ruskin Crs GSLY LS20 ....11 E3
Ruskin St PDSY/CALV LS28 ......41 H3
Ruskin Ter HIPP HX3 ....61 G5
Russell Av CUL/QBY BD13 ....52 B2
Russell Hall La CUL/QBY BD13 ..52 B2
Russell Rd CUL/QBY BD13 ....52 A2
Russell St CUL/QBY BD13 ....52 B1
HFAX HX1 ....5 H4
KGHY BD21 ....7 G4
SHPY BD18 ....28 D4
WBOW BD5 ....47 E2
Russell Wy BRIG HD6 ....71 G5
The Russetts HIPP HX3 ....60 B5
Rustic Av HIPP HX3 ....69 H4
Rustless Av CLECK BD19 ....77 H4
Ruswarp Crs IDLE BD10 ....30 D1
Rutland Cl BOW BD4 ....47 H3

KGHY BD21 .....14 A1
Ryan Gv HWTH BD22.....6 A3
Ryan St WBOW BD5.....47 E4
Ryburn Cl HFAX HX1.....4 B3
Ryburn St RPDN/SBR HX6.....67 H5
Rycroft Av BGLY BD16.....26 D3
Rycroft St SHPY BD18.....29 E4
Rydal Av HTON BD9.....28 D5
Rydal St KGHY BD21.....6 D5
Rydings Av BRIG HD6.....71 F5
Rydings Cl BRIG HD6.....71 F5
Rydings Dr BRIG HD6.....71 F5
Ryecroft BGLY BD16.....15 E5
Rye Cft LUD/ILL HX2.....51 E4
Ryecroft Crs LUD/ILL HX2.....58 C4
Ryecroft La LUD/ILL HX2.....58 C5
Ryecroft Rd BGLY BD16.....14 C4
Ryecroft Ter LUD/ILL HX2.....58 C4
Ryedale Wy WIL/AL BD15.....36 D2
Ryefield Av CLAY BD14.....45 E2
Ryelands Gv HTON BD9.....27 G5
Rye La LUD/ILL HX2.....58 B4
Rye St HWTH BD22.....2 A2
Rylands Av BGLY BD16.....23 F1
Rylands Meadow HWTH BD22...23 F1
Rylstone Gdns BAIL BD17.....18 A4
Rylstone St KGHY BD21.....7 G3
Ryshworth Av BGLY BD16.....13 G5
Ryton Dl IDLE BD10.....30 D5

S

Sable Crest ECHL BD2.....29 G5
Sackville St BFD BD1.....2 C5
Saddler St LM/WK BD12.....62 D1
Saddleworth Rd GTL/HWG HX4...76 B4
Saffron Dr WIL/AL BD15.....36 D3
Sage St WBOW BD5.....47 E4
Sahara Ct GIR BD8.....39 E2
St Abbs Cl WBSY BD6.....54 D3
St Abbs Dr WBSY BD6.....54 D3
St Abbs Fold WBSY BD6.....54 D3
St Abbs Ga WBSY BD6.....54 D3
St Abbs Wk WBSY BD6.....54 D3
St Abbs Ws WBSY BD6.....54 D3
St Aidan's Rd BAIL BD17.....19 E4
St Alban's Av HIPP HX3.....68 D5
St Albans Cft HIPP HX3.....69 E4
St Alban's Rd HIPP HX3.....68 D5
St Andrews Cl YEA LS19.....11 H4
St Andrew's Crs LM/WK BD12...63 H1
St Andrew's Dr BRIG HD6.....71 F4
St Andrews Rd YEA LS19.....11 H4
St Andrew's Rd GTHN BD7 *.....38 D5
St Anne's Rd HIPP HX3.....75 H1
St Anns Sq RPDN/SBR HX6.....67 F4
St Anuil GIR BD8 *.....58 C3
St Augustine's Ter BFDE BD3.....3 K1
  HFAX HX1.....4 C3
St Barnabas Rd LVSG WF15.....73 E3
St Bevan's Rd HIPP HX3.....68 D5
St Blaise Ct WBOW BD5.....2 D7
St Blaise Wy BFD BD1.....2 D6
St Chad's Av BRIG HD6.....70 D3
St Chad's Rd GIR BD8.....38 C3
St Clare's Av ECHL BD2.....40 C2
St Eloi Av BAIL BD17.....14 C4
St Enoch's Rd WBSY BD6.....54 C1
St George's Crs HFAX HX1.....4 A1
St George's Pl WBOW BD5 *.....47 F2
St George's Rd HIPP HX3.....59 F4
St Giles Cl BRIG HD6.....70 D5
St Giles Rd HIPP HX3.....59 G4
St Helena Rd WBSY BD6.....54 C1
St Helier Gv BAIL BD17.....19 E2
St Hilda's Ter BFDE BD3.....40 D4
St Ive's Gdns HIPP HX3 *.....68 D5
St Ives Gv BGLY BD16.....15 H4
St Ives Pl BGLY BD16.....15 H4
St Ives Rd BGLY BD16.....15 H4
  HIPP HX3.....68 C5
St James Ct HFAX HX1.....5 G3
St James Crs PDSY/CALV LS28...41 G3
St James Rd HFAX HX1.....5 G3
St James Sq HFAX HX1 *.....47 F2
St James St HFAX HX1.....5 G3
St Johns Cl CLECK BD19 *.....73 H1
St John's Ct BAIL BD17.....19 F4
  YEA LS19.....11 F5
St John's Crs GIR BD8.....37 H4
St John's Dr YEA LS19.....11 F5
St John's La HFAX HX1.....5 G6
St John's Pl BIRK/DRI BD11 *...57 F4
  HFAX HX1 *.....5 G6
St John's Rd AIRE BD20.....5 G5
  YEA LS19.....11 F5
St John St BRIG HD6.....78 B2
St Johns Wv HWTH BD22.....2 A3
  YEA LS19.....11 F5
St Jude's Pl BFD BD1.....2 B2
St Jude's St BFD BD1.....2 A2
  HFAX HX1.....68 C3
St Laurence's Cl ECHL BD2.....38 A3
St Leonards Ct HTON BD9.....38 A4
St Leonard's Gv GIR BD8.....38 A3
St Leonard's Rd GIR BD8.....38 A3
St Luke's Cl CLECK BD19.....73 E1
  WBOW BD5.....47 E2
St Margaret's Av BOW BD4.....48 D3
St Margaret's Pl GTHN BD7.....46 C2
St Margaret's Rd GTHN BD7.....46 C2
St Margaret's Ter BFDE BD3....46 C2
St Mark's Av LM/WK BD12.....63 G1
St Mark's Ter LM/WK BD12.....63 G1
St Martins GTHN BD7.....38 D5
St Martin's Vw HIPP HX3.....71 F5
St Mary Magdalenes Cl
  GIR BD8.....38 C4
St Mary's Av LM/WK BD12.....62 D3

St Mary's Cl LM/WK BD12.....62 C3
St Mary's Ct LM/WK BD12.....62 C4
St Mary's Dr LM/WK BD12.....62 C4
St Marys Ga ELL HX5.....76 D4
St Mary's Mt LM/WK BD12.....62 C4
St Mary's Rd AIRE BD20.....8 A1
  BOW BD4.....48 C2
  BFD BD1.....38 D2
St Mary's Sq LM/WK BD12.....62 C3
St Mary St HFAX HX1.....4 E5
St Matthews Cl WIL/AL BD15...25 G5
St Matthew's Dr HIPP HX3.....25 G5
St Matthews Gv WIL/AL BD15...25 G5
St Matthew's Rd WBOW BD5....55 E1
St Merrion Crs HIPP HX3.....69 F5
St Michael's Rd GIR BD8.....38 D4
St Oswalds Garth GSLY LS20....10 D2
St Paul's Av BIRK/DRI BD11.....57 G5
  WBSY BD6.....54 C2
St Pauls Cl GIR BD8.....38 D3
St Pauls Gv WBSY BD6.....54 C2
St Paul's Rd BIRK/DRI BD11.....57 F5
  GIR BD8.....38 D3
  HFAX HX1 *.....4 A7
  KGHY BD21.....7 G5
  SHPY BD18.....28 B2
  WBSY BD6.....54 C2
St Peg Cl CLECK BD19.....73 H1
St Peg La CLECK BD19.....73 H1
St Peter's Av RPDN/SBR HX6...66 C5
St Phillips Ct GIR BD8.....38 A3
St Stephens Ct HIPP HX3 *.....75 F1
St Stephen's Rd
  PDSY/CALV LS28.....31 F2
  WBOW BD5.....31 G2
St Stephen's St HIPP HX3.....75 F1
St Stephen's Ter WBOW BD5 *...47 F4
Saint St HFAX HX1 *.....46 B3
St Thomas Gdns HUDN HX2.....79 G5
St Wilfrid's St PDSY/CALV LS28..31 G2
St Wilfrid's Cl GTHN BD7.....46 A2
St Wilfrid's Crs GTHN BD7.....46 A2
St Wilfrid's Rd GTHN BD7.....46 A2
St Winifred's Cl LUD/ILL HX2 *...50 C5
Salcombe Pl BOW BD4.....48 D5
Salem St BFD BD1.....2 C4
  CUL/QBY BD13.....58 D1
Salisbury Av BAIL BD17.....19 E3
Salisbury Pl HIPP HX3.....59 G4
  PDSY/CALV LS28.....31 F3
Salisbury Rd CLECK BD19.....63 G5
  HTON BD9.....28 D4
  BFD BD1.....6 D5
  LM/WK BD12.....63 F3
Salisbury Ter PDSY/CALV LS28..31 F3
  RPDN/SBR HX6.....66 D5
  YEA LS19.....21 G2
Salisbury Ter HIPP HX3.....59 G4
Sal Royd Rd LM/WK BD12.....55 E3
Saltaire Rd AIRE BD20.....5 G1
  SHPY BD18.....28 B1
Saltburn Pl HTON BD9.....38 A2
Saltburn St HFAX HX1.....4 A3
Salterhebble Hl HIPP HX3.....76 A1
Saltterlee HIPP HX3.....60 B5
Salt Horn Cl LM/WK BD12.....63 H1
Salts Mill Rd BAIL BD17.....28 C1
Salt St GIR BD8.....38 D3
  HFAX HX1.....4 C2
Samuel St KGHY BD21.....7 F3
Sandale Wk WBSY BD6.....54 A3
Sandall Magna WBSY BD6.....54 A3
Sandals Rd BAIL BD17.....18 D4
Sand Beds CUL/QBY BD13.....52 B1
Sandbeds Rd LUD/ILL HX2.....58 D4
Sandbeds Rd LUD/ILL HX2.....58 D5
Sandbeds Ter LUD/ILL HX2.....58 D4
Sanderling Ct GIR BD8 *.....37 F5
Sanderson Av WBSY BD6.....54 D1
Sandfield Rd IDLE BD10.....30 A3
Sandford Rd BFDE BD3.....40 B5
Sandforth Av HIPP HX3.....59 H5
Sandhall Av LUD/ILL HX2.....67 G1
Sandhall Cl LUD/ILL HX2.....67 G1
Sandhall Gn LUD/ILL HX2.....58 C5
Sandhall La LUD/ILL HX2.....67 G1
Sandhall Fold IDLE BD10.....29 H2
Sandhill Mt IDLE BD10.....30 A3
Sandholme Crs HIPP HX3.....70 C1
Sandhurst Rd PDSY/CALV LS28..31 F2
Sandhurst St PDSY/CALV LS28..31 F2
Sandmead Cl BOW BD4.....48 D4
Sandmead Ct CUL/QBY BD13....44 B1
Sandmoor Gdns HIPP HX3.....61 E1
Sandmoor Garth IDLE BD10.....20 A5
Sandown Av LUD/ILL HX2.....58 D1
Sandown Rd LUD/ILL HX2.....58 D1
Sandpiper Ms GIR BD8.....37 F5
Sandringham Cl CLAY BD14 *...45 G2
Sandringham Ct CLAY BD14.....45 G2
Sandringham Rd CLAY BD14.....45 G2
Sandsend Ct HTON BD9.....37 H2
Sandside Cl WBOW BD5.....47 G5
Sand St HWTH BD22.....22 D5
  KGHY BD21.....7 F4
Sandy Banks BGLY BD16.....25 G1
Sandy Beck WIL/AL BD15.....36 D1
Sandy Ga AIRE BD20.....6 D5
Sandygate Ter BOW BD4.....48 C3
Sandymoor WIL/AL BD15.....26 D5
Sandy Wy YEA LS19.....11 G4
Sandywood St KGHY BD21.....7 F3
Sangster Wy WBOW BD5.....55 H1
Santa Monica Crs IDLE BD10....29 H2
Santa Monica Gv IDLE BD10.....29 H2
Santa Monica Rd IDLE BD10.....29 H2
Sapgate La CUL/QBY BD13.....44 B1
Saplin St GIR BD8.....38 C3
Savile Av IDLE BD10.....30 B3
Savile Cl BRIG HD6.....72 A5
Savile Ct HFAX HX1.....5 H4
Savile Dr HFAX HX1.....4 E7
Savile Gln HFAX HX1.....5 F6

Savile La BRIG HD6.....72 A5
Savile Lea HFAX HX1.....5 H5
Savile Pde HFAX HX1.....68 C3
Savile Pk HFAX HX1.....68 C3
Savile Park Gdns HFAX HX1.....68 C3
Savile Park Rd CLECK BD19.....64 C2
  HFAX HX1.....5 F6
Savile Park St HFAX HX1.....68 C3
Savile Park Ter HFAX HX1 *.....68 C3
Savile Rd ELL HX5.....76 C5
  HFAX HX1.....5 F6
Savile Royd HFAX HX1.....4 E7
Savile St CLECK BD19.....64 C4
Savile Ter HFAX HX1.....4 D7
Saville Wy ELL HX5.....76 D3
Saville Park Rd HFAX HX1.....4 E7
Sawley St KGHY BD21.....7 E5
Sawood La HWTH BD22.....33 G4
Sawrey Pl WBOW BD5.....2 B7
Saxilby Rd AIRE BD20.....8 C2
Saxon St GIR BD8.....38 D4
  HFAX HX1.....4 C2
Saxton Av WBSY BD6.....54 A1
Sayle Av BOW BD4.....56 A2
Scaley St BFDE BD3.....40 C5
Scarborough Gv HTON BD9.....28 B2
Scarborough Rd SHPY BD18.....28 B2
Scar Bottom La GTL/HWG HX4...75 E4
Scar Head Rd RPDN/SBR HX6...74 A1
Scarlet Hts CUL/QBY BD13.....52 C1
Scarr Bottom Rd LUD/ILL HX2..68 A4
Scar Top GTL/HWG HX4 *.....75 E4
Scarwood Cl BGLY BD16.....16 D2
Scholars Wk ECHL BD2.....40 A1
Scholars Wy AIRE BD20.....28 A5
Scholebrook La BOW BD4.....49 H4
Scholemoor Av GTHN BD7.....45 H2
Scholemoor La GTHN BD7.....45 H2
Scholemoor Rd GTHN BD7.....46 A2
Scholes La CLECK BD19.....63 G5
  GTL/HWG HX4.....75 F2
Scholes St BFDE BD3.....12 A5
Scholey Av BRIG HD6.....78 B5
Scholey Rd BRIG HD6.....78 B5
School Cl LUD/ILL HX2.....51 E3
School Cote Brow HIPP HX3.....51 G4
School Crs LUD/ILL HX2.....51 E3
School Gn BGLY BD16.....78 B5
  CUL/QBY BD13.....44 D1
School Green Av
  CUL/QBY BD13.....44 C1
School House Fold AIRE BD20...8 A1
School La HIPP HX3.....69 H5
  LUD/ILL HX2.....51 E2
School Pl LM/WK BD12 *.....62 D1
School Rd HWTH BD22.....22 D5
School Sq BFDE BD3.....40 C5
School St AIRE BD20.....27 E2
  BGLY BD16.....48 B4
  BOW BD4.....56 A2
  CLAY BD14.....45 E3
  CLECK BD19.....24 C3
  CUL/QBY BD13.....58 A1
  GTL/HWG HX4.....75 G3
  HFAX HX1.....5 J5
  LM/WK BD12.....63 H1
  LM/WK BD12.....63 H1
  WIL/AL BD15.....25 H4
School Wk HWTH BD22.....22 D5
School Yard Vw HIPP HX3 *.....59 H4
Score Hl HIPP HX3.....60 D1
Scoresby St BFD BD1.....3 F5
Scotchman Rd HTON BD9.....38 A2
Scotland Cl CLECK BD19.....64 A1
Scott La AIRE BD20.....7 H1
  CLECK BD19.....65 E4
Scott La West AIRE BD20.....7 G1
Scott St KGHY BD21.....7 E4
Scotty Bank BRIG HD6 *.....78 B2
Scotty Croft La BRIG HD6.....78 B2
Seaton St BFDE BD3.....3 J4
Second Av BFDE BD3.....40 B3
  HIPP HX3.....68 C4
  KGHY BD21.....73 E4
  LVSG WF15.....21 H1
  YEA LS19.....21 H1
Second St LM/WK BD12.....63 G5
Sedbergh Rd HIPP HX3.....5 J7
Sedge Gv HWTH BD22.....22 D1
Sedgefield Ter BFD BD1 *.....2 A4
Sedgewick Cl BFD BD1.....2 A3
Seed Hill Ter LUD/ILL HX2.....50 B4
Seed Rw BOW BD4.....56 A2
Seed St LM/WK BD12.....55 G4
Sefton Av BRIG HD6.....71 E3
Sefton Crs BRIG HD6.....71 E3
Sefton Dr BRIG HD6.....71 E3
Sefton Gv ECHL BD2.....40 A1
Sefton Pl KGHY BD21 *.....7 F3
Sefton St HFAX HX1.....4 D2
  KGHY BD21.....7 F3
Sefton Ter HFAX HX1.....4 D2
Selborne Gv HTON BD9.....38 C1
  KGHY BD21.....13 H1
Selborne Mt HTON BD9.....38 D2
Selborne Ter HTON BD9.....38 C1
  SHPY BD18.....28 A1
Selborne Vls CLAY BD14.....45 F4
  HTON BD9.....38 D2
Selby Rd LUD/ILL HX2.....50 C3
Selbourne St HFAX HX1.....50 B3
Selene Cl CLECK BD19.....64 A1
Sellars Fold GTHN BD7 *.....46 B3
Sellerdale Av LM/WK BD12.....63 E3
Sellerdale Dr LM/WK BD12.....63 E3
Sellerdale Ri LM/WK BD12.....63 E3
Sellerdale Wy LM/WK BD12.....63 E4
Senson Av ECHL BD2.....29 G4
Senior Wy WBOW BD5 *.....2 D7
Serpentine Rd CLECK BD19.....64 C5
Sevenoaks Md WIL/AL BD15.....37 E3

Seventh Av LVSG WF15.....73 E3
Severn Rd ECHL BD2.....39 H2
Sewell Rd BFDE BD3.....3 K6
Seymour St BFDE BD3.....3 H6
Shaftesbury Av BRIG HD6.....77 G2
  HTON BD9.....37 G2
  SHPY BD18.....
Shakespeare Cl BFDE BD3.....3 H3
Shakespeare Rd LS20.....10 D3
Shakespeare St HFAX HX1.....5 G6
Shalimar St HFAX HX1.....4 B4
Shann Av AIRE BD20.....6 C3
Shann Crs AIRE BD20.....6 C3
Shann La AIRE BD20.....6 C3
Shannon Cl BRIG HD6.....77 H4
Shannon Rd BRIG HD6.....77 H4
Shann St ECHL BD2.....29 E5
Shapla Cl HWTH BD22.....2 C5
Sharp Av WBSY BD6.....54 D2
Sharpe St WBOW BD5.....2 C7
Sharp St WBSY BD6.....54 D1
Shaw Gv LUD/ILL HX2.....5 J7
Shaw Hill La HIPP HX3.....5 J7
Shaw La ELL HX5.....77 H4
  GSLY LS20.....11 E2
  HIPP HX3.....52 C4
  HIPP HX3.....69 E4
  KGHY BD21.....14 C3
  RPDN/SBR HX6.....74 B2
Shaw Lane Gdns GSLY LS20.....11 E2
Shaw Leys YEA LS19.....11 F3
Shaw Royd YEA LS19.....11 F3
Shaw St CLECK BD19 *.....73 E1
  LM/WK BD12.....54 C4
Shay Crs HTON BD9.....27 H5
Shay Dr HTON BD9.....27 H5
Shay Fold HTON BD9.....27 H5
Shay Ga WIL/AL BD15 *.....26 B5
Shay La HIPP HX3.....28 A5
  HTON BD9.....27 H5
  WIL/AL BD15.....26 B5
Shay Syke HFAX HX1.....5 J6
Shearbridge Gn GTHN BD7.....46 D1
Shearbridge Rd GTHN BD7.....46 D1
Shearbridge Ter GTHN BD7.....46 D1
Sheed St KGHY BD21 *.....7 F4
Sheep Hill La CUL/QBY BD13...45 E5
Sheila Henry Dr WBSY BD6.....53 F1
Shelby Gra IDLE BD10.....30 B3
Sheldon Rdg BOW BD4.....56 A3
Sheldrake Av GIR BD8.....37 F5
Shelf Hall La HIPP HX3.....53 E5
Shelf Moor HIPP HX3.....53 E5
Shelf Moor Rd HIPP HX3.....53 E5
Shelley Cl BGLY BD16.....16 D5
Shelley Gv GIR BD8.....37 H4
Shelton Cl CUL/QBY BD13.....34 D3
Shepherds Thorn La HUDN HD2..78 D5
Sherborne Dr HWTH BD22.....2 A3
Sherborne Rd GTHN BD7.....46 D1
  IDLE BD10.....20 A5
Sherburn Cl BIRK/DRI BD11.....57 G4
Sherburn Gv BIRK/DRI BD11.....57 G4
Sherburn Rd BIRK/DRI BD11.....57 H4
Sheridan St BOW BD4.....48 C2
Sherwell La BGLY BD16.....17 F2
Sherwell Ri WIL/AL BD15.....36 C4
Sherwood Av CLECK BD19.....65 G5
Sherwood Cl ECHL BD2.....17 F1
  GIR BD8.....65 G5
Sherwood Gv SHPY BD18.....65 G5
Sherwood Pl ECHL BD2.....40 A2
Sherwood Rd BRIG HD6.....78 D1
Shetcliffe La BOW BD4.....56 C1
Shetcliffe Rd BOW BD4.....56 C1
Shetland Cl ECHL BD2.....29 G5
Shibden Garth HIPP HX3.....60 D5
Shibden Grange Dr HIPP HX3...60 C5
Shibden Hall Cft HIPP HX3.....60 C5
Shibden Hall Rd HIPP HX3.....60 C5
Shibden Head La
  CUL/QBY BD13.....51 H3
Shibden Vw CUL/QBY BD13.....52 A3
Shipley Airedale Rd BFDE BD3..3 H2
Shipley Fields Rd SHPY BD18...28 C4
Ship St BRIG HD6.....78 B1
Shire Cl WBSY BD6.....54 A3
Shirley Av CLECK BD19.....65 G5
  WBSY BD6.....54 A2
Shirley Crs LM/WK BD12.....62 C4
Shirley Gv CLECK BD19.....65 G5
  HIPP HX3.....71 F1
Shirley Mt CLECK BD19.....65 G5
Shirley Pde CLECK BD19.....65 F5
Shirley Pl CLECK BD19.....65 F5
  LM/WK BD12.....62 C4
Shirley Rd BOW BD4.....56 C1
  CLECK BD19.....65 G5
  GTHN BD7.....46 C1
Shirley St AIRE BD20.....28 B1
  SHPY BD18.....28 B1
Shirley Ter CLECK BD19.....65 G5
Short Cl LM/WK BD12.....62 C1
Shortway CUL/QBY BD13.....44 D1
  PDSY/CALV LS28.....41 F5
Shrike Cl WBSY BD6.....54 A3
Shroggs Rd HFAX HX1.....4 D2
Shroggs St HFAX HX1.....4 D1
Shroggs Vue Ter HFAX HX1.....4 D2
Shuttleworth La GIR BD8.....37 H4
Sickle La LUD/ILL HX2.....67 H5
Sickle St CLECK BD19.....64 B4
Siddal La HIPP HX3.....69 E4
Siddal Gr HIPP HX3.....69 E4
Siddal New Rd HIPP HX3.....69 E4
Siddal St HIPP HX3.....69 E4
Siddal Top La HIPP HX3.....69 E3
The Sidings HIPP HX3.....10 D2
Silk St HTON BD9.....38 B2
Silson La BAIL BD17.....19 F2

Silver Birch Av LM/WK BD12.....63 E3
Silver Birch Cl LM/WK BD12.....63 E3
Silver Birch Dr LM/WK BD12.....63 E3
Silver Birch Gv LM/WK BD12.....63 E3
Silver Birch St LM/WK BD12.....63 E3
Silver Ct AIRE BD20.....5 H2
  GSLY LS20.....10 D3
Silverdale Cl GSLY LS20.....10 D4
Silverdale Dr GSLY LS20.....10 D4
Silverdale Gra GSLY LS20.....10 D4
Silverdale Gv GSLY LS20.....10 C4
Silverdale Mt GSLY LS20.....10 C4
Silverdale Rd GSLY LS20.....10 C4
  WBOW BD5.....47 F5
Silverhill Dr BFDE BD3.....40 C4
Silverhill Rd BFDE BD3.....40 B5
Silver La YEA LS19.....11 H4
Silver St BFD BD8.....38 C3
  HFAX HX1.....5 G4
Silverwood Av LUD/ILL HX2.....58 B4
Silwood Dr ECHL BD2.....40 B1
Simm Carr La HIPP HX3.....60 A1
Simmonds La HFAX HX1.....5 J7
Simms Dene WIL/AL BD15.....26 D5
Simon Cl BOW BD4.....49 E5
Simpson Gv IDLE BD10.....20 B5
Simpson St KGHY BD21.....59 G3
  KGHY BD21.....
Sinclair Rd ECHL BD2.....29 G4
Sinden Ms IDLE BD10.....20 D4
Singleton St BFD BD1.....2 D2
Sion Hl HIPP HX3.....69 F5
Sir Isaac Holden Pl GTHN BD7...38 C5
Sir Wilfred Pl IDLE BD10.....30 A1
Siskin Dr WBSY BD6.....53 G1
Sixth Av BFDE BD3.....
  LVSG WF15.....73 E3
Sizers Ct YEA LS19.....21 F1
Skelton Rd IDLE BD10.....30 C2
Skinner La GIR BD8.....38 D2
Skipton Rd KGHY BD21.....7 F3
Skircoat Gn HIPP HX3.....75 H1
Skircoat Green Rd HIPP HX3....75 H1
Skircoat Moor Cl LUD/ILL HX2..68 B4
Skircoat Moor Rd LUD/ILL HX2..68 A4
Skircoat Rd HFAX HX1.....5 H7
Skirrow St BGLY BD16.....27 E3
Slack Bottom Rd WBSY BD6....54 B2
Slack La HWTH BD22.....12 C3
Sladdin Rw CUL/QBY BD13.....51 H2
Slade La AIRE BD20.....7 H1
  BRIG HD6.....78 A5
Sladen St KGHY BD21.....6 D4
Slaymaker La HWTH BD22.....2 C5
Slead Av BRIG HD6.....71 E4
Slead Ct BRIG HD6.....71 E4
Slead Crs BRIG HD6.....71 E4
Slead La BRIG HD6.....71 E4
Slead Royd BRIG HD6.....71 E4
Sleningford Gv SHPY BD18.....27 H1
Sleningford Ri BGLY BD16.....16 C1
Sleningford Rd BGLY BD16.....16 C1
  SHPY BD18.....27 H1
Slingsby Cl IDLE BD10.....30 C1
Slippy La LUD/ILL HX2.....50 B5
Sloan Sq GIR BD8.....38 C4
Smalewell Dr PDSY/CALV LS28..49 H1
Smalewell Gdns
  PDSY/CALV LS28.....49 H1
Smalewell Rd PDSY/CALV LS28..49 G1
Small Page Fold
  CUL/QBY BD13 *.....52 B1
Smiddles La WBOW BD5.....55 D5
Smith Av WBSY BD6.....54 D2
Smith Crs BRIG HD6.....77 H3
Smitherds St KGHY BD21.....7 F5
Smithfield Av HIPP HX3.....61 F5
Smith House Crs BRIG HD6.....71 E3
Smith House Gv BRIG HD6.....71 E3
Smith House La BRIG HD6.....71 G2
Smith La HTON BD9.....37 H2
Smith's Ter HIPP HX3.....59 F2
Smith St BGLY BD16.....27 E3
  BOW BD4.....56 A2
  GTHN BD7.....2 A5
  KGHY BD21.....6 D5
Smithville AIRE BD20.....8 A2
Smithy Carr La BRIG HD6.....71 F4
Smithy Hl CUL/QBY BD13.....42 D1
Smithy La WIL/AL BD15.....25 H3
Smithy St HFAX HX1.....5 J3
Snaith Wood Dr YEA LS19.....21 H5
Snaith Wood Ms YEA LS19.....21 G5
Snape Dr GTHN BD7.....45 G5
Snape St KGHY BD21.....6 D5
Snelsins La CLECK BD19.....64 B4
Snelsins Rd CLECK BD19.....64 B4
Snowden Rd SHPY BD18.....29 E3
Snowden St BFD BD1.....2 C3
Snowdens Wk CLAY BD14.....45 G3
Snowdrop Ms WIL/AL BD15.....36 C1
Soaper House La HIPP HX3.....61 F5
Soaper La HIPP HX3.....53 C5
Sod House Gn HIPP HX3.....59 F2
Soho St BFD BD1.....2 B5
  HFAX HX1.....4 B4
Somerset Av BAIL BD17.....18 C4
Somerset Rd HFAX HX1.....78 C4
Somerville Av BOW BD4.....48 C5
Somerville Gr BOW BD4.....54 C3
Somerville Pk WBSY BD6.....54 C3
Sonning Rd ECHL BD2.....37 E4
Sorrel Wy BAIL BD17.....19 G2
Sorrin Cl IDLE BD10.....30 D2
Sourehy Cross Wy BOW BD4....57 E3
Southampton St BFDE BD3.....3 F1
South Bank CUL/QBY BD13.....52 B1
South Bolton LUD/ILL HX2.....50 C3
South Brook Ter BFD BD1 *.....2 B6
South Cliffe CUL/QBY BD13.....44 B1
Southcliffe HIPP HX3.....69 G3
Southcliffe Dr BAIL BD17.....18 D5
Southcliffe Wy BAIL BD17.....18 D5
South Cl GSLY LS20.....10 A3

South Clough Head
   LUD/ILL HX2 ....66 D1
Southcote Pl IDLE BD10 ....30 A1
South Croft Av BIRK/DRI BD11 ...57 F4
South Croft Dr BIRK/DRI BD11 ...57 F5
South Croft Gv BIRK/DRI BD11 ...57 F5
Southdown Cl HTON BD9 ....37 H2
Southdown Rd BAIL BD17 ....18 C5
South Dr GSLY LS20 ....10 A3
South Edge AIRE BD20 ....6 D5
Southedge Cl HIPP HX3 ....27 H2
Southfield Av AIRE BD20 ....70 B1
   WBSY BD6 ....54 D2
Southfield Dr AIRE BD20 ....8 B1
Southfield La AIRE BD20 ....46 B4
Southfield Mt AIRE BD20 ....8 B1
Southfield Rd BGLY BD16 ....16 D5
   WBOW BD5 ....46 D4
Southfield Sq GIR BD8 ....38 D3
Southfield Ter BIRK/DRI BD11 ......8 B1
   HIPP HX3 ....61 F4
Southfield Wy AIRE BD20 ....8 B1
Southgate BFD BD1 ....5 F4
   ELL HX5 ....76 C4
   GSLY LS20 ....10 A4
   HFAX HX1 ....5 H4
South Gv BRIG HD6 ....70 C3
   SHPY BD18 ....27 G2
South Hill Dr BCLY BD16...............17 E3
Southlands BAIL BD17 ....18 C5
   LUD/ILL HX2 ....51 E1
Southlands Av AIRE BD20 ....8 B2
   BGLY BD16 ....16 D5
   CUL/QBY BD13 ....45 F1
Southlands Dr AIRE BD20 * 8 B2
   BGLY BD16 ....16 C5
   CUL/QBY BD13 ....45 E1
Southlands Gv West
   AIRE BD20 ....8 B1
Southlands Mt AIRE BD20 ....8 B1
Southlands Rd AIRE BD20 ....8 B1
South La HIPP HX3 ....53 E3
Southlea Av LM/WK BD12 ....13 F4
Southlea Cl LM/WK BD12 ....55 H5
Southmere Av GTHN BD7 ....46 B4
Southmere Crs GTHN BD7 ....46 B4
Southmere Dr GTHN BD7 ....46 B4
Southmere Gv GTHN BD7 ....46 B4
Southmere Ov GTHN BD7 ....46 A5
Southmere Rd GTHN BD7 ....46 B4
Southmere Ter GTHN BD7 ....46 B4
Southowram Bank
   HIPP HX3 ....69 F2
South Pde CLECK BD19 ....64 B5
   GIR BD8 ....2 B1
   HFAX HX1 ....5 J6
South Royde Av HIPP HX3 ....68 D1
South Sq CUL/QBY BD13 ....44 A1
South St BRIG HD6 ....71 F5
   CUL/QBY BD13 ....34 C4
   CUL/QBY BD13 ....36 A5
   HFAX HX1 ....5 F5
   KGHY BD21 ....3 K7
   LM/WK BD12 ....63 H1
   WBOW BD5 ....46 D4
South Vw AIRE BD20 ....8 C2
   BAIL BD17 ....18 D3
   HIPP HX3 ....69 H4
   HWTH BD22 ....22 D2
   IDLE BD10 ....30 C2
   PDSY/CALV LS28 ....41 H3
   YEA LS19 ....11 E4
South View Cl BOW BD4 ....56 D3
   YEA LS19 ....10 D4
South View Ct HIPP HX3 ....57 E3
South View Rd BOW BD4 ....56 D3
   YEA LS19 ....11 C4
South View Ter BAIL BD17 * 18 D3
   HFAX HX1 ....4 B2
   YEA LS19 ....11 C4
South Wk BGLY BD16 ....15 F5
South Wy BOW BD4 ....56 D3
   SHPY BD18 ....27 G2
Southway BGLY BD16 ....17 F1
   GSLY LS20 ....10 A3
Sovereign Pk BAIL BD17 ....19 F2
Sovereign St HFAX HX1 * 5 F5
Sowden Buildings ECHL BD2 ....40 A2
Sowden Gra CUL/QBY BD13 ....44 A1
Sowden Rd HTON BD9 ....37 G1
Sowden St GTHN BD7 * 46 C4
Sowerby Croft La
   RPDN/SBR HX6 ....67 E5
Sowerby New Rd
   RPDN/SBR HX6 ....66 B5
Sowerby St RPDN/SBR HX6 ....67 E5
Spa La BGLY BD16 ....16 D1
Spark House La
   RPDN/SBR HX6 ....67 E5
Spartan Rd LM/WK BD12 ....55 E5
Spearhead Wy KGHY BD21 ....7 F3
Speeton Av GTHN BD7 ....45 H5
Speeton Gv GTHN BD7 ....45 G5
Spencer Av GTHN BD7 ....46 B2
Spencer Rd GSLY LS20 ....11 H3
   GTHN BD7 ....46 A2
Spencer St KGHY BD21 ....6 D4
Spen Cl CLECK BD19 ....65 E5
Spen La GSLY LS20 ....11 E3
Spenser Ri GSLY LS20 ....11 E3
Spenser Rd GSLY LS20 ....11 E3
Spen Valley Heritage Trail
   BIRK/DRI BD11 ....56 D4
   CLECK BD19 ....64 D3
Spen View La BOW BD4 ....56 A3
Spicer St WBOW BD5 * 46 D4
Spiers Garth WBSY BD6 ....54 C5
Spindle St LUD/ILL HX2 ....51 F5
The Spinners HWTH BD22 ....22 D3
Spinners Wy CLECK BD19 ....63 G5
Spinney Ri BOW BD4 ....57 E1

The Spinney BRIG HD6 ....71 F3
   IDLE BD10 ....30 A1
Spinning Mill Ct SHPY BD18 ....27 H1
Spout Hl HIPP HX3 ....77 H5
Spout House La BRIG HD6 ....70 D2
Spring Av KGHY BD21 ....19 H5
Springbank YEA LS19 ....21 F2
Spring Bank Pl GIR BD8 ....39 E3
Spring Bank Ri KGHY BD21 ....19 H5
Springcliffe GIR BD8 ....38 C3
Springcliffe St GIR BD8 ....38 C3
Spring Cl BGLY BD16 ....17 E4
   KGHY BD21 ....7 H5
Spring Ct WIL/AL BD15 * 36 D1
Springdale Crs IDLE BD10 ....30 B1
Spring Dr KGHY BD21 ....7 H5
Spring Edge North HFAX HX1 ....4 C7
Spring Edge South HFAX HX1 ......68 B5
Spring Edge West HFAX HX1 ....68 A5
Spring Farm La BGLY BD16 ....15 F5
Spring Farm Ms WIL/AL BD15 ......25 H4
Springfield Av AIRE BD20 ....46 A2
Springfield Cl AIRE BD20 ....6 D3
Springfield Dr LVSG WF15 ....73 F3
Springfield Gdns AIRE BD20 ....6 C3
Springfield Gv BGLY BD16 ....16 C2
   BRIG HD6 ....70 C3
Springfield La LVSG WF15 ....73 H1
Springfield Rd AIRE BD20 ....6 D3
   BAIL BD17 ....18 C2
   ELL HX5 ....77 E4
   GSLY LS20 ....10 D3
Springfield St CUL/QBY BD13 ....44 B1
   GIR BD8 ....38 C2
Springfield Ter CLECK BD19 ....63 G4
   GSLY LS20 ....10 D2
Spring Gdns BFD BD1 ....2 B2
   BRIG HD6 ....71 F4
Spring Gardens La AIRE BD20 ....6 D2
Spring Gardens Mt AIRE BD20 * ...7 E2
Spring Gardens St HTON BD9 ....38 B1
Spring Garden St
   CUL/QBY BD13 ....52 B1
Spring Gv HFAX HX1 ....67 H1
Spring Hall Cl HFAX HX1 ....53 E5
Spring Hall Dr LUD/ILL HX2 ....67 H2
Spring Hall Gdns LUD/ILL HX2 .....67 H1
Spring Hall Gv LUD/ILL HX2 ....67 H1
Spring Hall La HFAX HX1 ....67 H1
Spring Hall Pl HFAX HX1 ....67 H1
Spring Head Rd
   CUL/QBY BD13 ....44 B1
   HWTH BD22 ....22 D1
   SHPY BD18 ....29 F2
Spring Holes La CUL/QBY BD13 ...35 H5
Springhurst Rd SHPY BD18 ....28 B2
Spring La GTL/HWG HX4 ....75 F4
Springlodge Pl GIR BD8 ....2 B1
Spring Mill St WBOW BD5 ....47 F2
Spring Mt KGHY BD21 ....14 D1
Spring Park Rd WIL/AL BD15 ....25 H4
Spring Pl CTHN BD7 ....46 D2
   KGHY BD21 ....7 H5
Spring Ri KGHY BD21 ....15 G5
Spring Rw KGHY BD21 ....15 G5
Springroyd Ter GIR BD8 ....38 A4
Springs Rd BAIL BD17 ....20 D1
Spring St BRIG HD6 ....78 B1
   IDLE BD10 ....30 A1
   KGHY BD21 ....7 F3
Springswood Av SHPY BD18 ....28 B2
Springswood Pl SHPY BD18 ....28 B2
Springswood Rd SHPY BD18 ....28 B2
Spring Ter KGHY BD21 ....5 J2
   RPDN/SBR HX6 ....66 C2
Springwell St GSLY LS19 ....11 H5
Springwell Dr WBOW BD5 ....47 F3
Spring Wood Av HIPP HX3 ....75 H5
Springwood Av WBOW BD5 ....47 G4
Spring Wood Dr HIPP HX3 ....75 G1
Spring Wood Gdns HIPP HX3 * 75 G2
   WBOW BD5 ....47 G5
Springwood Rd YEA LS19 ....21 F3
Springwood Ter ECHL BD2 ....39 F2
Sprinkwell Cl BFDE BD3 ....2 E1
Spruce Hts BRIG HD6 ....71 F2
Spruce St KGHY BD21 ....7 G3
Square Rd HFAX HX1 ....5 J4
Square St BOW BD4 ....47 H2
The Square GIR BD8 ....3 F3
Squire Gn GIR BD8 ....38 A3
Squire La HTON BD9 ....38 A3
Squirrel La CUL/QBY BD13 ....43 G2
Stable Fold LM/WK BD12 ....63 E3
Stable La HIPP HX3 ....59 G4
Stackgarth BRIG HD6 ....78 B3
Stadium Rd WBSY BD6 ....55 E2
Stafford Av HIPP HX3 ....68 D4
Stafford Pde HIPP HX3 ....69 E4
Stafford Rd HIPP HX3 ....68 D4
Stafford Sq HIPP HX3 ....69 E5
Stafford St BOW BD4 ....48 A3
Stainbeck Gdns HWG BD6 ....75 H5
Stainland Rd GTL/HWG HX4 ....75 H5
Stainton Cl WBSY BD6 ....55 G2
Staithgate La WBSY BD6 ....55 G2
Stallabrass St GIR BD8 * 38 B4
Stamford St BOW BD4 ....48 A2
Stanacre PI BFDE BD3 ....3 K1
Stanage La HIPP HX3 ....53 F5
Stanhope Dr BAIL BD17 ....38 C3
   HFAX HX1 ....4 A4
   HWTH BD22 ....13 H2
Stanley St BGLY BD16 ....16 D3
   BRIG HD6 ....78 D2
   CLECK BD19 ....64 C5
   HWTH BD22 ....23 F1
   IDLE BD10 ....30 A1
   KGHY BD21 * 7 H5

RPDN/SBR HX6 ....67 F4
   SHPY BD18 ....28 D4
Stanmore Pl GTHN BD7 ....46 B2
Stannary PI HFAX HX1 ....5 H3
Stanningley Av LUD/ILL HX2 ....50 A5
Stanningley By-Pass
   PDSY/CALV LS28 ....41 H3
Stanningley Dr LUD/ILL HX2 ....50 A5
Stanningley Rd LUD/ILL HX2 ....50 A5
Stansfield Cl HFAX HX1 ....4 D5
Stansfield Ct RPDN/SBR HX6 ....67 F5
Stapper Gn WIL/AL BD15 ....25 H5
Stariza St KGHY BD21 ....7 E5
Star St WBOW BD5 ....46 D4
Station Ct CSLY LS20 ....10 C2
Station La BIRK/DRI BD11 ....57 G4
Station Rd BAIL BD17 ....10 A5
   BAIL BD17 ....19 E3
   BRIG HD6 ....78 D1
   CLAY BD14 ....45 F3
   CUL/QBY BD13 ....24 B3
   CUL/QBY BD13 ....34 D4
   GSLY LS20 ....52 B1
   HIPP HX3 ....62 B5
   HIPP HX3 ....70 B1
   HWTH BD22 ....13 E4
   HWTH BD22 ....22 D2
   HWTH BD22 ....32 D2
   LM/WK BD12 ....55 F5
   LUD/ILL HX2 ....50 A1
   RPDN/SBR HX6 ....67 F5
   SHPY BD18 ....28 C1
   WIL/AL BD15 ....35 C3
Station Vw HWTH BD22 ....32 D1
Staups La HIPP HX3 ....60 C2
Staveley Cv HWTH BD22 ....19 E2
Staveley Gv HWTH BD22 ....13 H3
Staveley Ms BGLY BD16 * 16 D2
Staveley Rd BGLY BD16 ....16 D2
   GTHN BD7 ....46 C1
   HWTH BD22 ....13 H3
   SHPY BD18 ....29 G1
Staveley Wy HWTH BD22 ....13 H2
Stavely Ms BGLY BD16 * 16 D2
Staverton Gv CUL/QBY BD13 ....36 B5
Staverton St HFAX HX1 ....67 H1
Staybrite Av BGLY BD16 ....26 D2
Staygate Gn WBSY BD6 ....55 F1
Stead Hill Wy BAIL BD17 ....19 G5
Steadings Wy HWTH BD22 ....13 F1
Steadman St BFDE BD3 ....3 K6
Steadman Ter BFDE BD3 ....3 K6
Stead St HFAX HX1 * 4 B1
Steanard La HWTH BD22 ....56 D2
Steeplands HUDN HD2 ....79 G5
Stell Hl HWTH BD22 ....13 E1
Stephen Cl HIPP HX3 ....60 D4
Stephen Crs ECHL BD2 ....39 F1
Stephen Rd GTHN BD7 ....46 A4
Stephenson Rd WIL/AL BD15 ....36 A2
Stephenson St GTHN BD7 ....46 C4
Stepping Stones AIRE BD20 ....7 F3
Sterne Hl LUD/ILL HX2 ....68 A4
Stewart Ct ECHL BD2 ....30 D4
Stewart St HWTH BD22 ....23 F1
Sticker La BOW BD4 ....48 B4
Stirling Crs BOW BD4 ....48 C4
Stirling St HFAX HX1 ....4 E5
Stirrup Gv ECHL BD2 ....29 C5
Stirton St WBOW BD5 ....46 D4
Stockhill Fold IDLE BD10 ....30 C1
Stockhill Rd IDLE BD10 ....30 C2
Stock La LUD/ILL HX2 ....50 A2
Stocksfield Vw CUL/QBY BD13 .....53 E1
Stocks Hill Cl AIRE BD20 * 9 E2
Stocks La RPDN/SBR HX6 ....66 B5
   WBSY BD6 ....55 G4
Stod Fold LUD/ILL HX2 ....50 B2
Stone Arches WBOW BD5 ....47 F3
Stonecliffe LUD/ILL HX2 ....68 B4
Stone Ct AIRE BD20 ....9 E3
Stonecroft ECHL BD2 ....30 B5
Stonecroft Mt LUD/ILL HX2 * 60 B1
Stonefield Cl IDLE BD10 ....30 A4
Stonefield St CLECK BD19 ....72 D2
Stonegate BGLY BD16 ....16 D1
Stonegate Rd IDLE BD10 ....30 B3
Stone Hall Rd ECHL BD2 ....30 A5
Stonehouse Dr
   CUL/QBY BD13 ....51 E2
Stone La HWTH BD22 ....32 C2
Stoneleigh CUL/QBY BD13 ....52 C1
Stoneleigh Ct CLECK BD19 ....63 F4
Stone St BAIL BD17 ....20 D4
   BFD BD1 * 5 G2
   WIL/AL BD15 ....36 D1
Stoney Battery HIPP HX3 ....5 H1
Stoneycroft La AIRE BD20 ....7 E1
Stoney HI BRIG HD6 ....78 B1
Stoneyhurst Sq BOW BD4 ....48 C4
Stoney La HIPP HX3 ....59 F2
   HIPP HX3 ....71 F1
Stoney Ridge Av WIL/AL BD15 .....27 E5
Stoney Ridge Rd BGLY BD16 ....27 E4
Stoney Royd Ter HIPP HX3 ....69 E4
Stoneys Fold WIL/AL BD15 ....25 G5
Stoney St AIRE BD20 ....7 E1
Stony La ECHL BD2 ....30 B4
   GTL/HWG HX4 ....75 F3
   HIPP HX3 ....70 B4
   WIL/AL BD15 ....36 C2
Stony Royd PDSY/CALV LS28 ....41 H1
Stoodley Ter LUD/ILL HX2 ....67 H3
Storey Stones BGLY BD16 ....17 G1
Stormer Hill La RPDN/SBR HX6 ...74 C1
Storr HI LM/WK BD12 ....62 D1
Storr Hill Ter LM/WK BD12 ....62 D1
Stott HI BFD BD1 ....5 H2
Stott St CUL/QBY BD13 ....30 C5
Stotwell Mill St WBOW BD5 ....47 E3
Stradmore Rd CUL/QBY BD13 ....34 C4
Strafford Wy IDLE BD10 ....30 D1

Straightacres La IDLE BD10 ....30 C4
Straight La LUD/ILL HX2 ....50 C5
Straits BAIL BD17 ....18 D2
Strangford Ct IDLE BD10 ....30 C1
Strathallan Dr BAIL BD17 ....18 C2
Strathmore Dr BAIL BD17 ....18 C2
Stratton Cl BRIG HD6 ....78 C2
Stratton Pk BRIG HD6 ....78 C2
Stratton Rd BRIG HD6 ....78 C2
Stratton Vw BOW BD4 * 48 D5
Strawberry Flds KGHY BD21 ....7 F3
Strawberry St KGHY BD21 ....7 F3
Straw Vw IDLE BD10 ....29 G1
Stream Head Rd
   CUL/QBY BD13 ....35 G2
Street Hall HFAX HX1 ....5 F4
Street La AIRE BD20 ....9 E2
Stretchgate La LUD/ILL HX2 ....58 D5
Stringer Cl BOW BD4 ....56 A2
Strong Close Gv KGHY BD21 ....7 H4
Strong Close Rd KGHY BD21 ....7 H4
Strong Close Wy KGHY BD21 ....7 H4
Stubbings Rd BAIL BD17 ....18 A4
Stubbing Wy SHPY BD18 ....28 B3
Stubs Beck La CLECK BD19 ....64 B5
Studley Av WBSY BD6 ....54 C3
Studley Cl AIRE BD20 ....9 E2
Studley Crs BGLY BD16 ....17 E3
Studley Rd ECHL BD2 ....39 G2
Stump Cross HIPP HX3 ....60 D4
Stunsteds Rd CLECK BD19 ....64 C5
Sturges Gv ECHL BD2 ....40 A2
Sturton Gv LUD/ILL HX2 ....50 D3
Sturton La LUD/ILL HX2 ....51 E4
Styes La LUD/ILL HX2 ....66 A4
Sty La BGLY BD16 ....9 G5
Suffolk Ct YEA LS19 ....11 G4
Suffolk Pl ECHL BD2 ....29 G5
Sugden Cl BRIG HD6 ....78 B3
Sugden St BFD BD1 ....38 D5
   LM/WK BD12 ....63 G1
Sulby Gv IDLE BD10 ....30 D3
Summerbridge Crs
   ECHL BD2 ....65 G3
   IDLE BD10 ....30 C4
Summerbridge Dr IDLE BD10 ....30 C4
Summerdale CLECK BD19 ....65 G3
Summerfield Av BAIL BD17 ....71 G2
Summerfield Cl BAIL BD17 ....18 B3
Summerfield Dr BAIL BD17 ....18 B5
Summerfield Gn BAIL BD17 ....18 C5
Summerfield Gv BAIL BD17 ....18 B5
Summerfield Pk BAIL BD17 ....18 B5
Summerfield Rd BAIL BD17 ....30 B3
Summergate Pl HFAX HX1 * 4 A6
Summergate St HFAX HX1 * 4 B7
Summer Hall Ing
   LM/WK BD12 ....62 C1
Summer Hill St GTHN BD7 ....46 B2
Summerlands Gv WBOW BD5 * 45 H2
Summer Lea IDLE BD10 ....29 H1
Summerley Ct BGLY BD16 ....30 A2
Summerscale St HFAX HX1 * 4 C2
Summerseat Pl GTHN BD7 ....46 C2
Summer St HFAX HX1 ....4 A4
Summerville Rd GTHN BD7 ....46 D1
   PDSY/CALV LS28 ....41 H2
Summit St KGHY BD21 ....7 E3
Sunbridge Rd BFD BD1 ....2 C5
   GIR BD8 ....38 D4
Sunderland Ct BRIG HD6 ....71 F5
Sunderland Rd HTON BD9 ....38 C2
Sunderland St HFAX HX1 ....5 H5
   HWTH BD22 ....23 G1
   KGHY BD21 ....7 F5
Sundown Av GTHN BD7 ....45 H5
Sun Fold HFAX HX1 ....5 J6
Sun Hill Dr BAIL BD17 ....17 H5
Sunhurst Cl HWTH BD22 ....12 D5
Sunhurst Dr HWTH BD22 ....12 D5
Sunningdale GIR BD8 ....37 G4
Sunningdale Crs
   CUL/QBY BD13 ....24 D4
Sunny Av SHPY BD18 ....28 C2
Sunnybank Av BFDE BD3 ....41 E5
Sunny Bank Av WBOW BD5 ....55 E1
Sunnybank Cl CLECK BD19 ....72 C2
Sunnybank Crs GTL/HWG HX4 .....75 F4
Sunny Bank Dr
   RPDN/SBR HX6 ....67 F4
Sunnybank Gv BFDE BD3 ....41 E5
Sunnybank La BFDE BD3 ....41 E5
   GTL/HWG HX4 ....75 G4
Sunny Bank La HIPP HX3 ....70 A3
Sunny Bank Rd BRIG HD6 ....71 E5
Sunnybank Rd GTL/HWG HX4 .....75 F4
Sunny Bank Rd LUD/ILL HX2 ....55 E1
   WBOW BD5 ....55 E1
Sunny Bank St
   RPDN/SBR HX6 ....67 F4
Sunny Bank Ter HIPP HX3 ....59 H4
Sunnybrae Crs BGLY BD16 ....17 E4
Sunny Brow La HTON BD9 ....29 F2
Sunnycliffe AIRE BD20 ....8 E3
Sunnydale Av BRIG HD6 ....78 B5
Sunnydale Pk AIRE BD20 ....9 F2
Sunny Hill Cl HWTH BD22 ....13 G1
Sunny Hill Gv HWTH BD22 ....13 G1
Sunny Lea Ter WBSY BD6 * 55 E2
Sunny Mt AIRE BD20 ....8 D4
   BGLY BD16 ....15 G5
   KGHY BD21 ....7 F5
Sunnyside CLECK BD19 ....72 B3
Sunnyside Rd HIPP HX3 ....79 E5
Sunny Side St HIPP HX3 * 59 H4
Sunny View Ter
   HIPP HX3 ....51 H2
Sunshine Ct WBSY BD6 ....54 A3
Sun St BFDE BD3 ....3 H5
   KGHY BD21 ....7 F5

YEA LS19 ....11 H4
Sun Wy HIPP HX3 ....69 C3
Sun Wood Av HIPP HX3 ....61 E1
Suresnes Rd KGHY BD21 ....7 E4
Surgery St HWTH BD22 ....23 E3
Surrey Gv WBOW BD5 ....47 F5
Surrey St HFAX HX1 ....67 H2
   KGHY BD21 ....7 H3
Sussex St ECHL BD2 ....3 J5
Sutcliffe St LUD/ILL HX2 ....58 D5
Sutcliffe Wood La HIPP HX3 ....70 B2
Sutherland Rd HIPP HX3 ....61 H5
Sutton Av ECHL BD2 ....30 C4
Sutton Crs BOW BD4 ....48 D5
Sutton Dr CUL/QBY BD13 ....24 C4
Sutton La AIRE BD20 ....8 D2
Sutton Rd BOW BD4 ....48 D2
Swaine Hill Crs YEA LS19 ....11 F4
Swaine Hill St YEA LS19 ....11 F4
Swaine Hill Ter YEA LS19 ....11 H4
Swain House Crs ECHL BD2 ....29 H4
Swain House Rd ECHL BD2 ....29 H4
Swain Mt ECHL BD2 ....29 H4
Swales Moor Rd HIPP HX3 ....51 H5
Swallow Fold GIR BD8 ....37 F5
Swallow St KGHY BD21 ....7 F3
Swan Av BGLY BD16 ....17 F3
Swan Bank La HIPP HX3 ....70 A3
Swarland Gv WBOW BD5 ....47 F2
Swift Dr WBSY BD6 ....53 F1
Swincar Av YEA LS19 ....11 G3
Swincliffe Cl CLECK BD19 ....65 G4
Swincliffe Crs CLECK BD19 ....65 F2
Swine La AIRE BD20 ....8 C3
Swine Lane Br AIRE BD20 ....8 C3
Swinton Pl GTHN BD7 ....46 C2
Swinton Ter HFAX HX1 ....4 A6
Swires Rd ECHL BD2 ....40 A3
   HFAX HX1 ....4 E6
Swires Ter HFAX HX1 * 5 F6
Sycamore Av BGLY BD16 ....16 C4
   GTHN BD7 ....46 A3
Sycamore Cl BFDE BD3 ....3 G2
Sycamore Dr BRIG HD6 ....71 F2
   CLECK BD19 ....73 E1
   ELL HX5 ....76 A5
The Sycamores CSLY LS20 ....10 A3
   WIL/AL BD15 ....25 H5
Sydenham Pl BFDE BD3 ....39 H2
Sydney St BGLY BD16 ....16 D3
Syke House La GTL/HWG HX4 ......75 H4
Syke La CUL/QBY BD13 ....52 B3
   HIPP HX3 ....61 H4
   LUD/ILL HX2 ....42 C5
   SHPY BD18 ....38 B1
Syke Side AIRE BD20 ....70 B2
Sykes La HWTH BD22 ....13 E3
Sykes Rd CLECK BD19 ....63 H1
Sykes St CLECK BD19 ....73 C1
Sylhet Cl BFD BD1 * 2 B3
Sylvan Av CUL/QBY BD13 ....52 A2
Syringa Av WIL/AL BD15 ....26 D5

T

Tabbs Ct CLECK BD19 ....63 G4
Tabbs La CLECK BD19 ....63 F4
Tagore Ct BOW BD4 ....48 C1
Talbot St GTHN BD7 ....38 C5
   KGHY BD21 ....6 D4
Tamar St WBOW BD5 ....46 D3
Tamworth St BOW BD4 ....56 D3
Tanglewood Ct WBSY BD6 ....54 B1
Tanhouse Hl HIPP HX3 ....70 B1
Tan House La HIPP HX3 ....25 C3
   WIL/AL BD15 ....25 C3
Tanhouse Pk HIPP HX3 ....70 B1
Tanhouse Vw HIPP HX3 * 70 B1
Tan La BOW BD4 ....56 D3
Tannerbrook Cl CLAY BD14 ....45 G3
Tanner Hill Rd GTHN BD7 ....45 H4
Tanner St LVSG WF15 ....73 E3
Tannery Ct IDLE BD10 ....30 C1
Tanton Crs CLAY BD14 ....45 G3
Tanton Wk CLAY BD14 ....45 G3
Tarn BAIL BD17 * 19 H2
Tarn Ct AIRE BD20 ....6 C3
Tarnhill Ms WBOW BD5 ....47 E2
Tarn View Rd YEA LS19 ....11 H4
Taunton St SHPY BD18 ....28 D4
Tawny Cl BOW BD4 ....56 D1
Taylor La LUD/ILL HX2 ....43 F5
Taylor Rd WBSY BD6 ....55 E2
Taylor St CLECK BD19 ....63 H1
Teasdale St BOW BD4 ....48 A4
Teasel Cl LM/WK BD12 ....46 D4
Tees St WBOW BD5 ....46 D3
Teicombe Dr BOW BD4 ....48 C1
Temperance Flds CLECK BD19 ......63 G5
Templars Cl GTL/HWG HX4 ....75 H4
Templar's Wy GIR BD8 ....37 H4
Temple Rhydding Dr
   BAIL BD17 ....18 D4
Temple St HTON BD9 ....38 C2
   KGHY BD21 ....7 F3
Tenbury Fold BOW BD4 ....48 C1
Tenby Ter HFAX HX1 * 4 B2
Tennis Av BOW BD4 ....56 D1
Tennis Wy BAIL BD17 ....18 D5
Tennyson Av RPDN/SBR HX6 ....3 J2
Tennyson Pl BFDE BD3 ....3 J2
   CLECK BD19 ....64 D5
Tennyson Rd BAIL BD17 ....18 D4
Tennyson St GSLY LS20 ....11 E3
   HIPP HX3 ....14 A1
   KGHY BD21 ....7 E2
Tenterfields Rd HIPP HX3 ....60 D4
Tenterfields IDLE BD10 ....30 B4
   LUD/ILL HX2 ....66 B3
Tenter Hl CLAY BD14 ....45 E3

Tenth Av LVSG WF15 .....73 E3
Ten Yards La CUL/QBY BD13 .35 E3
Ternhill Gv WBOW BD5 .....47 F2
Tern St WBOW BD5 ....47 F2
Terrace Gdns HIPP HX3 ....59 G4
Terracotta Dr WIL/AL BD15 .36 D4
Terrington Crest CLAY BD14 .45 G3
Terry Rd LM/WK BD12 .....55 F5
Tetley Dr BIRK/DRI BD11 ...55 G1
Tetley La HIPP HX3 ....60 D5
Tetley Pl ECHL BD2 ....39 G1
Teville Ct BOW BD4 ....47 H3
Tewit Cl LUD/ILL HX2 .....51 E5
Tewit Gn LUD/ILL HX2 .....51 E5
Tewit Hall Gdns LUD/ILL HX2 .51 E4
Tewit Hall Rd BFDE BD3 ...40 B4
Tewit La LUD/ILL HX2 .....51 E3
Tewitt La CUL/QBY BD13 ...35 F2
Thackeray Rd IDLE BD10 ...30 C5
Thackley Av IDLE BD10 ....19 H4
Thackley Ct SHPY BD18 ....28 D1
Thackley Old Rd SHPY BD18 .19 F4
Thackley Vw IDLE BD10 ....19 H4
Thackray St LUD/ILL HX2 ...67 G1
Thatchers Wy CLECK BD19 ..65 F4
Theakston Md CLAY BD14 ...45 G3
Thearne Gn CLAY BD14 ....45 G3
Third Av BFDE BD3 ....40 B3
  HIPP HX3 ....68 C4
  KGHY BD21 ....7 E5
  LVSG WF15 ....73 E3
Third St LM/WK BD12 .....55 F4
Thirkleby Royd CLAY BD14 ..45 F3
Thirlmere Av ELL HX5 .....77 E4
  LM/WK BD12 ....63 F4
Thirlmere Gdns ECHL BD2 ..40 A2
Thirsk Gra CLAY BD14 .....45 F3
Thirteenth Av LVSG WF15 ..73 E5
Thomas Ct WBSY BD6 .....54 D1
Thomas St BRIG HD6 ......78 B2
  ELL HX5 ....76 D5
  HFAX HX1 * 4 A5
  HWTH BD22 ....23 E3
Thomas St South HFAX HX1 .4 A5
Thomas St West HFAX HX1 ..68 B3
Thompson Gn BAIL BD17 ...29 G4
Thompson La BAIL BD17 ...18 B4
Thompson St SHPY BD18 ...28 B1
Thoresby Dr CLECK BD19 ..65 G5
Thoresby Gv CLAY BD14 ...44 D5
Thornaby Dr CLAY BD14 ...45 G2
Thornacre Crs SHPY BD18 ..29 F3
Thornacre Rd SHPY BD18 ..29 F2
Thorn Av HTON BD9 ....27 F5
Thorn Bank Av HWTH BD22 .13 G2
Thornberry Dr LVSG WF15 ..73 E3
Thornbridge Ms ECHL BD2 ..30 A5
Thornbury Av BFDE BD3 ...40 C4
Thornbury Crs BFDE BD3 ..40 C4
Thornbury Dr BFDE BD3 ...40 C4
Thornbury Gv BFDE BD3 ...40 C5
Thornbury Rd BFDE BD3 ...40 C5
  HWTH BD22 ....6 C5
Thorncliffe Rd GIR BD8 ....39 E3
Thorne Cl PDSY/CALV LS28 .41 G4
Thornes Pk BRIG HD6 .....78 B4
  SHPY BD18 ....29 E4
Thorneycroft Rd AIRE BD20 .8 B2
Thornfield BGLY BD16 .....16 B2
Thornfield Av PDSY/CALV LS28 .41 H1
  WBSY BD6 ....54 D2
Thornfield Ms BGLY BD16 ..9 H4
Thornfield Pl ECHL BD2 ...40 A1
Thornfield Rd GTL/HWG HX4 .75 G4
Thornfield St GTL/HWG HX4 .75 G4
Thorn Garth AIRE BD20 ....6 D2
  CLECK BD19 ....73 F2
Thorn Gv HTON BD9 ......27 F5
Thornhill Av HWTH BD22 ..13 F3
  SHPY BD18 ....29 E4
Thornhill Bridge La BRIG HD6 .71 F5
Thornhill Cl PDSY/CALV LS28 .31 H1
Thornhill Dr PDSY/CALV LS28 .31 G1
Thornhill Gv PDSY/CALV LS28 .31 G1
  SHPY BD18 ....29 E4
Thornhill Pl BFDE BD3 ....40 D4
Thornhills Beck La BRIG HD6 .71 G4
Thornhills La BRIG HD6 ...71 H4
Thornhill St PDSY/CALV LS28 .31 G3
Thornhill Ter BFDE BD3 ...40 D4
Thorn La HTON BD9 ......27 G5
Thornlea Cl YEA LS19 .....21 E1
Thornmead Rd BAIL BD17 ..19 E4
Thorn Royd Dr BOW BD4 ..49 E5
Thornsgill Av BOW BD4 ...49 E4
Thorn St GIR BD8 ....38 A5
  HWTH BD22 ....23 F1
Thornton Ct GIR BD8 .....38 A4
Thornton La WBOW BD5 ...46 D4
Thornton Moor Rd
  HWTH BD22 ....33 H5
Thornton Old Rd GIR BD8 ..37 G5
Thornton Rd BRIG HD6 ....77 H5
  CUL/QBY BD13 ....43 E2
  GIR BD8 ....37 G5
Thornton St BFDE BD1 ....38 D5
  CLECK BD19 ....72 D2
  HFAX HX1 ....4 A2
Thornton Ter HFAX HX1 ...4 A2
Thornton View Rd CLAY BD14 .45 F3
Thorn Tree St HFAX HX1 ..4 A5
Thorn Vw HIPP HX3 ....59 H3
Thorpe Cl GSLY LS20 .....10 A3

Thorpe Dr GSLY LS20 .....10 A2
Thorpe Gv CUL/QBY BD13 ..45 E1
Thorpe La CUL/QBY BD13 ..44 D1
Thorpe St HIPP HX3 ......59 G3
  KGHY BD21 * 7 F3
Thorp Garth IDLE BD10 ...30 A2
Thorverton Dr BOW BD4 ...56 D2
Thorverton Gv BOW BD4 ..56 D2
Thread Cft LUD/ILL HX2 ...51 E4
Threshfield Crs BIRK/DRI BD11 .57 F4
Thrice Fold IDLE BD10 ....19 G5
Thrift Wy BGLY BD16 .....16 C4
Throstle Bank LUD/ILL HX2 .68 A3
Throstle Mt LUD/ILL HX2 ..66 C5
Throxenby Wy GSLY LS20 * .45 F5
Thrum Hall Cl HFAX HX1 ...67 H1
Thrum Hall Dr HFAX HX1 ..4 A3
Thrum Hall La HFAX HX1 ..4 A3
Thrush St KGHY BD21 ....7 G5
Thryberg St BFDE BD3 ....3 H6
Thurstone Ct AIRE BD20 ..8 C3
Thurley Dr BOW BD4 .....48 A5
Thurley Rd BOW BD4 .....48 A5
Thurnscoe Rd BFD1 ......2 B2
Thursby St BFDE BD3 .....3 J5
Thurston Gdns WIL/AL BD15 .37 E4
Thwaite Ga CLAY BD14 ....45 F3
Thwaites Brow Rd KGHY BD21 .8 A4
Thwaites La KGHY BD21 ...7 G5
Tichborne Rd WBOW BD5 * .47 F4
Tichborne Rd West
Tichborne St LVSG WF15 ..73 H4
Tickhill St BFDE BD3 ......3 J6
Tile St GIR BD8 ....38 C3
Tiley Sq WBOW BD5 ......47 F3
Till Carr La HIPP HX3 .....71 F1
Tillotson Av RPDN/SBR HX6 .66 D5
Timber St ELL HX5 ....76 C5
  KGHY BD21 ....7 H5
Timble Dr BGLY BD16 .....17 E2
Tim La HWTH BD22 ....12 C5
Timmey La RPDN/SBR HX6 .66 D3
Tinkler Stile IDLE BD10 ...29 G1
Tintern Av GIR BD8 ......37 G5
Tisma Dr BOW BD4 ....56 D2
Tithe Barn Wy BRIG HD6 ..78 D3
Tithe House Wy HUDN 79 F5
Titus St SHPY BD18 ......28 A1
Tivoli Pl WBOW BD5 ......46 D4
Toby La GTHN BD7 * 46 B2
Todd Ter GTHN BD7 * 46 C5
Todwell La WBOW BD5 ....46 D4
Tofts Av LM/WK BD12 .....62 D3
Tofts Gv BRIG HD6 ....78 A4
Tofts Grove Gdns BRIG HD6 .78 A4
Toftshaw Fold BOW BD4 ..56 D2
Toftshaw La BOW BD4 ....56 C2
Toftshaw New Rd BOW BD4 .56 C2
Tofts Rd CLECK BD19 .....73 G1
Toller Dr HTON BD9 ......37 H1
Toller Gv HTON BD9 ......38 A1
Toller La HTON BD9 ......38 A1
Toller Pk HTON BD9 ......38 A1
Tolworth Fold WIL/AL BD15 .36 D4
Tonbridge Cl SHPY BD6 ...54 A2
Tong La BOW BD4 ....57 H2
Tong St BOW BD4 ....56 C1
Toothill Av BRIG HD6 .....78 B4
Toothill Bank BRIG HD6 ...78 B5
Toothill La BRIG HD6 .....78 B5
Tor Av LM/WK BD12 ......62 D4
Tordoff Av GTHN BD7 .....45 H2
Tordoff Gn WBSY BD6 ....54 C2
Tordoff Rd LM/WK BD12 ..55 F4
Torre Crs WBSY BD6 .....53 G4
Torre Gv WBSY BD6 ......53 G3
Torre Rd WBSY BD6 ......53 G1
Torridon Crs WBSY BD6 ...53 H4
Tower Gdns LUD/ILL HX2 ..68 A4
Tower Hl RPDN/SBR HX6 ..67 E4
Tower La LUD/ILL HX2 ....68 A4
Tower St ECHL BD2 ......40 A2
Tower Vw HFAX HX1 ......67 H3
Town End GTHN BD7 ......46 B3
Town End Rd CLAY BD14 ..45 E2
Townfield WIL/AL BD15 ...25 H4
Town Fields Rd ELL HX5 ..76 C5
Town Ga CLECK BD19 .....65 G5
  GSLY LS20 ....10 D2
  HIPP HX3 ....60 D2
  PDSY/CALV LS28 ......31 G2
  RPDN/SBR HX6 ......66 A5
Towngate BRIG HD6 ......71 F5
  HIPP HX3 ....61 F5
  HIPP HX3 ....69 H4
  KGHY BD21 ....7 F4
  LM/WK BD12 ....62 D3
Town Hall Sq LS19 ....11 C4
Town Hall St ELL HX5 ....76 C5
  GTL/HWG HX4 ....75 G4
  RPDN/SBR HX6 ......67 E5
Town Hall St East HFAX HX1 * .5 F4
Town Hill St BGLY BD16 * .27 E3
Town La IDLE BD10 ....20 A5
Townley Av HFAX HX1 ....69 H4
Town St BIRK/DRI BD11 ...57 F4
  GSLY LS20 ....10 D2
  YEA LS19 ....11 G4
Town Wells Dr
  PDSY/CALV LS28 ......31 G3
Trackside LM/WK BD12 ...55 G5
Trafalgar Sq HFAX HX1 ...4 C3
Trafalgar St BFD1 ....3 G5
Tramways LM/WK BD12 ...55 G5
Tranbeck Rd GSLY LS20 ...10 A2
Tranfield Av GSLY LS20 ...10 B2
Tranfield Cl GSLY LS20 ...10 B2
Tranfield Gdns GSLY LS20 .10 B2
Tranmere Ct GSLY LS20 ...10 B2
Tranmere Dr GSLY LS20 ...10 B2
Transperience Wy

LM/WK BD12 ....55 G4
Tranter Gv BOW BD4 .....48 D2
Trees St GIR BD8 ....38 D3
Tree Top Vw CUL/QBY BD13 .43 H5
Trenam Park Dr IDLE BD10 .19 H4
Trenance Dr SHPY BD18 ..28 A3
Trenance Gdns GTL/HWG HX4 .75 F5
Trenholme Av LM/WK BD12 .54 C4
Trenton Dr GIR BD8 ......38 D3
Trevelyan St BRIG HD6 ...71 F3
Trimmingham La LUD/ILL HX2 .67 G2
Trimmingham Rd LUD/ILL HX2 .67 G2
Trimmingham Vls
  LUD/ILL HX2 ....67 H2
Trinity Cl LUD/ILL HX2 ....51 F4
Trinity Fold HFAX HX1 * ..5 G5
Trinity Dr BGLY BD16 .....16 D4
Trinity Pl BGLY BD16 .....16 D4
  HFAX HX1 ....5 G5
Trinity Rd HFAX HX1 .....5 G5
Trinity St HFAX HX1 ......5 G5
  KGHY BD21 ....7 F5
  LM/WK BD12 ....55 F3
Trinity Vw HIPP HX3 .....5 K6
Trinity Wk LM/WK BD12 ..55 F3
Tristram Av WBOW BD5 ...55 G4
Trooper La HIPP HX3 .....5 K6
Trooper Ter HIPP HX3 ....5 K6
Trough La HWTH BD22 ...33 H3
Trueman Ct LM/WK BD12 .55 E5
Truncliffe WBSY BD6 .....55 E1
Tudor Barn Ct SHPY BD18 .29 E2
Tudor Ct PDSY/CALV LS28 .41 H2
Tudor St WBOW BD5 .....47 E3
Tuel La RPDN/SBR HX6 ...66 D5
Tulip St HWTH BD22 .....22 D3
Tumbling Hill St GTHN BD7 .2 A6
Tunnard Rd GTL/HWG HX4 .54 D4
Tunstall Gn BOW BD4 ....48 D4
Tunwell La ECHL BD2 ....30 B5
Tunwell St ECHL BD2 ....30 B5
Turbury La GTL/HWG HX4 .74 D3
Turf Ct CUL/QBY BD13 ...45 E1
Turf La CUL/QBY BD13 ...24 B5
Turner Av GTHN BD7 .....46 A2
Turner Av North LUD/ILL HX2 .50 C5
Turner Av South LUD/ILL HX2 .50 D1
Turner La HIPP HX3 ......66 D1
Turner Pl GTHN BD7 .....46 C2
  LUD/ILL HX2 ....50 C5
Turner's Ct HIPP HX3 ....59 G3
Turner Vw LUD/ILL HX2 ..50 C5
Turney St HIPP HX3 ......59 G3
Turnpike St ELL HX5 .....76 D4
Turnstales Av CLECK BD19 .64 A5
Turnstales Cl CLECK BD19 .64 A5
Turnstales Dr CLECK BD19 .64 B5
Turnstales Mt CLECK BD19 .64 B5
Tweedy St WIL/AL BD15 ..25 H4
Twelfth Av LVSG WF15 ...73 E3
Twickenham Ct GIR BD8 ..59 E2
Tyersal Av BOW BD4 .....41 E5
Tyersal Cl BOW BD4 .....41 E5
Tyersal Crs BOW BD4 ....49 E1
Tyersal Dr BOW BD4 .....49 E1
Tyersal Garth BOW BD4 ..49 E1
Tyersal Gn BOW BD4 .....49 E1
Tyersal Gv BOW BD4 .....49 E1
Tyersal La BOW BD4 .....48 D1
Tyersal Pk BOW BD4 .....49 E1
Tyersal Rd BOW BD4 .....48 D1
Tyersal Ter BOW BD4 ....49 E1
Tyersal Vw BOW BD4 ....48 D1
Tyersal Wk BOW BD4 ....49 E1
Tyne St BFDE BD3 ....3 J1
  KGHY BD21 ....7 G4
Tyrrel St BFD1 ....3 G5
Tyson St HFAX HX1 ......67 H2

Ullswater Cl ELL HX5 .....77 E4
Ullswater Dr WBSY BD6 ..54 A4
Undercliffe La ECHL BD3 ..3 K3
Undercliffe Old Rd ECHL BD2 .40 A1
Undercliffe St BFDE BD3 ..3 J1
Underwood Dr YEA LS19 ..21 G5
Union House La CLAY BD14 .45 F7
Union La LUD/ILL HX2 ....50 C4
Union Rd GTHN BD7 ......46 C2
  WBSY BD6 ....54 A1
Union St BAIL BD17 ......19 E4
  BGLY BD16 ....16 C4
  CUL/QBY BD13 * 52 B1
  GTL/HWG HX4 ....76 A4
  HFAX HX1 * 5 G5
  RPDN/SBR HX6 ......67 F3
Union St South HFAX HX1 * .5 F5
Union Yd IDLE BD10 ......30 A1
Unity St North BGLY BD16 .16 C4
Unity St South BGLY BD16 .16 C4
Unity Ter HFAX HX1 ......67 E5
Unwin Pl HTON BD9 ......37 H2
Uplands AIRE BD20 ....8 A1
Uplands Av CUL/QBY BD13 .45 E5
Uplands Cl CUL/QBY BD13 .45 E5
Uplands Crs CUL/QBY BD13 .45 E5
Uplands Gv CUL/QBY BD13 .45 E5
Upper Ada St SHPY BD18 ..28 B1
Upper Addison St BOW BD4 .47 G2
Upper Allerton La
  WIL/AL BD15 ....44 C4
Upper Ashley La SHPY BD18 * .28 C1
Upper Bell Cft HIPP HX3 ..68 A5
Upper Bell Hall HFAX HX1 .68 B3
Upper Bolton Brow
  RPDN/SBR HX6 ......67 G3
Upper Bonegate BRIC HD6 .71 G5
Upper Butts CLECK BD19 ..73 G1

Upper Calton St KGHY BD21 .14 A1
Upper Carr La PDSY/CALV LS28 .31 F5
Upper Castle St WBOW BD5 .47 F2
Upper Chelsea St KGHY BD21 .14 A1
Upper Ellistones Ct
  GTL/HWG HX4 ....75 F5
Upper Ferndown Gn
  WIL/AL BD15 * 36 D3
Upper Forge HFAX HX1 * ..5 G4
Upper Fountain St
  RPDN/SBR HX6 ......67 E4
Upper Fyfe La BAIL BD17 ..19 F5
Upper George St WBSY BD6 * .54 C1
Upper Grange Av WIL/AL BD15 .37 E4
Upper Green Av CLECK BD19 * .63 G5
Upper Green La BRIG HD6 .77 G5
Upper Hall Vw HIPP HX3 ..60 D2
Upper Haugh Shaw HFAX HX1 .4 D7
Upper Headley
  CUL/QBY BD13 * 44 A2
Upper Heights Rd
  CUL/QBY BD13 ....35 H4
Upper Hird St KGHY BD21 .13 H1
Upper House La LVSG WF15 .73 F4
Upper House St BOW BD4 ..48 A2
Upper Kirkgate HFAX HX1 ..5 J4
Upper Lane BFD1 ....3 K6
Upper Lombard St YEA LS19 .21 F2
Upper Marsh HIPP HX3 ...69 G5
Upper Marsh La HWTH BD22 .22 A4
Upper Martin Gn
  GTL/HWG HX4 ....75 F4
Upper Mary St SHPY BD18 .28 A1
Upper Mdw CUL/QBY BD13 .52 B2
Uppermoor PDSY/CALV LS28 .41 H5
Upper Mosscar St BFDE BD3 .3 K6
Upper Park Ga BFDE BD3 ..3 H5
Upper Piccadilly BFD1 * ...5 H3
Upper Quarry Rd HUDN ...79 H5
Upper Range HIPP HX3 ...59 H4
Upper Royd HIPP HX3 * ..59 H3
Upper Rushton Rd BFDE BD3 .40 C3
Upper Seymour St BFDE BD3 .3 K6
Upper Sutherland Rd
  HIPP HX3 ....61 H5
Upper Washer La LUD/ILL HX2 .67 G2
Upper Willow Hall LUD/ILL HX2 .67 G2
Upper Woodlands Rd GIR BD8 .38 B5
Upwood La AIRE BD20 ....9 E1
Usher St BOW BD4 ....47 G2
Uttley St HIPP HX3 * 59 G3

Vale Gv CUL/QBY BD13 ...52 D3
Vale Mill La HWTH BD22 ..13 G5
Valentine Ct CUL/QBY BD13 .36 B5
Vale St BRIG HD6 ....71 F5
  KGHY BD21 ....7 H2
Valley Av HIPP HX3 ......60 D2
Valley Cl BFD1 ....39 F5
Valley Fold CUL/QBY BD13 .52 B2
Valley Gv LUD/ILL HX2 ...51 E3
Valley Hts CUL/QBY BD13 ..34 C3
Valley Pde GIR BD8 ......2 B1
Valley Ridge BFD1 ....2 E5
Valley Rd BFD1 ....2 D1
  CLECK BD19 ....64 D5
  KGHY BD21 ....7 H4
  SHPY BD18 ....28 C3
Valley Vw BAIL BD17 .....18 C5
  BGLY BD16 ....15 F5
  LUD/ILL HX2 ....50 B5
Valley View Cl HWTH BD22 .13 F3
Valley View Gdns
  HWTH BD22 ....23 F1
Valley View Gv ECHL BD2 ..39 H2
Valley Wy LUD/ILL HX2 ...51 E5
Vaughan St BFD1 ....4 A7
  HFAX HX1 ....4 A7
Ventnor Cl CLECK BD19 ...65 G3
Ventnor Dr BFDE BD3 ....3 H5
Ventnor Ter HIPP HX3 ....68 C4
Ventor Cl WBSY BD6 .....54 B2
Verdun Rd WBSY BD6 ....54 B2
Vere Sq WBOW BD5 .....47 E3
Verity St BOW BD4 ....57 E3
Vernon Ct HIPP HX3 .....60 A4
Vernon Pl ECHL BD2 .....40 A2
Vernon St HWTH BD22 ...23 F1
Vestry St BOW BD4 ......48 A4
Vicarage Cl LM/WK BD12 ..62 D3
Vicarage Ct CLECK BD19 ..65 G5
Vicarage Gdns BIRK/DRI BD11 .57 F5
Vicarage Rd HIPP HX3 ....78 A3
Vicarage Rd SHPY BD18 ..29 E1
Vicar La BFD1 ....5 J4
Vicar Park Dr LUD/ILL HX2 .58 A5
Vickerman St HFAX HX1 ..4 B6
Victor Dr GSLY LS20 .....10 D3
Victoria Av BRIG HD6 ....71 H5
  CLECK BD19 * 30 D2
  ECHL BD2 ....30 C5
  ELL HX5 ....76 B5
  HFAX HX1 ....68 D2
  HWTH BD22 ....22 D1
  RPDN/SBR HX6 ......67 F3
  SHPY BD18 ....28 D3
Victoria Cha BRIC HD6 ...62 C5
Victoria Crs ELL HX5 .....76 C5
  PDSY/CALV LS28 .....41 H5
Victoria Gdns
  PDSY/CALV LS28 .....41 H5
Victoria Ms ELL HX5 .....76 C5
  RPDN/SBR HX6 ......61 E2
Victoria Pk HFAX HX1 * ..4 C5
  SHPY BD18 ....28 D3
Victoria Park Gv KGHY BD21 .7 G4
Victoria Park Vw KGHY BD21 .7 G3

Victoria Pl BRIG HD6 .....71 F4
  YEA LS19 ....11 F4
Victoria Ri PDSY/CALV LS28 .41 H5
Victoria Rd BRIG HD6 ....71 G1
  CLECK BD19 ....30 B5
  ECHL BD2 ....30 B5
  ELL HX5 ....76 B5
  GSLY LS20 ....10 C3
  HFAX HX1 ....4 C3
  HIPP HX3 ....70 C1
  HWTH BD22 ....13 E4
  KGHY BD21 ....7 E5
  PDSY/CALV LS28 .....41 H5
  RPDN/SBR HX6 ......67 E5
  SHPY BD18 ....28 A1
  WBSY BD6 ....54 B2
Victoria St BAIL BD17 ....28 C1
  BFD1 ....2 B2
  BRIG HD6 ....71 H5
  BRIC HD6 ....76 D4
  CLAY BD14 ....45 E3
  CLECK BD19 ....64 C5
  CUL/QBY BD13 ....24 D3
  CUL/QBY BD13 ....52 C1
  ECHL BD2 ....40 B2
  GTL/HWG HX4 ....76 A4
  HFAX HX1 * 5 G3
  IDLE BD10 ....20 A4
  PDSY/CALV LS28 .....31 F3
  RPDN/SBR HX6 ......67 E5
  WIL/AL BD15 ....25 H5
Victoria Ter CLECK BD19 ..73 G1
  HFAX HX1 * 4 C5
  KGHY BD21 ....7 G4
  LUD/ILL HX2 ....66 C3
Victor Rd HTON BD9 .....38 C2
  HTON BD9 ....38 C2
Victor Ter HFAX HX1 .....4 C1
  HTON BD9 ....38 C2
View Croft Rd BAIL BD17 ..29 E2
View Rd AIRE BD20 ......6 D3
Vignola Ter CLAY BD14 ...45 F7
Village Ms WIL/AL BD15 ..25 H4
Village St HIPP HX3 ......62 A3
Villa Gv BGLY BD16 ......16 D2
Villa Mt LM/WK BD12 ....62 D4
Villa Rd BGLY BD16 ......16 D2
Villa St RPDN/SBR HX6 ...66 C5
Villier Ct WIL/AL BD15 ...37 E3
Vincent St BFD1 * 2 B5
  HFAX HX1 ....4 C3
Vine Av CLECK BD19 .....64 B5
Vine Cl BRIG HD6 ....79 E1
Vine Ct BRIG HD6 ....79 E1
Vine Crs CLECK BD19 ....64 B5
Vine Garth BRIG HD6 ....79 E1
Vine Gv BRIG HD6 ....79 E1
Vine St CLECK BD19 .....64 C5
  GTHN BD7 ....46 C2
Vine Ter CUL/QBY BD13 ..44 A1
Vine Ter East GIR BD8 ...37 H4
Vine Ter West GIR BD8 ...37 H4
Violet St HFAX HX1 ......4 C3
  HWTH BD22 ....22 D3
Violet St North HFAX HX1 .4 C3
Virginia St CLAY BD14 ....45 F3
Vivian Pl GTHN BD7 .....46 A4
Vivien Rd GIR BD8 ....37 F4
Vulcan St BOW BD4 ......56 C1
  BRIG HD6 ....78 D2

Waddington St KGHY BD21 .7 F5
Wade House Av HIPP HX3 ..53 F4
Wade House Rd HIPP HX3 ..53 F5
Wade St BFD1 ....2 C6
  HFAX HX1 ....5 J3
Wadlands Cl PDSY/CALV LS28 .31 H5
Wadlands Dr PDSY/CALV LS28 .41 H1
Wadlands Gv PDSY/CALV LS28 .41 H1
Wadlands Ri PDSY/CALV LS28 .41 H1
Wadsworth St HFAX HX1 ..4 A3
Wagon La BGLY BD16 ....16 D5
Wagtail Cl WBSY BD6 ....53 F1
Wainhouse Rd HFAX HX1 ..4 A7
Wainman St BAIL BD17 ...18 C1
  BFD1 ....28 C1
  HFAX HX1 ....4 B3
Wakefield Ga LUD/ILL HX2 .68 A4
Wakefield Rd BFD1 ......3 F7
  BOW BD4 ....48 A3
  BRIG HD6 ....70 D5
  HIPP HX3 ....71 F1
  RPDN/SBR HX6 ......67 G4
Walden Dr HTON BD9 ....37 F1
Walker Av GTHN BD7 .....45 H2
Walker Dr GIR BD8 ......37 F5
Walker La RPDN/SBR HX6 .66 C5
Walker Pl SHPY BD18 ....29 E1
Walker Rd LM/WK BD12 ..63 G1
Walkers Rw YEA LS19 ....11 F4
Walker St BOW BD4 ......56 A2
  CLECK BD19 ....63 G4
  GSLY LS20 ....10 C3
Walker Ter BOW BD4 .....48 H3
  CUL/QBY BD13 ....45 F5
Walker Wd BAIL BD17 ....18 A4
The Walk KGHY BD21 ....7 F5
  PDSY/CALV LS28 .....41 H2
Wallbank Dr SHPY BD18 ..28 D3
Wallingford Mt WIL/AL BD15 .37 E5
Wallis St GIR BD8 ....37 F4
  RPDN/SBR HX6 ......67 E4
Wall St HWTH BD22 ......7 G5
Walmer Vls GIR BD8 .....38 E3
Walnut St BFDE BD3 .....48 A1
  HFAX HX1 ....4 C4

KGHY BD21 ....14 A2
Walshaw St *GTHN* BD7 ....46 B3
Walsh La *BGLY* BD16 ....9 C5
HIPP HX3 ....59 G4
Walsh Sq *HFAX* HX1 * 68 B5
Walsh St *HFAX* HX1 ....4 B5
Walter Clough La *HIPP* HX3 ...70 A3
Walter St *ECHL* BD2 ....29 E5
IDLE BD10 ....29 F2
Walton La *BRIC* HD6 ....72 B3
Walton St *BOW* BD4 ....47 G2
RPDN/SBR HX6 ....67 E4
Waltroyd Rd *CLECK* BD19 .....73 F1
Wansford Ct *BOW* BD4 ....48 D5
Wanstead Crs *WIL/AL* BD15 ...37 E4
Wapping Rd *BFD* BD1 ....5 F4
Wardle Crs *KGHY* BD21 ....6 C3
Wardman St *KGHY* BD21 ....7 H2
Ward's End *HFAX* HX1 ....5 H5
Ward St *GTHN* BD7 ....46 B4
KGHY BD21 ....7 H2
Warehouse Cnr *BOW* BD4 ....48 D5
Warhurst Rd *ELL* HX5 ....76 D5
Warley Av *BFDE* BD6 ....40 C4
Warley Dene *LUD/ILL* HX2 ......67 E2
Warley Dr *BFDE* BD6 ....40 C5
Warley Edge La *LUD/ILL* HX2 ..67 E1
Warley Gv *BFDE* BD6 ....40 C4
LUD/ILL HX2 ....67 G1
Warley Rd *LUD/ILL* HX2 ....67 G2
Warley Town La *LUD/ILL* HX2 ..66 D1
Warley Vw *LUD/ILL* HX2 ....66 C3
Warley Wood Av *LUD/ILL* HX2 ..66 C3
Warley Wood La *LUD/ILL* HX2 ..66 B5
Warm La *YEA* LS19 ....21 F1
Warmlieigh Pk *CUL/QBY* BD13 ..51 G1
Warren Av *BGLY* BD16 ....17 E2
Warren Dr *BGLY* BD16 ....17 E2
Warren La *BGLY* BD16 ....17 E2
Warren Pk *BRIC* HD6 ....70 D2
Warren Park Cl *BRIC* HD6 ......70 D3
Warrenton Pl *GTHN* BD7 * 46 B2
Warton Av *BOW* BD4 ....56 A1
Warwick Cl *BOW* BD4 ....48 A5
Warwick Dr *BOW* BD4 ....48 A5
HFAX HX1 * 68 C3
Warwick Rd *BOW* BD4 ....48 A5
Washer La *LUD/ILL* HX2 ....68 A4
Washington St *GIR* BD8 ....38 A3
HIPP HX3 * 59 F4
Wastwater Dr *WBSY* BD6 ....54 A4
Watercock St *BOW* BD4 ....47 H2
Waterfront Ms *IDLE* BD10 ....30 D1
Watergate *HIPP* HX3 ....70 B1
Water Hill La *RPDN/SBR* HX6 ..66 D3
Waterhouse St *HFAX* HX1 ....5 G4
KGHY BD21 ....6 C4
Water La *BFD* BD1 ....5 J6
HFAX HX1 ....5 H5
KGHY BD21 ....7 E5
Waterloo Crs *IDLE* BD10 ....31 E1
Waterloo Fold *LM/WK* BD12 ...63 E3
Waterloo Gv *PDSY/CALV* LS28 ..41 G5
Waterloo Mt *PDSY/CALV* LS28 ..24 A5
Waterloo Rd *BGLY* BD16 ....16 C3
BRIC HD6 ....71 F5
PDSY/CALV LS28 ....41 G4
Waterloo Ter *LUD/ILL* HX2 .....67 F2
Waterside *BGLY* BD16 ....16 A1
HIPP HX3 ....59 G5
HWTH BD22 ....32 D2
Water St *BRIC* HD6 ....71 G5
RPDN/SBR HX6 ....67 E5
Watford Av *HIPP* HX3 ....62 A2
Watkin Av *CUL/QBY* BD13 ......44 C1
Watkinson Av *LUD/ILL* HX2 ....59 E1
Watkinson Dr *LUD/ILL* HX2 .....59 E1
Watkinson Rd *LUD/ILL* HX2 ....59 E1
Watmough St *GTHN* BD7 ....46 B4
Watson Mill La *RPDN/SBR* HX6 ..67 E5
Watts St *CLAY* BD14 ....45 C5
Watt St *BOW* BD4 ....48 A2
Watty Hall Av *WBSY* BD6 ....46 B5
Watty Hall La *WBSY* BD6 ....46 C5
Watty Hall Rd *WBSY* BD6 ....46 B5
Wauds Gates *BAIL* BD17 ....18 D5
Waverley Av *AIRE* BD20 ....8 C3
Waverley Crs *HIPP* HX3 ....70 B1
Waverley Pl *GTHN* BD7 ....46 C2
Waverley Rd *GTHN* BD7 ....46 C2
Waverley Ter *GTHN* BD7 ....46 C2
Waverton Gn *WBSY* BD6 ....53 H3
Wavertree Park Gdns
LM/WK BD12 ....62 D1
Wayside Ct *AIRE* BD20 ....6 D1
Wayside Crs *IDLE* BD10 * 30 A4
Weardale Cl *BOW* BD4 ....56 B1
Weatherhouse Ter
LUD/ILL HX2 ....58 C4
Weavers Ct *LUD/ILL* HX2 ....67 F2
Weavers Cft *IDLE* BD10 ....19 H4
Weavers Gra *GSLY* LS20 ....10 D2
Weavers Hl *HWTH* BD22 ....22 D3
Weavers La *CUL/QBY* BD13 .....24 C3
Weaverthorpe Rd *BOW* BD4 ...56 D2
Webb Dr *ECHL* BD2 ....39 H2
Webb's Ter *HIPP* HX3 ....4 A1
Weber St *BFDE* BD3 * 40 B5
Webster St *BFDE* BD3 ....3 J3
Wedgemoor Cl *LM/WK* BD12 ..62 D1
Weetwood Rd *GIR* BD8 ....38 A3
Welbeck Dr *ECHL* BD2 ....45 H3
Welbeck Rd *GTHN* BD7 ....45 G3
Welburn Av *HIPP* HX3 ....70 C1
Welburn Mt *WBSY* BD6 ....53 H2
Welbury Dr *GIR* BD8 ....38 D2
Weldon Ct *BOW* BD4 ....44 A3
Welham St *WBSY* BD6 ....3 G2
Wellands Gn *CLECK* BD19 ......73 E1
Wellands La *CLECK* BD19 ....63 G5
Wellands Ter *BFDE* BD3 ....40 B5
Well Cl *YEA* LS19 ....21 H3
Well Close St *BRIC* HD6 ....71 F5
Well Cft *SHPY* BD18 ....28 C2

Wellcroft Gdns *HIPP* HX3 ....61 F5
Wellesley Pk *LUD/ILL* HX2 * ...67 H1
Wellgarth *HFAX* HX1 ....5 F7
Wellgate *CTL/HWG* HX4 ....5 F5
Well Green La *BRIG* HD6 ....71 E3
Well Gv *BRIC* HD6 ....71 E3
Well Head Dr *HFAX* HX1 ....5 G6
Well Head La *HFAX* HX1 ....5 G6
Well Heads *CUL/QBY* BD13 .....43 F1
Well Hl *YEA* LS19 ....11 C4
Wellholme *BRIC* HD6 ....71 G5
Wellington Ar *BRIC* HD6 * 78 B1
Wellington Ct *BIRK/DRI* BD11 ..52 F4
LUD/ILL HX2 ....58 D4
Wellington Crs *SHPY* BD18 .....28 B2
Wellington Gv *ECHL* BD2 ....40 A2
PDSY/CALV LS28 ....41 H5
Wellington Rd *ECHL* BD2 ....40 A2
WIL/AL BD15 ....25 H5
Wellington St *BFD* BD1 ....2 E4
BGLY BD16 ....16 C3
BOW BD4 ....48 C1
CUL/QBY BD13 ....52 C1
ECHL BD2 ....40 A1
IDLE BD10 ....30 A2
WIL/AL BD15 ....30 A1
Wellington St South *HFAX* HX1 ..5 J5
Wellington St West *LUD/ILL* HX2 ..4 E6
Well La *BRIG* HD6 ....71 F5
GSLY LS20 ....10 D2
HFAX HX1 ....5 J3
YEA LS19 ....11 G5
Well Road Cl *LUD/ILL* HX2 ......67 G1
Well Royd Av *LUD/ILL* HX2 .....67 G1
Wells Rd *GSLY* LS20 ....10 D2
The Wells *LUD/ILL* HX2 ....67 H1
LUD/ILL HX2 ....67 H3
Well St *BFD* BD1 ....2 E5
CUL/QBY BD13 ....34 C4
KGHY BD21 ....7 E4
WIL/AL BD15 ....25 H4
Well Ter *GSLY* LS20 ....10 D2
Welwyn Av *SHPY* BD18 ....29 G2
Welwyn Dr *BAIL* BD17 ....18 D4
SHPY BD18 ....29 G2
Wembly Av *CUL/QBY* BD13 .....44 C1
Wenborough La *BOW* BD4 ....49 E4
Wendron Wy *IDLE* BD10 ....30 A2
Wenlock St *BFDE* BD3 ....3 G6
Wenning St *KGHY* BD21 ....7 H1
Wensley Av *SHPY* BD18 ....28 B2
Wensley Bank *CUL/QBY* BD13 ..43 H1
Wensley Bank Ter
CUL/QBY BD13 ....43 H1
Wensley Bank West
CUL/QBY BD13 ....43 H1
Wensleydale Ri *BAIL* BD17 ......19 F2
Wensleydale Rd *BFDE* BD3 .....40 D5
Wensley Gv *BRIC* HD6 ....77 H3
Wentworth Ct *BRIC* HD6 ....78 A4
Wentworth Dr *LUD/ILL* HX2 ....51 E3
Wentworth Gv *LUD/ILL* HX2 ...51 E3
Wesleyan Ter *BOW* BD4 * 48 B4
Wesley Av *LM/WK* BD12 ....55 E3
Wesley Av South *LM/WK* BD12 ..55 E3
Wesley Dr *LM/WK* BD12 ....55 E3
Wesley Gv *IDLE* BD10 ....20 B5
Wesley Pl *BOW* BD4 ....14 A3
Wesley Rd *PDSY/CALV* LS28 ..41 H5
Wesley St *CLECK* BD19 ....64 C5
West Av *BAIL* BD17 ....18 D2
HIPP HX3 ....68 C4
HIPP HX3 ....71 F1
West Bank *HWTH* BD22 ....6 C3
LUD/ILL HX2 ....58 C1
West Bank Cl *HWTH* BD22 ....6 C3
West Bank Gv *AIRE* BD20 ....7 H1
West Bank Ri *HWTH* BD22 ....6 C3
West Bank Rd *AIRE* BD20 ....7 G1
West Bolton *LUD/ILL* HX2 ....50 C5
Westbourough Dr *LUD/ILL* HX2 ..67 G1
Westbourne Crs *HIPP* HX3 ......69 E5
Westbourne Dr *GSLY* LS20 .....10 B2
Westbourne Gv *HIPP* HX3 ....69 E5
Westbourne Rd *GIR* BD8 * 38 C2
West Brook Ct *HFAX* HX1 * 4 E5
Westburn Av *HWTH* BD22 ....13 G1
Westburn Crs *HWTH* BD22 .....13 G1
Westburn Gv *HWTH* BD22 ....13 G1
Westburn Wy *HWTH* BD22 ......13 G1
Westbury Cl *BOW* BD4 ....48 C2
Westbury Mt *BOW* BD4 * 67 H2
Westbury Rd *WBSY* BD6 ....53 G1
Westbury St *BOW* BD4 ....48 C2
ELL HX5 ....76 D4
Westbury Ter *HFAX* HX1 ....4 E7
West Byland *HWTH* BD22 * 50 C5
West Cl *HWTH* BD22 ....18 C2
Westcliffe Av *BGLY* BD16 ....16 C1
Westcliffe Dr *BGLY* BD16 ....17 G1
Westcliffe Ri *CLECK* BD19 ....73 F1
Westcliffe Rd *CLECK* BD19 ......64 B5
SHPY BD18 ....28 C2
Westcombe Ct *LM/WK* BD12 ...63 E3
West Cote Dr *IDLE* BD10 ....19 G5
West Cft *LM/WK* BD12 ....62 D3
Westcroft Av *HIPP* HX3 ....5 H1
Westcroft Rd *GTHN* BD7 ....46 B3
Westcroft Rd *GTHN* BD7 ....46 B3
West Dr *HWTH* BD22 ....32 D1
West End *CUL/QBY* BD15 ....52 A2
HFAX HX1 * 4 C7
West End Dr *CLECK* BD19 ....73 E2
West End Rd *HFAX* HX1 ....67 H2
PDSY/CALV LS28 ....31 G3
Westend St *BFD* BD1 ....2 B4
West End Ter *ECHL* BD2 ....30 A4
GSLY LS20 ....10 B2
SHPY BD18 ....28 B1
Westercroft La *HIPP* HX3 ....61 F2
Westercroft Vw *HIPP* HX3 ....61 E2
Western Pl *CUL/QBY* BD13 .....52 B1
Western Wy *WBSY* BD6 ....54 B3
Westerton Ct *LM/WK* BD12 .....56 A5
Westfell Cl *HWTH* BD22 ....6 C5

Westfell Rd *HWTH* BD22 ....6 C5
Westfield Wy *HWTH* BD22 ....6 C5
SHPY BD18 ....28 A1
Westfield *CUL/QBY* BD13 ....44 D1
Westfield Av *AIRE* BD20 ....70 C1
YEA LS19 ....11 E5
Westfield Cl *YEA* LS19 ....11 E5
Westfield Crs *AIRE* BD20 ....8 A1
SHPY BD18 ....29 E5
Westfield Dr *AIRE* BD20 ....8 A2
HIPP HX3 ....70 C1
YEA LS19 ....10 D5
Westfield Gdns *HIPP* HX3 ....70 C1
Westfield Gv *IDLE* BD10 ....29 H1
SHPY BD18 ....29 E5
Westfield La *ECHL* BD2 ....29 G2
LM/WK BD12 ....63 E4
Westfield Mt *YEA* LS19 ....10 D5
Westfield Ov *YEA* LS19 ....10 D5
Westfield Pl *CLECK* BD19 ....63 F4
HFAX HX1 ....4 C6
Westfield Rd *AIRE* BD20 ....8 A2
CLAY BD14 ....44 B3
HTON BD9 ....38 B2
Westfield St *HFAX* HX1 ....4 E5
Westfield Ter *BAIL* BD17 ....18 D2
CLAY BD14 ....44 B3
ECHL BD2 ....40 A3
Weyhill Dr *WIL/AL* BD15 ....37 E4
Weymouth Av *WIL/AL* BD15 ....36 D4
Whack House Cl *YEA* LS19 ......11 F5
Whalley La *CUL/QBY* BD13 .....34 C2
Wharfedale Gdns *BAIL* BD17 ...19 F2
Wharfedale Mt *HIPP* HX3 * 53 E4
Wharfedale Ri *HTON* BD9 ....37 G2
Wharfedale Rd *BOW* BD4 ....55 H5
Wharf St *BAIL* BD17 ....28 C1
BFDE BD3 ....2 E3
BRIC HD6 ....78 C1
RPDN/SBR HX6 ....67 F4
Wharncliffe Crs *ECHL* BD2 .....30 C5
Wharncliffe Dr *ECHL* BD2 ....30 C5
Wharncliffe Gv *ECHL* BD2 ....30 C5
SHPY BD18 ....28 C3
Wharncliffe Rd *SHPY* BD18 ....28 C4
Wheater Rd *GTHN* BD7 * 46 B2
Wheathead Crs *HWTH* BD22 ...13 F1
Wheat Head Dr *HWTH* BD22 ...13 F1
Wheathead La *HWTH* BD22 .....13 F1
Wheatlands *PDSY/CALV* LS28 ..41 H1
Wheatlands Av *HTON* BD9 ....37 H2
Wheatlands Dr *HTON* BD9 ....37 H2
Wheatlands Gv *HTON* BD9 ....37 H2
Wheatlands Sq *HTON* BD9 ....37 H2
Wheatley City *HIPP* HX3 ....58 D3
Wheatley Gdns *HIPP* HX3 * 59 F4
Wheatley La *HIPP* HX3 ....59 F4
Wheatley Ri *HIPP* HX3 ....59 E5
Wheatley Rd *HIPP* HX3 ....58 D3
Whernside Mt *GTHN* BD7 ....45 H5
Wherwell Rd *BRIC* HD6 ....78 C2
Whetley Cl *GIR* BD8 ....38 D4
Whetley Gv *GIR* BD8 ....38 C4
Whetley Hl *GIR* BD8 ....38 C5
Whetley La *GIR* BD8 ....38 C4
Whetley Ter *GIR* BD8 ....38 D5
Whimbrel Cl *GIR* BD8 ....38 F5
Whinfield Av *HWTH* BD22 ....6 B3
Whinfield Cl *HWTH* BD22 ....6 C3
Whinfield Dr *HWTH* BD22 ....6 C3
Whin Knoll Av *KGHY* BD21 ....6 B5
Whinney Brow *IDLE* BD10 ....6 D5
Whinney Hill Pk *BRIC* HD6 ......71 F5
Whinney Royd La *HIPP* HX3 ....52 D5
Whin St *HWTH* BD22 ....6 D4
Whiskers La *HIPP* HX3 ....60 B2
Whitaker Av *ECHL* BD2 ....30 B1
Whitaker Cl *ECHL* BD2 ....30 B1
Whitaker Wk *HWTH* BD22 * 32 D2
Whitby Rd *GIR* BD8 ....38 B3
Whitby Ter *GIR* BD8 ....38 B3
Whitcliffe Rd *CLECK* BD19 ......64 B5
Whitcliffe Sq *CLECK* BD19 ......64 C5
White Abbey Rd *GIR* BD8 ....38 C5
White Birch Ter *HIPP* HX3 ....59 E3
White Castle Ct *CUL/QBY* BD13 ..43 C5
Whitefield Gv *HIPP* HX3 ....63 H5
Whitefield Pl *GIR* BD8 ....38 B4
Whitegate Dr *HIPP* HX3 ....69 E4
White Gate La *LUD/ILL* HX2 ....50 C3
Whitegate Rd *HIPP* HX3 ....69 E3
Whitegate Ter *HIPP* HX3 ....69 E4
Whitegate Top *HIPP* HX3 ....69 F4
Whitehall Av *LM/WK* BD12 ......57 G5
Whitehall Gv *BIRK/DRI* BD11 ..53 G5
Whitehall Rd *CLECK* BD19 ....63 G4
Whitehall Rd East
BIRK/DRI BD11 ....53 G5
Whitehall Rd West
BIRK/DRI BD11 ....65 F1
CLECK BD19 ....64 D3
Whitehall St *HIPP* HX3 ....61 G5
Whitehaven Cl *WBSY* BD6 ....54 A3
Whitehead La *ECHL* BD2 ....40 B3
Whitehead Pl *ECHL* BD2 ....40 B2
Whiteheads Ter *HFAX* HX1 * 3 K6
Whitehead St *BFDE* BD3 ....3 K6
Whitehill Crs *LUD/ILL* HX2 ......50 D5
Whitehill Dr *LUD/ILL* HX2 ....50 D4
Whitehill Gn *LUD/ILL* HX2 ......51 E4
Whitehill Rd *LUD/ILL* HX2 ....50 D5
White Lands *YEA* LS19 ....11 E5
Whitelands Crs *BAIL* BD17 ......19 E3
Whitelands Rd *BAIL* BD17 ....19 E3
White La *HWTH* BD22 ....12 A4
WBSY BD6 ....55 E2
Whiteley Av *RPDN/SBR* HX6 ...66 C5
Whitemoor Wy *CUL/QBY* BD13 ..34 D1
White's Ter *GIR* BD8 ....38 C3
Whitestone Crs *YEA* LS19 ....11 G4
Whitestone Dr *AIRE* BD20 ....8 C4
White's Vw *GIR* BD8 ....38 C4
Whiteways *ECHL* BD2 ....30 A1
Whitewell Green La *ELL* HX5 ...77 E4

Whitfield St *CLECK* BD19 ....64 C5
Whitlam St *SHPY* BD18 ....28 A1
Whitley Dr *LUD/ILL* HX2 ....51 E4
Whitley La *HIPP* HX3 ....69 H3
Whitley Rd *KGHY* BD21 ....7 H3
BGLY BD16 ....16 C3
Whittle Crs *CLAY* BD14 ....45 E2
Whitty La *LUD/ILL* HX2 ....67 E2
Whitwell Av *ELL* HX5 ....77 E4
Whitwell Dr *ELL* HX5 ....77 F4
Whitwell Gv *ELL* HX5 ....77 E4
Whitwell St *BOW* BD4 ....47 H2
Whitwood La *CLECK* BD19 ......71 H1
Whytecote End *LM/WK* BD12 ..62 D1
Whewsey Bank *WBSY* BD6 ......55 E1
Wibsey Park Av *WBSY* BD6 .....54 C2
Wicken Cl *IDLE* BD10 ....30 B3
Wicken La *CUL/QBY* BD13 ......35 H5
Wickets Cl *WBSY* BD6 ....55 E2
Wickham Av *WBSY* BD6 ....54 D2
Wickham St *CLECK* BD19 ....63 G4
Wide La *HWTH* BD22 ....12 B5
Wigan St *BFD* BD1 ....2 B4
Wightman St *BFDE* BD3 ....39 H2
Wignall St *AIRE* BD20 ....7 E2
Wild Gv *PDSY/CALV* LS28 ......31 E5
Wilfred Crs *CLAY* BD14 ....45 E2
Wilfred St *CLAY* BD14 ....45 E2
Wilkinson Fold *LM/WK* BD12 * ..62 D3
Wilkinson Ter *GTHN* BD7 ....46 A1
Wilkin St *KGHY* BD21 ....7 H2
William Henry St *BRIC* HD6 * ..71 F5
SHPY BD18 ....28 A1
William St *HFAX* HX1 * 48 C2
William St *BOW* BD4 ....56 C1
BOW BD4 ....56 C1
BRIC HD6 ....78 B2
CUL/QBY BD13 ....34 C3
WBOW BD5 ....2 C7
Willow Av *ECHL* BD2 ....54 A3
Willow Bank *HFAX* HX1 ....67 G2
Willow Brook *HIPP* HX5 ....58 B5
Willow Cl *LUD/ILL* HX2 ....67 G2
WBSY BD6 ....54 D3
Willow Crs *ECHL* BD2 ....30 B3
RPDN/SBR HX6 ....67 F5
Willow Cft *CLECK* BD19 ....73 F1
Willow Dene *LUD/ILL* HX2 ......67 G2
Willow Dr *LUD/ILL* HX2 ....67 G2
Willowfield Av *LUD/ILL* HX2 ....67 G3
Willowfield Cl *LUD/ILL* HX2 ....67 G2
Willowfield Crs *IDLE* BD10 ......29 H3
LUD/ILL HX2 ....67 G3
Willowfield Dr *LUD/ILL* HX2 ....67 G3
Willowfield Rd *LUD/ILL* HX2 ...67 G3
Willowfield St *GTHN* BD7 ....46 C1
Willowfield Ter *LUD/ILL* HX2 ...67 G3
Willowfield Vw *LUD/ILL* HX2 ...67 G3
Willow Gdns *ECHL* BD2 ....29 H3
GSLY LS20 ....10 D2
Willow Gv *ECHL* BD2 ....22 C3
Willow Hall Dr
RPDN/SBR HX6 ....66 C5
Willow Hall La *RPDN/SBR* HX6 ..67 F5
Willow Ri *LUD/ILL* HX2 ....67 G2
Willow Rd *PDSY/CALV* LS28 ...41 G2
The Willows *BGLY* BD16 ....17 H1
LUD/ILL HX2 ....50 D3
Willow St *CLECK* BD19 ....64 D3
GIR BD8 ....38 B4
HFAX HX1 ....67 H4
Willow Tree Cl *KGHY* BD21 .....14 C1
Willow Tree Gdns *BGLY* BD16 ..17 F1
Willroyd Dr *IDLE* BD10 ....19 H5
Wills Gill *GSLY* LS20 ....11 E2
Wilmer Dr *HTON* BD9 ....38 B1
Wilmer Rd *HTON* BD9 ....38 B1
Wilsden Hill Rd *WIL/AL* BD15 ..25 E4
Wilsden Old Rd *BGLY* BD16 ....15 C5
Wilsden Rd *KGHY* BD21 ....6 B4
WIL/AL BD15 ....16 B1
Wilson Rd *BGLY* BD16 ....16 C2
HFAX HX1 ....41 F5
LM/WK BD12 ....63 E1
Wilson Av *HIPP* HX3 ....38 D3
Wilton Av *HUDN* HD2 ....79 H5
Wilton St *BRIC* HD6 ....71 E5
GTHN BD7 ....2 B7
Wilton Ter *CLECK* BD19 ....73 C1
Wimborne Dr *HWTH* BD22 ....6 B3
WIL/AL BD15 ....37 E5
Winbrooke Ter *WBSY* BD6 ....54 B1
Winburg Rd *GTHN* BD7 ....46 A2
Winchester Gdns *BOW* BD4 ....48 C3
Windermere Ri *BRIC* HD6 ....71 G2
Windermere Ter *GTHN* BD7 * ..45 H4
Windhill Old Rd *IDLE* BD10 .....19 G4
Winding Rd *HFAX* HX1 ....5 G5
Windle Royd La *LUD/ILL* HX2 ..67 E2
Windmill Crs *HIPP* HX3 ....60 D3
Windmill Dr *HIPP* HX3 ....60 D3
Windmill Hl *PDSY/CALV* LS28 ..41 F2
WBSY BD6 ....54 B1
Windmill La *WBSY* BD6 ....54 B1
YEA LS19 ....11 H5
Windsor Crs *HWTH* BD22 ....6 C3
LUD/ILL HX2 ....58 D4
Windsor Gv *CUL/QBY* BD13 ....44 A1
HWTH BD22 ....12 C4
Windsor Rd *HWTH* BD22 ....12 C4
SHPY BD18 * 28 C3
Windsor St *BOW* BD4 * 47 H2
HFAX HX1 ....5 G6
Windsor Wk *BRIC* HD6 ....71 F2
Windy Bank La *HIPP* HX3 ....36 A1
LVSG WF15 ....65 H4
Windy Gv *WIL/AL* BD15 ....36 A1
Winfield Gro *BIRK/DRI* BD11 ...53 H2
Wingate Av *HWTH* BD22 ....6 C5
Wingate Wy *HWTH* BD22 ....6 C5
Wingfield Ct *BGLY* BD16 ....16 D2

Wingfield Mt *BFDE* BD3 ....3 J2
Wingfield St *BFDE* BD3 ....3 J5
Winnard Rw *WBOW* BD5 * 47 G4
Winrose Cl *LM/WK* BD12 ....62 D1
Winslow Vw *IDLE* BD10 ....30 D5
Winston Ter *GTHN* BD7 ....46 B2
Winterburn La *LUD/ILL* HX2 .....66 D2
Winterburn St *KGHY* BD21 ....7 F5
Winter Ct *WIL/AL* BD15 ....36 D1
Winter St *HFAX* HX1 ....4 B7
Winterton Dr *LM/WK* BD12 .....54 D5
Wistons La *ELL* HX5 ....58 D5
Witchfield Hl *HIPP* HX3 ....53 G4
Witham Rd *SHPY* BD18 ....29 E3
Withens Hill Ct *LUD/ILL* HX2 ....50 C3
Withinfield Ct *HIPP* HX3 ....69 H4
Within Flds *HIPP* HX3 ....69 H4
Withins Cl *WBOW* BD5 ....46 C5
Woburn Ter *CLAY* BD14 ....45 E5
Wold Cl *CUL/QBY* BD13 ....44 A1
Wolseley St *CLAY* BD14 ....45 F2
Wolseley Ter *HFAX* HX1 ....4 B2
Wolston Cl *BOW* BD4 ....48 D5
Womersley St *HFAX* HX1 ....4 B3
Woodale Av *HTON* BD9 ....37 G1
Woodbine Gv *IDLE* BD10 ....30 A2
Woodbine St *BFDE* BD3 ....3 G4
  HFAX HX1 * 4 C7
Woodbine Ter *HFAX* HX1 * 4 C7
  IDLE BD10 ....30 A2
Wood Bottom La *BRIG* HD6 .....70 D5
Woodbrook Av *LUD/ILL* HX2 ....50 B5
Woodbrook Cl *LUD/ILL* HX2 ....50 B5
Woodbrook Pl *LUD/ILL* HX2 ....50 B5
Woodbrook Rd *LUD/ILL* HX2 ....50 B5
Woodbury Rd *GIR* BD8 ....38 C2
Wood Cl *BAIL* BD17 ....18 C4
Woodcot Av *BAIL* BD17 ....19 E4
Wood Cft *BRIG* HD6 ....78 A2
  RPDN/SBR HX6 ....66 B5
Wood End Cl *HIPP* HX3 ....68 C5
Woodend Ct *WBOW* BD5 ....47 G5
Wood End Crs *SHPY* BD18 ....29 F3
Woodfield Av *GTL/HWG* HX4 ...75 G4
Woodfield Cl *IDLE* BD10 ....30 C5
Woodfield Dr *GTL/HWG* HX4 ...75 G5
Woodfield Rd *CUL/QBY* BD13 ..24 D2
Woodford Av *HIPP* HX3 ....69 E4
Woodgarth Gdns *BOW* BD4 .....49 E4
Woodhall Av *BFDE* BD3 ....40 D4
Woodhall Cl *PDSY/CALV* LS28 ..41 F2
Woodhall Ct *PDSY/CALV* LS28 ..31 F4
Woodhall Cft
  PDSY/CALV LS28 ....41 F2
Woodhall La *PDSY/CALV* LS28 ..41 F1
Woodhall Park Av
  PDSY/CALV LS28 ....41 F2
Woodhall Park Crs West
  PDSY/CALV LS28 ....41 F2
Woodhall Park Cft
  PDSY/CALV LS28 ....41 G3
Woodhall Park Dr
  PDSY/CALV LS28 ....41 F3

Woodhall Park Gv
  PDSY/CALV LS28 ....41 F3
Woodhall Park Mt
  PDSY/CALV LS28 ....41 F3
Woodhall Pl *BFDE* BD3 ....40 D3
Woodhall Rd *BFDE* BD3 ....40 D4
Woodhall Ter *BFDE* BD3 ....40 D4
Woodhall Vw *BFDE* BD3 ....41 E3
Woodhead La *BRIG* HD6 ....79 F2
Woodhead Rd *GTHN* BD7 ....46 C1
Woodhead St *CLECK* BD19 ......73 H2
Woodhill Ri *IDLE* BD10 ....30 D1
Woodhouse Av *KGHY* BD21 .....14 B1
Woodhouse Cl *KGHY* BD21 ......14 B1
Woodhouse Dr *KGHY* BD21 .....14 B2
Woodhouse Gdns *BRIG* HD6 ....78 D5
Woodhouse Gv *KGHY* BD21 .....14 B1
Woodhouse La *BRIG* HD6 ....78 D3
  HIPP HX3 ....68 B5
Woodhouse Rd *KGHY* BD21 .....14 B2
Woodhouse Ter *WBSY* BD6 ......55 E2
Woodhouse Wy *KGHY* BD21 ....14 B1
Woodkirk Gv *LM/WK* BD12 .....62 D4
Woodland Ct *HTON* BD9 ....27 F5
Woodland Crs *BGLY* BD16 ....16 A1
Woodland Crs *BGLY* BD16 ....27 E5
Woodland Dr *BRIG* HD6 ....71 E5
  LUD/ILL HX2 ....67 G5
Woodland Gv *HTON* BD9 ....27 F4
Woodlands *BAIL* BD17 * 19 F2
  HWTH BD22 * 12 D4
Woodlands Av *CLECK* BD19 .....65 F4
  HIPP HX3 ....59 H4
  PDSY/CALV LS28 ....41 H3
Woodlands Cl *HUDN* HD2 ....70 H5
  IDLE BD10 ....21 E5
Woodlands Crs *CLECK* BD19 ....65 F5
Woodlands Dr *CLECK* BD19 .....65 F4
  IDLE BD10 ....21 F4
Woodlands Fold
  BIRK/DRI BD11 ....57 G5
Woodlands Gv *BAIL* BD17 ....18 A4
  BGLY BD16 ....22 E2
  CUL/QBY BD13 ....52 D1
  HIPP HX3 ....59 H4
  PDSY/CALV LS28 ....41 H3
Woodlands Mt *HIPP* HX3 ....59 H4
Woodlands Pk
  CLECK BD19 ....64 A2
Woodland Sq *BRIG* HD6 * 78 D2
Woodlands Ri *HWTH* BD22 ....22 D5
Woodlands Rd *BGLY* BD16 ....17 F2
  CLECK BD19 ....66 A4
  CUL/QBY BD13 ....52 D1
  ELL HX5 ....76 C3
  GIR BD8 * 38 B3
  HIPP HX3 ....59 H4
  PDSY/CALV LS28 ....41 H3
Woodlands St *GIR* BD8 ....38 C4
Woodlands Ter
  PDSY/CALV LS28 ....41 H3
Woodlands Vw *HIPP* HX3 ....59 H4

Woodland Vw
  PDSY/CALV LS28 ....31 F2
Wood La *ECHL* BD2 ....29 G4
  HIPP HX3 ....61 G4
  LUD/ILL HX2 ....77 G1
  PDSY/CALV LS28 ....31 G2
  RPDN/SBR HX6 ....66 B4
Woodlark Cl *WBSY* BD6 ....53 G1
Woodlea Ap *YEA* LS19 ....11 E5
Woodlea Cl *YEA* LS19 ....21 E1
Woodlea Dr *YEA* LS19 ....11 E5
Woodlea Gv *YEA* LS19 ....11 E5
Woodlea Mt *YEA* LS19 ....11 E5
Woodlea Rd *YEA* LS19 ....11 E5
Woodleigh Av *WBOW* BD5 ......55 F1
Woodlesford Crs
  LUD/ILL HX2 ....49 F2
Woodman St *WBSY* BD6 ....53 H4
Wood Nook La
  RPDN/SBR HX6 ....67 F3
Wood Nook Ter
  PDSY/CALV LS28 ....41 H3
Woodpecker Cl
  WIL/AL BD15 ....37 E5
Wood Pl *GIR* BD8 ....38 D4
Wood Rd *HTON* BD9 ....28 D5
  WBOW BD5 ....47 G5
Woodrow Dr *LM/WK* BD12 ......55 F5
Woodroyd Av *WBOW* BD5 * 47 H5
Woodroyd Dr *HIPP* HX3 ....58 D3
Woodroyd Gdns
  RPDN/SBR HX6 ....66 C3
Woodroyd Rd *WBOW* BD5 ....47 F5
Woodroyd Ter *WBOW* BD5 ......47 F5
Woodside *AIRE* BD20 ....6 D2
  SHPY BD18 ....29 E1
Woodside Av *BGLY* BD16 ....26 C2
  SHPY BD18 ....27 H1
Woodside Ct *CUL/QBY* BD13 ....24 C3
Woodside Crs *BGLY* BD16 ....26 C2
  HIPP HX3 ....59 H4
Woodside Dr *BGLY* BD16 ....26 C2
Woodside Gv *GTL/HWG* HX4 ...75 H5
  HIPP HX3 ....59 H4
Woodside Mt *HIPP* HX3 ....55 F1
Woodside Pl *HIPP* HX3 ....59 H4
Woodside Rd *LM/WK* BD12 .....62 D1
Woodside Ter *HIPP* HX3 ....59 H4
Woodside Vw *BGLY* BD16 ....26 C2
  HIPP HX3 ....59 G4
Woodsley Rd *IDLE* BD10 ....21 E5
Wood Sq *HIPP* HX3 ....59 G3
Woodstock Wk
  WBOW BD5 * 47 F2
Wood St *BAIL* BD17 ....18 D5
  BGLY BD16 ....26 C2
  BRIG HD6 ....78 C1
  CLECK BD19 ....73 F1
  ELL HX5 ....76 D5
  GIR BD8 ....38 D4
  KGHY BD21 ....14 B3
  WIL/AL BD15 ....37 F3
Wood St North *HIPP* HX3 * 59 G3

Woodthorpe
  CUL/QBY BD13 ....34 B4
Wood Top *BRIG* HD6 ....70 D5
Woodvale Cl *BOW* BD4 ....48 D2
Woodvale Crs *BGLY* BD16 ....16 D1
Woodvale Gv *WBOW* BD5 * 45 H2
Woodvale Rd *HIPP* HX3 ....71 G5
Wood Vw *HWTH* BD22 * 13 G2
Woodview Av *BAIL* BD17 ....19 G2
Wood View Dr *ECHL* BD2 ....40 B2
Wood View Gv *BRIG* HD6 ....71 E4
Woodview Rd *HWTH* BD22 ......13 G2
Wood View Ter *HWTH* BD22 ....14 A2
Woodville Gv *HWTH* BD22 ......23 G1
Woodville Pl *HTON* BD9 ....28 A5
  HUDN HD2 ....79 F5
Woodville Rd *AIRE* BD20 ....7 E3
Woodville St *HIPP* HX3 ....59 F4
  SHPY BD18 ....29 E1
Woodville Ter *WBOW* BD5 ....47 G2
Wood Vine Rd
  PDSY/CALV LS28 ....41 H3
Woodworth Gv *KGHY* BD21 .....14 A3
Woolcomb Ct *HTON* BD9 ....38 B2
The Wool Ex *BFD* BD1 ....2 D5
Wooller Rd *LM/WK* BD12 ....55 E5
Woolrow La *BRIG* HD6 ....71 H2
Woolshops Sq *HFAX* HX1 * 5 H4
Wootton St *WBOW* BD5 ....47 E5
Worcester Pl *BOW* BD4 ....47 H5
Worden Gv *CLAY* BD14 ....45 H3
Workhouse La
  GTL/HWG HX4 ....76 A5
  LUD/ILL HX2 ....66 D1
Worsnop Buildings
  LM/WK BD12 ....62 D1
Worsnop St *LM/WK* BD12 ....55 E4
Worstead Rd *HWTH* BD22 ....23 G1
Worth Av *KGHY* BD21 ....7 H2
Worth Bridge Rd *KGHY* BD21 * .7 H2
Worthing Head Cl
  LM/WK BD12 ....63 E2
Worthing Head Rd
  LM/WK BD12 ....62 D2
Worthing St *LM/WK* BD12 ....63 E2
Worthington St *GIR* BD8 ....38 C4
Worthville Cl *KGHY* BD21 ....14 B3
Worth Wy *HWTH* BD22 ....23 E5
  HWTH BD22 ....23 H1
  KGHY BD21 ....7 F5
Wortley St *BGLY* BD16 ....17 E3
Wren Av *GTHN* BD7 ....45 H2
Wren St *KGHY* BD21 ....7 F3
Wright Av *HWTH* BD22 ....13 E3
Wright St *HWTH* BD22 ....13 E4
Wrigley Av *BOW* BD4 ....56 A1
Wrigley Hl *LUD/ILL* HX2 ....50 D4
Wroe Crs *LM/WK* BD12 ....62 D2
Wroe Pl *LM/WK* BD12 ....62 D2
Wroe Ter *LM/WK* BD12 ....62 D2
Wrose Av *ECHL* BD2 ....29 H4
  SHPY BD18 ....29 E3

Wrose Brow Rd *SHPY* BD18 .....29 E1
Wrosecliffe Gv *SHPY* BD18 ......29 E1
Wrose Dr *SHPY* BD18 ....29 E3
Wrose Gv *ECHL* BD2 ....29 G3
  SHPY BD18 ....29 E3
Wrose Hill Pl *ECHL* BD2 ....29 E4
Wrose Mt *SHPY* BD18 ....29 E3
Wrose Rd *SHPY* BD18 ....29 E5
Wrose Vw *SHPY* BD18 ....29 E3
Wycliffe Gdns *SHPY* BD18 ....28 B1
Wycliffe Rd *SHPY* BD18 ....28 B1
Wycoller Rd *LM/WK* BD12 ....62 D1
Wycombe Gn *BOW* BD4 ....48 D4
Wyke Crs *LM/WK* BD12 ....63 E3
Wyke La *LM/WK* BD12 ....63 F2
Wykelea Cl *LM/WK* BD12 ....63 E3
Wyke Old La *BRIG* HD6 ....71 F1
Wyncroft Ri *SHPY* BD18 ....29 E4
Wyndham Av *ECHL* BD2 ....39 G1
Wyndy Rdg *CUL/QBY* BD13 .....35 H5
Wynford Wy *WBSY* BD6 ....55 F2
Wynne St *GIR* BD8 ....2 A3
Wyvern Cl *GTHN* BD7 ....46 A1
Wyvern Pl *LUD/ILL* HX2 ....58 D5
Wyvern Ter *LUD/ILL* HX2 ....58 D5

Y

Yarborough Cft *HIPP* HX3 ....60 D1
Yardley Wy *LM/WK* BD12 ....55 F4
Yarwood Gv *GTHN* BD7 ....45 H4
Yate La *HWTH* BD22 ....32 D1
Yates Flat *SHPY* BD18 ....29 E3
Yeadon Dr *HIPP* HX3 ....69 H4
Ye Farre Cl *BRIG* HD6 ....71 E4
Yewdall Wy *IDLE* BD10 ....30 B3
Yew Tree Av *GIR* BD8 ....37 G3
Yew Tree Cl *SHPY* BD18 ....28 D3
Yew Tree Crs *GIR* BD8 ....37 H3
Yew Tree La *WIL/AL* BD15 ....36 H4
Yew Trees Av *HIPP* HX3 ....60 D2
York Crs *BGLY* BD16 * 16 D4
York Pl *CLECK* BD19 ....64 C5
Yorkshire Wy *GTHN* BD7 ....46 C4
York St *BGLY* BD16 ....16 D4
  BRIG HD6 ....78 B2
  CUL/QBY BD13 ....52 B1
  GIR BD8 ....37 H5
  HFAX HX1 ....5 K5
York Ter *HIPP* HX3 ....59 G4
Young St *GIR* BD8 ....38 A5

Z

Zealand St *BOW* BD4 ....48 C3

Index - featured places

Abbey Park Primary School
  LUD/ILL HX2 ....50 C4
Acorn Park Industrial Estate
  BAIL BD17 ....19 F4
Adwalton Moor Business Park
  BOW BD4 ....57 G3
Aireborough Leisure Centre
  GSLY LS20 ....10 D2
Airedale Centre
  KGHY BD21 ....7 F4
Aire Valley Business Centre
  KGHY BD21 ....7 F5
Aireview Business Centre
  BAIL BD17 ....28 B1
Alhambra Theatre
  BFD BD1 ....2 C6
Allerton Clinic
  WIL/AL BD15 ....37 E4
Allerton Primary School
  WIL/AL BD15 ....37 E3
All Saints CE Primary School
  HIPP HX3 ....75 H1
  WBOW BD5 ....46 D3
Alston Retail Park
  KGHY BD21 ....7 G2
Armytage Road
  Industrial Estate
  BRIG HD6 ....78 D1
Arndale Shopping Centre
  SHPY BD18 ....28 C2
Ash Green Primary School
  LUD/ILL HX2 ....50 B5
Atlas Community
  Primary School
  GIR BD8 ....38 D3
Aylesham Industrial Estate
  LM/WK BD12 ....55 E4
Baildon CE Primary School
  BAIL BD17 ....19 F2
Baildon Golf Club
  BAIL BD17 ....18 D1
Baildon Recreation Centre
  BAIL BD17 ....18 C5
Bailiff Bridge J & I School
  BRIG HD6 ....71 G1
Bankfield Museum
  HIPP HX3 ....59 H4
Bankfoot Primary School
  WBOW BD5 ....47 E5
Barkerend Primary School
  BFDE BD3 ....3 H3

Barplas Industrial Park
  WBOW BD5 ....47 F4
BBC North Studio
  BFD BD1 ....2 D6
Beacon Business Centre
  HIPP HX3 ....69 F2
The Beaconsfield Centre
  HIPP HX3 ....69 F3
Beckfoot Grammar School
  BGLY BD16 ....16 D5
Beech Hill Primary School
  HFAX HX1 ....4 E2
Beeties Gallery
  Restaurant & Hotel
  BAIL BD17 ....18 A5
Belle Vue Boys
  Upper School
  HTON BD9 ....27 G5
Belle Vue Girls School
  BGLY BD16 ....27 F4
Benton Park School
  YEA LS19 ....21 G1
Bitton Medical Centre
  GIR BD8 ....38 D4
Bingley Grammar School
  BGLY BD16 ....16 B2
Bingley Health Centre
  BGLY BD16 ....16 B3
Bingley Hospital
  BGLY BD16 ....17 E3
Bingley Little Theatre
  BGLY BD16 ....16 C3
Bingley St Ives Golf Club
  BGLY BD16 ....15 H3
Birch Lane Medical Centre
  WBOW BD5 ....47 F4
Birkenshaw CE First School
  BIRK/DRI BD11 ....57 F4
Birkenshaw Health Centre
  BIRK/DRI BD11 ....57 F4
Birkenshaw Middle School
  BIRK/DRI BD11 ....65 G1
Birksland Industrial Estate
  BOW BD4 ....48 A2
Blakehill Primary School
  HTON BD9 ....29 H3
Blue Sox RLFC (The Shay
  Stadium)
  HFAX HX1 ....5 H7
Bolling Hall
  BOW BD4 ....47 H4

Bolling Special School
  BOW BD4 ....48 A4
Bolton Brow
  Primary School
  RPDN/SBR HX6 ....67 G4
Bolton Villas CC
  IDLE BD10 ....29 H3
Borough Market
  HFAX HX1 ....5 H4
Bowling Community College
  & Swimming Pool
  BOW BD4 ....47 H4
Bowling Court
  Industrial Estate
  BOW BD4 ....48 B1
Bowling Park
  Primary School
  WBOW BD5 ....47 G4
Brackenhill Primary School
  GTHN BD7 ....46 A3
Bradford & Bingley RFC
  BGLY BD16 ....17 E5
Bradford Bulls RLFC
  (Odsal Stadium)
  WBSY BD6 ....55 F2
Bradford Business Park
  BFD BD1 ....2 D2
Bradford Cathedral
  Community College
  BOW BD4 ....48 A4
Bradford Christian School
  SHPY BD18 ....29 E4
Bradford City FC (Bradford
  & Bingley Stadium)
  GIR BD8 ....39 E3
Bradford College
  BFD BD1 ....2 B5
Bradford College
  (McMillan Campus)
  WBOW BD5 ....47 E2
Bradford
  Grammar School
  GIR BD8 ....37 H3
Bradford Grammar School
  HTON BD9 ....28 D5
Bradford & Ilkley
  Community College
  GTHN BD7 ....46 D1
Bradford Industrial Museum
  & Horses at Work
  ECHL BD2 ....40 B1

Bradford Moor Community
  Primary School
  BFDE BD3 ....40 B4
Bradford Moor Golf Club
  BFDE BD3 ....40 A3
Bradford Royal Infirmary
  HTON BD9 ....38 A2
Bradford Royal
  Infirmary Remedial Unit
  HTON BD9 ....37 H2
Bradford Salem RFC
  HTON BD9 ....27 H5
Bradford University
  PDSY/CALV LS28 ....41 F3
Bradley Park Golf Club
  HUDN HD2 ....79 E5
Bradshaw Primary School
  LUD/ILL HX2 ....51 E1
Bramall Business Park
  WBOW BD5 ....47 F3
Branshaw Golf Club
  HWTH BD22 ....13 E3
Branshaw Special School
  HWTH BD22 ....6 D5
Branxholme
  Industrial Estate
  BRIG HD6 ....71 G2
Brathwaite Special School
  HWTH BD22 ....6 B3
Brighouse High School
  BRIG HD6 ....71 E3
Brighouse Sports Centre
  BRIG HD6 ....71 G5
Brighouse Sports Club
  BRIG HD6 ....71 G5
Broadway
  (due to open 2007)
  BFD BD1 ....2 E5
Broadwood School
  LUD/ILL HX2 ....58 C4
Bronte House School
  IDLE BD10 ....21 E4
Brontë Parsonage Museum
  HWTH BD22 ....22 C2
Brookfoot Industrial Estate
  BRIG HD6 ....78 A1
Brow Quarry
  Industrial Estate
  HIPP HX3 ....70 C2
Brunswick Industrial Estate
  HFAX HX1 ....4 E6

Bull Royd Industrial Estate
  GIR BD8 ....37 H4
Business Enterprise Centre
  BFD BD1 ....2 E4
Butterfield Industrial Estate
  BAIL BD17 ....19 E5
Buttershaw High School
  WBSY BD6 ....54 A2
Buttershaw Primary School
  WBSY BD6 ....53 H3
Byron Primary School
  BFDE BD3 ....3 K3
Calderdale Business Centre
  HFAX HX1 ....4 B4
Calderdale Business Park
  LUD/ILL HX2 ....59 E2
Calderdale College
  BRIG HD6 ....78 A2
  HFAX HX1 ....4 D5
Calderdale College
  (Princess Mary Centre)
  HFAX HX1 ....4 C5
Calderdale Industrial Museum
  HFAX HX1 ....5 J4
The Calderdale Royal Hospital
  HIPP HX3 ....68 D5
Calder Industrial Estate
  BRIG HD6 ....71 G2
Calder Trading Estate
  HUDN HD2 ....79 H5
  RPDN/SBR HX6 ....67 F5
Calverley CE
  Primary School
  PDSY/CALV LS28 ....31 G2
Calverley Golf Club
  PDSY/CALV LS28 ....41 F1
Calverley Medical Centre
  PDSY/CALV LS28 ....31 F3
Calverley Parkside
  Primary School
  PDSY/CALV LS28 ....31 F3
Carlisle Mills Business Centre
  GIR BD8 ....38 D3
Carlton Bolling College
  BFDE BD3 ....3 H1
Carr Green J & I School
  BRIG HD6 ....78 A4
Carrwood Primary School
  BOW BD4 ....49 E3
Cartwright Hall Art Gallery
  HTON BD9 ....38 C1

Castlefields Industrial Estate
BCLY BD16 ....16 A1
Castlefields Infant School
BRIG HD6 ....78 A2
Cavendish Primary School
IDLE BD10 ....30 B4
Challenge College
HTON BD9 ....38 D1
Chapel Grange Special School
GIR BD8 ....37 F4
Chohan Medical Centre
WBOW BD5 ....47 E3
Christ Church CE
Junior School
RPDN/SBR HX6 ....67 F3
Christ Church CE
Primary School
LUD/ILL HX2 ....58 C5
Cineworld
BFD BD1 ....2 E5
City Link Industrial Park
BOW BD4 ....40 D5
Civic Theatre
HFAX HX1 ....5 G5
Clayton Cemetery
CLAY BD14 ....45 G2
Clayton CE Primary School
CLAY BD14 ....45 F3
Clayton Golf Club
CLAY BD14 ....45 F4
Clayton Village
Primary School
CLAY BD14 ....45 G3
Cleckheaton
& District Golf Club
CLECK BD19 ....64 A3
Cleckheaton Sports Club
CLECK BD19 ....64 B3
Cliffe Castle Museum & Gallery
AIRE BD20 ....7 E2
Cliffe Hill Primary School
HIPP HX3 ....71 E2
Clifton Cemetery
BRIC HD6 ....79 F1
The Colour Museum
BFD BD1 ....2 B5
Common Road
Industrial Estate
LM/WK BD12 ....55 E4
Cooper Lane Primary School
WBSY BD6 ....53 F1
Copley Primary School
HIPP HX3 ....75 G2
Copthorne Primary School
GTHN BD7 ....46 D2
Copwood Mental Health Clinic
BOW BD4 ....48 D3
The Coronation
Business Centre
KGHY BD21 ....7 G2
Cottingley Clinic
BGLY BD16 ....26 D2
Cottingley Village
Primary School
BGLY BD16 ....9 E5
Crossflatts CC
BGLY BD16 ....9 E5
Crossflatts Primary School
BGLY BD16 ....9 F5
Crossley Hall Primary School
GIR BD8 ....37 H5
The Crossley Heath School
HFAX HX1 ....68 B4
Crossley Retail Park
HFAX HX1 ....4 E2
Cuckoo Nest
Industrial Estate
GTHN BD7 ....38 D5
Cullingworth Medical Centre
CUL/OBY BD13 ....24 C3
Cullingworth Primary School
CUL/OBY BD13 ....24 C3
Dalesgate Hotel
AIRE BD20 ....6 D1
Days Inn
BRIC HD6 ....72 C3
Denholme Clinic
CUL/OBY BD13 ....34 C3
Denholme Primary School
CUL/OBY BD13 ....34 C3
Dixons City
Technology College
WBOW BD5 ....47 F3
Dockfield Industrial Estate
BAIL BD17 ....28 C1
Dominion Industrial Park
HIPP HX3 ....61 F5
Drakes Industrial Estate
LUD/ILL HX2 ....59 E1
Drummond Trading Estate
GIR BD8 ....2 A2
East Bierley CC
BOW BD4 ....56 D3
East Bierley First School
BIRK/DRI BD11 ....57 E3
East Bierley Golf Club
BOW BD4 ....56 D3
East Morton CE
Primary School
AIRE BD20 ....8 D3
Eastwood Primary School
KGHY BD21 ....7 G3
Eccleshill CC
IDLE BD10 ....30 C4
Eccleshill Clinic &
Health Centre
IDLE BD10 ....30 C4
Eccleshill United Sports Club
IDLE BD10 ....29 G4
Eldwick Primary School
BGLY BD16 ....17 F2
Elizabeth Industrial Estate
HFAX HX1 ....4 D1
Elland CE J & I School
ELL HX5 ....76 C4

Ellar Carr School
IDLE BD10 ....20 B5
Ellen Royde Health Centre
ELL HX5 ....76 B4
Empire Business Centre
ELL HX5 ....59 F1
Esholt & Aire Bronians
Sports Club
BAIL BD17 ....20 A1
Essex Park Industrial Estate
BFD BD3 ....3 G7
Eureka! The Museum
For Children
HIPP HX3 ....5 J5
Euroway Trading Estate
BOW BD4 ....55 H4
Fagley Primary School
ECHL BD2 ....40 C2
Fardew Golf Club
AIRE BD20 ....8 D3
Farfield Primary School
PDSY/CALV LS28 ....41 G2
Farnham Primary School
GTHN BD7 ....46 C2
Farrow Medical Centre
BFDE BD3 ....3 F2
Farsley Community Clinic
PDSY/CALV LS28 ....41 H1
Fearnville Primary School
BOW BD4 ....48 C2
Fentham Industrial Estate
BRIC HD6 ....78 B2
Fieldhead Business Centre
BRIC HD6 ....46 D1
Field Lane Primary School
BRIG HD6 ....77 H4
Forster Square Retail Park
BFD BD1 ....2 C2
Four Lanes Business Park
GIR BD8 ....38 A5
Fowler Street Industrial Estate
BOW BD4 ....48 A2
Foxhill Primary School
CUL/OBY BD13 ....44 A5
Friars Industrial Estate
IDLE BD10 ....30 A2
Frizinghall Medical Centre
HTON BD9 ....28 C5
Frizinghall Primary School
HTON BD9 ....28 D4
Fulford Grange Hospital
YEA LS19 ....21 F3
The Gleddings School
HIPP HX3 ....68 B5
Glenaire Primary School
BAIL BD17 ....18 B4
Glen Cable Tramway
BAIL BD17 ....18 A4
Gomersal CE Middle School
CLECK BD19 ....65 H4
Gomersal First School
CLECK BD19 ....65 G4
Gomersal Lodge Hotel
CLECK BD19 ....65 H3
Gomersal Park Hotel
CLECK BD19 ....65 H2
Grange Road Primary School
GTHN BD7 ....46 B2
The Grange Technology
College
WBOW BD5 ....46 C5
Great Horton Industrial Estate
WBSY BD6 ....45 G5
Greenfield Special School
IDLE BD10 ....19 H5
Greengates Primary School
IDLE BD10 ....30 D2
Greenhead Athletics Track
AIRE BD20 ....7 E2
Greenhead High School
AIRE BD20 ....7 E1
Green Meadows School
GSLY LS20 ....10 B2
Green Mount Retail Park
HFAX HX1 ....4 E3
Greetland Cricket &
Bowling Club
GTL/HWG HX4 ....75 H4
Greetland Primary School
GTL/HWG HX4 ....75 G4
Gresley Road
Industrial Estate
KGHY BD21 ....7 F4
Grove House Primary School
ECHL BD2 ....29 H5
Grove Mills Industrial Estate
ELL HX5 ....76 D4
Guard House Primary School
KGHY BD21 ....6 B4
Guide Post Hotel
LM/WK BD12 ....55 E4
Guiseley AFC
CSLY LS20 ....10 B2
Guiseley Infant School
GSLY LS20 ....10 D2
Guiseley School
GSLY LS20 ....10 C3
Haigh Hall Medical Centre
IDLE BD10 ....30 C2
Halifax Building Society
HFAX HX1 ....5 G5
Halifax Cricket Ground
HFAX HX1 ....67 H1
Halifax Golf Club
LUD/ILL HX2 ....50 B1
Halifax High School
HFAX HX1 ....5 G6
The Halifax High School
HFAX HX1 ....68 B3
Halifax Industrial Centre
HFAX HX1 ....4 D2

Halifax Leisure Centre
HFAX HX1 ....5 H5
Halifax RUFC
LUD/ILL HX2 ....59 E1
Halifax Ski Centre
HFAX HX1 ....59 H2
Halifax Swimming Pool
HFAX HX1 ....5 H6
Halifax Town FC
(The Shay Stadium)
HFAX HX1 ....5 H7
Halifax West End Golf Club
LUD/ILL HX2 ....58 B5
Hanson Upper School
ECHL BD2 ....29 G5
Harden Primary School
BCLY BD16 ....15 F5
Hartshead Moor
Special School
CLECK BD19 ....72 C2
Haycliffe Special School
WBOW BD5 ....46 C5
Headley Golf Club
CUL/OBY BD13 ....44 A2
Heathfield Industrial Estate
ELL HX5 ....76 D5
Heaton Ave First School
CLECK BD19 ....73 F1
Heaton Primary School
HTON BD9 ....27 G5
Heaton Royds Hospital
HTON BD9 ....27 G4
Heaton Royds Special School
SHPY BD18 ....28 A4
Heaton St Barnabas Aided CE
Primary School
HTON BD9 ....28 A5
Hebble Brook Business Park
LUD/ILL HX2 ....50 B3
High Bank First School
CLECK BD19 ....73 E3
Highbury Special School
BRIC HD6 ....77 H4
High Crags Primary School
SHPY BD18 ....28 D3
High Fernley
Primary School
LM/WK BD12 ....62 D2
High Royds Hospital
ILK LS29 ....10 A1
Hightown First School
LVSC WF15 ....73 F3
Hillside Works
Industrial Estate
CLECK BD19 ....64 D5
Hill Top CE Primary School
LM/WK BD12 ....54 D4
Hipperholme Clinic
HIPP HX3 ....61 G5
Hipperholme Grammar School
HIPP HX3 ....61 F5
Hipperholme & Lightcliffe High
School & Sports College
HIPP HX3 ....71 E1
Hockney Road
Industrial Estate
GIR BD8 ....38 B4
IDLE BD10 ....30 A4
Holdsworth House Hotel
LUD/ILL HX2 ....51 F3
Hollingwood Primary School
WBOW BD5 ....45 G4
Holme Wood Health Centre
BOW BD4 ....48 C3
Holmfield Industrial Estate
LUD/ILL HX2 ....51 F5
Holybrook Primary School
IDLE BD10 ....30 C3
Holycroft Primary School
KGHY BD21 ....7 E5
Holy Family RC School
AIRE BD20 ....6 D2
Holy Trinity CE
Primary School
HFAX HX1 ....4 E6
Holy Trinity CE Senior School
LUD/ILL HX2 ....51 F4
Horsfall Stadium
WBSY BD6 ....54 C3
Horton Park Primary School
WBOW BD5 ....46 C5
Hoyle Court Primary School
BAIL BD17 ....19 F3
Huddersfield Amateurs FC
ELL HX5 ....77 E3
Huddersfield Crematorium
HUDN HD2 ....78 B5
Idle CE Primary School
IDLE BD10 ....19 H5
Idle CC
IDLE BD10 ....30 B2
Idle Medical Centre
IDLE BD10 ....30 A1
Immanuel CE
Community School
IDLE BD10 ....20 A5
Imperial Crown Hotel
HFAX HX1 ....5 J5
Ingrow Primary School
HWTH BD22 ....13 H2
Inland Revenue Office
BFD BD1 ....2 D4
Innkeeper's Lodge
HFAX HX1 ....7 G3
IQRA Community
Primary School
GIR BD8 ....38 D5
Keelham Primary School
CUL/OBY BD13 ....43 E2
Keighley Business Centre
KGHY BD21 ....14 A1
Keighley CC
KGHY BD21 ....7 F2

Keighley College
KGHY BD21 ....7 F4
Keighley Crematorium
HWTH BD22 ....12 B3
Keighley Industrial Park
KGHY BD21 ....7 F2
Keighley Retail Park
KGHY BD21 ....7 G3
Keighley and Worth
Valley Railway
HWTH BD22 ....13 G4
HWTH BD22 ....22 D2
KGHY BD21 ....14 B1
Kensington Street
Health Centre
GIR BD8 ....38 B4
Kents Sports Club
ECHL BD2 ....30 A5
Kershaw Drive Health Centre
LUD/ILL HX2 ....66 A1
Killinghall Primary School
BFDE BD3 ....40 B3
Kirkfields Business Centre
YEA LS19 ....11 F4
Kirkgate Shopping
Centre & Market
BFD BD1 ....2 C5
Knowle Spring
Industrial Estate
KGHY BD21 ....14 A1
Knowleswood
Primary School
BOW BD4 ....48 C4
Lady Lane Park School
BGLY BD16 ....16 D1
Lady Royd Junior School
GIR BD8 ....37 H3
Laisterdyke Clinic
BFDE BD3 ....40 D5
Laisterdyke High School
BFDE BD3 ....40 C5
Lapage Primary School
BFDE BD3 ....40 D4
Laura Mitchell
Health Centre
HFAX HX1 ....5 G3
Lee Bridge Industrial Estate
HFAX HX1 ....4 D1
Leeds Road Hospital
BFDE BD3 ....3 J5
Lee Mills Industrial Estate
HFAX HX1 ....4 E1
Lee Mount Primary School
HIPP HX3 ....59 F4
Lees Primary School
HWTH BD22 ....23 F1
Leisure Exchange
BFD BD1 ....3 F6
Ley Top Primary School
WIL/AL BD15 ....37 E4
Lidget Green Primary School
GTHN BD7 ....46 A1
Lightcliffe CE J & I School
HIPP HX3 ....70 D1
Lightcliffe Golf Club
HIPP HX3 ....61 H5
Lightcliffe
Preparatory School
HIPP HX3 ....61 G5
Lilycroft Primary School
HTON BD9 ....38 C2
Ling Bob Primary School
LUD/ILL HX2 ....58 C5
Lister Lane School
ECHL BD2 ....39 H1
Littlemoor Primary School
YEA LS19 ....21 H2
Long Lee Primary School
KGHY BD21 ....7 H5
Longroyde Junior School
BRIG HD6 ....78 A2
Low Ash Primary School
SHPY BD18 ....29 E3
Lower Fields Primary School
BOW BD4 ....48 B3
Lower Grange
Medical Centre
GIR BD8 ....37 F5
Lowfields Business Park
ELL HX5 ....77 E3
Low Moor Business Park
LM/WK BD12 ....55 F4
Low Moor CE Primary School
LM/WK BD12 ....55 E4
Luddendenfoot
Primary School
LUD/ILL HX2 ....66 B3
Lynfield Mount Hospital
HTON BD9 ....37 G2
Manningham Baths &
Sports Centre
GIR BD8 ....38 C3
Manningham Clinic
GIR BD8 ....38 D3
Manor Leisure Centre
YEA LS19 ....11 F4
Mantra House
Business Centre
KGHY BD21 ....7 F5
Manywells Brow
Industrial Estate
CUL/OBY BD13 ....24 C4
Margram Business Centre
AIRE BD20 ....4 E3
Marsfield Primary School
WBOW BD5 ....46 D5
Midland Hotel
BFD BD1 ....2 D4
Mid Point Business Park
LM/WK BD12 ....41 E4
Mirriam Lord Community
Primary School
GIR BD8 ....38 C3

Mixenden Clinic
LUD/ILL HX2 ....58 C1
Mixenden Community
Primary School
LUD/ILL HX2 ....50 A4
Moorend CE First School
CLECK BD19 ....64 B4
Moorlands Small
Business Centre
CLECK BD19 ....64 C4
Moorside Community
Primary School
BOW BD4 ....59 E1
Moorview Business Park
IDLE BD10 ....19 H5
Mount Pellon J & I School
HFAX HX1 ....4 A1
Municipal Baths
BRIG HD6 ....78 C1
Myrtle Park Primary School
BGLY BD16 ....16 C4
Nab Wood Cemetery
SHPY BD18 ....27 G1
Nab Wood Crematorium
SHPY BD18 ....27 G1
Nab Wood School
BGLY BD16 ....27 F2
Napoleon Business Park
BOW BD4 ....48 A2
National Museum of
Photography, Film
& Television
WBOW BD5 ....2 C7
Neil Hunt Memorial
Ground & RFC
BOW BD4 ....48 B2
Nessfield Primary School
HWTH BD22 ....13 G1
Netherlands Avenue
Special School
WBSY BD6 ....55 E3
Netherleigh &
Rossefield School
HTON BD9 ....28 B5
Netherleigh School
HTON BD9 ....38 A2
Newbridge Industrial Estate
IDLE BD10 ....7 G4
Newby Primary School
WBOW BD5 ....47 E4
New Cross Street
Health Centre
WBOW BD5 ....47 E4
Newhall Park Primary School
WBOW BD5 ....55 H1
Newlands Industrial Estate
SHPY BD18 ....28 D1
New Line Clinic
IDLE BD10 ....30 D2
New Road Primary School
RPDN/SBR HX6 ....66 D5
Newspaper Office
BFD BD1 ....2 E5
Norcroft Industrial Estate
BFD BD1 ....38 D5
Norland CE Primary School
RPDN/SBR HX6 ....74 C1
North Bridge Leisure Centre
HFAX HX1 ....5 H2
Northcliffe Golf Club
SHPY BD18 ....27 H3
North Dean Business Park
HFAX HX1 ....75 H2
North Dean RFC
GTL/HWG HX4 ....76 A4
The North Halifax
Grammar School
LUD/ILL HX2 ....51 E4
Northowram Hall Hospital
HIPP HX3 ....60 D1
Northowram
Primary School
HIPP HX3 ....60 D2
Norwood Business Park
LM/WK BD12 ....62 C3
Novotel
BOW BD4 ....55 H4
Oakbank School
AIRE BD20 ....13 G2
Oakwell Hall Country Park
BTLY WF17 ....65 H2
Oakworth Health Centre
HWTH BD22 ....13 E4
Oakworth Primary School
HWTH BD22 ....12 D4
Oastler Centre
BFD BD1 ....2 C4
Odeon Cinema
BFD BD1 ....2 C6
BFDE BD3 ....41 E4
Old Bear Brewery
KGHY BD21 ....7 G4
Old Earth CE Primary School
ELL HX5 ....77 E4
Old Rishworthians RUFC
HIPP HX3 ....75 F1
Old White Lion Hotel
HWTH BD22 ....22 D2
Our Lady Of Victories
RC Primary School
HWTH BD22 ....6 C4
Our Lady & St Brendans
RC Primary School
IDLE BD10 ....30 C3
Oxenhope CE Primary School
HWTH BD22 ....32 C1
Parkhouse Industrial Estate
LM/WK BD12 ....55 F4
Parkinson Lane Community
Primary School
HFAX HX1 ....4 C6
Parkland Primary School
IDLE BD10 ....30 C2
Park Road Medical Centre
WBOW BD5 ....47 F2

Parkside School
CUL/QBY BD13 ....24 D3
Park Wood Crematorium
ELL HX5 ....76 C2
Parkwood First School
KGHY BD21 ....7 G5
Parkwood Primary School
KGHY BD21 ....7 G5
Parkwood Street
Industrial Estate
KGHY BD21 ....7 H4
Peckerwell College
HFAX HX1 ....5 E3
Pellon Industrial Estate
HFAX HX1 ....4 B2
Penistone Hill
HWTH BD22 ....22 B3
Phoebe Lane
Industrial Estate
HIPP HX5 ....69 E4
Pictureville Cinema
BFD BD1 ....1 ....
Piece Hall
HFAX HX1 ....5 J4
Pitt Street Business Centre
KGHY BD21 ....7 G4
Playhouse & Film Theatre
BFD BD1 ....3 F6
Playhouse Theatre
HFAX HX1 ....5 F4
Pollard Park Health Centre
BFDE BD3 ....3 G2
Poplars Farm Primary School
ECHL BD2 ....29 F5
Premier Travel Inn
AIRE BD20 ....8 D4
HIPP HX3 ....76 A1
HUDN HD2 ....79 C3
Priestthorpe School
PDSY/CALV LS28 ....41 G2
Priestley Centre
BFD BD1 ....3 F5
Priestthorpe Medical Centre
BGLY BD16 ....16 C2
Priestthorpe Primary School
BGLY BD16 ....16 C2
Prince Of Wales Business Park
BRIG HD6 ....78 C1
Princeville Primary School
GTHN BD7 ....38 C5
Princeville Road
Industrial Estate
GIR BD8 ....38 B5
Pudsey Bolton
Royd Primary School
PDSY/CALV LS28 ....41 F4
Q F Industrial Estate
BOW BD4 ....48 A3
Queensbury Golf Club
CUL/QBY BD13 ....52 C2
Queensbury Health Centre
CUL/QBY BD13 ....52 A2
Queensbury School
CUL/QBY BD13 ....52 B2
Queens Road School
HFAX HX1 ....4 A3
Queens Sports Club
HFAX HX1 ....4 E7
Queensway Primary School
GSLY LS20 ....11 F3
Ramada Hotel
BGLY BD16 ....27 F1
Rastrick High School
BRIG HD6 ....78 A2
Rastrick Preparatory &
Nursery School
BRIG HD6 ....78 A3
Rastrick Squash Centre
BRIG HD6 ....78 B2
Ravenscliffe First School
IDLE BD10 ....30 D5
Ravenscliffe High
Special School
HIPP HX5 ....75 G1
Rawdon CC
YEA LS19 ....21 H2
Rawdon Golf &
Lawn Tennis Club
YEA LS19 ....21 F3
Rawson J & I School
HFAX HX1 ....5 G3
Rawson Market
BFD BD1 ....2 B4
Red House
CLECK BD19 ....65 G4
Reevy Hill Primary School
WBSY BD6 ....54 A1
Revival Industrial Estate
BOW BD4 ....47 H2
Rex Cinema
ELL HX5 ....76 C5
Rhodesway School
GIR BD8 ....37 F4
Richard Dunn Sports Centre
WBOW BD5 ....55 E1
Riddlesden St Marys CE
Primary School
AIRE BD20 ....7 H2
Ridings Business Park
HFAX HX1 ....4 A5
The Ridings School
LUD/ILL HX2 ....59 E2
Riverside Business Park
BAIL BD17 ....28 D1
Rm Grylls Middle School
LVSG WF15 ....73 E4
Royal Halifax Infirmary
HFAX HX1 ....68 C3
Royal Industrial Park
HFAX HX1 ....4 A4
Royd Mill Business Park
BRIG HD6 ....78 C1
Rufford Park
Primary School
YEA LS19 ....11 G5

Russell Hall Primary School
CUL/QBY BD13 ....52 B1
Ryburn Brewery
RPDN/SBR HX6 ....67 G4
Ryburn Golf Club
RPDN/SBR HX6 ....74 B2
Ryecroft Primary School
BOW BD4 ....49 E5
Sacred Heart RC
Primary School
RPDN/SBR HX6 ....66 D5
Sai Medical Centre
BFD BD8 ....38 D2
St Andrews CE
Infant School
BRIG HD6 ....71 F4
St Andrews CE Junior School
BRIG HD6 ....71 F5
St Annes RC Primary School
HWTH BD22 ....6 D5
St Annes RC Primary School
KGHY BD21 ....7 E3
St Anthonys RC
Primary School
CLAY BD14 ....45 G2
IDLE BD10 ....29 G1
St Augustines CE
Primary School
HFAX HX1 ....4 C2
St Bedes Catholic
Grammar School
HTON BD9 ....38 B1
St Catherines Catholic
High School
LUD/ILL HX2 ....51 F4
St Chads CE Primary School
BRIG HD6 ....70 D3
St Clares RC Primary School
ECHL BD2 ....40 B2
St Columbas Catholic
Primary School
BOW BD4 ....48 C5
St Cuthberts & The First
Martyrs Primary School
HTON BD9 ....38 B2
St Francis RC Primary School
ECHL BD2 ....29 H5
St George's Hall
BFD BD1 ....2 E6
St James Business Park
BFD BD1 ....3 F6
St James Church
Primary School
WIL/AL BD15 ....36 D5
St James Market
BFD BD5 ....3 G7
St Johns CE Primary School
BOW BD4 ....56 B1
BRIG HD6 ....79 F1
St Johns Health Centre
HFAX HX1 ....4 C3
St John The Evangelist RC
Primary School
WBSY BD6 ....53 H1
St Josephs Catholic College
HTON BD9 ....38 D1
St Josephs Catholic School
BRIG HD6 ....71 E3
St Josephs RC Primary School
BGLY BD16 ....16 D3
St Josephs RC
Primary School
HIPP HX5 ....5 J1
St Josephs RC Primary School
KGHY BD21 ....14 A1
WBOW BD5 ....47 E3
St Lukes CE First School
CLECK BD19 ....73 E1
St Lukes CE Primary School
ECHL BD2 ....30 C5
St Lukes Hospital
WBOW BD5 ....47 E3
St Malachys RC
Primary School
LUD/ILL HX2 ....58 D2
St Marys Catholic
Primary School
HFAX HX1 ....4 E6
St Marys CE (A) First School
CLECK BD19 ....65 G5
St Marys RC Primary School
BFD BD1 ....2 E4
St Matthews Catholic
Primary School
WIL/AL BD15 ....37 E4
St Matthews CE
Primary School
WBSY BD6 ....47 F5
St Michaels & All Angels CE
Primary School
HIPP HX3 ....53 G4
St Oswalds CE Junior School
GSLY LS20 ....10 D3
St Oswalds CE
Primary School
GTHN BD7 ....46 B3
St Patricks Catholic
Primary School
GTL/HWG HX4 ....76 A5
St Pauls CE Primary School
WBSY BD6 ....54 C2
St Peter & St Paul RC
Primary School
YEA LS19 ....11 E5
St Peters Cathedral
BFD BD1 ....2 E4
St Peters CE Primary School
BFDE BD3 ....3 K5
St Philips CE First School
GIR BD8 ....38 A4
St Philip's CE Primary School
BFD BD8 ....38 B3
St Stephens CE
Primary School
WBOW BD5 ....47 F4

St Walburgas County
Primary School
SHPY BD18 ....28 A1
St Williams Catholic
Primary School
BFD BD8 ....38 B4
St Winefrides RC
Primary School
WBSY BD6 ....54 C2
Saltaire Medical Centre
SHPY BD18 ....28 A1
Saltaire Primary School
SHPY BD18 ....28 A1
Salterhebble J & I School
HIPP HX3 ....69 E5
Salterlee Primary School
HIPP HX3 ....60 C3
Salt Grammar School
BAIL BD17 ....18 A4
Sandal Primary School
BAIL BD17 ....18 C3
Sandy Lane Primary School
WIL/AL BD15 ....26 D5
Scholemoor Cemetery
GTHN BD7 ....45 H1
Scholemoor Crematorium
GTHN BD7 ....45 H1
Scholes First School
CLECK BD19 ....63 F4
Sdh Industrial Estate
RPDN/SBR HX6 ....67 E5
Shaw House School
HTON BD9 ....38 B1
Sheibarg Industrial Estate
BOW BD4 ....48 C5
Shelf Health Centre
HIPP HX3 ....53 F4
Shelf Primary School
HIPP HX3 ....53 E5
Shibden Hall & Folk Museum
HIPP HX3 ....60 C5
Shibden Head
Primary School
CUL/QBY BD13 ....52 A2
Shipley Baths
SHPY BD18 ....28 B2
Shipley CE Primary School
SHPY BD18 ....28 B1
Shipley College
SHPY BD18 ....28 B1
Shipley Golf Club
BGLY BD16 ....16 C5
Shipley Health Centre
SHPY BD18 ....28 C2
Shipley Hospital
SHPY BD18 ....28 B2
Shires Business Park
GTHN BD7 ....46 B3
Shirley Manor Primary School
LM/WK BD12 ....62 D4
Siddal Primary School
HIPP HX3 ....69 E5
Silver Blades Ice Rink
BFD BD1 ....2 C7
South Bradford Golf Club
WBSY BD6 ....55 F2
South Halifax High School
HIPP HX3 ....76 B2
Southmere Primary School
GTHN BD7 ....46 B4
South View Business Centre
GSLY LS20 ....10 D1
Southview Business Park
GSLY LS20 ....10 D1
GSLY LS20 ....10 D4
Sowerby Bridge Clinic
RPDN/SBR HX6 ....67 F5
Sowerby Bridge CC
RPDN/SBR HX6 ....67 E4
Sowerby Bridge
High School
RPDN/SBR HX6 ....67 F3
Spen Valley Industrial Park
CLECK BD19 ....73 H2
Spen Victoria Cricket,
Bowling & Athletic Club
CLECK BD19 ....65 E5
Springwood
Primary School
GIR BD8 ....38 D4
Stafford Hall
Education Resource
HIPP HX3 ....59 G3
Standard Industrial Estate
ECHL BD2 ....40 B1
Station Industrial Park
LUD/ILL HX2 ....66 A1
Station Works
Industrial Park
KGHY BD21 ....7 H4
Stocks Lane Primary School
CUL/QBY BD13 ....53 E1
Stoney Ridge Hospital
BGLY BD16 ....27 F4
Stoney Royd Cemetery
HIPP HX3 ....69 E3
Swain House
Primary School
ECHL BD2 ....29 H5
Taison Industrial Park
GTHN BD7 ....46 A4
Tannery Business Park
HIPP HX3 ....60 D2
Temple Bank Special School
HTON BD9 ....37 H2
Tenterfields Business Park
LUD/ILL HX2 ....66 B3
Thackley AFC
IDLE BD10 ....19 H4
Thackley CC
IDLE BD10 ....20 A4
Thackley Primary School
IDLE BD10 ....20 A4
Thornbury Primary School
BFDE BD3 ....40 D3

Thorncliffe Park
Industrial Estate
BFD BD8 ....39 E2
Thorncliffe Square
Industrial Estate
BFD BD8 ....39 E3
Thorn Park School &
Service for Deaf & Hearing
HTON BD9 ....27 G5
Thornton Baths
CUL/QBY BD13 ....44 B1
Thornton Grammar School
CUL/QBY BD13 ....45 E1
Thornton Medical Centre
CUL/QBY BD13 ....43 H1
Thornton Primary School
CUL/QBY BD13 ....43 H1
Thorpe Primary School
IDLE BD10 ....30 A1
Thrum Hall Industrial Park
LUD/ILL HX2 ....67 H1
Tong School
BOW BD4 ....57 F2
Tong Sports Centre
BOW BD4 ....57 F2
Top Rank Theatre
HFAX HX1 ....5 G3
Tranmere Park
Primary School
GSLY LS20 ....10 A3
Travelodge
BFDE BD3 ....41 E4
HIPP HX5 ....5 F1
Trinity All Saints CE
Primary School
BGLY BD16 ....16 D4
Tuel Lane Infant School
RPDN/SBR HX6 ....67 E4
Tyersal Family Clinic
BOW BD4 ....49 E1
Tyersal Primary School
BOW BD4 ....49 E1
Undercliffe CC
ECHL BD2 ....40 B2
Undercliffe Cemetery
BFDE BD3 ....39 H3
Undercliffe Primary School
ECHL BD2 ....39 H2
Union Business Centre
ECHL BD2 ....30 C5
University of Bradford
GTHN BD7 ....2 A6
University of Bradford
Sports Centre
GTHN BD7 ....46 D1
Usher Street Primary School
BOW BD4 ....47 H2
Valley Mills Industrial Estate
IDLE BD10 ....30 D1
Venio Industrial Estate
BOW BD4 ....48 B5
Victoria Baths
ELL HX5 ....76 D5
Victoria Industrial Estate
ECHL BD2 ....30 B5
Victoria Primary School
KGHY BD21 ....6 D4
The Victoria Theatre
HFAX HX1 ....5 G4
Vine Industrial Estate
BRIG HD6 ....71 E5
Vintage Railway
Carriage Museum
HWTH BD22 ....22 D2
Walnut Business Park
HFAX HX1 ....4 C4
Warley Road Primary School
LUD/ILL HX2 ....67 H2
Warley Town Primary School
LUD/ILL HX2 ....66 D2
Waterloo Primary School
PDSY/CALV LS28 ....41 H5
Weavers Restaurant & Hotel
HWTH BD22 ....22 C1
Wedgwood Special School
BOW BD4 ....49 E5
Wellington Business Centre
ELL HX5 ....76 D4
Wellington Primary School
BRIG HD6 ....40 A1
Wellington Shopping Arcade
BRIG HD6 ....78 B1
Wellwoman Clinic
HFAX HX1 ....5 G5
Westbourne Primary School
GIR BD8 ....38 C2
West Bradford Golf Club
WBOW BD5 ....55 H1
West Bowling Golf Club
HTON BD9 ....37 E1
Westcliffe Medical Centre
SHPY BD18 ....28 B2
West End Middle School
CLECK BD19 ....73 E1
Westfield Industrial Estate
YEA LS19 ....11 F5
Westfield Junior School
YEA LS19 ....11 E5
Westgate Hill First School
BOW BD4 ....57 F3
West Side Retail Park
GSLY LS20 ....11 E4
West Vale Primary School
GTL/HWG HX4 ....76 A4
Westwood Park Primary School
HIPP HX3 ....53 G2
West Yorkshire
Industrial Estate
BOW BD4 ....56 C1
Wharfedale Business Park
BOW BD4 ....56 C1
Whetley Primary School
GIR BD8 ....38 B4

The Whitcliffe Hotel
CLECK BD19 ....73 G1
Whitcliffe Mount School
CLECK BD19 ....64 A5
Whitcliffe Road First School
CLECK BD19 ....64 C5
Whitechapel Middle School
CLECK BD19 ....64 A4
Whitehall Primary School
LUD/ILL HX2 ....50 D4
The William Henry
Smith School
BRIG HD6 ....77 G3
Willow Industrial Complex
RPDN/SBR HX6 ....67 G5
The Willows Medical Centre
CUL/QBY BD13 ....52 B1
Willow Valley Golf &
Country Club
BRIG HD6 ....72 B3
Wilsden Primary School
WIL/AL BD15 ....25 H4
Windhill CC
SHPY BD18 ....19 E5
Windhill CE Primary School
SHPY BD18 ....29 E1
Windhill Green Medical Centre
SHPY BD18 ....28 D1
Withinfields Primary School
HIPP HX3 ....69 G3
Woodhall Hills Golf Club
PDSY/CALV LS28 ....31 E5
Woodhouse Grove School
IDLE BD10 ....21 E5
Woodhouse Primary School
BRIG HD6 ....78 C3
Woodlands CE Primary School
LM/WK BD12 ....55 H5
Woodlands CC
LM/WK BD12 ....55 G5
Woodroyd Industrial Estate
LM/WK BD12 ....55 F5
Woodside Clinic
WBSY BD6 ....54 B4
Woodside Primary School
WBSY BD6 ....54 B4
Woolshops Shopping Centre
HFAX HX1 ....5 H4
Worthinghead Primary School
LM/WK BD12 ....63 G2
Worth Valley Primary School
HWTH BD22 ....13 H3
Wrose Health Centre
ECHL BD2 ....29 G4
Wycliffe CE Primary School
SHPY BD18 ....28 B1
Wyke Manor Upper School
LM/WK BD12 ....63 G2
Yeadon Cemetery
YEA LS19 ....11 H3
Yeadon CC
YEA LS19 ....11 H4
Yeadon Health Centre
YEA LS19 ....11 G4
Yeadon Westfield
Infant School
YEA LS19 ....11 E5
Yorkshire Clinic
BGLY BD16 ....27 F2
Yorkshire Martyrs Catholic
Sports College
BOW BD4 ....57 F2
Young Street Industrial Estate
GIR BD8 ....38 A4

The Post Office is a registered trademark of Post Office Ltd. in the UK and other countries.

Schools address data provided by Education Direct.

Petrol station information supplied by Johnsons

One-way street data provided by © Tele Atlas N.V. Tele Atlas

Garden centre information provided by

Garden Centre Association   Britains best garden centres

Wyevale Garden Centres

The statement on the front cover of this atlas is sourced, selected and quoted from a reader comment and feedback form received in 2004

Notes

Notes

Notes

AA **Street by Street** QUESTIONNAIRE

Dear Atlas User
Your comments, opinions and recommendations are very important to us.
So please help us to improve our street atlases by taking a few minutes
to complete this simple questionnaire.

You do not need a stamp (unless posted outside the UK). If you do not want to remove this page from your street atlas, then photocopy it or write your answers on a plain sheet of paper.

Send to: The Editor, AA Street by Street, FREEPOST SCE 4598,
Basingstoke RG21 4GY

ABOUT THE ATLAS...

Which city/town/county did you buy?

_____

Are there any features of the atlas or mapping that you find particularly useful?

_____
_____
_____

Is there anything we could have done better?

_____
_____
_____

Why did you choose an AA Street by Street atlas?

_____
_____
_____

Did it meet your expectations?

Exceeded ☐   **Met all** ☐   **Met most** ☐   **Fell below** ☐

Please give your reasons

_____
_____
_____
_____
_____

continued overleaf

Where did you buy it?

For what purpose? (please tick all applicable)

To use in your own local area ☐   **To use on business or at work** ☐

Visiting a strange place ☐   **In the car** ☐   **On foot** ☐

Other (please state)

LOCAL KNOWLEDGE...

Local knowledge is invaluable. Whilst every attempt has been made to make the information contained in this atlas as accurate as possible, should you notice any inaccuracies, please detail them below (if necessary, use a blank piece of paper) or e-mail us at *streetbystreet@theAA.com*

ABOUT YOU...

Name (Mr/Mrs/Ms)

Address

                                                                Postcode

Daytime tel no   **Mobile tel no**

E-mail address

Please only give us your e-mail address and mobile phone number if you wish to hear from us about other products and services from the AA and partners by e-mail or text or mms.

Which age group are you in?

Under 25 ☐   **25-34** ☐   **35-44** ☐   **45-54** ☐   **55-64** ☐   **65+** ☐

Are you an AA member?   **YES** ☐   **NO** ☐

Do you have Internet access?   **YES** ☐   **NO** ☐

The information we hold about you will be used to provide the product(s) and service(s) requested and for identification, account administration, analysis, and fraud/loss prevention purposes. More details about how that information is used is in our Privacy Statement, which you will find under the heading "Personal information" in our Terms and Conditions and on our website. Copies are available from us by post, by contacting our Data Protection Manager at AA, Fanum House, Basing View, Hampshire, Basingstoke RG21 4EA.

We may want to contact you about other products and services provided by us or our partners but please tick the box if you DO NOT wish to hear about such products and services from us by mail or telephone. ☐

Thank you for taking the time to complete this questionnaire. Please send it to us as soon as possible, and remember, you do not need a stamp (unless posted outside the UK).   ML13